# CUBA
## *Unchained*

### A NOVEL

SECOND EDITION

GERARD DION

Copyright © 2024 Gerard Dion.

All rights reserved. No part of this book may be reproduced, stored, or transmitted by any means—whether auditory, graphic, mechanical, or electronic—without written permission of both publisher and author, except in the case of brief excerpts used in critical articles and reviews. Unauthorized reproduction of any part of this work is illegal and is punishable by law.

ISBN: 979-8-89419-530-8 (sc)
ISBN: 979-8-89419-531-5 (hc)
ISBN: 979-8-89419-532-2 (e)

Because of the dynamic nature of the Internet, any web addresses or links contained in this book may have changed since publication and may no longer be valid. The views expressed in this work are solely those of the author and do not necessarily reflect the views of the publisher, and the publisher hereby disclaims any responsibility for them.

One Galleria Blvd., Suite 1900, Metairie, LA 70001
(504) 702-6708

# CUBA
## *Unchained*

GERARD DION

# DEDICATION

*To those men and women in Cuba, America
and elsewhere,
fighting for democracy in Cuba.*

# AUTHOR'S NOTE

*"Those with the ability have the responsibility."*

# PROLOGUE

## REUTERS NEWS SERVICE

**Miami, Florida**

OCTOBER 4
10:30 A.M.

Earlier this morning, a derelict, 38-foot wooden sailing scow came ashore in Miami Beach, Florida, in bad weather and heavy surf. Crowded aboard were 21 illegal immigrant Cubans seeking a better life in America, including six women, four children and a baby.

The heavy old boat floundered in the surf line 50 yards offshore, spilling its occupants into the sea. Several of the Cubans could not swim and drowned in the surf, while early morning pedestrian exercisers watched the tragedy from the beach. Others watched from State Route A1A and high-rise condos and hotels overlooking the scene.

The U.S. Coast Guard was not at sea in this area this a.m., but had been alerted concerning the suspicious approaching vessel, and seven Coast Guard men and six police officers were defending the beach from illegal Cuban immigrants trying to make it to dry sand, safety and freedom before being arrested in the water. The beach defenders also kept a few civilians, wanting to assist those in the water, from helping the Cubans get to shore.

What was this disastrous scene all about?

It's the U.S. Government's "Wet Foot—Dry Foot" Cuban immigration policy, which, believe it or not, provides freedom in the United States for any illegal Cuban immigrant able to reach dry U.S. soil, or a free trip back to Cuba for those who get caught out at sea or in one foot of water before putting their wet feet on dry U.S. land.

This extremely unusual U.S. immigration law applies only to Cubans. Some believe that this U.S. policy actually encourages Cubans to try to illegally immigrate to the United States, thus endangering their lives at sea. Two men, two women and the baby drowned in their efforts to reach freedom and opportunity in the United States. Four other men remain missing.

The law applied here is officially called the U.S./Cuban Adjustment Act.

# I

## THE HARVEY TOWNHOUSE

*NOVEMBER*
*Twenty-Four Months Before the Next U.S. Presidential Election*

Nickolas and Elizabeth Harvey live in downtown San Diego in a two-story townhouse with a street-level entrance in a high security condo building called City Front Place. The building was designed by a Chicago architect with a Midwestern turn-of-the-century style, finished in brick with black wrought iron railings, fencing and gates. City Front Place had been one of the earliest large, new residential buildings built in downtown San Diego in the late 1980s and had helped lead the downtown renaissance of the '80s and '90s and the redevelopment of the Marina and Gaslamp Districts.

As empty nesters and heavy travelers, the convenience of living downtown within walking distance to San Diego Bay, Seaport Village, the grocery store, Horton Plaza and the ballpark, plus the excitement of the Gaslamp's many restaurants, bars, nightclubs, boutiques and hotels, helped Nickolas and Elizabeth simplify their lifestyle as Nickolas entered semi-retirement a few years ago and purchased the yacht, *Glory*, which they kept in Fort Lauderdale, Florida. The boat was a key element of Nickolas' retirement planning.

Nickolas and Elizabeth both had worked hard following their graduations from college. Nickolas' active duty in the Marine Corps and early years at Baxter Industries lead him to start his own company.

Nickolas became very successful quite quickly, providing them far more in the way of income and net worth than they had ever dreamed. However, in spite of their rapidly growing wealth, they were both happy to moderately improve their lifestyle and otherwise, live conservatively. The exception, perhaps, was the rather large 20-year-old yacht Nickolas had purchased in Fort Lauderdale and their cruising trips in the Caribbean over recent years with family, friends and business associates.

Nickolas and Elizabeth had been happily married since college, and had raised two children: a boy, Evan, and girl, Michelle. They had managed to guide them to adulthood without either of them getting hooked on drugs, creating any illegitimate children or spending time in jail. Both eventually graduated from college, and now had good jobs, earning a living and paying their taxes. Nickolas and Elizabeth felt fortunate that they had succeeded in executing their responsibility to their children and society at large. It wasn't easy, but perseverance had paid off in all aspects of their life, including marriage, child rearing and careers.

Nickolas' initial plan to semi-retire at 40, and then fully retire at 50 or 55 was not working out as planned. Five years of semi-retirement at a rate of about 50% had revealed to him that he was way too young and energetic to go beyond the 50% level— even 50% sometimes bored him and left him feeling like he was wasting valuable time and should be doing something more productive and mentally challenging.

Over the past year or two, Nickolas had discussed his disillusionment about full-time retirement with Elizabeth, and she had encouraged him to spend more time at work in San Diego or to find something compelling that he wanted to do in Fort Lauderdale or elsewhere.

Nickolas considered all the options, and over time decided to go back to work full time for another three or four years in a risky plan he called his "Signature Event." Three of the seven people with whom he initially shared his idea thought he was nuts. Two were afraid to comment pro or con, and two had encouraged him.

About a year ago, without telling anyone other than Elizabeth, Nickolas initiated his Signature Event plan by purchasing a large, older brick apartment building in the Georgetown area of Washington,

D.C. He then hired a good architect, who created plans for a major remodeling of the ground floor into retail space and the basement into a parking garage. The updating and refurbishing of the second floor into offices, and the third and fourth floor into rental apartments, followed.

This construction work now was largely completed and Nickolas was ready to soon make a series of announcements that would ultimately put his Signature Event plan onto the front page of every major newspaper in America and ultimately on the six o'clock news everywhere.

# II

# AT THE HARVEY HOUSE

*Preparing for the Evening*

Nickolas was in that state of self-hypnosis that frequently occurs when a man commences his rituals of toiletry and grooming and discovers 15 or 20 minutes later that he is done, but doesn't remember how, because his mind was elsewhere. In the early morning, the businessman's mind is focused on the imminent day's activities and priorities. In the evening, the same man's mind goes to the important dinner companions and the social strategy necessary to perpetuate his business goals. Day, night, weekend, at his desk or at play, it was all the same to Nickolas Harvey. He enjoyed it all. Work had not been work to him for many years. Work, as most call it, was simply a part of his daily lifestyle, and he lived and loved life.

The floor-to-ceiling mirror behind Nick revealed the six-foot, 190-pound body of a man 30-something years old, even though Nick was pushing 50. Although Nick had worked hard and long all of his adult life, the years had been good to him. He had good genes, and although his diet was consistently under investigation by his wife, Elizabeth, he also watched his diet and weight, ran 15 miles a week and worked out with heavy weights.

Nick paused as he finished shaving, stood straight, threw his shoulders back, tucked his chin in, and playfully snapped a perfect

Marine Corps salute to himself in the mirror. He thought, "I may not be as good as I once was, but I damn near look as good."

Then Nick stepped back with his right foot, bent his knees, raised his hands and leaned into a karate offensive position. He raised one leg and foot, waving it menacingly at his mirror image, while balanced on the other. Then he emitted a karate attack shriek, which started at a low frequency and ended on high, as he feinted with his left foot, set it down and spun, bringing his right foot around his body and into his mirror image, stopping his foot at the glass close enough to tap the mirror with his big toe, while smiling and saying, "I've still got it! I'm telling you, I still got it!"

Nick's antics were interrupted by his wife, Elizabeth, in the next room by simply calling his name from the bedroom in a certain tone, "Nickolas!" Nick recognized in that tone the unsaid statement understood by most married men, which meant, "Husband! Stop being foolish and get back to business!" He smiled to himself, slapped on some after-shave and moved to the threshold between the rooms. Elizabeth was standing at the foot of their bed, laying out Nick's tuxedo and accessories. She was dressed in black bra and panties—a lean and mean 120 pounds of beauty. She saw him in the doorway and asks, "Red or black tie and cummerbund?"

"I think red. This evening is a celebration. Everyone is supposed to have a good time, especially you and me," he says, as he moves into the bedroom.

"Well, I always do. You need to remember it will be a long night and you need to pace yourself."

"I know, dear, I will, and if I don't, I know you'll remind me."

"Yes, I will. Just remember, about everybody who is important to you in business, as well as friends and family will be there, not to mention all your management staff."

"Yes, dear," says Nickolas, as he starts to dress.

As Nickolas is buttoning his shirt, Elizabeth affixes his tie. "This party will last five to six hours," she says. "Have a good time, but don't overdo it, okay? And, you don't need to eat everything they put in front of you!"

"Okay dear, I have the message. Twice, I think. If you'll hurry up a little, we can have a quick drink before Abraham picks us up. Get the edge off, know what I mean?"

"Yes, okay, but just half of one. You get it ready. I'll be down in 15 minutes. You can start without me because I know you'll have a full glass anyway."

Nickolas finished dressing and headed out of the bedroom down the hall to the staircase to the lower level of the townhouse and then to the bar and the under-counter wine cooler, where he selected a bottle of Chardonnay. He quickly dispatched the seal and cork, and poured a frosty glassful. He then made Elizabeth a half-glass Cosmo. He looked at his glass and said, "Yep, that's half a glass."

Nick exited the dining room to the hall, forward in the townhouse to another short stairway down to the large living room with a two-story entryway and a front wall of glass, which looked out onto a sidewalk heavy with trees past the front entrance patio. He sat in a large, well-worn, burgundy leather chair to the side of the fireplace, facing the front window of glass and the street. He took a generous sip of the cold Chardonnay and a few deep breaths to relax himself. He was in a good mood, but yet a little nervous. Even after 20 years in business, the discomfort of social situations and public speaking still stressed him although most people would not know that from his performance. And, performance is what it was, as it was not natural for him to be outgoing. It was not in his genes nor his upbringing.

He looked around, admiring the environment his hard work had created. His mind began to circle back to business and what he needed to achieve that night. He thought, I need to remind everyone once again that this event is primarily the celebration of the company's 20th year anniversary in business. We need to focus on the employees, not my change of status in the company. My move to Washington is secondary and as Chairman, I will be around in the future anyway, if only for the Board meetings. No, he thought. It's too late to remind anyone of anything. At this point, it will be what it is. I just need to relax and have a good time. Nickolas had another sip of wine. His mind moved on, no sense worrying about things you can't control.

Evan was master of ceremonies tonight and he would do a good job; he always did. Where he got that skill, Nick could never fathom. He had another sip. He could hear Elizabeth singing to herself upstairs—the song coming over the second-floor balcony into the entryway atrium. Nickolas smiled, an Irish lullaby. He yelled in the direction of the atrium,

"Your Cosmo is getting warm!"

"I'm coming!" Elizabeth yelled back.

Nickolas smiled and thought, whatever would I do without this amazing woman? Would I have gotten to where I am? I may have gotten here, but probably not with all the pieces intact. I've been a lucky man since I graduated college on the NROTC program. Or, maybe I just got away from a bad environment. Or, maybe I just grew up. I don't know. But the transition seemed to occur in the Corps where he discovered that nothing, *nothing* besides death itself, could stop him from achieving anything he set his mind to do in the long term.

Nickolas' reverie was surprisingly interrupted by Elizabeth's sudden appearance in the living room, where she discovered him in a trance.

"Nickolas, Nickolas. Are you okay? You must have been a million miles away. What were you thinking about?"

Nickolas rises to meet Elizabeth, with her drink in one hand and his in the other. He hands Elizabeth her drink and says,

"Dear, I was thinking of you and how you are more beautiful this night than ever before. How do you do it, year after year, just getting more beautiful?"

"I do it, Nickolas, because each year your eyesight deteriorates just a little more."

"Not true! Not true! You are taking some sort of anti-aging medicine and I want to know what it is. It's not fair that you do not share your secret of youth with your husband!"

"If I did have a secret potion, I would not give it to you until I caught up with you! Men seem to get better looking with age while women do the opposite."

"Maybe some women, but not you."

"Okay, let me sit down. I'm already tired just from getting ready to go out. Let me drink my Cosmo."

Elizabeth settles into a chair next to Nick, with their drinks on the table between. Nickolas asks, "How much time before Abraham gets here?"

"Fifteen minutes if he's on time."

"He's always on time."

"Yes, he is. That's one of his most important position description responsibilities as a company chauffeur."

"Abraham is not a chauffeur. He's a personal transportation and security specialist."

"You're right, I agree."

"Have you got the edge off yet?"

"Maybe not, but it'll come soon. I'm in a celebratory mood."

"Me, too. We deserve it. You deserve it, I should say. I'm just along for the ride."

"Not true, dear. I couldn't drive without you along for the ride. You're the co-pilot, or better said, navigator. By myself, I would get lost."

"You're sweet, but we both know that isn't true. You are the pilot and the navigator. I am just happy you chose me as a passenger."

"Well, you're right about one thing, it's been a helluva an exciting ride! Who could have *'thunk'* it?"

"You *'thunk'* it and you did it. Don't underestimate yourself. Relish in it. Enjoy it. This is your life, Charlie Brown!"

"Charlie Brown! Hey, don't confuse me with one of your early boyfriends."

"Well, you know what I mean. Your whole life will pass before your eyes before this night is over. Relax and enjoy it."

Elizabeth and Nickolas finished their drinks. They stood up and walked to the front door just as the grandfather clock started striking seven bells.

# III

## EN ROUTE TO PRADO BALLROOM, BALBOA PARK

Nickolas and Elizabeth walked out the front door of their two-story townhouse onto the front patio, down the steps and through their front wrought iron gate, which locked after them. The black Lincoln limousine was at the curb, and Abraham was at the left door to assist Elizabeth into the rear seat. Nickolas made his way to the street-side door and entered. As he sat down, he patted Elizabeth's hand and gave her an affectionate smile and says,

"Elizabeth, do you realize this evening will be another one of those milestone events in our life that will conclude one book and start another? Tonight is chapter one."

"Yes, I know, and frankly it scares me a little."

"Well, it scares me a little too, dear, but are you ready? We've been talking about this for quite awhile."

"Yes, I am ready. I am with you 100%, as usual."

Abraham enters the car and lowers the privacy window between the driver and passenger sections.

"Long time no see, boss. What's it been, three hours since the last board meeting?" Abraham says.

"Yes, that's about it, but here we are, another beautiful evening in paradise. Are you and Mrs. B ready to have a good time?" Nickolas asks.

"Yes, we are. We've been looking forward to this party for months. I just dropped Marjorie off at the Prado 15 minutes ago."

"Abraham, you didn't need to drop her off before picking us up; she could have rode with us," Elizabeth says.

"I know, Mrs. Harvey. I suggested she do that, but you know Marjorie, she has a mind of her own. She said she wanted to get there a little early to help the girls with the special table decorations."

"That sounds like Marjorie," Elizabeth says.

Abraham Brown had been Nickolas' personal and family driver for 20 years. Abraham, his wife, Marjorie, and their two grown children, Beth and Andy, were charter members of the greater Harvey Defense Industries (HDI) family. The Brown kids and the Harvey kids had grown up together, meeting at all the various HDI family and holiday functions that had occurred over the two decades of growth and prosperity HDI had enjoyed.

Abraham was turning left on Fifth Street in the Gaslamp Quarter, when he asks in a concerned voice,

"Is this the last night I'll be seeing you in a while?"

"No, I'm sure you'll see me in San Diego another time or two before I see you in Washington."

"When Elizabeth moves, you and Margaret will move."

"Sounds good, boss. We're looking forward to the change and the potential adventure."

"Well, let's hope it is *only* adventure. However, as you know, we are leaving for Fort Lauderdale in the morning and a week or 10 days on the boat."

"Yes, I've been looking at that plan on the schedule for a month or so." Laughing, Abraham says, "You sure after the next six hours of partying, you and Mrs. Harvey are going to feel like flying in the morning?"

"Abraham, I've trained all my life to do these kinds of things. If you can't stay out late, party and go to work at eight o'clock in the morning and get the job done, you simply don't do it, because the people you work with and the job come first. How many mornings have you had to wait for me in the past 20 years?"

"None that I remember, boss. You must have the constitution of a 25-year-old."

"No, Abraham, it's all in the training. I keep myself in top condition. I work out with barbells *and barstools* at least three times a week."

Abraham pulled up to a four-way intersection red light in the extreme right lane for a right turn and waited for the traffic to clear. Nickolas was in the back, sitting on the right. He noticed a man standing on the corner, holding a sign asking for money. The man was just a few yards opposite his window. In one all-encompassing look, he assessed the man. He was in his early 50s, significantly overweight and unkempt—wearing military fatigue trousers cut off to affect shorts, a very tight military green T-shirt and dirty untied sport shoes. He had long blond hair to the shoulders and blue eyes.

The man caught Nickolas' stare and a smirk appeared on his face. They locked eyes for a moment, the top of the food chain and the bottom. The "bottom" pulled a cigarette from a pack in his T-shirt, fished a lighter from his cargo pocket, and flipped the cigarette into his mouth. He then snapped the old Zippo lighter lid open in a one-hand manipulation of fingers and thumb in a flourish and snapped fingers of the other hand, which activated the flint wheel and lit the lighter and cigarette all in one quick fluid motion. Just as quick, the lighter was back in his pocket, but not before Nickolas got the glint of the faded brass Marine Corps emblem on the side. The man sucked in a long, apparently enjoyable drag, with his eyes never leaving those of Nickolas. This entire little drama all occurred in perhaps three to four seconds.

Nickolas had seen this little act performed a thousand times in the Corps, but not in a long while. Nickolas gave the man a knowing nod of understanding and mouthed Semper Fi. The man nodded back almost imperceptibly with a slight smile and pointed an index finger at Nickolas. Nickolas pointed back. They both knew they had a common experience that made them brothers at some elemental level. As the limo turned right, they were both left thinking about this fact, and nodding the truth of it to themselves, each pleased knowing the truth of the other.

Shortly, the limo arrived at the historic Prado Ballroom in Balboa Park, only blocks from downtown San Diego. Many of the out-of-town guests had flown within 1,000 feet of the Prado as they landed at the downtown San Diego International Airport.

Abraham pulled up to the building behind three other limos, dropping their special guests, and waited for his turn to pull to the curb and drop the couple who were the focus of the whole event—the owner, the ex-CEO/Chairman, now Chairman, and his wife, of one of San Diego's top ten private companies and defense contractors, Harvey Defense Industries.

# IV

## PRADO BALLROOM PORTICO

Elizabeth and Nickolas were a respectable one drink late, giving their guests time to get relaxed and socialize before the boss arrived.

The evening was perfect, with the temperature in the low 70s. It had been a sunny day and the sky was beautiful as the sun started its descent in the west.

The large Prado Ballroom entrance patio was full of HDI employees, who were already having a good time. Everyone was dressed to the nines, particularly the ladies, some of whom were barely recognizable in comparison to their daytime business appearance. The four bars in the corners of the patio had lines awaiting the busy bartenders mixing drinks to order. An attractive female violinist was strolling throughout the crowd playing "Ave Maria." When she noticed Elizabeth and Nickolas' arrival, she smiled a big welcome and played a few bars of "Hail to the Chief."

Nickolas said, "Shit" under his breath, "Now everyone knows we're here."

At the same time, many heads turned to the portico of the patio to see the boss and his lady. Among many smiles, welcomes and a short, smattering of applause and a few backslaps, Elizabeth and Nickolas walked into the center of the happy crowd and into many warm and affectionate congratulatory embraces. Moments later, Elizabeth and Nickolas were rescued by Phil Bowen, one of Nick's oldest and dearest friends and a member of his HDI Board of Directors, who had shouldered his way through the crowd with a big smile on his face and a drink in each hand, a Cosmo for Liz and a Chardonnay for Nick. Phil, grabbing Nick by the arm, says,

"Bette is right over there by the fountain. You need to get the water to your back so you can only be attacked by a frontal assault. Follow me!"

They reached Bette, who was beautiful in a black full-length evening gown framed by the patio fountain to her rear. She was holding their two drinks, the usual Manhattan on the rocks for Phil and a glass of Merlot for herself. They all embraced and welcomed one another with genuine affection and enthusiasm. Everyone seemed supercharged for this evening's event, thought Nickolas.

"Bette, I don't think I've seen that beautiful black dress before. You look lovely."

"Thank you Nick, you're always so observant. Yes, it is new. Liz and I were up in La Jolla shopping yesterday while you guys were at your Board meeting and I saw this dress and just had to have it. I bought the dress, and Liz bought lunch at the Marine Room. It was a beautiful day. We had fun, did a little shopping and enjoyed a lot of girl talk."

"Good, that's why you're here to have a good time. Tonight will be the best time of all."

Phil, with a smile, interjects, "I believe, Nick, that it was more than a *little* shopping."

Bette replies defensively, "Well, it was all on sale—30% off!"

Phil says jokingly, "That's after they mark it up 100%!"

Liz, defending Bette, says, "Well, I am here to assure you all that if it was not a good deal, she would not have bought it."

Nicholas says, "Okay, okay, you can't take all that money with you anyway so you might as well enjoy it while you can. We're here to have a good time. Don't remind me that this soiree is costing a bundle. We've had another record business year, our third in a row, and this event is part of everyone's reward for a lot of hard work, including *yours*, Phil, and mine."

Nick tips his drink in a toast to Liz and his best friends and says, "Here's to all of those who helped us get to where we are and those who will help us get to where we are going. Life is a trip, enjoy the ride—that's all there is."

"Liz, you and Bette need to make the rounds. Find Kate and take her with you. Say hello to all the ladies. Phil and I'll do the same with the men after we find Tim and Mike. You guys go that way, we'll go the other. We'll see you in the ballroom at table number one when it opens up at eight o'clock."

Nickolas and Phil were left standing together as their wives moved off through the crowd to a very animated series of conversations, meeting and greeting many employees and their spouses. Nickolas and Phil moved toward the bar, Nickolas saying, "Let's top off these drinks before we go to work. By the way, have you seen Tim and Mike? They should have been ahead of me?"

"Yeah, they're here. I saw them earlier at the hors d'oeuvre table."

"Okay, good. Bartender," looking at his badge, "Fred, please top off these two drinks, will you please? A Chardonnay and a Scotch on the rocks."

"Absolutely, Mister Harvey, it is my pleasure. Here you go. It certainly looks like the start of a great party, sir."

"Yes, Fred, it does, and that is the plan, but don't over-serve anybody. We want everyone getting home safe."

"Yes, sir, we know. We got the word."

Nickolas and Phil elbowed their way through the happy and noisy crowd. More people were arriving who were late, accidentally or on purpose. The crowd was getting larger and the related cacophony more intense. The violinist was playing "Somewhere Over the Rainbow." Nickolas and Phil caught up with Tim, Kate and Mike behind one of the hors d'oeuvre tables with drink glasses in one hand and small food plates in the other.

Nickolas says, "Hey guys, how you doin'? Looks like you have your hands full."

Phil says, "And your mouth's full, too! How did you get that food in your mouth with no hands?"

"Necessity is the root of all invention or whatever that famous saying is," Tim says.

"Well," Phil says, "the only invention I can imagine right now is your power to suck that meatball off the plate!"

"Okay now, leave it to Phil to bring sexual innuendo into every conversation," says Mike, with a smile and wink.

"Only among good, old friends can we get away with this kind of conversation," Nickolas says laughing.

"Give me a hug," says Nickolas to Kate.

Hugs then went around the group of five as Nickolas watched with a big smile, relishing this old demonstration of friendship, which he never ceased to enjoy. He fell into deep thought. How many years? How many business meetings, vacations and inter-family events had this been going on?

How many years, about 20 he thought. A long time since their early days at Baxter Industries. A lot of time. A lot of water under the bridge. Marriages, children, divorces, sickness and even death, including his own struggle with colon cancer. These five people were Nickolas' closest business associates and oldest, closest friends, and he loved them dearly. All of them had worked for Nickolas at one time or another in their early years with Baxter.

Phil was the oldest friend, as they had met in college before any of them crossed paths at Baxter. Nickolas was a senior when Phil was a junior at the University of Illinois. They both were starters on the varsity football team with the Fighting Illini. Nickolas was the quarterback and Phil was a tight end. Phil got himself into trouble by consistently arguing with the coach during games about play calling. Phil was on a football scholarship and thought he knew more about how to play his position than the coach, and maybe he did. After an animated sideline argument during a play-off game on the way to a Regional Conference Title, Phil was suspended by the coach. Phil's ability to graduate the following year was at stake, because if he didn't play, he had no scholarship. He was a good student. He was intelligent, but he had an ego that wouldn't quit when he was competing and challenged—particularly when challenged unjustly.

He likely could have gotten back into play immediately by apologizing to the coach and admitting the error of his ways. However, he couldn't bring himself to do it. He came to Nickolas after missing the second game of the play-off series, which was won by the Fighting Illini without Phil. He had received a notice from the Dean that his scholarship would be revoked at the end of the season. There was one game left—a bowl game, the league championship. When he came to Nickolas, it was almost too late. No, it *was* too late. However, Phil was one helluva good tight end. As a quarterback, Nickolas really appreciated his ability to catch the ball almost regardless of where Nickolas threw it. Phil was a great athlete. He could have been drafted by the pros except he was a rebel. Nickolas really liked him although he couldn't understand why Phil seemed so intent on self-destruction.

Phil came to Nickolas to tell his side of story for the tenth time, to tell Nickolas why the coach was wrong. Nickolas already knew the coach was wrong. However, he was still the coach. Nickolas listened again. He was sympathetic. The championship game was on Saturday, five days away. As the quarterback, Nickolas wanted the great tight end to play, and he wanted to win the game. Although Nickolas was a senior, he had no aspirations to play pro ball. He wasn't that great a quarterback, but he was a great leader and understood the strategy. He led the team and won games, even as an average quarterback, and he had a contract with the U.S. Marine Corps to serve four years after college.

Nickolas knew his options. As leader, he could do nothing and thereby sacrifice Phil, and maybe win the game and maybe not. Or, he could put his reputation on the line and try to save Phil, and maybe increase the odds of winning, or maybe not. It wasn't a real big gamble because he knew he held all the cards. But, on the other hand, he was going to graduate with honors in six months with a reputation on the field and in the classroom— so why risk it all even if you felt you could control the situation? But, he did. He did it because he felt the coach had been too defensive, too concerned about who he was and his desire to control the situation, right or wrong. And lastly, Nickolas did believe that Phil knew more about the play calling for a tight end than the coach did, and that the coach should have listened before he started putting his control lever into gear. They both made big mistakes. But the coach is supposed to be smarter than his players, and apparently, the coach was willing to lose the championship before admitting that he went overboard in suspending Phil indefinitely. So Nickolas pushed all his chips into the center of the table and bet his reputation to save Phil and, for that matter, the coach, the school and the team from their committed course of potential career suicide.

Nickolas met with the coach for a burger and a beer after practice on the Tuesday evening before the Saturday final bowl game of the year for the league championship. Nickolas told the coach that he would not play and that he would tell everyone why if the coach did not reverse his decision to suspend Phil by Thursday at noon. Nickolas said that he had three other starters who shared his position and would get the flu on Friday unless Phil was starting.

The coach was surprised, amazed and upset that Nickolas would take the position that he did. He said,

"You're not that kind of guy, I can't believe this. This will not go down in a beneficial way for you. This will cost you. You're a senior with six months to go. You're a good student, a great athlete, and leader. You are respected by the entire student body and faculty. You could be drafted by the pros. I've had several calls about you. You don't want to do this, son. Listen to me, don't do this."

"Coach," Nickolas said, "you're right, I don't want to do this and I know it's going to hurt me. But I have to do it. I am not going to let Phil get flushed down the shitter because the coach's staff got a little embarrassed in public. Phil gets emotional on the field because he's a fanatical competitor, he hates to lose. He's a passionate guy. Those qualities are desirable in a football player and necessary to win games. Coach, those qualities overcome his emotional immaturity. You are risking the entire team's ability to win the league championship by not letting Phil play. What about them? They've worked hard to get to this point. Why should they be punished?"

"Nickolas," the coach said. "We play football hard at U of I for two or three different reasons and one of them is to teach young players how to lead and how to follow and to realize how getting anything done in life requires that you learn how to do both well. How long do you think Phil would last in corporate America telling the top boss how to run his company? It takes teamwork whether here on the football field or in corporate life or marriage. No one, two or three people on any football team or any business team of consequence can achieve success alone. It always takes everybody working hard together toward a common goal to achieve success. In that process, the head coach or the president of the company, or for that matter, even the president of the United States isn't always right all the time. But in those cases, that doesn't mean that the team or the employees get to revolt or publicly vent and rave in frustration. What they do is hunker down together. They dig in, they plan better together, and together they fight harder the next time out."

"Coach, I agree with you. I understand that principle. I learned that lesson some time ago. But Phil didn't. I believe he's learning now. But, it's not a lesson he needs to learn in one single traumatic event that might result in his losing his scholarship and his will to play the game."

"Nickolas, he won't lose his scholarship, for Christ sakes! What kind of man do you think I am? He'll be playing again in his senior year. I didn't kick him off the team! We suspended him for two games. It just so happens to be the last two games."

"Yes, and perhaps the most important game of his, your or my career. With half the starters graduating this year, it is unlikely, in my opinion, that you'll go to a bowl game next year. Besides, you're assuming that Phil will stay at U of I for his senior year. If he doesn't play in this game and the team loses, he will blame himself, and he will blame you and he will blame the administration. He's a proud guy. He has a big ego. He will be gone!"

"How do you know that?"

"He's my best friend."

"What school would he play for?"

"He wouldn't."

"What would he do?"

"He's in the NROTC program with me. He would join the Marines by the end of next week. But he wouldn't be going in as an officer without his degree."

"Nickolas, I'll re-visit this decision with the coaching staff and we'll determine what we can and want to do. Can you convince him to come before the staff and apologize for his unacceptable behavior on the field?"

"Yes, just let me know tomorrow where and what time you want him and I'll take him there myself."

"Okay, I'll see what I can get done."

Nickolas was still in a state of reverie as his friends talked and laughed and enjoyed the fancy celebration. Nickolas looked at Tim, recalling their time together at Baxter Industries in San Diego.

Nickolas had just been promoted to V.P. of Marketing for Baxter, and one of his first objectives was to interview and evaluate existing key personnel and confirm their ability to get the job done technically and get the job done working for him interpersonally. He had been with Baxter Industries for two years and had been promoted and moved two times, including his one year of accelerated management development training. He, therefore, was well-informed about the organization, his career opportunities, the competition and the industry relating thereto. He played his politics from the top down and he played his performance from the bottom up. Those who worked for him respected and admired his willingness to work as hard as they worked and his pure managerial and political skills that had brought him out of nowhere to an officer in the corporation in only two years. During that time, most all of those he had helped and supported had proven themselves to be strong, successful managers in their own right and had progressed even after Nickolas had moved on beyond his ability to directly influence their careers. However, his career advice was sought by many of them as time went by, and they all climbed the ladder of success—some fast, some slow.

The ones who didn't progress could get the job done for Nickolas with his leadership style, but not for someone else with a different style, or perhaps no style at all. In those cases, it was a mutual failure—first, one of leadership, and secondly, one of followship. There are casualties in all wars; you can't save everyone in every battle no matter how much you want to.

Nickolas hadn't relocated quickly so that he could work all day and all night, seven days a week if needed. As a result, he spent a good deal of time interviewing personnel and working with his 10 key people the first 90 days. His secondary priority was to socialize and politick with fellow constituents in other company departments who had to interface with his marketing people, and with outside vendor people, like the corporate advertising agency who interfaced almost daily with key members of his staff as his budget of $100 million dollars was expended each year. He didn't want to make any impetuous decisions so he had decided to work closely with everyone for 90 days before making any major changes. He understood that his directives would be life-changing to the people involved, whether negative or positive, and to his image and reputation as a manager both up and down the organization.

In this process Nickolas had discovered that the manager of market research was pretty much an old, empty-suit surrounded by several highly qualified young men and women who made their boss look good, but the department was not doing its best possible work because it went through the screen of the old man who had reached the height of his market research intellectual ability perhaps a dozen years ago. He had been smart enough to keep his job, but not smart enough to optimize the potential in his organization. As a result, his annual and quarterly forecasts for the various segments of the industry were always on the conservative side, compared to other competitive manufacturers. When the business cycle was improving, the CEO raised production too late to take advantage of the increasing market, and the opposite was true when certain segments declined, and Baxter was producing at a higher level and increasing very expensive inventory in a declining market.

The accountability process had not been working under the prior V.P. of Marketing. It was just one of two dozen problems Nickolas had been appointed to correct.

Ultimately, Nickolas made an early retirement deal with the aging Marketing Manager and replaced him with a young, obscure Market Research Analyst who had only been with Baxter four years. His name was Timothy Sutton and he was brilliant and courageous and unbelievably accurate in his market research and related forecasts. Nickolas had discovered Tim's ability over a series of Annual Business Planning brainstorming meetings wherein Tim revealed an acute understanding of what the complete process of market research and forecasting should look like, and what it could achieve for the corporation. He was careful not to criticize his boss while enthusiastically suggesting all the ways they could improve the accuracy of the forecasts by segment and in total. Following the meeting, Nickolas invited Tim for a private drink in the lobby bar, which lasted until midnight. Following a very complete and broad discussion of market research and forecasting, as it related to the overall marketing job, Nickolas made up his mind that Tim was his new guy. It would take a real selling job to get it done as Tim was still a young man not yet 30 years of age. But, Nickolas knew he could get Tim sold, and he did.

Nickolas smiled as his attention returned to his friends and the party.

# V

# PRADO BALLROOM

At 10 p.m., as scheduled, the band took a 30-minute break so that Evan Harvey could make a small speech about the status of Harvey Defense Industries business, his new role as President and CEO, and to present some 20-year service awards.

With those assignments complete, Evan says, "Ladies and gentlemen, it is now my honor to introduce my father, the founder of HDI and its Chairman, Nickolas Harvey!" Everyone in the ballroom stands, yells and applauds as Nickolas makes his way to the podium and a warm embrace from his son. The applause continues for another 30 seconds even though Nickolas tries to dissuade them. Finally, most of the audience settles down and takes their seats and Nickolas says,

"Thank you, ladies and gentlemen. What a night! Isn't the Prado Ballroom a beautiful venue?" *(The audience hoots and claps.)* "I am so pleased that we can all be here together to celebrate the 20th year anniversary of our company." *(There's more applause and yelling.)*

"This event is only possible because all of you, spouses included, work efficiently and effectively together to help maintain our leadership within the markets we choose to compete. Our company cannot share the wealth we do not earn, and it takes every one of us working closely together as a team to create profit in our very competitive industry. I thank each and every one of you for your personal sacrifices and contributions to our common enterprise." *(There's more applause and yelling.)*

"As you know, tonight is my last appearance before you as a President and Chief Executive Officer. Tonight at midnight, Evan Harvey is promoted from Chief Operating Officer to President and Chief Executive Officer. I shall retain only my title and role as your Corporate Chairman of the Board over the next several years as Evan continues to increase his HDI ownership shares to a majority. I cannot express my great pride and satisfaction in all that we have accomplished together. I know that our progress will continue into the foreseeable future. I am not retiring from our company, but I'll be moving into a less visible role. However, be assured that from time to time you will see me, and that I will be watching over our common financial future for some time to come. I will never be more than a cell phone call away from any of you if you should need me." *(There's more applause and yelling.)*

"Many of you have asked me what I intend to do in my semi-retirement. I can only say at this time that you will likely be surprised and I hope proud of my decision, which will become obvious to all of you in the next 60 to 90 days. As I undertake this new and exciting major activity, I want you to know it is only possible because of each of you and your contributions for over 20 years to our company. In closing, I thank you on behalf of the entire Harvey family and urge you to enjoy yourself this evening, but remember you still have to drive home safely."

Nick steps back and to the side of the podium and bows to the audience. The audience is on its feet and yelling and applauding enthusiastically. The band is back and plays "Hail to the Chief."

Nick bows a few more times, and throws a few kisses while touching his heart. He is sincerely touched and close to tears, his eyes welling. He leaves to stage right and into the embrace of Elizabeth, who is wiping tears from her eyes and smiling with admiration and love for her husband.

# VI

## PRADO BALLROOM

*Later that Evening*

Nickolas and Elizabeth return to their table and to their special guests. The band is playing "Last Dance."

Tim says, "Nick, you have not lost your touch for throwing a great party. This was the best ever. You didn't overlook a thing. Great venue, good drink, good food, good music, best friends!"

"Thanks Tim, after 20 years you're supposed to know how to do it. This party was really for the employees. They are the ones who make the money. I just provide the resources. It's been a great, great journey."

"Nick, you hinted at a new beginning in your semi-retirement life. What do you have in mind? Will the current Board be involved?"

"We will talk about that in Key West, but yes, there will be an opportunity for you guys. At least I think it's an opportunity, but I am not sure you guys will agree. We'll see what you think in December."

"Hey guys," Nickolas says, as he looks around the ballroom, "as usual it looks like we'e going to close the bar. It's last call and last dance for us until Key West in three weeks!" Nickolas stands, yells at the band, "One more time please, 'Last Dance.'"

Nickolas and Elizabeth dance slowly, romantically to "Last Dance." He kisses her sweetly and says, "Dear, was this a great night or what?"

"The best. You and your people did a great job. Perfect planning as usual, no detail overlooked. But more importantly, are you happy with the party? You spent a small fortune tonight," Elizabeth says.

"Well, you can't take it with you, and every now and then you have to celebrate the milestones in your life. Tonight was a big one. My move to Chairman will reduce my daily role in the company substantially. Daily operations and results are pretty much in the hands of Evan as of midnight tonight, and you and I are off to two weeks holiday in New York, followed by ten days on the boat, then to our next and possibly last great adventure."

# VII

## GUANABO, CUBA

*DECEMBER*

Rose and Manuel Rodriquez live on the distant eastern outskirts of Havana, Cuba, in a fishing village called Guanabo. The greater beach area was populated long ago by four to five thousand Cubans whose income was largely related to the fishing and canning industry. In recent years, the major industry has been tourism. Therefore, the fishing industry in Guanabo has been in a period of transition, and it has become increasingly difficult for independent fisherman to make a living. The Cuban Government has basically taken charge of production and distribution and has slowly forced the small, local fisherman out of business. Only the most determined fishermen have been able to remain independent.

Manuel Rodriquez and his 20-year-old son, Miguel, are two of those fishermen still putting their own aged boat to sea every day except Sunday, chasing the seasonal fish up and down the northern coast of Cuba.

Rose and Manuel's 18-year-old daughter, Maria, and new baby son, Jon, also share their small home along with Miguel. Rose Rodriguez awoke her husband Manuel at 3 a.m. by calling his name softly through the curtained doorway. Rose had already started his breakfast and the smell of strong, dark coffee filled the small cottage. It was inherent with Manuel's occupation that she wake him at that hour since Manuel was a commercial fisherman by trade.

Manuel responds with a "yes, dear," after rubbing his eyes. He sleepily swings his legs off the steel-framed bed and places his feet onto the worn rug over the old wooden floor. He hesitates in the sitting position for a minute or two before raising himself erect with a soft grunt. He straightens his back, rubs his eyes and scratches his butt while weaving slightly, acquiring his balance following six hours of sleep in the horizontal position. In a minute his feet and brain are oriented enough to stiff-leggedly walk to the basin of water on the bureau a few steps away, where he undertakes his daily morning toilet. He washes his face, head and upper body with a washcloth, using the bowl of fresh water Rose had prepared. He brushes his teeth, hair and short beard. He shaves around the beard and trims here and there with a pair of ancient barber scissors. He slowly emerges from the fog of early awakening as he dresses by the bed and prepares for another day.

Manuel goes to the open window. The night air is as cool as it gets in December at this hour of the day in Havana. The slight breeze is out of the southwest and is refreshing on his still moist skin. Like all good men of the sea, he inspects the sky. It is clear, as far as he can see. The stars are as vivid as diamonds on black velvet. It would be another clear, sunny, warm fall day, he thinks, so hopefully the fishing will be good. The yellowtail should begin biting soon. Manuel enters the small kitchen, the main room in the cottage. Rose is at the stove basting Manuel's three eggs in the fat left from the bacon now warming on the back of the stove atop two thick slices of homemade bread slathered with bacon bits and grease. He comes up behind her, as she knew he would, and kisses her on the side of her neck. In a hushed tone he says,

"It's Saturday. Tomorrow after church, we shall go downtown and walk the Marcione, and I shall buy you ice cream and cake at Tomlies. We will spend an afternoon together like we used to when we were young. And when we get home, we shall make love like we were 20 again!"

"Manuel, the loving will be no different unless you can love like you were 15!"

"Rose, you could always sweet-talk me into anything. How about a cup of coffee?"

Manuel sits down at the small oilcloth-covered kitchen table and Rose serves him a big cup of steaming black coffee.

Manuel sips his coffee carefully and lets the delicious smell of frying eggs, bacon, fresh bread and beans waft over him as his mind starts to review the day's plans and tasks. It's Saturday and he would normally be going fishing with Miguel; however, this particular Saturday he has to go work on his new boat. They would fish on the way there and back.

Slowly, his mind switched gears and came into focus on the new boat project and the current status of work and the timetable for completion. He had 10 months to go to finish on plan and put the boat to sea before the hurricane season began next year. He was basically on schedule, but the most difficult portion, the construction, was in front of him. He needed to gain time in the next month or two on the schedule, or he might finish too late to go next year, and his special cargo was counting on him. He had given his word to Rose that this coming year was the year. He instinctively knew his schedule needed a measure of safety. Everything to do with boats and the sea required planning ahead for unforeseen, unknown emergencies. That which could go wrong, would go wrong. He had been a fishing boat captain for 15 years on his own boat and on his father's boat 10 years before that. He had learned from his father like his own son was learning now.

He knew all there was to know about boats and fishing in the waters surrounding Cuba. Knowledge and experience of boats and the sea was Manuel's and Rose's only security because since Fidel, the civilian domestic fishing industry did not have one new boat in almost 50 years. The money for a new boat simply couldn't be earned.

Fisherman simply continued to make-do with boats, which in some cases were built in the 1940s. Spare parts and materials were almost impossible to find and when found, very expensive. Fisherman had long ago become accustomed to putting their lives on the line every time they went to sea.

Manuel's reverie was interrupted by Rose's serving of their breakfast. It was 3 a.m. They always ate breakfast together. It was one of their rituals long ago established, except on Sunday, when they slept late, went to church and occasionally ate their Sunday breakfast in the city.

"Manuel, were you able to find the lumber you were looking for?" Rose asks.

"Yes, I think so. It's from an old wreck Miguel and I found in the sand dunes below Cristopal sometime ago. Most of what's left of this old sailing schooner is pretty dry. But the wood two to three feet below the sand still has life in it. The hull was screwed to its frames with brass screws, which means the hull of the ship was built post-1920. Even the brass screws appear reusable."

"So what are you going to do today? Will you work a full day?"

"Today will be an easy day for me. I'll be working in a sand hole on the shady side of the hull unscrewing all the good wood I can get to. I dug the hole Wednesday night so that no one could see me at the site during the day, which is unlikely anyway, as you can't see there's a wreck there unless you almost walk upon it. It's miles from the nearest road. *Resolute* anchored offshore and my dinghy on the beach could attract the attention of someone at sea but not likely. The alternative is to do all the work at night, but then I would need a light and that would attract more attention."

"The main reason I am working in daylight is that I need to gain some time on our schedule. I've only six months to build this boat. Everyone is counting on me to be ready no later than next July."

"I know you will be ready in time, don't worry. You always get done that which you say you will do. How are you feeling? Any more chest tightness?"

"I'm feeling fine. Maybe a little tired and stressed. I'm trying to slow my life down as the doctor suggested."

"Are you carrying your niacin? They are important. Are you taking an aspirin every day? The other day you left it on the side of your coffee cup. You have to take one every day. You know what the doctor said. I think you're working too hard and worrying too much. Also you haven't been coming home early and taking a nap every day. We should have never started this whole idea. You're too old for all this stuff. You're not a young man anymore. You're not in good health. What would I do without you?" she cries. "Isn't it bad enough you're taking Maria and the baby away from me? What if none of you ever return? What if you all die at sea? What then?" she asks.

"Rose, Rose, that isn't going to happen. I am not going to let it happen. That's why I am handling all this myself, so it's done right. I've put together a perfect plan. I've spent all my life on the sea. It's only a 90-mile sail. Our daughter wants her child to grow up in America with all that that means. She convinced me that one way or another she's taking the baby to America. Would you rather I take them or someone else?"

"I know all that, but I'm so afraid something will go wrong. If you're caught, even on the way back, you'll go to prison. At your age, you could die in there just like Antonio will."

"Rose, we been through all of this a dozen or more times. We've agreed on this. You, me and Maria, we all want the same for baby Jon. We're all long overdue in taking control of our own lives and future. It may be too late for you and me, but not for our son and daughter and baby Jon and those grandsons and granddaughters to come. There is no opportunity in Cuba except more of the same. It has been more than 50 years. Our chance to change things came and went, but the young people, Rose, the young people, they want much more than you and I did."

"Manuel, we wanted more. You fought in the Revolution. You almost died fighting for our freedom, what greater price is there?"

"None, you are right, but it all got away from us and it's gone now. Young people today know what lies 90 miles away and they want it. They don't understand why they can't have it here in Cuba. Many keep thinking tomorrow it will come, but tomorrow never arrives. Each new day is yesterday in Cuba. Rose, it's been more than 50 years! Maria and little Jon will wait no longer and I will not entrust them to someone else. No one else but me, Rose. I have the plan, the experience at sea. I can do this. I love Maria and baby Jon. I will get them to America safely. I have to do this, Rose. I have to do it now. As you say, I am getting old and my health is starting to go. That's why I must do this. It is the last important mission of my life. It is my last fight, my last big contribution to our family, a new beginning for our future family in a new world. Perhaps, it's the most important accomplishment in our entire life. I said, *our* life, Rose, because I must believe that we have made this decision together, regardless of the outcome. The risks are large but worth the rewards for our daughter and grandson, who will carry on the family name and heritage in America long after we are gone."

"Rose, one of my greatest regrets in my life is that you and I didn't do this very thing ourselves 20 or 30 years ago. It's my fault that we didn't. I was just too optimistic all those years that Cuba would change, that America would force the change if Fidel didn't do it himself. But, that didn't happen. When I finally realized that simple fact, it was too late for you and me to give up what we had and start over. I am so sorry. I'll go to my grave regretting this mistake in my judgment."

"Manuel, don't be silly. We've had a wonderful life together here. We worked hard and are better off than most. We have family, good friends. We've never really needed anything other than one another. We created a beautiful son and daughter. Our daughter has conceived a beautiful child. We have truly been blessed. Who could have guessed the outcome of Fidel's Cuba. No one did. Certainly America, as smart as they are, did not." Rose pauses, then continues,

"Probably Fidel himself didn't know where he was going until he got there. Probably he still doesn't know. I live in constant fear of what you're planning. But I understand that you must do it and the reasons why. I know you'll get it done the best way you know how and I pray that you will return to me safely and thereafter, simply arise early every morning, have breakfast with me and then go fishing every morning with Miguel and return to me every afternoon, this I pray."

"Manuel, hold me for a moment before you go. I'm so afraid."

# VIII

## KEY WEST, FLORIDA

*DECEMBER*

Nickolas, Elizabeth, their captain and engineer aboard their classic 70-foot Hatteras motor yacht, *Glory*, had departed their home dock in Fort Lauderdale 10 days earlier for a leisurely cruise to Key West. They had steamed each day for no more than four hours per day, or 40 or 50 miles, stopping first at the Miami Beach Marina and at Bayside Marina in Miami the second night. The third night was Dinner Key Marina in Coconut Grove, then Key Largo, Hawk's Key and Marathon. They had thoroughly relaxed, sleeping late, walking the docks, seeing the sights, catching a few fish, gunkholing in the dinghy, reading, sunning and eating a gourmet meal every night ashore. They had worked long and hard to achieve this lifestyle and they enjoyed the reward.

However, the R & R was coming to a quick end as they rounded the point into the Key West Channel heading for the Galleon Marina. It was 3 p.m. and they were right on schedule.

Nickolas and Elizabeth are standing forward of the pilothouse, leaning on the Portuguese bridge deck rail with arms around one another, looking rested, tanned and happy. Nickolas says to Elizabeth,

"Dear, it has been a wonderful couple of weeks. It couldn't have been better. You've been an absolute joy to be with. I love you with all my heart, but it's back to work in about an hour. The biggest challenge of our life starts tonight and the biggest adventure, maybe the last."

"Nickolas, you know what I say. It will be what it is. I know you'll be successful. You always have been. You always will be, because it isn't within you to give up, or, for that matter to stop working. You're not happy in the retirement mode. I used to pray that you would retire, but I now know that you can't do it and that it wouldn't be good for you or us. You know that I'll support you all the way, no matter what you choose to do." Elizabeth gives Nickolas a kiss and says,

"I just want you to be happy. If you're happy, I'm happy. I know you will get the job done with your friends or you will get the job done without them. I know you want to do it with them and I believe you will. But, you must remember, there's always the chance you won't. You're asking an awful lot not only from them but from their wives and family. They are not going to have the interest in this project that you do. You've been thinking about it for three years. They haven't thought about it all. Be prepared for disappointment and don't oversell your ideas if they resist. Give them time to come around. Give them room to say no without believing they are going to lose your respect and friendship."

"I understand and I agree. But, I believe that what I want to do would be very good medicine for these guys. There they are at the end of the pier."

"Fine, just don't overdo it. You've been friends with these guys half of your life. I'm returning to the pilothouse, see you in few minutes."

"Okay, I got it. I got it. We're almost in. I have to get the forward lines." Nickolas moves forward on the deck to the bow.

"Hey, Mike! How are you doing?"

"Hey, how's it going?" Mike asks. "Throw me a line."

"Tim! You doin' okay? Watch that cleat behind you! Loop your end. I'll adjust the lines from my end," Nickolas says.

"Hey, where's Phil?" Nick asks.

"Phil is at the dockmaster's office, checking you in," Mike says.

"Well," says Nickolas, while securing the boat's forward lines, "that's nice, very convenient."

While Nickolas secured the two bow lines, the engineer was securing the aft lines working with a dock boy. This done, the engineer helped to secure the spring lines, followed by affixing the vessel's dock ladder to the side of *Glory*. Once completed, Nickolas says,

"You guys are a sight for sore eyes! Welcome aboard! We missed you! Get aboard, get unpacked, get a shower, relax for an hour and then get dressed for Louie's Backyard. I'll meet you on the aft deck at six for cocktails."

# IX

## KEY WEST HYATT HOTEL

The evening at Louie's Backyard restaurant had been full of the kind of raucous fun and conversation only true old friends can enjoy after a few drinks and a good meal. The evening's conversation had covered a wide variety of subjects that had brought each of them up-to-date with the lives of the others and their near-term plans following the special board meeting at the Key West Hyatt commencing the next day at lunch.

As usual, following the taxicab ride back to the Galleon Marina, everyone opted for an after-dinner drink.

Nickolas, Phil, Tim and Mike are sitting at a table enjoying after-dinner drinks at the Tiki Bar behind the Hyatt Hotel and adjacent to the Galleon Marina. It had been a long but enjoyable day for everyone, and all of them were relaxed. Nickolas had been hesitant to bring up the subject of his Signature Event but decides it is now or never. During a pause in the conversation, Nickolas says,

"Guys, let me say a few words. Thank you so much for being here. This day has been special and important to me and one I will never forget. I want to tell you why. Please permit me to introduce the subject matter completely, withholding your questions until the end. At that point, I know we'll have a lively discussion. The subject is my plan to undertake what I call a Signature Event, as I approach the end of a very successful business career in my life."

"What is a *Signature Event?*" Tim asks. Nickolas gives Tim a look.

"In my opinion, it's the last and final major achievement in your life, for which you wish to be remembered, and potentially the last challenge of your public life. Perhaps a challenge, if you've been financially successful in life, which has a social component—like the betterment of man, or the elimination of hunger in the world, as a classic example. Perhaps it's some goal that necessitates using all of your career experience and personal skills to achieve, but is a chance to 'give back' to mankind in appreciation for all that a successful career, a great life, and good health has provided to you and yours. Or, perhaps, it's the achievement of your 15 minutes of fame, your last hurrah, the final fight before you retire from the battlefield forever!

"Have you ever considered such an idea? I have, and I want to share my thoughts with you. Maybe in the sharing of my aspiration, I will arouse your imagination and interest. I believe in the value of a positive point of view regarding the future, so at this time in my life, as you know, I believe I can do about anything that I set out to do, and I do believe in the power of one man to change the world. Other men have done so, some for good, some for bad. I have a dream, and I believe dreams lead to visions, and big visions to big plans and potentially to big achievements. I believe dreams and visions are the cornerstones of inspiration, and when coupled with planning and organization and focus, result in a powerful, powerful force. HDI is a good example.

"As you will recall, it was those exact beliefs that brought each of us from where we were in college to where we are now in the present—successful, retired, wealthy businessmen.

"Somewhere in the beginning, you had the dream, then the vision and then the plan. You believed. You made others believe. In the end, you made your dreams become reality!

"You had the ability to initiate a vision, gather all the necessary intelligence and resources and focus upon converting the vision into an organized plan. Then enlist the manpower and other support requirements. Then achieve consensus on strategic directions, priorities, budgets, controls and timing in a comprehensive, detailed and organized fashion. Then initiate action, measure and report results, and recommend changes to strategy and tactics as needed to achieve the desired results.

"The other night, we talked about the rewards of leadership that we used to enjoy so very much as young executives with Baxter Industries. For many of us, those years were the apex of our managerial careers and leadership roles. The benefits we talked about missing are related to playing upon the larger stage of big multi-national corporate America. Simply stated, it was the glory of it all that we miss!

"Command, esteem, respect, honor, dignity, recognition, excitement. Betting big and winning big!

"We've all missed that level of excitement. Our current or past business situations, although far more financially rewarding, did not provide the height of those emotional highs.

"Therefore, I have searched for a worthwhile Signature Event that would provide those benefits to me on an even larger scale then Baxter or HDI did, because today I am a more experienced leader with greater skills than before. Thus, a greater challenge and bigger stage are necessary.

"I believe I want to experience all of these benefits just one more time before I retire. And, not just for myself, but to relive these satisfying experiences with those I admire and love and those with whom I have shared these experiences before. I'm talking about you three guys principally, and others who are waiting for our call, although they do not know it as we speak.

"More importantly, I would sincerely like to make a significant contribution to society, or mankind in general, that makes the world a better place to live in, because I was here, if I can.

"Guys, my life is full of everything good. I've been extremely fortunate and 'my cup runneth over' with appreciation and gratitude, which I strongly desire to share. You can't take all that money with you."

"What is this Signature Event?" Phil asks.

"It's called the Americans for Reconciliation with Cuba coalition or ARC for short. The objective of this coalition is to change current U.S.-Cuban Foreign and Economic policy from what it is today and has been for more than 50 years to a normal relationship similar to U.S.-Canada and U.S.-Mexico relations, our other two nearest neighbors. This goal is to be achieved in three years or less."

"What's wrong with the relationship now?" Mike asks.

"Here is the situation. In the past and currently, 900,000 organized South Florida Cubans over many, many years have determined U.S.-Cuban Foreign Policy through special interests political influence, that influence being money and votes. This situation has continued to exist without any significant political opposition or change for more than 50 years! As a result, 12,000,000 Cuban people, who are U.S. neighbors, 90 miles off the coast of the United States, continue to lead a life of poverty, hopelessness and quiet desperation. The situation is ridiculous if you think about it.

"The only way to turn around this situation is to organize a larger, stronger more influential opposing U.S. political organization, which shall overcome all the political obstacles that currently exist between the historical U.S.-Cuban relationship of the past 50 years and the one which the ARC organization believes needs to exist.

"I believe this can be done, and that the timing is right, by capturing the *'moral high ground'* opportunity that exists and by recruiting a grassroots campaign organization in every U.S. state and county to enlist broad public support, financing and superior political power. Secondarily, if necessary, organize corporate America on this issue, specifically those who have reparations at stake from the past and those who have a major nearby market opportunity at risk for the future.

"There are tides in the affairs of men when taken at their ebb unleash a flood of change of unparalleled strength. My dream has a spiritual component and it's telling me that the Cuban people, the American people and the world community is ready, willing and able to join this crusade, and are impatient for someone to lead it.

"Think about it. Consider making my Signature Event yours, as well. Join me in this major, worthwhile effort to free the Cuban people. Our neighbors and their families are in trouble and they need our help."

Nickolas finished his statement largely without interruption from his surprised friends although he had been able to tell from some of their facial expressions and body language that they had wanted to interrupt and question or comment on some of his statements. They now sat passively, stone-faced, alternately looking at their hands on the table, at Nick or at one another, waiting for someone to take a leading position on Nick's plan. They were totally surprised by Nickolas' commentary.

Phil took a slow sip on his drink as he looked over the edge of the glass at his friends. Tim straightened his back in his chair looking around. Mike spoke,

"Nick, you've worked your ass off, night, day and weekend for 20 years, not counting four years of college and four years in the Corps. You're pushing 50! Isn't it time to rest? Why take on a new challenge and particularly one you're ill-prepared to win? You're no politician outside of your business circles."

"Good question, Mike, but I've already answered it. However, I'll speak to it again. But first, I'm interested in everyone's initial point of view regarding my proposal. Phil, what do you think?"

"Nick, I don't know what to think. I think you've caught us all pretty flat-footed on this one. You've been working most of the time right up to two weeks ago. The rest of us sold our businesses some time ago and retired. I don't think any one of us has considered returning to any kind of serious full-time work. I don't know if any of us is willing to do that. Personally, I would have to hear a lot more."

"Phil, I fully understand and obviously the need for more discussion is a foregone conclusion for all of us, assuming you would even consider the concept."

"Mike, what do you say?"

"Well, Nick, I don't want to piss you off, but I'm wondering how well you've thought this idea through. First, as I understand your goal, your activity would likely be in conflict with the U.S. Government's long-standing Cuban Foreign Policy and federal laws relating thereto.

"Second, Castro is a Communist, who has run a dictatorship in Cuba for more than 50 years. Five or six U.S. Presidents, both Democrat and Republican, have more or less maintained the same U.S.-Cuba Foreign Policy for all that time without change. I don't understand how a man with your background and experience is going to change that long-standing policy." Mike pauses, then smiles and says, "Unless, of course, you had our help."

"Third, do you realize that the activity you wish to engage in and the changes you hope to achieve could become very dangerous? Dangerous not only to you, but to us and all of our families. In fact, the more I think about it, the more I understand that you would likely be pissing off everyone who has been a stakeholder in maintaining the status quo not only in America but in Cuba, as well. And, everybody includes the U.S. Government, the Cuban Government, U.S. Cubans, U.S. citizens, some other foreign governments, certain U.S. business interests and Cuban business interests; the list goes on and on!

"Most of these guys do not play fair, if you know what I mean. To some extent, you're asking us to put our lives in danger. The more I think about it, the more I think this is a bad idea, a dangerous idea."

"Mike, I appreciate your candor. I wouldn't disagree with anything that you said. However, I believe that if I fully explained what I want us to do and how we would do it, I could change your mind. I realize that my concept and your suggested involvement is a major surprise and that you'll need time and much more information to make an informed decision. I also understand that you, too, have worked hard all of your careers, built a business and sold it in order to pursue the good life, as they say, and enjoy the fruits of your labor. But, I also know that each one of you has grown tired and bored with full-time retirement and that you miss the action of your past business lives.

"You are still all young men with 20 to 30 years of active life ahead of you. You all are 10-15 years away from being able to draw Social Security, assuming there's any left to draw. I know that each of you has considered returning to business in a less-challenging, time-consuming situation. We've all talked about some of the ways we could do that together. A couple of years ago, we almost did that Florida real estate development thing. Remember?

"All I really expect at this time from each of you is to keep an open mind on this possibility and take the time to listen and consider my complete plan over the next few days.

"I can tailor your involvement in ARC to be full or part time, but no less than three consecutive days a week, including travel time. You can return home every Thursday evening through Tuesday mornings if you desire to do so. Or, I'll put all of you and your wives temporarily in a nice townhouse or condo in Georgetown for the full period of this mission, which I project to be 24 to 36 months. This is what Elizabeth and I intend to do, and I will make the same offer to certain other key personnel that I will transfer from HDI in San Diego.

"All your traditional IRS-approved business travel and relocation expenses, vehicle expenses, etc., will be paid by the new corporation that we'll form soon.

"Liability insurance, health and welfare, disability and life insurance will be provided for you and your wives for a minimum of three years—perhaps longer if you choose to stay with the new company beyond the Cuba project.

"I'll pay each of you $100,000 after tax and benefits the first year and more the second and more the third if you stay. I know you're worth a lot more, but I also know if you come to work with me and each other again it won't be because of the money. You're all very wealthy men. Secondly, if you're not motivated by the cause, I believe that no amount of money would attract you.

"You'll be motivated by the idea that you, too, would enjoy sharing the work and rewards associated with our, your Signature Event, perhaps your last big hurrah and the lifestyle enhancing opportunity for all of us to work closely together again to move mountains. But this time, moving mountains will change the world we live in for the better.

"I suggest that we now postpone further discussion on this subject until breakfast at eight in the morning on the aft deck of *Glory*. Agreed?"

"Hell no, Nick!" says Tim. "You said we would have Q&A at the conclusion of your speech. You can't drop a bomb like this on us and then say we'll revisit the issues in the morning!"

"Tim, I know the Q&A is going to be emotional and I wanted us to enjoy the rest of the evening, that's all," Nickolas says.

"Well, Nickolas, you've already shot that idea all to hell. If you want us to sleep tonight, we have to talk about this idea of yours!"

# X

# ABOARD THE YACHT GLORY

Nick slipped quietly into the dark master cabin of *Glory*, trying not to awaken Elizabeth. The passageway light briefly lit the bedroom through the open door, revealing Elizabeth apparently sleeping peacefully. He closed the door and moved to his side of the bed and the dresser, removing his watch and rings and unloading his pockets in the faint moonlight coming through the portholes. He was being careful not to make any noise when Elizabeth says, "I'm awake. You can turn on the lamp if you wish."

"Hello dear, did I wake you?"

"No. I've been awake. What time is it?"

"It's 11:45."

"I've been awake since about 10:30 when you guys came home from dinner and had that last drink."

"Were we too loud?"

"No, although I heard you coming down the deck. Then it was just the anticipation of your coming to bed that kept me awake. How did it go? Do you want to talk? Did you get the job done?"

Nick crawled into bed in his Skivvies and T-shirt, saying, "Well, it was a long serious evening after dinner. Not much fun, mostly business. I had to sell my butt off all night, but I finally got them all to commit. None of them are very excited about the whole idea, but they're in—at least for the first 90 days. I had to give them an out to make them comfortable with proceeding. Phil was the most difficult. He has an endless list of problems with the project. We know he's very conservative, but I had no idea how super-conservative he was until now."

"But, he finally agreed?"

"Yes, but he's not a happy camper. I doubt he will go beyond the first 90 days, and he's probably only going that far because he knows that he owes me big time."

"Nick, I hope you didn't use the '*you-owe-me card.*' He's been a good, loyal friend of yours for more than 20 years."

"No, I didn't. I wouldn't do that."

"Well, I'm glad it's all working out for you. You knew it wouldn't be easy. Personally, I'm surprised you got them all lined up. You've asked an awful lot of them, and their families."

"Yes, I know, and if this project doesn't fly the way I've planned, I'm going to look like a total idiot, and our net worth is going to take a big negative hit."

"Your goal is worthy, your motivation noble and you've never failed at anything you made up your mind to do. I'm not worried about anything except your safety. I couldn't face life without you."

"Nor I without you, dear. Think you can go to sleep now?"

"Yes, all I need is a kiss and a big hug."

Nick turned off the light, rolled on his side, gave her a long, sweet kiss and a hug and said, "Are you sure that's all you need?"

# XI

## ARC HEADQUARTERS

### (Americans for Reconciliation with Cuba)

**Georgetown, Washington, D.C.**

*FEBRUARY*
*Twenty-One Months to Election*

Nickolas and Elizabeth had been living temporarily at the Georgetown Marriott Suites the past six weeks. Phil, Bette, Tim, Kate, Abraham and Marge had only recently arrived and were staying at the Marriott while looking at more appropriate, longer-term living accommodations. Mike had been staying at the Harvey Building in the only completed, remodeled apartment, overseeing the installation of the building's security system and keeping an eye on things until the security system was installed, tested and effective. Nickolas had been personally involved in the final remodeling of his new apartment building and more importantly, the ARC headquarters and first-floor commercial space, including a new bar, grill and jazz club called the Blue Note. The primary ARC Conference Room was to be completed today, and Nickolas was looking forward to seeing it.

The four-story, 40-year-old brick building encompassed a half-city-block with two levels of below-street parking, retail space on the first floor, ARC headquarters on the second, and apartments on the third and fourth floor. An alley split the block. The area was a combination of commercial buildings on the main streets and mixed single-family homes and apartment buildings beyond the main streets.

Nickolas had purchased the building two years ago after deciding what activity his Signature Event would require.

The building was internally as solid as the Rock of Gibraltar, but, in appearance, was in disrepair. They don't build buildings like this one anymore. It was in the D.C. area where he had decided they needed to headquarter to best get ARC's job done. Georgetown was expensive, but had location, location, location. That only meant it was popular to those who could afford it, and those who could, would always be able to afford it. Investment-wise, he knew it was good, disregarding the outcome of ARC, and he had the money to invest.

The remodeling of the building was almost complete, inside and out, with a recent focus on the ARC headquarters, the parking garage, the Blue Note and the building's basic high security system. Nickolas was very pleased with the outcome and excited about the opportunity to show it off to Phil and Tim.

Nickolas arrived at his building this day by cab and was pleased to see that all the trees in the front were starting to bud and that the street parking was full of pickup trucks and SUVs, revealing the various contractors' commitment to finishing all the final plumbing, electrical, painting and trim issues. He knew it could take another 60 to 90 days to finish the building, but his plan required that the first two floors, ARC Headquarters and the Blue Note be done by the end of the month, perhaps in another two to three weeks.

Nickolas exited the cab, waved at some of the foreman and workers he knew, and entered the lobby portion of the building through the main front door. The lobby was not yet complete. He took the elevator to the second floor, where halls went forward left and right from the second-floor reception area. He went left, heading for his and Phil's executive offices. Mike's section would be straight ahead and Tim's to the right. Nickolas had planned for each of his associates to have their own separate space. As he turned left down his hall, he noticed there was a lot of 'moving in and setting up' activity. Inside were carpet layers, painters, desk installers and others.

Nickolas entered the conference room. It appeared complete with new paint, carpet, a table for 12 with leather chairs, coffee bar with lower fridge on the right side, and a pop-up large-screen TV monitor on the far end. There was a large built-in buffet at the other end of the room and matching chairs to the right along the wall. Soft yellow walls were replete with artwork in dark wood frames. Overhead lights were controlled with dimmers and a variety of lighting options. The large windows to the left and right of the TV monitor were fitted with folding white shutters, all recently installed and painted.

Seated at the table in casual business attire were Phil, Tim, Mike and Judy Austin. To the right, seated independently of one another in the gallery, were two men and four women dressed in business attire.

"Atten-hutt!!" yells Mike as he jumps up, startling everyone, and causing those in the gallery to rise unexpectedly. One drops her portfolio. Mike laughs at most everyone's startled response as he sits back down, saying,

"Just a little humor, folks. Sorry I woke you up."

The gallery persons look at one another with raised eyebrows.

"Yes, damn little humor, but you didn't catch Tim and me," Phil says.

"Mike, you shouldn't do that before I've had my second cup of coffee," Nickolas says. "I'm not as young as I used to be, you know." Nickolas takes his seat at the head of table. He punches a button on a mini-screen PC to his right and a large pop-up TV monitor silently rises in the console at the forward wall and drapes close automatically over the shuttered windows. Another button is pushed, and a large clock appears on the screen revealing the time as eight o'clock in the morning.

"Ladies and gentlemen, it is with great enthusiasm, satisfaction and expectation that I welcome you all to the first official business meeting of the Americans for Reconciliation with Cuba coalition, or ARC if you like acronyms, and an ARC of influence, if you like logos." Nickolas brings the ARC logo up on the screen.

"It has taken some of us several months of planning to get to this point, and I know that those of us involved are excited and gratified to finally be here.

"Permit me to introduce the leadership of our coalition.

"I'm Nickolas Harvey. I'm married, 48 years old and have two children. I was born and raised in Burlington, Vermont, on the beautiful shores of Lake Champlain. I graduated from the University of Illinois. I was in the NROTC while there and took the Marine Corp option. I served in the Corps four years. I was a basic *'gravel cruncher,'* a reconnaissance team leader. I saw active duty in 1979, 1980 and in 1982–83. I left the Corps and went to work for Baxter Industries in San Diego where I proceeded to do well, saved some money, left Baxter and started my own business called Harvey Defense Industries. I took HDI public five years later and semi-retired two years ago.

"Life has been very good to me. I've been very fortunate in almost all ways. I'm very appreciative. What I'm trying to do now is to give something back. The effort we're about to commence will take some unknown period of time to complete—likely at least two years, and an unknown amount of capital, but obviously several million initially. Our cause will become self-funding within a year or so if we're successful. That concludes my personal introduction. You will become aware very soon of a lot more information in the normal course of our start-up activity.

"To my left is Judy Austin, my personal Administrative Assistant. Judy has been with me since we started HDI 20 years ago. She has agreed to take a leave of absence from HDI to spend the next two years or so working for me in my capacity as Chairman/CEO of ARC. Phil, Tim and Mike already know Judy well, and the rest of you will get to know her quickly as she is my right arm and knows me better than I know myself. You'll discover Judy is very capable, knowledgeable, effective and efficient."

"Judy, what would you like to say?" Judy stands.

"Thank you, Mr. Harvey. Only that I am very pleased to be here. I look forward to getting to know Phil, Tim and Mike better and to meet and work with the rest of you on this exciting, unique and very challenging project. My job will be to help you get your job done quicker and easier by being your liaison to Mr. Harvey when he's not personally available to you or your issue requires a decision but perhaps is not worthy of a personal meeting, or phone conversation with him. I'll be monitoring all of Mr. Harvey's communications, business and personal, including e-mail, on a strictly confidential basis, of course. Thank you."

"Folks, you can trust Judy. If you'd say something to me, you can say it to her. Her purpose is to help you, not slow you down. She will prove that to be true, I guarantee you. Thank you, Judy."

"Next, I would like to introduce our newly appointed Chief of Staff, Phil Bowen. Phil and I, and for that matter Tim and Mike, too, go back 20 years or more. We were all young executives at Baxter Industries initially. We all left at various times to start our own businesses. At one point, we all worked in the same department. Actually, I've known Phil and his wife, Bette, since college. We all have been meeting at various industry events every year for 15 years or more. Phil sold his business about three years ago and I was fortunate to be able to appoint him a Board Director for HDI. Phil has been a tremendous asset at HDI and has agreed to go to work full time on the ARC project. Phil is a very experienced, successful executive with especially strong financial and administrative management skills. We are very lucky to have Phil on our team."

"Mr. Bowen, what have you got to say to these people?" Phil stands.

"Mr. Harvey, I'll be brief. I think you've done a great job of selecting this particular property and building as our Corporate Office. I've noted it is very close to a number of attractive bars, restaurants, hotels and public transportation. Some of the bars I have already interviewed while the Blue Note is being finished and would like to show you. Further, I see your personal influences in this particular conference room, and you have done an outstanding job here, as well. However, I note this is the only completed room above the first floor! I sense that my first job is to complete the Corporate Office as soon as possible."

"Phil, you're very astute. However, in the interest of controlling future expense, your first job really is to complete the 32 apartments on the third and fourth floors. Young people at our rate of pay cannot afford to live in Washington, D.C., so one of the benefits of the lowest paid 20 is free housing. Also, there are two other completed rooms you haven't seen yet, a wine storage room and a workout room on the first level of the garage."

"I see," Phil says. "Nick, you're always thinking. What about the other 12 apartments?"

"Well, at least temporarily, you, Tim and Mike and I will use four of them. That way, we can work 16 hours a day, at least until we move into more permanent housing."

"Well, that covers all four levels. Quite a remodeling job, I would say," Phil replies.

"You're right," Nick says. "It's a challenge, but it's all been planned, is under way and nearly complete. You just need to bring it home as quickly as possible and watch the budget. Oh, by the way, the basement is being turned into a two-level parking garage and there is some danger the whole building could collapse, so keep an eye on that to please.

"Next, I would like to introduce our Director of Communications, Tim Sutton. Tim's married to Kate, and they have two children in college. Tim, like Phil and Mike, go back with me 20 years or more. Tim also worked with me long ago at Baxter Industries, left the company, went into business, sold the business and retired with a small fortune. Hey! This is the second old friend of mine I've introduced who sold his business and retired with a small fortune! What am I doing still working every day, and I am older than any of them? I digress, excuse me. Tim was the Vice President of Sales and Marketing for Baxter and did a hell of a job for them for several years before he left. Tim is a professional marketer among other management skills in every sense of the words. He has experience with multimillion dollar communications budgets in print, radio, TV and public relations.

"Do you remember the TV campaign 'Who's got the beef?'" The gallery nods their heads. The conference table just smiles.

"Well, Tim didn't do that one, but he dated the star of the commercial for a while. Just joking. He didn't date her. She wouldn't go out with him.

"Tim, you know I love you. What would you like to say?"

Tim stands. "That last part of the story is not true. She did date me up to the time she died of a coronary. You may not realize it, but she was only 19 when she made those commercials. Too many burgers and fries. Let that be a lesson to you fast food fanatics." Tim pauses, smiles and says,

"Ah, thank you. I think Nick, I'll be brief too. I am sincerely pleased to be here and part of something so much bigger than anything that I've done all of my life. Retirement has not set too well with me and very well may have cost me my marriage with my third wife, 22-year-old Annabelle! Just joking. What I'm trying to say is I'm already feeling good about being back in the traces as they say, and in pursuit of a major challenge. The challenge I'm referring to is the fact that in Washington, D.C., the women outnumber men four to one. I want you all to know that I'll do my very best to do my fair share. Or more! Just joking.

"Seriously, I'm serious when I say seriously, I am more than pleased to be here. Our goal has been unrecognized by anyone else in 50 years. Hundreds have died, hundreds imprisoned unjustly, millions now live in unnecessarily poverty, fear and oppression. There has been no hope for many years that the Cuban situation will ever change. Very soon, you and I, at the very minimum, will for the first time provide hope. At the very best, you and I will, in fact, achieve a major significant change for the better in the lives of 11 million Cuban neighbors, who live just across the street from Key West—neighbors we've ignored for way too long. Thank you, Nick, for bringing us back together again."

"Thank you, Tim, it's my honor. It's going to be a lot of work, but it's also going to be a lot of fun as some of us have tried to demonstrate. We believe if we can't have fun doing the work that we don't want to do it. I don't like work!

"Last, but certainly not least, I introduce another old friend and my Krav Maga training instructor Mike McLean. Mike and I also go back to my early years at Baxter; however, we actually met as Marine Corps Reserve Officers in San Diego. Mike was smarter than me and spent his active duty time as a Marine Corps Intelligence Officer. Among his many varied adventures and experiences was a two-year special assignment to the Navy's Adjutant General's Office Criminal Investigation Unit, right here in Washington, D.C., where among other successes, he led a C.I.D. unit that investigated and busted a major, big-time fraud and theft ring that was looting the Navy's supplies and distribution system worldwide.

"Having served his country with distinction, Mike opened his own corporate security and investigations company, which he managed very successfully for a number of years before selling to a major, international security firm. As you probably have figured out at this point, Mike is our Director of Security Operations which, in addition to key personnel security, will include responsibility for transportation, travel, lodging, investigations, training, background checks, etc., heavy on *the etc.*

"Mike is fully qualified for this very important assignment and I request, on his behalf, your full cooperation. Mike's decisions on security-related issues are final. He will, after all, only be concerned about your good health, safety and security, and the security of all of our data, activities and communications. Mike has been on the job for the last six months, making sure our building security is everything it should be. Mike is a single guy, divorced, no children, one dog.

"Mike, what would you like to add at this time?"

"Thank you, Nick. I'll add that I am very pleased to be here and a part of your Signature Event, which surprisingly I believe is rapidly becoming my Signature Event, as well. I can't quite understand why previously I had very little, if any, concern with Cuba or the Cuban people. I guess I haven't ever questioned our country's Foreign Policy. I didn't understand that policy in Cuba as being strictly political until recently. Once I understood the weight of consequence caused by this travesty, it's overwhelming. I'm off point. Nick, I'm just trying to say that I've become a believer. Back on point.

"We are all thoughtful people or we wouldn't be in this room today. Therefore, you know there is an element of danger in this project. My job is to eliminate and reduce that danger from affecting our mission or assets, including personnel, in any way. You can help me best by remaining constantly aware that our opposition will be seeking information about our organizations, plans, strengths, weaknesses, etc., in an effort to initiate measures counter to our mission. As we successfully go through time, these opposition efforts will intensify in frequency and threat level. All of us, and the people who will work for you, need to remain alert. Not worried. Not in fear, but alert. My people and I will do the worrying. Trust us. If threats develop that you should fear and actually defend against, I'll advise you. Much, much more to come on this subject, but that will do for now. Thank you."

"Thank you, Mike. I think everyone will agree that your role in our organization could become the most important to us collectively and individually. Don't let this subject dampen your spirits. Take it very seriously, but don't let it worry you. Worry is a waste of time as it won't change anything other than your attitude. When evaluation of potential threats and action to correct them is needed, Mike and his people will address them.

"You have now met the senior leadership of our organization. Reporting to the four of us are only seven people, at least initially, and six of them are in the room. Judy reports to me and she has been introduced. Another reporting to me is our CFO, who is Joyce Johnson. Joyce is my CFO at HDI in San Diego, and some of you know her. She will remain in San Diego. Our PC-based systems needs will be connected to the HDI mainframe computers by secure, direct, digital satellite access to all of our information, data files, etc. As a military weapons supplier, our HDI computers are secured by the very best and latest technology. Therefore, there is no need to reinvent that particular wheel. We're actually up and running as we sit here with secure, computerized, departmentalized Financial Accounting, Inventory Control, Asset Management, Receivables, Payables, HR, Communications, Word Processing, web access; you name it, we have it. We intend to operate our business as paperless as possible. Everything possible will be on line with very strict access coding."

Nick pushes buttons once again on the mini-keyboard to his right and the computerized clock appears with the current time, 9:30 a.m. "This clock is part of one of our San Diego software programs coming to you real time from HDI in San Diego. So, as you can see, we're ready to do business.

"Phil is our Chief of Staff. Phil, please introduce your people."

"Nick, that won't take long, I have only one at this time."

"She is Carmen Benson who is, effective this date, our Office Manager. Carmen is an American-born, single, Cuban woman, born and raised here in Washington, D.C. She's a graduate in accounting from Virginia State University and has been working in the defense industry the past three years. Carmen, will you rise?"

Carmen stands and waves. "Hello everyone, I'm glad to be here and I'm excited about your cause, which I do believe in very much. Phil, thank you so much."

"Carmen speaks Spanish and is fluent in all the Spanish dialects, including Cuban. I thought that asset may come in handy at some point. As our in-house manager of our financial, accounting inventory and secretarial pool and related administrative duties, including our receptionist, she will, of course, be interfacing frequently with Joyce Johnson at HDI in San Diego and with our senior managers. Carmen is a very good communicator and you'll enjoy doing business with her.

"As Chief of Staff, I am in charge of managing our financial plan budget, and manpower, which likely will be our greatest cost. My philosophy has always been to run my business as lean and mean as possible. I, therefore, intend to run my personal department lean and urge my fellows to run theirs the same way. Thus, Carmen and I are challenging each other to see how far we can go without hiring another chief. We obviously have to hire five or six Indians—figuratively speaking, of course."

"Thank you, Phil. Those Indians are now called Native Americans. Tim, please introduce your people."

"Nick, at this time I only have two to introduce, and they are the other two ladies. First is our Manager of Marketing Research and Planning, Casie Scott. Casie is a recent graduate of Delaware University with a degree in marketing. She is a single lady and will live in our building as soon as the space is available. Casie graduated 'cum laude' in her class and plans to continue her education at nights going for her master's degree at nearby Northeastern."

Casie stands and waves. "Good morning."

"Next is Lisa James, reporting to Casie, who is our new Manager of Public and Media Relations. Lisa is a graduate of the University of Vermont with a degree in communications and has a distinguished background in television, radio, print and advertising sales. Most recently, she was a Senior Sales Executive for Young & Rubicam in Manhattan. Lisa will obviously be a key contributor to our success, by assuring that our message gets optimum attention in the media. Lisa, thank you for being with us."

Lisa stands and waves. "Good morning, glad to be here."

"Thank you, Tim," Nickolas says. "You've obviously pulled the wool over the eyes of these ladies or exceeded your authorized budget! Welcome ladies. We look forward to working with you. Let us know how to make the job easier for you—and more fun. Remember, if we can't make it fun, instead of work, we really don't want to do it."

"Mike, what's happening here? There's no beautiful women left! Only some "hairy legged guys." *(One guy in the gallery pulls his pant leg down.)* "It looks to me that you need to take 'recruiting training' from Phil and Tim!" Nick says.

"Well, Nick, I do have some surprises for you guys, but not today. Today I am pleased to introduce to you two old friends of mine from the 'Crunch' and from my old company SM One. Fortunately, my no-compete, no-hire agreement with SM One expired six months ago and these two guys agreed to contract with us for two years. However, as part of our deal I have to set them up in their own security business at the end of their contract, which I am willing to do since I'm beginning to get bored with retirement, but Nick, I might need you to buy a few thousand shares of stock or change security providers for HDI."

"Mike, is there no end to your entrepreneurship promotion? You're unbelievable! Bringing this up in front of all these witnesses, including the two guys who are going to put up every dollar they have! Right!"

"Obviously," Mike says.

"Okay. If I have any money left after this mission, the four of us or the six of us, if Phil and Tim want in, and your two guys will figure out how to fund this new company," Nickolas says.

Mike answers, "Jesus, that was pretty easy." Looking at his two associates, he says, "We should have gone for more. He's getting soft in his old age!"

"Well, I said, if there is any money left after this mission, which means you guys have a large stake first in keeping me alive, and second, helping me get this job done before I go broke!" Nick answers.

"I did tell you there was a quicker, cheaper way to get to the end," Mike says.

"Yes, yes, I know. Let's not go there!"

"Okay Mike, let's return to the business at hand. Who are these guys?" Nick asks.

"Okay, here we go. Both of these guys are very experienced ex-Marine reconnaissance NCOs, which is the only accreditation they need to work for me and you. I've known them both for more than 10 years and in that time, they both worked for me several times. We've shared some very serious times together. It's my privilege to introduce Gunny Sergeant Tony Diego on the right and Gunny Sergeant Pete Alvarez on the left. Both these guys are Cuban Americans, and speak the language fluently. Tony is from Miami and Pete is from New Jersey. As Cuban-Americans, they are attracted to our mission. And, as I said, I made them an offer they couldn't refuse. What do you have to say guys?"

"We're real glad to be here and to work with Captain Mike again," Tony says. "We believe in what you're going to try to do and you all can count on Pete and me to do our share and more. We look forward to meeting and getting to know everyone."

"Mr. Harvey, we really appreciate the opportunity to be here," Pete says. "We'll take good care of you and your people. You can count on that 24/7/365."

Nickolas replies to Pete and Tony, "You guys call me Nick. I've read your files. I know where you've been and what you have done. I have every confidence in both of you. Welcome aboard. Mike, I heard you were in Israel for further Krav Maga training? Do you have to go that far these days to be trained?"

"Yes, if you want to be assured of getting the pure form of the art."

"How long did it take?"

"Ten days. Ten hard days."

"Was it worth it?"

"Yes, I believe it could save my life some day, or perhaps yours, realizing current circumstances."

"Can you teach me the advanced course?"

"Sure. Tony has asked, too. I'll teach you both at once."

"Great!" says Nickolas. Then says,

"Ladies and gentlemen, in conclusion, I wish to say, that today is the first day of the rest of your lives and that includes me. We're starting from zero. You only need to look around the building to understand that. Much basic planning has been completed, but much, much, more needs to be done. You are the nucleus of our new organization. It is your job starting today to undertake a complete, simple, straightforward, but professional business and financial plan for the next two years plus one. Phil will lead a meeting with all of you on this subject after our ten o'clock break." *(A small alarm from Nick's mini PC sounds.)*

"It's now ten o'clock. How's that for meeting management? I know that each of you has a hundred questions; however, please hold them for Phil's planning meeting, as most questions will be answered as a result of the planning discussion activity.

"Phil, as you know, I have a luncheon meeting to get to, and you and I have a meeting with the building contractor after that, so I'll see the rest of you guys at about 4 or 4:30. Phil, you have the helm. Call me on my cell if you need me. I'll see you at two."

"Okay Nick, I'll see you later," Phil says. "Mike and I will see you downstairs at the Blue Note at five," Tim says.

"I'll be there!"

# XII

## LATER THE SAME DAY, AT THE BLUE NOTE

Nickolas and Phil were in the ARC-designated large corner booth of the bar in the almost completed Blue Note. It was five o'clock. They had both arrived a little early and were waiting for Tim and Mike to join them for after-work cocktails to be served by Annie, acting bartender and waitress.

Annie was the second non-management person Nickolas had hired for the Blue Note, following Betty Lou, who had been hired as day-shift hostess. Annie was hired as a waitress and bartender trainee. Until the Blue Note officially opened, in another week or two, they were helping Sam the nighttime bartender and bar manager, and Alphonse, the chief chef, stock the bar, kitchen, wine cellar and pantry.

The Blue Note's construction was complete, including the installation of all furniture, fixtures, kitchenware and equipment. However, the barstools, tables and chairs were still stacked along the walls and on the small oak dance floor fronting the small stage. Even though it was after 5 p.m., the lighting and sound contractors were still making final adjustments. Cases of beer, liquor and wine were everywhere, awaiting storage.

Phil says, "I know you have a few bucks, but this project will cost millions! It will likely be a big percentage of what you have."

"Yes, it is, but it's within my capacity," Nick says.

"You realize $6 million to $10 million in three years is just a forecast. Perhaps, a conservative forecast. Hell, none of us really know what could happen when we get into this thing. Security costs could double or triple if the shit hits the fan, you know."

"Yes, I do know and if they tripled, I would be spending Liz's and my retirement money, particularly, if we can't raise the money from the donations that I've forecasted. However, I am prepared to take the risks. Phil, I believe in this mission of ours. I do want to give back. I do want to change a small part of the world for the better. I do believe that you, Tim, Mike, and I can do it. Imagine the satisfaction you'll have if we can. This is a noble campaign of magnificent dimensions and potential humanitarian benefits."

"I know, Nick, but your ability to fund this thing does have a limit. Bette and I don't want you and Liz living with us, at least not full time, you know."

"It wouldn't be full time if Tim, Kate and Mike do their share of taking care of Liz and me. Or, if you tight assholes ante up a couple million a piece for this cause!"

"I wouldn't count on that! We are not in your league!"

"I'm just joking. The fact that you're here, participating, is more than I had hoped for. I appreciate your concern. You're the most conservative of the four of us, and that's why you're the Chief of Staff and in charge of the finances. But you're forgetting the income-side potential of our venture. I believe our projections for donations could be way short."

"Well, I agree, but to protect you, I would rather present a conservative scenario—*'shit happens'* and *'Murphy's Law'* is always at work! Right now we have no idea how successful we might be and what level of support we can attract. In a year, we'll know, but we don't know now," Phil says.

"And in two years, we'll either have succeeded or failed."

"How do you know it won't take three years or even more?"

"Because I won't let it. We will not be beat by special interest groups or stonewalling, procrastinating politicians or the indecisive and uninformed silent majority! We are going to get this job done! We only need to change the minds of a couple of million U.S. voters and/or one tough, bearded old man in Cuba and one tough guy living in a big white house across town. The second part is easier said than done. The first part we are focused on. You get the first part done and the second part gets a lot easier," Nickolas says.

"Maybe. It could get a lot harder and more dangerous. There's a lot of big money involved here that doesn't want anything to change."

"And there's a lot of big money sitting on the sidelines just hoping that something will change."

"Here comes Tim and Mike," Phil says.

"Hey guys! How you doin'? Did you have a good day? Get in here. Mike is going to hold an executive security meeting as soon as Annie brings you a drink. Annie," yells Nickolas, "we have two more thirsty guys here!"

"It was a great day, we got a lot done. The girls are smart as whips. They're picking up our story and methodology real quick," Tim says.

"Mike, how did your day go?" Nickolas asks.

"Just like Tim said, it's a pleasure to deal with professionals. Tony and Pete are contributing heavily to our planning already. We're going to make a great security team, Nick, as I said we would."

Annie arrived with another round for Nickolas and Phil and drinks for Tim and Mike. Nickolas thanked her and then says,

"Okay, we need to do a little business here so I can write this evening's expense off. I think you'll find Mike's subject very interesting. A toast to Mike and his security team. May they always remain paranoid. Mike, you have the stage." They all clicked glasses and drank.

"Thank you, Nickolas. Guys, what I want to talk about is the Blue Note security and intelligence plan and equipment."

"As you might imagine, considering our business philosophy and traditions, when we are together we're likely to be spending a lot of time down here in the Blue Note—not only because Nick's designed a real cool bar, restaurant and nightclub, but because whenever we are here, we have planned to be relatively secure and safe in this specific oversized corner booth. Now, I must say up front, if my security does its job right, none of us will ever be on the defensive. But, *'Murphy's Law'* and the *'shit always happens'* rules always apply, particularly in the security business. Thus, the following features of this booth are its high back and sides, and it's bulletproof up to .50-caliber."

"Jesus!" Tim says. "That's the good news and bad news! I haven't really considered the fact that I might get shot on this job!"

"Well, the odds are you won't unless you happen to be with Nick when somebody tries to take him down," Mike says.

Nickolas says, "Oh, well, thanks a lot, Mike. I feel a lot better now!"

"Mike," says Phil, "continue your good news."

"Okay, continuing. Number two, Allan, the daytime bartender, and Sam, the nighttime bartender, are also security personnel. Behind the bar is enough weaponry to defend the White House from attack! The bar is also bulletproof. If gunplay is necessary, they'll do it, not you.

"Number three, the Blue Note is tied into the primary ARC building video/audio surveillance and security system monitored 24/7/365 upstairs.

"Number four. You're going to like this. Feel exposed to the rest of the bar area? Pick up and hold your drinks a moment and lean back." All four men do as suggested and Mike pulls a lever under the tabletop and manually flips the table on edge and pushes it outward, thereby closing off the entranceway into the booth. As they all sit, they're facing one another over the table post. Mike continues,

"And the tabletop is bulletproof. If you keep your head below the booth top and the tabletop, you are secure.

"Number five. See those four compartments on the bottom of the tabletop. You open them like this." Mike hits the top outside corner of each with the flat of his hand quite hard. A panel is released revealing on each end and top and bottom four tasers.

"You have 50,000 volts here to use to protect yourself. We don't want to shoot up Nick's new bar in gunplay." Mike pulls a black leather cushion off the bench, lifts a panel, releases two bolts, and pulls down the front panel of the seat to reveal a hole in the wall behind the booth to the kitchen storeroom.

"You can simply disappear into the wall. It's bulletproof. What do you think?"

Phil says, "I like number six best."

"Well, I understand the security measures, which are simple but very innovative. But, what about the intelligence piece?" Tim asks. Mike responds,

"Well, I alluded to it when I said that the entire Blue Note is connected to our video/audio building security system upstairs. You cannot have a private, unrecorded conversation in the Blue Note, which will seat 200, unless security elects not to video or audio record you."

"Is that legal, Mike?" Phil asks.

"Larry, our attorney, is willing to defend it on the basis of the many security disclaimers we have in various areas of the club and in the beverage and food menus."

"I see," Phil says.

"Obviously we don't anticipate a need to video or record 99% of the Blue Note customers; however, if we recognize a bad guy, or a suspicious guy, or we are having a meeting with certain people in this booth, we'll collect the video and audio," Mike says.

"I see," Tim says. "Makes sense. Could be a helpful tool."

"Absolutely," Mike says.

"Is that it?" Phil asks.

"Yes, that's it for tonight," says Nickolas, starting to laugh. "It was appropriate realizing that this evening was our first meeting in the Blue Note. We didn't cover the fact that the clarinet player is an accomplished Amazonian poisoned dart blower, and when the piano player hits a high C note, all doors close up the club like a vault. However, we'll cover those features in the next security meeting. Annie, another round of drinks and two of those cheeseboards with fruit that we're considering for the menu," Nickolas says.

# XIII

## ARC HEADQUARTERS

*MARCH*

Nickolas, Phil, Carmen Benson and Judy Austin are gathered, along with other personnel, in the main ARC Conference Room. The conference table is covered with the business tools and the aftermath of a long meeting. The angle of the sun, through mostly closed shutters, reveals the time as late afternoon. Nickolas' computerized world clock, seen in the lower right-hand side of the large television monitor, reveals the time as 4:06 p.m.

"So Nick, what do you think? In the past hour you've reviewed about a normal two months output of labor that was finished in just one month. Everybody has worked long and hard to complete our formal Business and Financial Plan and have it ready for review today, ahead of schedule."

"Phil, I'm very impressed with your planning results and the quality of the output. I believe you understood our goals and achieved them. Great job! I like it a lot! Good work! Obviously, I have some questions but we'll deal with those on Monday morning. You and your staff have been working day and night for the better part of two weeks. It is now time to relax and celebrate a job well done. It's Friday evening and I realize some of you may have other plans. This is not a command performance. However, for those of you who wish to join me, clean up your desk, visit the head if necessary and meet me out front at 4:30. I'm buying cocktails and an early dinner. The limo will bring you back here at 8 p.m. For those with other plans, we'll see you at 8 a.m. on Monday, and enjoy your weekend."

Nickolas' satisfaction provided much relief and enthusiasm as the meeting ended. The room vacated. The key executives lingered for an extra few minutes with Nick, and to congratulate one another. Others left, saying they'll see Nickolas in the limo. Phil and Nick remain.

"Okay, Nick, now tell me what you really think?" Phil asks.

"Phil, I did tell you. We've been meeting almost every night for a month, always discussing the plan. How could I not be happy?"

"Well, we couldn't present a consolidated financial plan until we completed all the business plan detail and costing with Tim and Mike. That was complete only on Wednesday evening. So you couldn't have known the projected actual cost until about an hour ago. And $3 million a year for two to three years is a helluva lot of money where I come from. I know you have some bucks, but this is serious after-tax money! Do you have it?"

"Yes, Phil, as I've said before, I have it, but obviously I don't want to spend it unless I have to."

"How do we avoid it?"

"We'll talk about that as it becomes necessary to do so, but obviously we have to do a good job of getting donation commitments and collecting the cash."

"Okay, you're the boss. I know you *always* have a contingency plan."

# XIV

## ARC HEADQUARTERS

*FOLLOWING WEEK*

It's the following Monday afternoon and time for Nickolas' review of Tim's Marketing Financial Plan and Business Action Plans. Nickolas is sitting at the head of the conference table, reading material relating to the meeting about to begin. He is alone in the conference room when Tim rushes in with four three-ring binders, five file folders and a computer disc.

"Nick, are we ready, am I late?" Tim asks.

Nickolas doesn't move but hits a button on his personal PC, and the large-screen monitor rises from the console at the front of the Conference Room. He pushes another button and the clock comes up at 3:03 p.m. Nickolas says, "Close, Tim, but not a 'ringer,' maybe a 'leaner.' You're three minutes late, but not to worry. I've read your Financial Plan so we can focus on the Marketing Plan first."

"Do you want Casie and Lisa in this meeting now?" Tim asks.

"No, we'll start and call them if we need them. They're standing by?"

"Yes."

"Okay, let's get started. I have a one-line index of the Marketing Business Action Plans from the Business Plan. I'm simply looking for a brief update on where we've been, where we are, and where we're going. And how long before we get there."

"I'm ready. Where do you want to start?" Tim asks.

"Let's start by you giving me a quick, general overview of where you're at, organizationally."

Tim gets up and puts his CD into the PowerPoint, brings up his first page on the screen, and says,

"We organizationally arrived at full strength for Phase I as of last Monday. We still have two telemarketing people working in one of the mini-conference rooms, but their cubicle should be completed later this week. Everybody else has a desk, chairs, phones, PCs, etc. We have basically hit all of our timing objectives although we've been delayed several times by slow securities approval of various venders. Nick, do you feel that we really need that level of security at this time? We've only recently sent our PR releases to the media and got the ARC website up and going. Very few people know we exist."

"I understand your consternation and you're probably right— we don't need it now. But, security isn't very challenged at this point and they want to contribute and do their part so they're doing what they can do at this time. They will have much bigger priorities to worry about soon—not that they're not doing important things now. For example, I just finished reading this investigative report from Mike covering all the major South Florida, New Jersey and U.S. Cuban registered lobbyists. Very interesting. His next job is to research every organization with a website, pro or con, trying to influence U.S.-Cuban relations. I digress. We're here to talk about your plan and activities. I just wanted you to know that Mike was getting some seriously important results, although I agree that investigating our vendors at this time may not be among them. However, I'm not the security expert, he is."

"No problem. I'm just letting you know why we were late on some sub-projects."

"I understand. You mentioned that we mailed our initial public relations packages. When did they go? How many?"

"We mailed 2,000 of them last Monday to the top news-gathering organizations in the country. All media. Everybody from San Diego to Bangor, Maine and Seattle to Key West. Completed under budget and on time. Good stuff, too. You approved it, remember?"

"Yes, I do. It was good. I just didn't know if it went. Have we heard from anybody?"

"Well, it's a little early to quantify the total results, but yes, we've had a few phone calls, maybe eight or ten. Some of these media types don't look at their regular mail for two or there weeks at a time. Even then they probably use less than 5% of what they get or see from the national news agencies or directly. The next two weeks will give us a better idea if anybody out there thinks that you, or our cause, is newsworthy, anywhere outside of Miami. Also, as you know, we've subscribed to a national news-gathering service so whatever makes the newspapers in the top 100 markets of interest to our cause we will see, including our new PR."

"Good. We had to start somewhere and that mailing, along with the website, was it. When was the website activated?"

"It was activated maybe a month ago. But, it wasn't completed with all the bells and whistles until about a week ago."

"How many hits to date?"

"About a thousand, most out of South Florida. They all count, but particularly in South Florida, due to the high interest there and the word-of-mouth effect. I wouldn't be surprised if in six months we had 100,000 hits out of South Florida."

"Me neither. Maybe sooner, depends how hot we get how fast."

"Have you been able to get any research done? We talked about some focus groups and surveys?"

"Nick, I haven't made up my mind that the investment would be worth the expense. This is such an old issue that I don't know what we could learn that hasn't appeared in the media a hundred times."

"Well, if you're talking about South Florida, you're right. But I'm not certain at all about Middle America. I think we need to understand what rural America knows and thinks about the whole situation."

"From that point of view, I agree. However, if our goal is to offset the Florida Cuban vote two to one, we should be able to achieve that over the course of our presentations, the associated Q&A and follow-up media reports, telemarketing and meeting participant report follow-up. Focus groups, national surveys, etc., cost a helluva lot of money and when complete, nobody agrees with the questions or the answers anyway. I would rather put that budget money into reserve."

"Okay, you're the professional marketer. I agree. Proceed accordingly. You're the first guy to totally complete one of his business action plans—by voiding it! But, that counts when you save money."

"It just occurred to me, Tim, did we send a PR package to Fidel?"

"No, not yet. The foreign language PR mailing just began development. They are another week or two away to complete. Each group of foreign language mailings are being converted by hand by an outside firm and will be ready for the printers soon."

"Okay. The plan to put somebody on the road to personally visit key opposition organizations—where are we on that?"

"Phil, Mike and I talked about that plan and agreed that it would be of greater overall benefit to the organization and cost less if security took that one. Security can make those visits while they are undertaking their on-site security plans in advance of our road shows."

"You're right, Tim. That makes sense. Good! What about the personal visit with the writers and editors who specialize in U.S.-Cuba news?"

"I've also thought further about this issue. I don't see any reason to rush to visit these people personally at this time. In fact, I see the opposite. Right now we have no image, no reputation and we are *not* newsworthy. Over time, if and when we are truly successful, we'll be newsworthy. You and I are best qualified to hold these meetings with the press; therefore, let's simply get it done as we hold meetings in each city. The longer we wait, the more newsworthy we'll be. This will also save money."

"You're right again. As long as somehow someway those particular people know we are alive and why."

"They will. I have a list of these people and I will confirm that they know the who, what, where and why of ARC as we move through time."

"Agreed. Proceed accordingly. Have you figured out what we have to do to get our key people to Cuba when the time comes?"

"No, not yet. But I'm working with the federal Office of Foreign Assets Control at Treasury to find out. I do know there is no major issue in Havana with including the HDI private jet. The problems are Federal Law, the State Department and the OFAC political and bureaucratic process."

"Well, it's not a short-term need, but if we are successful, we'll definitely be going to Havana to see Fidel. We need legal approval well in advance of the need to go. So stay on top of that one."

"I also remember you personally want to go unofficially, as soon as possible, and before you become a celebrity."

"I remember saying before I become *notorious*."

"Either way, that's my first objective with OFAC. We're working on that one now."

"Speaking of Cuba, are we getting the daily newspaper, etc.? Have we got someone translating?"

"We haven't quite found the right person yet. But we're working on it. You may recall that your suggested profile for this person was specific and extensive."

"Yes, I want a fluent, very attractive, mature, professional, U.S. Cuban, single, smart, intelligent, discreet, worldly woman 35-45 years of age, who believes in our cause, without any negative baggage regarding the male species. Someone I can work closely with and trust completely."

"Well, you realize all those specifications leave a lot to interpretation and *miss*-interpretation and either way, it's a tall order—particularly the *trust totally* part."

"The last time I was in Miami I saw a hundred of them!"

Tim laughs, "At what time of the night?"

"Granted, it was late. Probably 9 or 9:30."

"Right! That's late for you! Seriously—we actually have a Miami-based female, a professional headhunter looking for this woman. This particular Business Action Plan will likely cost a few bucks! But, I know you, and I know you have your reasons. I intend to find you three candidates who fit your profile. One will have long black hair and dark eyes. The second one will have long black hair and dark eyes and the third one will have long black hair and dark eyes. They all will have long legs and full, high breasts. Have I got it right?"

"You forgot the butt that you can set a champagne glass on at a cocktail party."

"Nick, you never fail to surprise me with your urbane and sophisticated manner!"

"I know. I love it! Hey, I've just realized we've forgotten to bring in any of your people. They're going to be disappointed!"

"Not to worry. I didn't make any promises. Although all of these people want to get to know you better and 'strut' their stuff. You know that, right?"

"Yes, I do, and I want to let them do it—they're all essential to our cause. They are *all* a part of the team and I want them to be happy in their work and feel important to the leadership. In the end, I want them to feel the satisfaction in a job well-done that you, Phil, Mike and I want. Do you want to bring them in and open a bottle of wine? Go to Anthony's or the Blue Note for a couple of drinks or what?"

"Well, there's no problem here. I didn't promise them they would get on stage. It's up to you. I know they would be impressed and appreciative."

"Who we talking about?"

"It would be Casie, Lisa and Joyce."

"Are you saying, I have to have a glass of wine with those three beautiful young women?"

"Well, yes, if you put it that way. That's exactly what I'm saying."

"Okay, get them into my office in 20 minutes. I'll get in the fridge and open some wine. I have to hit the head and make a short phone call so give me 10 minutes, okay?"

"Done, I'll be back in 10."

# XV

## THE WHITE HOUSE

*MARCH*

President Brendon Downing is at his desk in the Oval Office at the White House. His door opens and the President's Chief of Staff, Wayne Rogers, enters and says,

"Mr. President, that story in *The Times* and on CNN regarding that Nickolas Harvey guy seems to be gaining momentum in the media. I've had several calls from Senators Gonzales and Gibson and Congressmen Jones and Whitehall. Stewart from OFAC also called. He has an application from Harvey requesting official approval to visit Cuba. What do you want to do? I don't think this guy is a temporary irritation."

"What reason is he using to qualify himself to visit Cuba?"

"Humanitarian aid."

"Ouch. That's a hard one, under the circumstances, to deny. But, at this point, no one knows whether this guy is for real or just a fart in a hurricane."

"Well, personally, I don't believe he's the latter, but I've called the Bureau and the IRS to check him out further. I do know he is a card-carrying, long-term consistent donator to the national and California Replication Party. He was one of our Republican Businessmen of the Year in California the past six years. Additionally, he's a mid-sized defense contractor who has been doing business with the Pentagon for more than 20 years. He is an ex-Marine reconnaissance officer. Rank at exit was captain. Very good record. Some of his file is Top Secret. Even I couldn't pull it up. You can request it if you wish."

"He sounds impressive, intelligent, committed!"

"I'm sure he is."

"Well, hell then! He's a smart guy and we need to have someone visit with him. Let him know that what he's doing is not good for the party! Get him to join the team effort! Marines understand teamwork! Get on it, Wayne. Have Colonel Williamson from NSA have a talk with him. One Marine to another ought to do the trick."

# XVI

## CUBAN OFFICE OF FOREIGN AFFAIRS, WASHINGTON, D.C.

The second assistant to the Deputy Secretary of the Cuban Office of Foreign Affairs in Washington, D.C., is at his desk this morning. He puts down the Washington newspaper, picks up his interoffice phone and punches the numbers for his secretary, Mereeda, who says,

"Yes, sir, how can I help you?"

"Mereeda, please call Colonel Lonzo Moralis in Havana for me. Advise him that I'll be returning to Havana for a home visit next Friday evening and that I'd like to have a private dinner with him at the Tropicana Hotel at 9 p.m. Saturday evening, concerning this Nickolas Harvey person and his ARC organization. Tell him I've gathered some information I believe is important, which I wish to share with him confidentially before I disseminate the information through regular foreign office channels and make any related recommendations. Let me know immediately after he confirms the meeting."

"Yes, sir, I'll call his secretary right now."

# XVII

## AFCA HEADQUARTERS

### (Americans for a Free Cuba Association)

**Miami, Florida**

The president of the Americans for a Free Cuba Association, one of the oldest, largest, Cuban-American associations in America, is headquartered in Miami. Martin Alonso is 83 years of age and has been president of his association since day one, building its membership from nothing to one of the most powerful in South Florida.

Martin had evacuated his family from Cuba to Florida during the Batista regime in 1953. He was in Florida when Fidel began his revolution with the ill-fated attack on the Moncada Barracks, which led to his capture and imprisonment. At that time Martin became excited about the possibility of a Cuban revolution of sorts and tried to influence the U.S. Government to help Fidel get out of jail in the hopes that if he did, he would restart his revolutionary plan. Martin was only marginally successful because, at that time, the U.S. was officially behind Batista, and Martin had little in the way of resources or political leverage with which to achieve his goals. In the years that followed, Martin worked hard and focused on building both his personal wealth and political clout. He created a very powerful financial and political dynasty that continues to this day.

Martin is in his business office, sitting at his desk. His assistant sits in a guest chair to his front.

"Who the hell *is* this guy?" Martin says to his vice president assistant.

"He's made the front page of the *Miami Herald* four times in the last ten days! What is he up to? He's getting too much attention, too long! Get Senator Gonzales on the phone for me. If he's not available, make sure his chief of staff knows it's me calling, and I want a return call today even if it's after business hours! Secondarily, get me hard copy of everything that's on that ARC website before 4 p.m. Also, call Michael Costello in New Jersey for me and tell him that I have a job for him and to call me on my satellite phone."

# XVIII

## NEW YORK CITY

*APRIL*

Big Ed arrived at the double glass doors to the 26th floor restaurant of the Klatt Tower in lower Manhattan at 11 a.m. The restaurant wasn't open yet so Big Ed used his own key to unlock the door just before the daytime manager arrived on the other side of the door to let him in. Ed says,

"Good morning, Albert, how are you?"

"Good, Mr. Ed, thank you. The others are all here sitting at your usual table. We've served coffee and water. Will you need anything else?"

"No, Albert, just privacy. If you open before we're done, do not seat anyone near us until I give you the high sign, okay?"

"Yes, sir, no problem."

Big Ed walked into the restaurant from the lobby and some distance through tables, now set for lunch, to a large round corner table with a panoramic view of Lower Manhattan. There were three men and one woman sitting at the table. The men looked like business people and the woman, an aging model. Two of the men were Italian, one was Irish, and the female was a mixed Hispanic. Big Ed greeted everyone with a handshake and a grin. He greeted the female with a smile and a hug, which she did not rise to receive, nor did she put down the cigarette in her right hand that got dangerously close to Big Ed's $1,500 silk suit. He shook his head at her in disapproval. Big Ed took the last open seat, which was in the corner and provided no view except back into the restaurant.

"Well, I see you saved the best seat for the boss. Thanks," Big Ed says.

The lady answers, "You snooze, you lose."

"That's cute, Tara. Do you mind if I write that down and use it myself sometime?"

"It's all yours, sweetie pie. Be my guest. I have more of those if you need them."

"I know you do. By the way, you know this is a no-smoking establishment. Please cease."

"Why, does it matter? No one is here but us." She continues to smoke.

"Okay, I'll give you until 11:30 when the doors open, but that's it. Let's get down to business. Maurice, Angelo, Mike, Tara, I appreciate you guys being here. Thanks for meeting on such short notice. Drinks and lunch are on me following this meeting. I assume you saw yesterday's newspaper or today's or perhaps CNN in the past three to four days. Here is the page three article from *The Times* on Tuesday and the page two article today. I've brought a photocopy for each of you, in case you missed it."

"Yes, Ed, I saw it, but what about it?" Maurice asks.

"Yeah, I saw it, too. So what?" Angelo says.

Mike and Tara were reading the articles, having not seen them.

"Well, I guess that's why I'm the head honcho in this outfit, because you guys don't have any imagination or ability to think beyond next weekend. This new organization, ARC, I think they call it, Americans for Reconciliation with Cuba, if it creates some momentum and collects some political clout, they might just change the status quo on Cuba and open it up to American tourism and business and to us. Havana could be a future Las Vegas or Atlantic City once again!"

Maurice interrupts saying, "Yeah. Well, we've been saying that for 30 or 40 years and it's never happened. Castro has the country locked up and the U.S. politicians all are in bed with the Cuban expatriates who want that business for themselves. The Cuban expatriates control a million votes in Florida. That's a lot of influence. Those guys are well-organized and backed by a lot of big money—sugar interests being one of them, rum another one."

"Rum? You may or may not be right," says Ed, "but the difference is no one has ever challenged the U.S.-Cuban bloc politically before with a major, long-range strategy. A lot of things have changed in Cuba and in the U.S. in the past 20 years. The economic situation, timing and politics may be just right now. This guy Nickolas Harvey sounds like the kind of guy committed for the long haul, with the savvy, commitment and money to maybe get something done—particularly if a new President gets elected."

"Okay Ed. I'm starting to get the picture," Tara says. "What have you got in mind?"

"Tara," Mike says, interrupting, "whatever it is I bet it's going to cost us all a lot of money."

"Well," says Ed, "I don't know yet what it's going to cost. Maybe we should just stand on the side and watch the Seminoles take it over. However, if Harvey gets it done, we move in and do our usual thing. If he doesn't, nothing ventured, nothing lost. On the other hand, a little investment up front might get us a highly leveraged inside track if Cuba opens up. A small investment could help assure quicker and bigger dividends by getting us into Havana first, maybe exclusively."

"What is a small up-front investment in your mind, Ed?" Angelo asks.

"Well, we don't want to donate to this cause, we want to invest; therefore, we have to investigate the situation and the return-on-investment opportunities. With your agreement that this situation may be worth a close look-see, my people will undertake the investigation and initial discussions and I will report back to you. In the meantime, you should scratch together about $250,000 a piece in cash. If we are to proceed, we'll initially ante up a million as a group and cover it through some of our smaller companies."

"You realize that there are likely other ways to get this job done without potentially pissing away a a million bucks, right?" Mike asks.

"We're trying not to do things that way anymore, remember? Besides, it didn't work last time if you remember your history," Ed says.

"Right, Ed. But a million bucks is a lot of money."

"Mike, look at it long range. If we are successful, we can earn a million bucks a day!"

"Yeah, after three years of design, engineering and building and probably two or three hundred million more in investment capital!" says Tara.

"Well, Tara, it takes a little longer to do it the old-fashioned way—earning it! Legally earning it!" Maurice says.

"Well," Tara responds to Maurice, "I'm not sure we'll earn it, but gambling is legal these days, at least most places in the U.S."

"However, it's not currently legal in Cuba," Mike says.

"True, but it was legal even after the Castro brothers took over—at least in the beginning," Ed says.

"Yeah, and that job originally took 10 years and $60 million bucks of influence and investment! That deal didn't last. Remember?" Angelo asks.

"Okay, we're agreed. We have a plan. Let's be optimistic. This could be fun for a change. It's 11:30, and the place needs to open. Drinks and lunch are on the house. I recommend the Angus steak sandwich today, with the steak fries. They're homemade, very nice. Tara, you may prefer the cottage cheese and fruit, both are fresh this morning," Ed says.

# XIX

## MIAMI BEACH, FLORIDA

*MAY*

Jesus Hernandez has managed the Beach House Bar and Grill on Miami Beach for 20 years for his good friend Michael Costello, a New Jersey restaurateur. Every now and then Michael asks Jesus to do other odd jobs in the Miami area or elsewhere somewhat distant from the food and beverage business.

Jesus is a tall, lanky man in his 60s with sparse white hair combed straight back on his head. Jesus runs a tight ship at the Beach House and is a hard guy to work for, particularly if you're a young female. When he's not terrorizing the waitresses and bartenders, Jesus sits at a desk on a riser in the near right corner of the restaurant, raised up three or four steps where he can keep a close eye on everything that's happening. He was in his eagle's nest this day until he noticed two guys coming off the sidewalk and making their way through the sidewalk tables to the open bar. He flew his perch and was at the bar before they sat down. Before they could order, he had poured two shots of Jack and drawn two glasses of Budweiser.

Jesus asks, "Okay, Bones, what you got?"

"Well, Butt and I flew up there on Monday, rented a car and got to the business address you gave us pretty easy. Not much to say about the business. It's an old brick four-story apartment building in Georgetown south of the city. Old, but nice. Lot of BMWs, Mercedes, parked in the neighborhood. We did not see a lot of coming and going until the end of the day, then maybe a dozen men and women left the building walking, getting into taxis or cars. Mostly younger people, some of them kids. Butt followed two to a nearby apartment house. I followed two to a local bar and restaurant called the Westend. They looked like regular working stiffs to me and Butt," Bones says.

"You were supposed to follow this Nickolas Harvey guy!" Jesus says.

"I'll get to that. He wasn't there or he didn't come out at 5 p.m. that first day."

Bones reads his notes. "We didn't see the guy until the next morning, Tuesday. He showed up in a Dodge Charger limo at 7 a.m. He and an apparent bodyguard went into the building and didn't reappear until 11:30 a.m. At 11:30 they went to lunch at the Edgewater Hotel until one o'clock when they left and returned to their building. At 4 p.m., Harvey, his guard and three other guys left and went to the Edgewater again for what appeared to be drinks and a meeting followed by dinner. We tried to listen, but there was too much action in the place to hear anything."

"Those guys work hard, drink hard and play hard. I thought it would be a long night. They were getting into it, if you know what I mean. But at 9, they gave it up and left. We followed them all back to the Harvey Building where apparently they are all living."

"Did you check that?" Jesus asks.

"Yes, he and his wife are in rooms on the top floor. We did hear that Mr. Harvey runs every other morning. Mrs. Harvey wasn't seen."

"Did you physically look at the rooms in the building?"

"No boss. It's a secure building—no legal way in above the first floor."

"Are there balconies on the top floor?"

"Yes, two little tiny ones—one on each side of the corner surrounded by wrought iron."

"Are the balconies accessible from the rooms on each side?"

"Yes, if you're not afraid of heights and you have the right gear."

"Very good! It sounds like you've done a good job. Here's your bonus check. Now I want you to forget we've ever done business," Jesus says.

"Thanks, let Butt and I know if we can be of further service. As you know, we can do anything you need to get done in a very professional and confidential manner."

"Yes, I know. I may be in touch. We'll see. I have to get back to work. Enjoy your drinks. Al will give you a couple more on me, if you like."

The three shook hands and Jesus returned to his perch in the corner and got on the phone to Michael Costello in New Jersey.

# XX

## ABOARD RESOLUTE

**Guanabo, Cuba**

Manuel and his son, Miguel, arrived at their boat, *Resolute,* at 5:30 a.m. It is still dark. Their habit when going fishing was to be at the boat at 4 a.m. However, today they weren't going fishing, although they were going to look like they were fishing. Instead of going to the outer reefs, they were going to appear to troll inside the reef and head east down the coast to an area of sand dunes where the old schooner wreck finally had been discovered by Manuel after two months of looking twice a week, sometimes more.

Manuel is in the pilothouse preparing to start the old engine, and Miguel is on the forward deck preparing the lines to leave the dock after their special guest passenger arrives.

Dawn is breaking, the sun's light showing over the distant curvature of the earth like an eyebrow some minutes before the eye of the sun itself peeks over the horizon, commencing another day in the short lives of humanity and the quad-billionth cycle in the life of earth.

Manuel and Miguel are now in the pilothouse, awaiting their passenger and drinking coffee.

"Papa, another beautiful day begins," Miguel says.

"Yes, son, enjoy every one of them. The older you get, the faster they go. Any day you wake up without dirt in your face is a good day. Actually, awakening is a blessing from God himself. Look at that sunrise. Is it not one of the most beautiful things a man can look upon? In the early morning, God reminds you how lucky you are to have awakened. In the evening, at sunset, he reminds you to remember how great life has been that day by providing an equally beautiful sunset."

"I understand, Papa. But the effort each day to get from sunrise to sunset can be a difficult journey that many cannot complete."

"True, son, and vice versa, the night takes many. But most of it is in the natural order of things. Try to stay within the natural order of things and you'll be happy with your life every sunset. Don't defer happiness looking for an easy way to get there or believe in the idea that happiness is only important tomorrow, not today."

"Papa, where's our guest? I thought he was suppose to be here at dawn."

"He was, but remember, he is coming from afar. He will be here soon. It is in his character to do as he says he will do."

"Who is this man anyway? You haven't told me very much?"

"He is a carpenter, and old friend, and his name is Rufus, Rufus Caruso, son, and he's going to build the boat we need."

"Tell me more."

"Okay, let's see. Rufus and I as young men fought in the Revolution. We met in the mountains. We were there in the beginning and in the end. We fought many battles together and one time early on I saved his life, and one time later he saved mine. He was my best man at your mother's and my wedding 25 years ago. He is a carpenter by trade and has built many houses in Cuba and built a few boats and repaired a lot of boats— wooden boats, no steel. He is the kind of friend that once made, is a friend for life. That kind of friend is hard to find these days. I hope you find one, or two, in your lifetime."

"Papa, you're my best friend."

"Thank you, son, and you and your mother and Maria are mine. And now baby Jon. But, you know what I mean, lifelong friends outside of the bond of blood. They can be just as important to you as a family and they give you this and you give it to them—freely, totally and forever, without the blood connection. It's a valuable gift—the most valuable gift."

"Yes, Papa, I understand. When did you last see Rufus?"

"Oh, perhaps three or four years ago at the funeral of an old mutual comrade in arms from the Revolution."

"Anyone I know?"

"No. He was not a man you would want to know. He was not a man that I would introduce to you. Rufus and I did not attend his funeral to pay our respects. We attended to assure he was dead and in his coffin. He was a great warrior in the beginning of the Revolution, but somehow he lost his way. Achieving power along with his weaknesses of character corrupted him. He did not die naturally, although that is the common opinion."

"How do you know?"

"I know."

"When was that again?"

"Three or four years ago."

"Papa, there he is," Miguel pointed down the old dock pier.

Manuel stood to look toward the pier head. He saw Rufus in the distance chaining his old three-wheel bicycle to a dock bollard just behind the warehouse. That done, Rufus turned to the large wooden toolbox carried over the two-wheel rear axle of the cycle and started unchaining it from its mount.

"Jesus," Miguel says. "That's an overweight old man! I thought he was your age?"

"Rufus is 10 years older than me, but I've never thought of him as an overweight old man. You best wait to judge Rufus, son."

At that instant Rufus completes disengaging his chains, leans over with two large arms and in one movement grabs the large toolbox and lifts it to his right shoulder. With his left hand he grabs a large military green seabag and throws it over the left shoulder and steps off down the dock toward the boat maneuvering over and around the various holes in the pier deck, walking like a much younger man.

As Rufus gets closer, Miguel says, "Jesus, he's even older than I thought, but he's not fat, he's a giant! Let's get out there and help him aboard. If he falls in with that toolbox, he will go straight to the bottom."

Manuel and Miguel exit the pilothouse and proceed to the forward port side deck to help Rufus with his gear.

Miguel says to Rufus as he approaches the rail, "Hold on there, old man. Give me a minute to get out there to help you with that box."

Rufus picks up on the implication and says, "Stand still, son, the seabag is coming first."

Before Miguel can move or say anything, Rufus, with his left arm, has removed the seabag from his shoulder and thrown it into the chest of Miguel, as if it were a pillow off a bed. Miguel falls back two or three steps stumbling with the bag, which drops to the deck. He looks at Rufus befuddled and surprised.

Rufus says to Miguel, winking at Manuel, "Sorry, son, I thought you were ready."

"I thought I was, too. What the hell you got in there? I thought your tools were in the toolbox!"

"They are son. Now are you ready for the box?"

"Yes, if you'll kind of step up to the rail, I believe I can take it right off your shoulder."

Rufus smiles, looks at Manuel and says, "I better hand it up to you and make sure it gets over the rail. If you drop my tools into the drink, your father is going to get real upset with both of us." With that said, Rufus reaches up with his left hand and pulls the toolbox off his shoulder, catching the other end with his right. He lowers the box to his waist and says again,

"Are you ready?" Miguel nods in the affirmative and Rufus lifts the box above his shoulders and places the box on the rail of the forward deck.

"Now, this box is heavy. Don't drop it on your toes or you're won't be going fishing for a while."

Miguel grabs the box by its end handles and lifts. He doesn't move it off the rail, but it's now off balance and coming at him. He struggles, puts all his power into the lift and control of the box. Nothing. It goes straight to the deck with a crash, barely missing his toes.

"Jesus, what the hell you got in there, rocks? Damn!"

Rufus and Manuel both laugh. Rufus comes aboard to the open arms of Manuel. They hug and then each holding the other's shoulders at arm's length inspect one another in welcome and in enjoyment at seeing one another again.

"Rufus, you old sea dog, it's so good to see you! It's been way too long! What have you been doing?" Manuel asks.

"Yes, it has been too long, but true friendship does not weaken with age like our bodies do, captain. I've kept track of you from afar through our old friend Angelease. Or, I should say, at least I did until Fidel put him away again."

"Rufus, do you remember Miguel? Miguel, you finally get to meet Rufus in person. Rufus knew you when you were a boy. Rufus, how long since you last saw Miguel?"

"Miguel was this high," Rufus' hand is at his waist, "maybe 15 years ago. You and Rose were living in San Cabania at that time on the northwest coast. Miguel, you're lucky to be learning the fishing business from your father, he's the best in all of Cuba!" Rufus and Miguel shake hands. Rufus forces a hug upon Miguel.

"Okay, enough talk now, let's get this gear stowed and cast off. The coffee pot is on and we can talk more in the pilothouse when we get underway. It's going to be a great day. Rufus, it is so good to see you again. I've missed you."

# XXI

## EN ROUTE TO DES MOINES, IOWA

*MAY 2015*

Nickolas, Tim, Tony, Casie and Lisa were aboard the Harvey Defense Industries' Learjet 60, heading west about an hour out of Reagan International. Everyone had just finished a box lunch and was settling into the next two and a half hours of the flight. Tim was sitting across the small table from Nickolas.

"Well, Nick, how do you feel? You wanted the first road show to be ready in 90 days and here we are at 25,000 feet headed for Des Moines," Tim says.

"I feel great, Tim. You and your people have done an amazing job getting us ready for this. I'm very excited. In my opinion, this event is the true beginning—our first major effort to capture the hearts and minds of the American people."

"Well, I feel we have a good story to tell in a compelling fashion. Casie and Lisa have done a great job."

"I agree. But we are biased and untested on the field of battle. We'll know a lot more about our audience by ten o'clock tonight, that's for sure."

"We can't get into too much trouble with a meeting this size."

"That's the idea. We are just putting our toe in the water to check the temperature in Middle America. This is the first preseason football game, so to speak."

Both men were anxious and nervous in anticipation of the first road show presentation, now only a few hours away. Their conversation slowly ceased as they returned increasingly to their own inner thoughts.

Nickolas closed his eyes, trying to find a little private time to think and relax. Was there anything he had overlooked in planning this event that could cause the meeting to fail? He reviewed a series of *'what ifs'* that he had already considered several times. The review brought no new potential problems to mind. Was he worrying or was he verifying? He thought, I'm worrying. Anything that needed to be done was done. If it wasn't, it was too late anyway.

Public speaking always made him nervous before the event. After the first three or four minutes, he was usually okay. The more he did it, the better he got. But it had been awhile since he had done much of it, outside of speaking to his own employees and friends, which was usually an extemporaneous speech that was easy for him, harder for most others. Giving him a simple outline and letting him fly was not troubling. But give him 30 minutes of text, and he was nervous. If the prompting equipment or operator let you down, it was easy to panic. Once, a long time ago, in an audience of 500, that had happened to him. He had been forced to instantly BS his way through the last half of a 20-minute speech, which he did, but later he had no recollection of what he had said. And the 10 minutes of pure internal terror and embarrassment assured that it would never happen to him again!

He had learned a valuable lesson. The avoidance of excessive tension is a result of being fully and properly prepared, and assuring that the text uses words, phrasing and structure that is comfortable to the speaker. And, have a backup script in large type, if you're using prompting equipment.

Nickolas knew he had taken all these precautions, but he was still a little nervous. He knew a glass of Chardonnay about 30 minutes before showtime would settle him down and oil the old vocal cords a little. They were meeting at the Des Moines Marriott not far from the airport, using one-third of the main ballroom. Twenty rounds of 10 would be seating for 200. Attendance was by invitation only. A cross section of Des Moines' movers and shakers from several key segments of the community had received invitations requiring RSVPs. The ARC telemarketing people had followed up last week to assure attendance.

The 25 or so attendees whose plans had changed were replaced by other candidates on the master list of Des Moines' 500 most influential citizens.

Since this was the first test show, TEAM 2 lead by Phil was invited along so that they could become personally familiar and comfortable with the meeting methodology, mechanics, security measures, etc., in anticipation of putting on their first show the next week. Secondarily, they would judge the audience reaction during the presentation and later in Q&A. TEAM 1 would be identified as hosts and handle all aspects of the show. TEAM 2 would be unidentified and spread among the audience to gather the more subtle audience reactions, if any. If questioned, these people were to tell their table mates they were freelance independent researchers from Washington, D.C., traveling with the ARC people—a partial truth in support of quality marketing research. It happens every day somewhere. A rationalization, he asked himself. I guess, maybe, a small one. Not the first and not the last, he thought as he nodded off to the sound of the twin turbojet engines pushing their plane through the rarefied air at 400 miles per hour. Two hours to touchdown and two more to kickoff was his last lucid thought before drifting off to sleep.

# XXII

## DES MOINES, IOWA

Nickolas and Tim leading TEAM 1 and TEAM 2 arrive in two local limos at the Des Moines Marriott. Nickolas and Tim are the first ones out of each vehicle, walking toward Mike at the front doors of the hotel.

"Mike, what the hell are you doing here?" Nickolas asks.

"It's the first show, the first significant security challenge, and I thought at the last minute that I should experience this first meeting personally, just like you guys. My advance team arrived two days ago and I arrived yesterday. We are ready. There's nothing to concern us at this meeting that we know of. We've dotted the i's and crossed the t's. Everything is ready and you go on stage in an hour. I'll show you the room," Mike says.

Nickolas follows Mike into the lobby and down a hall to the conference room area and into the meeting room. Nickolas found everything as planned, went to the podium, laid down his portfolio with backup script, turned on the microphone and said. "Testing, one, two, three. One, two, three." He also was satisfied as he looked the room over and said, "Mike, it looks good to me. Two entrances in, four out. We'll have security at all four points?"

"Yes, of course. But it's all local security, except Tony and me. I have rehearsed them all. I believe they are adequate for this size and type of audience."

"Okay. Is the room secure now? Can I leave my stuff here?"

"Yes. It's been thoroughly checked and it's clean, been clean since I got here."

"Okay. There's only one important thing we need to do."

"What's that?"

"Have one slow glass of Chardonnay in the bar."

"I remember," Mike says. "Let's do it."

Mike and Nickolas go back down the hall to the lobby and to the lounge off the lobby. They both sit at the end of bar. It's 6:15. In mid-America that is the middle of the dinner hour. The bar is maybe half full.

The bartender comes over, "What can I get for you? It's the happy hour and drinks are two for one."

"What is the house Chardonnay?" Mike asks.

"Copper Ridge. Two for one during the happy hour."

"That'll do. Give us two."

"A poet and doesn't know it!" Nick replies.

"You, too!"

"Hey, that's a great band!"

"You beat me again. I've no quick response for that one."

"That's okay. That's why I'm the boss."

"No argument from me."

The bartender returns. "There you go. I gotta charge each of you for one drink even though you're only drinking one."

"Does that make sense, Nick?"

"I think we know what he means."

Mike lifts his glass. "Nick, here's to you, Phil, Tim, and me, but particularly to you for bringing us all back together. It's only the beginning and I'm already having more fun than I've had in three years of retirement. You were right about all of us benefiting from doing something important together! Further, I want you to know, if you don't already, that your intimate friends have all adopted your Signature Event. They are talking about it and selling it like it was their idea."

"I knew they would as soon as we all got in the groove of getting into something bigger than any one of us alone, and Mike, you're right, this is just the beginning. We don't even know yet what the big challenges are. And, we haven't got anything done yet as it relates to the mission, beyond planning. When we start winning these skirmishes, battles and, ultimately, the war, we are going to be very well-known, very influential, happy campers!"

"I agree. I'm starting to see the whole picture in a way that I couldn't before. It's very exciting! But, this has to be costing you a fortune!"

"Yes, Mike, right now it is. But I believe in our capacity to build a self-funding national organization within 12 months or so."

"I don't doubt your creativity. But it's hard to imagine it right now."

"Survival is the mother of invention."

"It's 6:45. Should we go in? Do you want another one?"

"Yes, I want another one. But I'm not going to have one. One makes me smart. Two make me sleepy. Three make me aggressive. Four make me romantic. Five make me real romantic. And six make me incapable of being romantic!"

"It must be the wine. I'm a Scotch drinker unless I am just having a drink or two with you, in which case I enjoy a nice $5 or $6 premium Chardonnay."

"You should know I do not drink wine for the taste. I'm only interested in the *effect*—a slow, even effect."

"Then you should drink gin or vodka or tequila."

"I used to do that when I was young. In my older age, I simply couldn't handle the hard stuff anymore. So I stopped and switched to something I could handle."

"Yes, I think I remember when you received that message from God."

"Let's not go there. We better get into the auditorium and get ready to rock 'n' roll."

# XXIII

## MARRIOTT HOTEL

Nickolas enters the hotel ballroom through a front door, turns left to the wall and walks forward to the edge of the raised platform stage. Behind the platform is a large screen on the forward wall. A 10-minute PowerPoint presentation is flashing black-and-white, with color photographic images of significant events in Cuban history covering the past 120 years. Classical background music by the Cuban National Orchestra is somber but beautifully done in support of a male vocalist and is uplifting, matching the sequence of changing photographs. The pre-presentation was played through twice simply to reveal the rich and tumultuous history of the Cuban people and the interaction of the American people with Cubans over the years. No effort was made to color the content in any way. The music, however, had been chosen to first match the sequence of film and secondly, to calm and relax the audience and put them in a contemplative mood.

Nickolas, standing in the left corner of the room, had been surveying the audience. He noticed that almost all the tables were full. Conversations were subdued, with only an occasional laugh above the murmur of 200 patient Des Moinesians, most in dressy casual attire, some less, some more well-dressed. All were registered voters. None were attending with a spouse. It was a carefully concocted mix of men and women, young and old, for marketing research purposes, all fitting into four carefully selected demographic categories.

The lights blinked and came up somewhat. It was 7 p.m. Tim walked to the podium and into an overhead spotlight, which featured him.

Tim, using his command voice, said, "Ladies and gentlemen, it is my honor to present your host for this evening's event, Mr. Nickolas Harvey, founder and chairman of ARC, the Americans for Reconciliation with Cuba coalition!" A respectable amount of applause followed Tim's introduction. Nickolas took the stage, walking to the podium.

"Thank you, ladies and gentlemen, for allocating some of your valuable personal time this evening to learn more about our cause and why we at ARC feel so strongly about it. First, please let me share a little of my personal history with you. I'm 48 years old, a graduate of the University of Illinois, with a degree in business. While in college I joined the NROTC and after graduation spent four years in the U.S. Marine Corps. I was a reconnaissance officer in the beginning of my military career and in Intelligence at the end. I served my country another six years as a Marine Reserve officer in San Diego, California, where I had started a small defense company. I remain Chairman of that company today. My son is CEO.

"When I started to plan my semi-retirement a couple of years ago, I knew that I had an awful lot to be thankful for. Life has been very good to me. I knew I wanted to give something back to my fellow man, and especially those at the very bottom of the economic ladder—those who were down and held down, disadvantaged to the degree that few Americans can really understand. My time in the Marine Corps, and in the defense industry, has given me the opportunity to travel much of the world.

"I can tell those of you who are not well-traveled that when you leave this great country of ours, you'll discover that most of the rest of the world lives in abject poverty. Yes, there are a lot of reasons why, but, in general, the reasons are political, educational, economic, and the greed of their leadership. In my judgment, America—as far and away the most wealthy, well-educated, largest, most influential economy in the world—has not, does not always, assume a proper leadership role. Foreign policy-wise, in my opinion, we cause as many problems as we correct. Are Americans a generous people? Yes, we give away billions every year! But, we're not smart enough to require proper accountability for the hard-earned money we send offshore. I am not sure our politicians really even care, as long as they get their share of the pork.

"Look at New Orleans—our politically focused leaders can't effectively manage money right here in the United States when U.S. citizens are desperate for help. Look at the billions we've sent to Iraq, for which there is not even a proper paper trail to track its disappearance. How about the billions we're spending on the war on drugs. Has that changed drug use in the United States? In the war on drugs, U.S. citizens are the problem, not the Colombians or Afghans. And there's the war on illegal immigration. We're spending billions on walls and fences to protect us from our next-door neighbor Mexico. Come on! Does that make sense to you? Did the Great Wall of China protect the Chinese? Did the Berlin Wall protect Russia? Long, tall walls went out as protection following the Medieval Age.

"My point! The foreign policy of the United States in some cases has been, and is, a failure perpetuated by Republican and Democratic politicians alike, who spend most of their time and energy developing strategies and tactics in a very expensive battle for control and supremacy of their political careers and party. That which is ethical, moral, legal, and in the spirit of our great Constitution, are the ideals to which our founders subscribed, but not the ideals to which many of our elected politicians aspire.

"The initiative that I am here to represent is perhaps the best, most easily understandable example of what I'm talking about, and therefore is my chosen cause, my Signature Event, my last great effort to show that any one man or woman can change the course of mankind on the world stage, including each of you.

"I'm here to talk about Cuba. There are 11 million oppressed people in Cuba. They've been oppressed for more than 50 years. They are our neighbors. The only nations closer to us are Canada and Mexico. Cuba and Havana are only 90 miles from the most southerly point in the U.S.—Key West. If you could drive it, it would be an hour and 20 minutes. By air, it's 20 minutes. By boat, perhaps two and half hours, depending on what you're driving. If you could walk it, it would take less than 30 hours. I'm trying to say, '*Cuba is close.*' Realize Cuba is our very close neighbor—always has been, always will be. But it's even closer today, due to the speed of travel and modern communications.

"The Cuban people are our friends. The vast majority, if not all of them, love America and American ideals. The Cuban people are a lot like Americans were back in the 1950s. They've been caught in a time warp caused by Fidel's Revolution and stubbornness. Fidel, of course, has been an American political leadership nemesis and bad guy poster child for many years. But, why did he, how did he, gain power? That is a historical question, with an answer that is not frequently remembered in the 21st century. But, the answer is not unlike the answers explaining our failed foreign policy right here in the Western Hemisphere with many of our neighbors in the Caribbean, Central America, South America and Mexico. Mass mismanagement!

"To refresh your memory, in Cuba, Fidel came to power to depose the American-supported dictator by the name of Batista, remember him? The U.S. helped him arrange a military coup because we didn't like the prior dictator the U.S. put in power. We believe, we say, in democracy, rule of law, free markets and power to the people. But what do we do to our neighbors, the Cuban people? Do you doubt that what we've done, and do now, is for any reason other than the economic gain of some special interest group with lots of money, influence and votes?

"If we, the U.S. Government, put someone in power and keep them in power, are we not smart enough and powerful enough to make a deal that assures a democratic future? I think yes.

"Ladies and gentlemen, the United States directly or indirectly put Fidel in the driver's seat. Then we proceeded to mismanage him, the situation deteriorated and unbelievably, we lost friends and neighbors only 90 miles away. And before we could figure out what was going on in Cuba, we were on the outside looking in. Folks, that can only happen when you are so big, fat, dumb, and happy that you get stupid. The accountability process fails, the communication process fails, leadership fails! Democracy, I'm confident, is the best system in the world, history proves it, but it is only as good as the stewards we elect to protect and perpetuate American ideals.

"Therefore, the failure of America's elected politicians and their Cuban policy brought, permitted, Fidel to come to power, and then another series of leadership bad decisions, bad foreign policy, permitted Fidel and his revolution to become perhaps the last, or certainly the best, well-known dictatorship in the world over the next 50-plus years. Ninety miles off the coast of the United States is our closest noncontiguous neighbor, 11 million depressed, oppressed neighbors! They are hungry for freedom, democracy and the American way, but intent upon retaining their rich heritage, culture and control of their way of life. They want help, but not domination, and interference by the United States.

"As their closest neighbors, we should have addressed those needs, probably through Fidel in the beginning and before he nationalized U.S. assets in Cuba. American business lost hundreds of billions of dollars. The IRS lost hundreds of millions in taxes. The U.S. lost what should have been a strategically located ally 90 miles off our coast. Worse, we wasted 50 years of influence in Cuba and permitted Russia—Russia!— six thousand miles away—to endanger every American son and daughter during the years of the Cold War!

"So, you're wondering, what am I trying to say? I'm trying to say that, in my judgment, the current Cuban mess was America's own fault, continues to be our own fault, and that now is way past time to correct the problem. And, that is my mission, my personal Signature Event as an ordinary American, a citizen diplomat with many resources, to try to lead the American people to a peaceful coexistence with 11 million of our good neighbors to the south, the people of Cuba.

"Here's the past and current situation as I see it. It's pretty simple, but not well understood by ordinary Americans, many who are called the silent majority. Some of you are here tonight. U.S.-Cuban foreign policy, certainly since the Cold War ended years ago, if not before, is all about politics, votes and influence and money. Money in U.S. politics buys votes. Votes then are influence. It does not matter who is in office, Democrats or Republicans. They are both really most motivated by the various supporting constituencies, disregarding their moral, ethical, economic, humanitarian or religious veracity—and getting and retaining control, prestige and power. Political people at the top of the food chain are enjoying the supreme ego trip! It's very addictive!

"Here's the bottom line. There are about 800,000 Cuban Americans in South Florida, maybe 100,000 in New Jersey, and 100,000 more spread around the United States. Some of them are quite well-to-do and influential. Some are politically very astute and over most of the past 40-some years have voted as a bloc, giving their 1 million votes to the political candidates who would most likely continue the embargo against Fidel and the Cuban people by association. Many of them have dreams of returning to Cuba as influential conquering heroes and/or recovering the cost of abandoned property and business. In many cases, the leadership of these influential pro U.S.-Cuban embargoists are depending on U.S. Government officials, in some future cooperative resolution of the relationship, to help appoint them to high office in the future U.S.-supported Cuban Government. I do not say the view of these people is wrong. I just say, it is biased and has exercised great power without offset, and the Cuban people do not want that kind of 19th century solution! They won't accept it!

"The U.S-Cuban bloc of 1 million votes is a big bloc. You will remember how close the vote was in Florida in 2002. The Cuban-Americans took credit for getting Mr. Bush number two elected. You'll recall that shortly after, the embargo was strengthened, primarily against the interest of ordinary Cubans. Business conditions, primarily agricultural products, actually improved. Make sense? Hell no! The whole issue does not make sense and that is why I'm here tonight! Is it moral? Absolutely not! No! Ethical? No! Good business? No! Good militarily? No! Humanitarian? No! Good foreign policy? No! A bad example to the whole Western Hemisphere? Yes! A bad example for the world? Yes!

"The United States of America! The very cradle of democracy! The champion of the poor and disenfranchised of the world for two centuries-plus. The largest, richest, most generous, forgiving society in the world, 300 million strong, has its big heavy foot on the neck of the little island of Cuba and its people like they really pose some kind of threat! Folks, it is absolutely ridiculous! It's ludicrous! It's absurd! Cuba is about the size of the state of Michigan. What are we doing? Why? As American citizens, we can't let our elected politicians get as far out of control as we've let them get in recent years. We have to get control of them and put our foot on their necks when they demonstrate un-American ideals!

"Cuba, as I said earlier, is a perfect example of politics taking precedence over American ideals. But, it is only one good example. My goal is to correct this miscarriage of American foreign policy, and I need your help to do so. I need 2 million American voters to vote in behalf of correcting this unjust policy against our neighbors in Cuba to offset 1 million biased, special interests U.S. Cuban votes. The next U.S. national election is 18 months away. You don't need to change political parties, you just need to advise your Congressmen and Senators and the President that you're not going to permit them to play these political games with your and my American goodwill. As we proceed through the election process, if my organization is successful, which will be a product of your activism, you'll see candidates adopt your point of view on this subject. For many years, there has not been an offset of voters to the U.S. Cuban voter bloc.

"Please join me in getting this job done!" *(Music comes up and applause.)*

"We're now at the point in our presentation where we've set aside about 15 minutes for questions and answers. If you have a question, simply raise your hand and one of our assistants will bring you a wireless microphone. Please stand, state your name, city of residence, occupation and question.

"Please seriously consider what we have said this evening. Read the material that was placed on the table in front of you. Use the sample letters, addresses and envelopes we've provided for you. If you have not already done so, complete the request for further information and leave it on the table or email it to us later.

"Now, who will present the first question?"

Initially, for a moment or two, no one raised a hand. The assistants holding microphones looked around expectantly. The audience looked around, too. Then, as if on cue, about 10 people raised their hands all at once. The assistant on the left was the first to reach an older gentleman.

She turned the microphone button on, handed it to him, and reminded him to stand. He did so, while saying a little testily, "My name is Jerome Whitfield. I'm a retired farmer living in Des Moines. What I want to know is how you can support the idea that America should be getting friendly with a Communist country just because they are our neighbors? Fidel, our neighbor as you say, was in cahoots with the Russians to build nuclear missile sites just 90 miles from the U.S.!"

"Thank you for your question, Jerome. It's a good one and worthy of a longer answer than I can provide tonight, but the short answer is that, in my judgment, Fidel is no longer a Communist and hasn't been one for many years. A socialist might better describe his actual philosophy in action. China was Communistic for many years, and some still think they are, and we have elected to do business with them and have done so quite successfully. I could go on to name quite a few more countries that were Communistic and/or led by dictators, whom we now support and with whom we have open trade. A major inconsistency exists in this regard because our U.S. politicians cater to the U.S. Cuban special interest groups for the sole purpose of garnering money and votes, to the direct disadvantage of the people of America and the people of Cuba's best interests—humanitarian, economic and other. In my opinion, it's immoral, unethical, unfair, bad foreign policy and un-American.

"Jerome, I hope I answered your question. I'll ask a member of my staff to assure that you receive our longer, more complete response to that question by mail.

"Now, next question, please."

A younger, professional looking woman stood, microphone in hand, turned the microphone on, and said, "Mr. Harvey, my name is Amie Butler. I'm an attorney living here in Des Moines. My question relates to your comment regarding certain pro-embargo U.S. Cubans who only desire an outcome that permits them to return to Cuba in high-ranking office or assures them the real property they abandoned—or lost by whatever means— is returned to them or in cash reparations paid, equal to current market value. Do you follow?"

"Yes, I am with you, Amie, your question?"

"Well, realizing the amount of property, personal and commercial, including U.S. corporate property nationalized, how could a poor country like Cuba ever afford to legally settle those claims?"

"A great question Amie. I can only share with you my personal opinion. To my knowledge, there has never been an in-depth analysis of this potentiality—probably because the U.S. is still as far away from attempting to negotiate a reconciliation as we were in the 1960s. That's a long time. I do not know of any other country in the world where that country's relationship with the U.S. has remained almost totally unchanged for more than 50 years! Therefore, there is little current data or related information on this subject. Further, I do not believe that the Cuban Government at this late date would agree to negotiate that particular issue. However, being the optimist that I am, I would not agree that resolution of this issue is beyond feasibility if the participants in the negotiation are willing to be creative, imaginative, reasonable and flexible in arriving at the solution. Thank you, Amie. Next question, please."

Amie, who had resisted handing over the mike, continued, "Mr. Harvey, I appreciate your answer. However, it begs a follow-up question. What might a creative solution be? You sound like you have an idea?"

"You're very perceptive, which is a talent that will serve you well in your profession. Yes, I do have some ideas that I feel might work, but I have no idea how they would be accepted by the two parties most involved. And, at this early date, it would be a mistake to reveal my endgame strategies. And, I, we, may never get to the endgame unless this national grassroots effort, started here tonight, gains support and is successful. Obviously, any successful negotiation has to conclude in a win-win for both parties. Thanks, Amie, for both your questions."

"Next question, please—yes, the mike on the right—you, sir."

Nickolas looked to the opposite side of the room for microphone number two and found it at the right rear in the hands of an older gentlemen in a blue shirt and a tie. "Yes, sir, your question please."

"My name is Wilford Bernham and I'm from rural Des Moines. My question is, you mentioned earlier a list of nations the United States has more-or-less forgiven for post-transgressions. Most of them, however, were, or are now, democracies. Doesn't that make for a hollow argument?"

"Perhaps I wasn't clear. I think I was referencing countries that, at one time or another, were a military threat to the U.S. However, the United States maintains proper, effective relations with many nations that are definitely not democratic. The best examples are Russia and China, which, of course, are on the other side the world and enjoy most-favored-nation trading status. These two countries, and many others with whom we do business, are pure Communistic or dictatorships and do not have good human rights records. They do business with our enemies, intimidate and attack their neighbors, routinely vote against the U.S. at the United Nations and make many other decisions we don't like. But, the U.S. evaluates the total relationship on balance and continues to do business with these nations and otherwise interact. So, therefore, why can't we do the same with our neighbor 90 miles away? Obviously, we can, and already should have done so, in my judgment. Thanks for the question, Wilford."

Looking left, Nickolas called upon a young executive-looking fellow in a blue sports coat, tan slacks and tie. "Yes, young man, your question please?"

"Thank you, my name is Ken Woods. I just graduated this summer from Iowa State, and I work for the Bank of Des Moines. My question is, how did this whole mess get started?"

"In the late 1950s, following Cuba's successful Revolution, followed by the failed U.S.-sponsored Bay of Pigs invasion, Fidel turned his back on the United States and sought protection and financial assistance from Russia, which obviously Russia was pleased to offer. Shortly thereafter in 1962, Russia, with Fidel's approval, started building missile-launching sites in Cuba, which led to a very dangerous military confrontation between the U.S. and Russia. Soon after turning back Russia's missile shipments to Cuba at sea, the U.S. imposed an economic embargo on Cuba under provisions of the Trading with the Enemy Act.

"However, these actions by the U.S. only strengthened the resolve of Fidel and the Russians to create a strong communist regime in Cuba 90 miles from U.S. territory. For the following 25 years, the Cuba and

U.S. relationship was very inflammatory. After the Berlin Wall came down, signaling the end of the Cold War in 1990, Russia discontinued its presence in the Caribbean and significantly reduced Fidel's resources with which to continue his efforts to spread communism or socialism in the Caribbean, Central America or South America.

"Since the early 1990s Fidel has ceased to be a threat to anyone except his own people and has otherwise confidentially shown a great deal of willingness to discuss and resolve mutual issues with the U.S. However, at the same time Fidel was trying to ease tensions, the U.S. decided to tighten the squeeze the embargo was causing on Fidel and the Cuban people, although the U.N. General Assembly and the Organization of American States had voted twice for the U.S. to end the embargo. The embargo's political and economic objectives have not been achieved in almost 30 years; however, the embargo has inhumanely oppressed the Cuban people. In my judgment, U.S. Foreign Policy regarding Cuba has been and is tragically flawed, strictly for internal U.S. political purposes. This policy has been in contradiction to those ideals the United States was founded upon. Thank you, Ken, good question."

Ken is still in control of the microphone and asks, "Mr. Harvey, for what purposes?"

"The usual reasons, the money, power and influence of special interests. In this case, there's a large segment of the right-wing Cuban-American community in South Florida. Several U.S. Presidents have taken a public stand on Cuba that they know full well will produce nonpositive results, thereby allowing domestic, special interests politics to dictate U.S. National Foreign Policies and actions, in exchange for political donations and votes."

Nickolas looks to the opposite side. A 30s-something stylish young woman has the microphone. "Yes, ma'am?"

"My name is Nancy Bancroft, and I live in Ames. I'm a reporter from the *Ames Gazette*. I appreciate the opportunity to be here for your very first national meeting. Thank you. My question follows your last answer.

"Mr. Harvey, where is all this special interest activity heading?"

"In my opinion, it appears that South Florida Cubans will only accept a bloody coup resolution, which will permit them to return to

Cuba as the new Cuban leadership. However, this violent outcome has not occurred in more than 50 years, and hopefully it never will. You can imagine a U.S military intervention in Havana, having watched the U.S. depose of Saddam Hussein on television. A violent overthrow of the Cuban Government will result in much death, injury of helpless and innocent Cubans, and destruction of Havana. But, if it happens any other way, the Cuban exiles in Florida get left out of the new Cuba. Thank you, Nancy."

Before Nickolas can recognize the next person with a question, an older man on the left says, "Mr. Harvey, what have we got to do to get this train wreck back on the tracks? My name is Don Abernathy and I'm from Des Moines."

"Thanks for the question, Don."

"What we have to do to get this train wreck back on the tracks? Join ARC, tell the ARC story. Write your senators and congressmen and demand they do the right thing, right now." Don asks a follow-up question,

"Remember that guy Chavez in Venezuela? He appeared to be taking lessons from Fidel in dictatorship. Do we want to do business with Fidel if he's still trying to expand his revolution into South America?"

"In my judgment on this question, I would say that Fidel and Chavez were each using the other to achieve different political and economic objectives. Fidel needs oil on credit and Chavez liked sticking his finger into Uncle Sam's eye. I don't see much more going on here, but I'm not looking very hard either. More importantly, I believe the U.S. needs an aggressive Latin-American/Caribbean policy which significantly improves all of our relationships to the south. A proper, consistent, continuous strategic Western Hemisphere Foreign Policy will help the U.S. avoid the Fidels and Chavezes of the future and strengthen all the countries in the Western Hemisphere in a period of time when U.S. influence in the world is weakening, as other major national economics strengthen, like China, India and Egypt, not to mention the resurgence of Russia.

"For a decade the U.S. has been pissing everybody off in a very arrogant manner, and it is way past time that we started to repair some of the damage we have done, pay more attention to our old friends and try to make some new ones all over the world, but particularly in the Western Hemisphere, where there are many emerging markets, resources, oil, minerals, low-cost labor, etc., to which the U.S. has the most dependable, low-cost convenient access. If we must lose our manufacturing capacity to India, Egypt and China, a gazillion miles away by boat, why not lose it to our neighbors in Central and South America, immediately available to us by boat, rail and highway and easily defensible from North America. Isn't a little insurance against the unknown future world order a prudent plan? Think about it. We should start by showing our neighbors south of our borders that we can forgive and forget the perceived transgressions of the past. Nations that cannot forgive and look forward are not held in high esteem or considered good future partners."

The audience has figured out the left and right rhythm of the questions. As soon as Nickolas turned his face to the other side, a tall, heavyset older man, in a jean jacket and cowboy hat, says,

"Mr. Harvey, I have great trouble forgetting the fact that in the 1960s the Cubans had made a deal with the Russians to place nuclear missiles in Cuba pointed at America. As I recall, the world had never been closer to a nuclear holocaust! How do you forgive and forget a lethal threat of that magnitude? My name is Jesse Bitwell and I am from Atlantic, Iowa."

"Jesse, the U.S. leadership hasn't forgotten that threat to date. In retaliation, we have made Fidel, and more importantly the Cuban people, pay for it, for more than 50 years. We forgave our WWII enemies, the Germans and Japanese, in far less time, and they caused far more U.S. deaths and destruction than the Cuban missile crisis, and don't forget that the U.S. sponsored an invasion of Cuba, called the Bay of Pigs. When our government sponsors the invasion of another country in an attempt to overthrow the government, we should expect a massive, long-term negative reaction.

"In the case of Cuba, we caused it and we got it—very bad policy and very bad planning. Fidel was trying to protect his little country from the largest most powerful country in the world, which had already tried to assassinate him and had tried to invade his country and overthrow his government. What would you do if someone you knew had tried to break into your house and kill you and probably would try it again? You'd likely go get the biggest guns you could find and call upon your friends to help you defend your home and family. That's what Fidel did. His only capable friends at the time were the Russians. The U.S. chose to be his enemy."

"Mr. Harvey, in follow-up, how do we know he won't do it again?"

"How do Fidel and Raul know that we won't do it again? We all have friends and we all have enemies. Do you know what the difference is? The difference is that we forgive the shortcomings and transgressions of our friends. And we don't forgive the shortcomings and transgressions of our enemies. It's that simple. Look into your own experiences and relationships. None of us is perfect. No nation has been or is perfect. The mission of ARC is not retribution; it is reconciliation. After more than 50 years, don't you believe it's time for us to reconcile with our Cuban neighbors just 90 miles south of Key West? If not now after 50 years, when do you want to do it? In a hundred years? Two hundred years? When?

"It is an American tradition to bring people together. What do the words say on the Statue of Liberty, which was the first sight of millions of our forebearers who settled this country and made it the shining example of freedom, tolerance and democracy that it has been? Those words mean we bring people together. We don't tear them apart. America is the melting pot of the world. We seek peace, not conflict—not peace at any price and not conflict without provocation."

"Mr. Harvey, my name is Ann Smith. Oh, I'm from Des Moines. Wasn't Cuba one of the axis of evil countries identified by President Bush?"

"Yes, Ann. However, President Bush, in my judgment, had his own political agenda as it relates to Cuba, which has more to do with South Florida's political special interests than whether the Castro regime is currently evil. Evil is a big word." Ann interrupts with a follow-up question,

"In terms of U.S. Foreign Policy or politics, what does evil mean?"

"Ann, Webster's Dictionary would define evil as morally wrong, bad, immoral, wicked. Obviously all these words leave a lot to interpretation by the user and the reader or listener. Words like evil and wicked do not have much legitimate application in the 21st century beyond religion or theatrics, in my opinion. Thank you, Ann."

A young, black American is standing in the center aisle next to one of ARC's hostesses, holding the microphone.

"Yes, in the center aisle, your question please," Nickolas says.

"Disregarding calling certain nations that are dictatorships evil, how can we negotiate with leaders whose very leadership would end if these countries became democratic and who, in most cases, are not trustworthy, hate the United States, and in several cases, want to destroy us?" the young man asks.

"In my opinion, the issue isn't whether the U.S. should negotiate with dictators or not. The issue is to have an aggressive, prioritized, realistic, rational, intelligent national strategic plan to achieve U.S. Foreign Policy objectives with all nations. Special emphasis should be placed on the Western Hemisphere, Canada, Mexico, Central and South America, and the Caribbean, as these countries are our closet geographical neighbors. In the final analysis, they should be part of our greater defensive perimeter. Secondarily, they should become our favored trading partners. The United States needs to significantly increase its goodwill and favorable influence in all the Americas and in the Caribbean in a sustainable consistent fashion over the long-term for the strategic mutual benefit of all. We need to ensure the security, well-being and economic vitality of our neighborhood before we go across town to make other major investments."

"Does that mean that we refocus resources away from Great Britain, Western Europe, the Middle East and Asia-Pacific? My name is Elwin Brewer. I'm from Des Moines."

"Thanks for the question, Elwin. No, I don't think so. I believe that on an inflation-adjusted basis, we've been reducing foreign investments in those areas over the past 25-30 years following WWII, and the Korean and Vietnam Wars. As a result of these much earlier investments, we have many permanent good friends in those areas who share American ideals and values, and with whom we are bound by a common destiny. However, like your friends or mine, we cannot take them for granted. We must continue to invest in the relationships or they will decline. Therefore, I see a return to major investments in our future foreign policy, while we maintain and enhance existing good relationships and invest in new ones, particularly in the Western Hemisphere."

Nickolas sees and hears a disturbance at one of the rear tables. Mike is at the table, gesturing in a manner revealing there was a problem of some sort that he now controls.

"Mr. Harvey, my name is Marjorie Withers. I'm in banking in Des Moines. What has all this talk about Latin American Foreign Policy got to do with Cuba? I just don't get the connection."

"Well, first of all, I was responding to a question regarding the issue of the United States negotiating with nations being lead by dictators and secondly, where was the money going to come from to pursue a more aggressive foreign policy plan in the Western Hemisphere. Hopefully, you've understood my answer. Now, to your question. What is the connection between my talk about Latin America Foreign Policy and Cuba? I would first say there is no connection; there is a disconnection in Cuba that has lasted more than 50 years. That is why there is an ARC and why I am here. I believe we've been punishing Cubans and certain Cuban-Americans way too long for strictly political reasons, namely the U.S. Cuban voting bloc, which does not want a peaceful solution to the long-standing antagonistic relationship.

"Thank you, sir. Next question please, don't be bashful."

A middle-aged, middle-class looking women was standing halfway down aisle two with the microphone. "My name is Sandy Windward and I'm from Des Moines, Iowa."

"Yes, Sandy, your question?"

"I understand that the Cubans have recently discovered oil in the Gulf between Cuba and Florida. Is that true? And, what does it mean to ARC's program?"

"Thank you, Sandy. That is a very good question."

"As I understand the situation, Cuba has announced that it has made a deal to drill for oil in the Gulf with the Canadians or the French, I am not sure, in areas off the northwest coast up to 50 miles from Key West, in which there are oil reserves that have been well-known for some time. They are very deep in the Florida Straits and, therefore, expensive to drill. I assume it is only the high cost of fuel that makes these particular oil fields economically attractive. If they started a plan to exploit these fields today, it would likely be five years before anybody made any money. It's ARC's plan to free the people of Cuba in the next 24 months. If we are able to do so, we may establish a political, legal and economic environment in which U.S. oil producers could directly benefit, as opposed to giving this business to the Canadians, French, Germans or Spanish."

"Thank you, Mr. Harvey."

"Thank you. Next question please."

"Mr. Harvey, my name is Winston Johnston and I'm from Iowa City."

"Thank you for coming all this way. What is your question?"

"My question may sound simple, but the simple answer may satisfy a lot of Iowans here tonight not as sophisticated as you and me."

"I understand, go ahead."

"Is Cuba, in any sense of this question, a threat to the United States?"

Nickolas smiles and looks around as the audience mumbles.

"Mr. Johnston, some people have a knack for cutting through all the BS and getting to the root of the question. I think you're one of those very special people. The United States is the richest, most powerful country in the world. Cuba is a third-world country of 11 million poor citizens with no Army, Navy or Air Force of significance, compared to the United States. Going to war with Cuba would be like the United States going to war with the state of Michigan. As a U.S. citizen, I'm embarrassed that our big, rich, powerful country has bullied a little country like Cuba for 30 or 40 years for strictly political reasons."

"Mr. Harvey, my name is Exavior Vieterov. It seems to me that we should continue to invest in relationships in Western Europe where most of us in the United States came from in the first place, such as England, Ireland, Scotland, France, Germany, Poland, Hungary, the Netherlands, even Russia?"

"Exavior, you've just named about all the white Anglo-Saxon countries. Are you saying, 'All of us white people ought to stick together?'"

"Well, I didn't think that was what I was saying, but now that you've said it, why isn't that a logical path? The Muslims seem to be organizing for a big showdown. They are committed to killing all of us white Christians, infidels they call us. By the way, what the hell is an infidel anyway?" Exavior asks.

"We continue to get far afield from Cuba and its relationship to foreign policy in Central and South America, but I'll give you a brief answer. My analysis tells me that the Muslim fundamentalist fanatics, as a percentage of all Muslims, are less than 10%. A small minority. If you've been in the U.S. military, you'll know what I mean when I say there is always 10% who don't get the word, which is to say, that the extremes of human knowledge include 10% who are ignorant and 10% who are genius. The rest of us are somewhere in the other 80%. We can't make rules for that 20% who are too dumb or too smart. They always have to be handled as exceptions to all rules. This is the situation with the radical Muslim fundamentalist—he or she is only 10% of the total and the only percentage that is a problem. He or she needs to be managed as an exception. We can't throw the baby out with the bath water! You understand what I'm saying?"

"Yes, I think I know that, but I needed you to tell me. Thank you."

"You're welcome, Exavior. Good question. By the way, an infidel is a nonbeliever in the Muslim faith," Nick replies.

"Mr. Harvey, my name is Oliver Wiggins. I am professor of Eastern studies at Iowa State. I'm impressed with some of your indirect observations regarding the changing U.S.-world-geopolitical situation. I think we're of like mindset, but you've only referred to these changes as future major developments. Could you please be more direct on that subject?"

"Again, Oliver, we seem to be getting further afield from the U.S.-Cuba relationship. However, I've promised to answer every question as directly and honestly as I can. I'll be brief as this subject's only relationship to my objective is in terms of first resolving the U.S.-Cuba issue as a preliminary event to a larger effort to develop and consolidate a self-sufficient, competitive Western Hemisphere political/economic power base capable of competing in the future with other major emerging geo-fiscal international global partnerships. That said, here we go.

"I believe, based on current facts in evidence, including economic development forecasts and recent American financial investment in Iraq, lack of investments at home, out-of-control health costs, energy costs and other major mistakes by our government, that the increasing costs of living and debt service will bring the U.S. to the threshold of very serious risks to our way of life for the first time since WWII. America has expended and wasted a huge amount of its capital at a time when its natural resources, low-cost energy availability being number one, are at an all-time low, all unnecessary and due to a lack of intelligent leadership in energy use and conservation since the 1970s. We had more than 30 years to think, plan and initiate low-cost alternatives. In recent times, we were not even smart enough to return to a 55 mph speed limit on our federal highway system, which would save 10% of our fuel use! Don't get me started here! I could give you two hours on how inept our leadership has been on energy over the past 30 years, which, by the way, includes plenty of time in office by Democrats and Republicans to realize that petroleum-based fuel is a declining, infinite natural resource.

"Excuse me, I got off point again, but only because I'm so frustrated with the outcome of the American political process and its inability and ineffectiveness at giving us the kind of strategic leadership we need, deserve and must achieve.

"Back on point, Mr. Wiggins, here's your answer. In my opinion, the world, *she-is-a-changin'*. Further, I believe most of the rest of the world knows, understands and welcomes the change with open arms. But the U.S. Government leadership and its' citizens don't see it. Our government leaders have been power fat, dumb and happy for a half century and arrogant for a decade. They aren't going to tell us that for the first time in a century we are now in a race we may not win for the world's super power title. They aren't going to tell you this race has already started and is leaving the U.S. at the starting gate. They aren't going to tell you the race started at a time when U.S. power was the weakest on a worldwide basis that it ever has been.

"Nobody is calling the U.S. trying to expand their relationship. U.S influence all over the world is at an all-time low. Why? Because the worldwide balance of power for the first time in 200 years is changing and Americans have lost the moral high ground in the eyes of many around the world. We have compromised our integrity—an integrity earned by thousands of American patriots who preceded us and gave their lives to preserve what were the traditional American ideals. Earning the moral high ground back may take a decade of very focused earnest efforts. It will be a long time before many of the world's current generation forget our transgressions, while trying to make the world conform to our expectations way faster than we achieved them ourselves. People forget, but the most costly war America has ever fought was the American Civil War. That was only a century and a half or so ago. My great grandfather's father fought in that war.

"I digress again, forgive me, back on point. China, India, Russia, Brazil and even smaller nations are slowly moving up on America in terms of economic self-realization, energy self-sufficiency and a willingness and ability to compete and influence. In the past, Americans have taken their leadership and past accomplishments, past image and reputation for granted. Our lack of focus on this factor now has us in a hole and we now must dig our way out, shovel by shovel. This, of course, is a simplified answer to a complex political question."

Another question comes from the right side of the audience.

"The U.S. policy seems to me to require that Fidel exit the scene, before the U.S. will commence any serious discussions. Is this true? My name is Nelson Green."

"Nelson, that's what some U.S. politicians say. However, in my opinion, that's simply their way of avoiding and deferring dealing with the problem. There is no major plan that I know of that can be initiated should Fidel or Raul or both die tomorrow."

"Mr. Harvey, my name is Mary Beth Albertson. I'm from Des Moines. Immigration policy seems to be an increasingly important issue in America. We hear a lot about our problems on the U.S.-Mexico border. What is the situation, generally speaking, with Cuba?"

"Approximately 20,000 Cubans legally immigrate to the United States annually. I estimate another 10,000 or so immigrate illegally to America each year, and many others lose their lives while trying. No one knows how many."

"Mr. Harvey, I know you're a wealthy man and I've read that you've worked hard to get to where you are. So why do you risk your wealth and possibly your life for this particular cause?"

"As you recognize, I have achieved my American dream. I want to help others on as large a scale as possible to achieve their dreams, if I can. I want to give back to society some of my good fortune while I can."

"Thank you. My name is Albert Swiss, and I work for Tomlinson Industries locally. I'm an engineer."

"Yes, I know Tomlinson, and we're in the same industry— defense. I know you're CEO, Peter Walker. Give him my regards. Albert, thank you for being here. What's your question?"

"Obviously, I know about your company, as well. You guys are tough competitors. Mr. Harvey, I've visited your website to gather information before attending this meeting, and noted that you're funding this national campaign personally. Realizing that you are not financially supported by either Republicans or Democrats and that even a senatorial race within a state can cost $100 million, how long can you sustain your effort?"

"A fair question. Obviously there are many variables. But, the biggest variable is the amount of campaign funds we can raise for this purpose. This is a grassroots campaign, at least initially, which will be supported or not by ordinary Americans who believe as we do. We need a minimum of 2 million of them to become our active supporters over the next couple of years. If they will, on average, send us $5 per month each, I believe we can change the balance of power and votes in the next election and in the process begin to establish a normalized relationship between Cuba and the United States. Thank you for your question."

"Next question, to the left. Yes, ma'am?"

"My name is Muriel Davis. I'm an office manager for the local Caterpillar distributorship. I've lived in Des Moines all of my life. Mr. Harvey, I, too, am troubled by this idea that Americans should establish a relationship with Cuba, which, in no time at all, would provide many more American dollars to one of our oldest and worst enemies. Of all the cases out there, why this one? How do we know Fidel won't use the new money to spread his hatred of Americans all over Central and South America?"

"Well, as you may know, this is my life's Signature Event. It is an effort to give back something to my fellow man in appreciation for all the good luck I've had in my life. I've tried to pick a project that will challenge my ability, and one of a size and consequence to have a major beneficial effect on mankind and, in fact, affect a change for the better for our greater worldwide society of mankind.

"The injustice that has occurred, is occurring, in Cuba is a situation I have long felt was correctable and which is occurring in the backyard of the United States, home of freedom, liberty and justice. Cuba is one of our very closest neighbors—granted they are a politically estranged neighbor, but a neighbor nonetheless. This estrangement, in my judgment, was initially avoidable, and should have been avoided through diplomacy. However, U.S. leadership took a hard line and drove Fidel into the waiting arms of the Russians and ultimately into a crisis that could have destroyed the world—all because we were not properly taking care of business in our neighborhood, which to me appears to be a continuous problem. More than 50 years later we are still ineffectively dealing with strategically sensitive problems in our own backyard while we focus on the Mideast and other expensive problems outside the Western Hemisphere. The situation is ridiculous and inexplicable if you really think about it.

"Lastly, I desire to try to achieve as large a social beneficial result as I believe I can financially afford.

"Thank you, Albert, for your thoughtful question.

"Next question please."

"Yes, the gentleman on the right. Sir, your name, please."

"Mr. Harvey, my name is Allan Jones and I'm from Atlantic, Iowa. It appears that you have influenced some Iowans here tonight, but not me. I see you for what you are—a card-carrying liberal Democrat trying to influence the outcome of the next election. Or, a disguised representative of U.S. big business who wants to get back into the Cuban market. You say you're not a politician, but everything I've read and heard about you and what I've seen and heard tonight sounds like pure bullshit to me—which is another word for politics here in Iowa. You won't get a cent out of me or another minute of my valuable time! I am out of here, and I suggest that everyone here follow me!"

Mr. Jones pushes his way through the tables and chairs and strides toward the back door, microphone still in hand. A security guard steps in front of Mr. Jones. Mr. Jones tries to push past. The security guard holds his position, asking Mr. Jones for the microphone, which he hesitatingly gives up to the security man, who then lets him pass. Behind Mr. Jones are two other men who were sitting at the same table, and follow Mr. Jones out the door. The audience has become uneasy and is talking with one another as a result of Mr. Jones' outburst and departure.

Nick, trying to regain control, says, "Ladies and gentlemen, please. Ladies and gentlemen, let me respond to Mr. Jones question, or better said, to his statement. Please, keep your seats.

"Thank you. Thank you for not letting someone emotionally intimidate you into doing something illogical. I want to respond. I wish Mr. Jones and his two friends would have remained here to listen. First, I am not a liberal Democrat or a liberal Republican. You've heard me criticize both Democrats and Republicans. If you analyze just a little bit, you will realize I am critical of elected officials who are more concerned with their politics, political party and re-election than they are with their oaths of office, ethics and responsibility to the American people who elected them. The U.S. historic and current situation in Cuba is a perfect storm of an example of what I mean, and that which I deplore. My approach to correcting this situation is bipartisan. I'm not a secret agent for any special interest group. I am, or intend to be, an agent for change. I'll lead those who wish to join me in seeking this change in the U.S.-Cuba relationship and thereby removing 8 million Cubans from the oppression of Fidel and the United States.

"I have been and I am now a businessman, an entrepreneur, who at the age of 28 started his own small business with personal savings and borrowed money and slowly grew that business into a major mid-sized defense manufacturing company. I was very lucky in my pursuit of the American dream.

"I'm not a politician. I've never run for any elective office and I do not intend to do so. I assure you that I am who and what I say I am. These facts are a matter of public record. My motivations are only what I've said they are. If you will come to understand my cause, believe in it and support it, I will not let you down. In the end, I assure you, you will only have pride and satisfaction in having been a part of changing the world we live in for the better. I give you my word as a Marine officer.

"Now, we asked for one hour of your time, and that hour is now up. There are self-addressed, stamped envelopes on your tables. You may take them home, fill them out, and mail or e-mail them to us. E-mail is preferred. We'll answer every one. We appreciate your donations. It will take several million dollars to do what we need to do. My personal wealth will get us organized and up and going, but is not enough to get the total job done. For your financial support, we'll return a monthly newsletter and a quarterly ARC financial report.

"In conclusion, I thank you very much for being here. Don't forget your envelopes when you leave. Communicate with us. You'll be glad you did."

Nickolas, still at center stage, paused a moment, thinking about what had happened. Near the end, the meeting had gotten somewhat out of control. One question was, had it been staged or was it real emotion? Fortunately, he regained control with sheer force of character near the end. At that point, Nick knew more security was needed and better control of communications, or his message could be diluted by radicals in the audience. This wasn't about freedom of speech. This was about the good guys winning and majority rule. The extremes of society or politics needed to learn how to communicate with the majority or learn to become the majority. Civilization cannot advance in any other way.

Nick concluded the meeting by saying, "Ladies and gentlemen, thank you very much for being with us this evening and listening to our story. You have been an important part of that for which our country stands—democracy! You've evidenced democracy in action tonight—Americans debating important issues about which some disagree, in an attempt to clarify, understand and resolve those issues.

"You have a lot of new information as it relates to America's past and current relationship with the Cuban people. You have a lot of good reasons to believe it should change in the future and you've heard from some of your fellow citizens on why it shouldn't. Believe it or not. Having heard these arguments, you will decide. Whatever your verdict, realize that the political world we live in is constantly changing for the better or the worse because politics is a human manifestation and humans make lots of mistakes, and some humans, on purpose or accidentally, are forces for good and some are forces for their own power and greed. One of the weapons of greed is ignorance. You are now educated. Become a force for good. Reach out to your neighbors in Cuba. Trust them with your helping hand and support so that they will do the right thing.

"Thank you, and drive carefully if you're leaving. There is fresh coffee and cake if you would like to stay a little longer and visit on a less formal basis."

By nine, almost everyone who had stayed for coffee and cake had left. At the end of the formal meeting, the two pilots who had been in the audience as additional security and to gather opinions had left for the plane to assure she had been fueled and otherwise checked out ready for the flight back to Washington's Reagan International. Moxie, the airplane's flight attendant, had stayed on board the plane in the three and half hours it was on the ground in Des Moines to assure no one came aboard the aircraft or otherwise tampered with it.

The flight back, flying with a favorable easterly wind, would be about a half-hour quicker than the flight west against it.

Nick, Tim and Mike stood in a circle in the lobby near the door to their meeting room, following the departure of the last six or eight hangers-on. Everyone was coming down from the stress and tension of the meeting, now that it was finally over after 30 days of presentation, planning and rehearsing. The group in another fashion was ebullient from the relief and pleased with the outcome, which they expectantly needed to have confirmed by their leader, Nick.

Nickolas understood that need as he looked at the mostly smiling faces around him. But he was enjoying their happy anticipation of his confirmation of their opinions and he continued to be mute for another moment or two as he looked at them all in turn, with just the faint hint of a smile at the corner of his lips, his eyes giving him away to those who knew him best. Then, quite surprisingly and out of character, Nick jumped into the air with a big smile, yelling, "We've done it! We've done it! We've influenced some people! We've done it!" Spontaneously, without realizing it, everyone else randomly started yelling, clapping and jumping, too. Nick started yelling "Hoorah" at the height of each jump, and soon they were all jumping in unison and hoorahing in unison. Nick stopped. They stopped, exhilarated and excited, but relaxed by the tension relief.

"Thank you all so much for all your very hard work. We're off and running as of tonight. I don't think we'll benefit from any further test meetings. We'll meet Monday morning in follow-up to this meeting, having analyzed much further what we got done here today. But I feel very confident that the analysis will show that we should proceed directly to initiate our campaign of meetings around the nation. Good work. Very good work! I am proud of each and every one of you!

"Let's get our gear packed up and head for the airport. Mike, you pay the hotel bill. Tim and I will round up the limo drivers, who I think are parked on the side of the building back here somewhere."

# XXIV

## MARRIOTT BALLROOM PARKING LOT

Nickolas and Tim exited a metal side door in the rear corner of the hotel meeting room into the loading area and parking lot. They both looked around for their limos and drivers and did not see them. They had finished a little early. Tim let the self-locking door close with a click. It was then that three overweight biker types in black leather jackets, jeans too long and boots too big, got out of an old dirty van with darkened windows, and started walking toward Nickolas and Tim. One biker was carrying a tire iron, two others, cans of beer. Tim pulls on the steel door trying to get back inside but, no movement. He then starts pounding on the door and yelling,

"Open up! Open up!" Surprisingly, the door opens up.

"It's open, Nick, let's go!" Tim says.

"Get in there, quick, Tim." But, Nickolas doesn't move or take his eyes off the advancing three men. Tim hesitates and then steps inside.

Nickolas yells, "Don't open this door until you hear me tell you."

The biker types are smiling and surprised.

The apparent leader responds, "You're one stupid old motherfucker! Coming to Des Moines to test your pro-communist plan to help Castro take over the Caribbean! We're going to change your mind about that right now, right here. We're going to teach you a lesson you will never forget. Come to daddy," he shouts, gesturing with the tire iron. "Daddy's going to spank your skinny ass in a way you'll never forget."

"This is your party. You're the teacher. Come and teach me. But I must warn you that you'll be fucking with a United States Marine. The Corps doesn't teach its Marines how to defend themselves in hand-to-hand combat. They teach us how to disable our enemies in hand-to-hand combat. If you engage me, you'll be putting your life and limbs in serious danger. I only know how to fight one way—for keeps. Think about it. If you have family who depend upon you, don't do this. Please, you could be out of work for a month or even permanently," Nickolas says.

The other two rednecks look at one another with a little nervous surprise and doubt. One says, "I was in the Corps. I will not attack a fellow Marine. I'm going home. I think you guys should, too. This guy could be a real bad ass. Not like me. I was a Hollywood Marine." He leaves, walking toward the front of the hotel. One of the remaining two backups replies,

"Shit. Two to one against a Marine can be less than even odds. I'm going home, too. I just spent $1,000 on new bridgework. See you, Burt. Good luck!" This guy heads back to the van.

The biker leader shouts. "Okay, jarhead. It looks like you got a pass tonight. But there will be another time and another place. This isn't over until I say it's over!"

"Okay, I believe you. However, I want it over now!" Nickolas runs toward the biker who drops the tire wrench, turns around to run, but gets tackled by Nickolas and put into an arm and headlock.

"Burt, I'm only going to ask you once. Is it over?" *He applies pressure.* Burt screams, "Yes, yes, it's over! It's over! Jesus! That hurts, let up! Let up!"

"Okay, Burt. I'm going to let you go without any bodily harm. But, if I ever see you again, I'm going to break either your arm or leg. You can decide which you prefer. Now go home and sober up!"

Burt runs off holding his head. Nickolas goes to the conference room door and knocks. Tim and the girls come out looking around, concerned. The van is speeding away. Tony appears around a corner where he had been watching the action.

Tony approaches, smiling and says, "Boss, you're something else! Let's go home."

# XXV

## AT 30,000 FEET ALTITUDE

**SEPTEMBER**

Nickolas was in deep thought as the large G5 executive jet headed south for Miami and the most important series of ARC presentations to be held in the field. He was pleased with ARC's work to date, particularly the fact that the average American registered voter awareness about ARC had increased from 30% to 60%. What he had planned was occurring faster than he had expected, and the media response had been much better than planned. The average American was grasping the incongruity of U.S.-Cuba Foreign Policy much more easily than he thought they would and, more importantly, they believed it should change, that U.S. suppression of the Cuban people for political reasons was immoral, unethical, inconsistent and un-American.

Nickolas thought, we've come a long way from Des Moines in May to Miami in September. But here they were preparing for a week of meetings in South Florida, including two major meetings in Miami—one downtown and one in the western suburbs—and two others, in Fort Lauderdale and West Palm Beach. Minor luncheon meetings would also be held in Marathon in the Keys, and in Coral Gables, Tampa, Orlando and Jacksonville.

Three presentation teams would be put into action, led by Nickolas, Phil and Tim. Each team would be equipped with a small business jet out of Miami International as each team was scheduled for the three major and five minor meetings over the period of Monday morning through Friday morning. The Miami area meeting schedule was purposely aggressive—get in, get it on in the opposition's backyard, do all you can, as well as you can, and then get out of Dodge, hoping you got it done. Nick didn't want to have to come back to South Florida. He didn't need to change everyone's mind, just half of them, the right half. He knew that at some time in the near future that ARC's influence on the basic issue would reach the tipping point and take on a life all of its own. The Phase I objective would be achieved. However, the budget was taking a beating.

Nickolas started thinking of all the things that he and Mike and the security planning team had identified that could go wrong in Miami. He went over those threats and his teams countermeasures again and again. He found everything as he had found it before. Their planning was as good as planning could be, but he knew the biggest threats were the rules of *'Murphy's Law'* and *'shit happens!'* He also knew worry was not productive. The presentation teams were ready. Security was ready. They were experienced, flexible and innovative. They would get the job done. In the end, what would be, would be.

# XXVI

## MIAMI, FLORIDA

All three teams arrived in Miami aboard a big Gulf Stream G5 executive jet at 3 p.m. The pilot had announced that the temperature was 90 degrees with 90% humidity, as they touched down at Miami International. A few minutes later they disembarked at the executive jet terminal, where Mike, Tony, Pete and his other security people awaited them and transferred them into the waiting limousines. Ten minutes later they were in the late Sunday afternoon traffic on I-812 headed east for I-95 south toward the downtown Marriott on Biscayne Boulevard. Two motorcycle officers preceded and two followed the motorcade, consisting of three limousines and three SUVs.

They were all a little nervous and tense, realizing that they were in South Florida for the first time, in the hometown of the major organized opposition. Anything could happen tonight, even though they had tried to plan for everything they could imagine. Late afternoon traffic was heavy. They were in the right lane looking for I-95 south when Nickolas suddenly noticed that all the cars in front of them, beside them, and behind them were flying Cuban flags over their rear side windows. Passengers in the cars, including many women with children, were gesturing wildly and screaming at them, although they could hear nothing. The occasional upraised middle finger, however, was easily understood. Nickolas quickly realized that their arrival time at the airport had not remained a secret. Further, someone had organized and orchestrated this reception to Miami for them. There were perhaps 10 or 12 cars in this flotilla of demonstrators, all anti-ARC.

Mike had anticipated and planned for this possibility, and the forward-most security vehicle moved left one lane and slowed the demonstrators' cars on their left in the center lane, then kept their station next to their assigned limousines, eliminating the harassment and potential for the vehicles to clash. As they exited into heavy traffic from the freeway exit onto Biscayne, the demonstrators' cars were dispersed and became less of an immediate harassment, although the horn blowing had become contagious on Biscayne as they made the final turn toward the hotel. The street was lined with flag-carrying demonstrators screaming and yelling.

At the hotel it was bedlam, although half of Miami's finest appeared to be there along with a forest of television antennae supporting live broadcasts for the 5 o'clock and 7 o'clock news, now only an hour away. The main hotel entryway had been cleared for them and they pulled up to the door immediately. The police had cordoned this area off from a small crowd of supporters and a large crowd of critics who must have numbered 200 or 300 excited flag- and banner-waving Miamians, mostly Cuban in origin from what Nickolas could see. ABC, NBC, CNN, Fox and CBS news crews had been granted access to the arrival area and moved quickly toward the two limos as they stopped to unload at the hotel entryway.

Phil and his team were in the lead car with their two security people. Nickolas, his team and his two security people were in the second car, and Tim's team were in car number three. By plan, all of the security exited first, securing the area quickly, and then opened Nickolas' limo door first.

Judy and Nickolas exited and met Carrie Carlisle of CNN News a few feet away. Tim had planned this event.

Carrie said, "Mr. Harvey. Welcome to Miami! As you can see, your visit has stirred the emotions of Miamians to a level not seen since the 'Little Evan' situation. What do you hope to accomplish here in the next two nights and two days?" This question meant more to Nickolas than Carrie thought it would, as no one was supposed to know that Nickolas was in Miami for a second night. All of ARC's advance news releases had indicated the usual one day, one night event. Nickolas wondered how she knew about the second night, which was information only Nickolas' staff was supposed to know.

However, unless the contraction of Nickolas irises gave him away he was quick and normal with his response.

"Carrie, my people and I are here to do that already reported upon in Des Moines, Omaha, Newark and many other cities across our great country. Simply stated, I am here to communicate on the reasons, ways and means to normalize U.S.-Cuban relations, which have been more than strained since the beginning of the Cold War in the 1950s. There are young people listening to us who don't even know what the Cold War was all about, how it started, or how it ended. This is how old and out-of-date this whole issue has become. This issue is perpetuated by U.S. egocentric politicians on both sides of the issue with no concern for the negative humanitarian and economic implications imposed upon the Cuban people and many Americans, or concerns for the real pursuit of justice, freedom and democracy in the Western Hemisphere!"

"Mr. Harvey, what can you say or do that hasn't been said or done before in the past 50 years?"

"Well, Carrie, that's an easy question to answer as there hasn't been anything positive done in more than 50 years! I intend to remove this issue as a tool of partisan politics for both parties and South Florida expatriate Cubans, and set it squarely in front of average Americans all across the U.S. to analyze for what it is—a failed U.S. Foreign Policy strategy. They will decide in the next election, now 14 months away, if not earlier, what our national policy should be with the people of Cuba, and elect leaders who want to change it."

"Mr. Harvey, don't you believe the Castro brothers will have something to say about all that, as well?"

"Carrie, yes, I do. However, I believe the Castro brothers are wise men who have learned a lot since their revolution began more than 50 years ago, just like the rest of us. We all tend to get a little smarter as we grow older. I believe Fidel, in the final analysis, will do the right thing for his people. I believe that Fidel realizes that he can go down in history in one of two ways. One way, as a stubborn old man stuck in the past with no reasonable or intelligent understanding of his people's future needs and leave them with extremely limited resources and options. Or, he can go down as a visionary leader who has always tried in his own way to do what he thought was best for the Cuban people when all else was said and done. He can hinder or help the process of transition that Cuba ultimately absolutely must and will undertake. But he can't stop it. He knows the last train to tomorrow is leaving the station. I think he wants to get on. I intend to help him do that in a respectable, acceptable manner."

# XXVII

## LATER THAT NIGHT

It was 1 a.m. Nickolas had been tossing and turning for an hour after watching the 11 o'clock news with Mike, Tim and Phil. He was wound up like a $3 watch. He knew his security instructions were to not leave the room. Tony was in an adjoining room and the door between was ajar, but he didn't feel threatened and he didn't want company. He felt like a quiet glass of wine or two would do the trick. It had been a big day and he felt good. The 11 p.m. news on ARC's first Miami meeting was positive and extensive and he wanted to think about it some more—relish the success a little while, relaxing with a good Chardonnay.

He dressed quickly and quietly and slipped out the door for the hotel club bar on the top floor. He put on his sunglasses as he exited the elevator on the 20th floor of the hotel. The bar and small dance floor were still crowded—probably as a result of the thousand people who attended the ARC presentation. He felt no malice as he carefully looked around the bar. In this atmosphere at this time of night, he didn't believe anyone would recognize him, dressed casually and wearing the sunglasses.

He chose a quiet booth and ordered a Chardonnay from the attractive, scantily clad young waitress, who shared a large tip-awarding smile with him. The wine came, he sipped, and he thought about the successful meeting and he felt good. He relaxed a little, making a few notes in his iPod. Shortly, he noticed a couple of guys sitting next to the dance floor, facing him. Their heads were close together in quiet conversation. What had caught Nickolas' eye a moment ago was one of them gesturing at him with the hand with which he now raised his drink to his mouth. Now the furtive glances in his direction revealed their interest in him.

Nickolas, being a little paranoid, started to feel a little apprehensive, but there was no other reason to be concerned at this time. But then they arose and headed in his direction. There was no one other than Nickolas in that corner of the club. His first thought was to get out of the booth and over to the bar where he would at least be on his feet if this was trouble coming. His second thought was that there wasn't time. He palmed the pepper shaker on the table and moved a couple of spaces in the circular corner booth to the front edge position. They were smiling like old friends as they approached. The big guy had his hand out, offering a shake. "Hey, pardner," he said, "we saw your show tonight. You were great. You had that audience in the palm of your hand. Hey, scoot in there will you, we'd like to talk."

"Hey, guys, thanks a lot, but it's kinda late. I've had a big day and I am just about ready to close up shop, but I'll be in the lobby restaurant for breakfast at 7 a.m. Why don't you stop by then? I'll buy the omelets."

"Scoot in there, partner. We'll only take a few minutes of your time."

Ignoring their request to move into the middle of the booth, he said, "Okay, I have a couple of minutes, you scoot in right over there." Nickolas pointed to the other side of the table. "What will you have to drink? Same thing? Buds and shots? Buds and Jack okay? I'll get it. Be right back." As they slid in, one guy's sports coat dragged on the table, revealing to Nickolas a shoulder-holster strap.

Nickolas got up and stepped toward the bar before they could say anything. At the bar, he ordered the drinks and asked for the Tabasco. He poured half the bottle into each beer and returned to the table and served them their drinks. "Well, guys, what should we toast to tonight? Normalized relations with Cuba?"

"Well, Mr. Harvey, that's what we want to talk to you about. Our idea about how to normalize Cuban relations and yours are a little different, and we've been working on ways to do it our way for a long time. You aren't even a Cuban! You shouldn't have anything to say about it!"

"Well, friend, you don't look very Cuban or Latin to me either. Where you from? New Jersey? Vegas? Miami?"

"Where I am from doesn't matter. My friends are Cubans and have been a long time. It's my job to see that they are not disappointed."

"Sounds to me like your friends are Floridians who want to be Cubans again."

"Who better? They've paid a big price for the chance to go home."

"What price? They left a third-world dictatorship country to come to America to enjoy freedom and democracy and pursue the American dream in the richest country in the world. They should thank the good Lord every day."

"They do. But Cuba is their home country. They want to set it free."

"Hey, I said, I can understand that point of view, but not all the Italians, Irish and Polish in America are trying to return to their homeland and take over the country! Not to mention Native Americans, who were really here first, you know. But I understand what you're saying. Let's drink to their success! Bottoms up!"

They hesitated a moment, not knowing whether Nickolas was sincere or not. But he was smiling in an innocent, encouraging manner, and holding their eye, so they lifted their shots and threw them down in one large gulp. They then grabbed their beer chasers and chugged about half the bottle in three to four gulps! It was at that point that their lips, palates, teeth, gums, throats and stomachs caught fire big time. Their eyes bulged, they lost their breath, they made noises only animals make, they grabbed their throats, and reached for something to drink, but there was nothing but the beer. They looked around in a panic, sweat broke out on their brows, they couldn't breathe, their eyes teared and rolled, they grabbed the table, and finally they ran to the men's room.

Nickolas had watched them, slightly surprised and amused, but otherwise unconcerned. He took another sip of Chardonnay, looked around, caught the eye of Tony Diego at the end of the bar and motioned him over and said, "Those two guys in the john drinking water, disarm them and escort them out of the hotel. Make sure they get in their car, leave and don't come back. Thanks for watching my back."

"I wouldn't have missed it for anything. Nick, you are something else!" They both smiled, then laughed, then laughed harder.

# XXVIII

## UNIVERSITY OF MIAMI'S SCHOOL OF POLITICAL SCIENCE

The University of Miami's School of Political Science, for the Americas Department, has kept a studious eye on Cuba and Castro for more than 50 years. Among the several professors in this department is Rolando Cardero, a first-generation Cuban-American born in the United States to parents who escaped Cuba in the mid 1960s. His parents were educators like Rolando, who came to the U.S. with nothing other than the clothes on their backs. They took menial jobs while living in a house with two other Cuban families. They each worked two jobs hard, saved their money, learned how to speak English, applied for citizenship, studied for their Florida teacher's license, passed the exam and like all good thoughtful Americans joined the "crabgrass wars" in a lower middle-class Cuban community by buying a little two-bedroom, one-bath starter home in near West Miami.

Twenty years later they had graduated two children from college, one with a master's degree. They lived in Weston Park in a $500,000 home and each drove a new Japanese SUV. Between the two of them, they were earning more than $120,000 a year and, in spite of paying for college educations, had accumulated more than $400,000 in savings for retirement. Rolando was their star player. As a professor at U of Miami,

Rolando had published a book on the Cuban economy and occasionally submitted articles to the *Miami Sun Tribune* for the Caribbean/ South American section of the newspaper. Sometimes, special interest groups asked him to speak on various subjects regarding Cuba, for which he charged $5,000 plus expenses, working through a National Speakers Bureau.

Rolando was holding court in front of one of his classes. It was Monday so it was Cuban History from 9-11 a.m. They were near the end of the two-hour session, and Rolando was asking for questions and comments on that morning's lesson plan. A white female from the left rear of the class says, "Professor Cardero, I heard on CNN this past weekend about some new national Cuban organization called Americans for Reconciliation with Cuba or something like that. Have you heard about that organization and its' founder, a Nickolas Harvey, from San Diego, as I recall? What can you tell us about this new organization?"

"I can tell you that Mr. Nickolas Harvey is a successful businessman from San Diego who has started an organization called Americans for Reconciliation with Cuba. He disagrees with past and present U.S. Foreign Policy as it relates to Cuba, and as a citizen diplomat and activist, he is trying to change the relationship for the better. He sees the Cuban people as needing help to enter the 21st century and he sees U.S. Foreign Policy as suppressing their ability to do so. You can all learn more about ARC by visiting their website at www.arc.com. In fact, I encourage you to do so. You may agree that Nickolas Harvey's efforts are an excellent example of the ability of one man to change the world—something you may wish to do yourself one day. Mr. Harvey is a political activist or citizen diplomat, or both, I'm not sure. Are there other questions? We have about 10 minutes left."

Rolando points at a young women directly to his front in a yellow dress and says, "Yes, ma'am, your question please."

"Professor Cardero, my question is, are we more likely to see the Cubans themselves revolt against their government at some future date?"

"No. I don't believe so. If that was a realistic possibility, it would have happened already. Cubans, by nature, are not militaristic or an aggressive, self-assertive people. They are peaceful non-combative people. Besides that, they do not have the capability to fight the Cuban Government beyond peaceful demonstrations and even that can be dangerous in Cuba." Rolando pauses, then continues,

"I see no future change that will save the Cuban people from the inhumanity of Fidel's regime and the inhumanity of past and current U.S. Foreign Policy on Cuba, except a major change in the U.S. position. It is ARC's mission, as I understand it, to see that policy change does occur as soon as possible. Further, ARC believes the time is now. It's possible that Fidel and Raul are rational and intelligent men and that they also believe the time is now. The Castro brothers are not getting any younger. Fidel is not getting healthier. He knows, as we do, if he dies before resolving the U.S.-Cuba issues that the outcome could be disastrous; it would be very uncertain and perhaps a resolution delayed for years. The Castro brothers know, as we do, that if the U.S. settles with them, they can assure a safe, effective, quick, peaceful, well-organized transition. Therefore, the time may be right. Next question?"

"Professor Cardero, the way I was brought up was to trust my government and its leaders. That's why we vote them into office, to figure out these complex issues and to do the right thing for America. I didn't vote for the ARC people to do what they are doing, which seems contrary to what the government is doing. I'm a loyal American. What do you say to that?"

"Billie, I'm glad to hear you say you voted for your elected officials so that they would do the right thing for America. But, you surely realize that our elected politicians all too frequently don't do the right thing for America. They do the right thing for themselves by catering to special interests, who help them get elected and re-elected, and when they do, the American voter has got to raise all kinds of hell to get them back on track or out of office, assuming it's not already too late to correct the error. All of our elected politicians work for you and I who voted them into office. As voters, we need to be their severest critics. However, unfortunately, we are not. We have a large silent majority in the United States who only take part in the political process once every four years. We have a lot of citizens who develop their opinions solely on the basis of the nightly ABC, CBS or NBC television newscast. In most cases, it's way too much entertainment and way too little news, or way too much news on non-important issues and way too little on what is important. The main business of all media news is business. They are all chasing viewers or readers. They run a business and, therefore, have a lot of advertisers to keep happy and don't necessarily concentrate on creating a well-informed public.

"Therefore, in the final analysis, you and I need to do a good job of keeping ourselves informed from a balance of sources and to take part in the political process when we discover a need for our intervention. That is the American way. It is also a civic responsibility that many avoid. Thanks for the question, Billie."

"Yes, Mr. Jones, your question please." A young black American male stands.

"Professor Cardero, I don't believe it is commonly understood, but Cuba, even though it's not a white, Anglo-Saxon culture, is racist and bias in its attitude toward blacks. I realize that sounds strange as Cubans are of color themselves. But, in spite of that they see blacks as below their class and, therefore, exclude them from their equal rights and opportunities. Did you know that?"

"Yes, Andrew. I did. I can only say that in my experience, racism is not just an American experience, nor one existing only between whites and Afro-Americans. Racism exists almost all over the world in one form or another. It exists not only between black and white, but between brown and dark brown, or dark brown and black, or black and yellow, or red or white, or Catholic and Protestant, or Christian and Jew, or Jew and Muslim, or more recently, Christian and Muslim. I could go on here to other categories of racism, but it would be redundant. In summary, for a lot of different reasons, there has been trouble between the races and religions of people all over the world forever. Race is declining as an issue and religion seems to be increasing. Is it deplorable? Yes. Should it end? Yes. Is it slowly going away? Yes. Will it end soon? No.

"As it relates to the Cuban culture, if we can bring them into the 21st century by making them our friends and communicate to them our American values and experience their culture, brown, white and black will benefit. I hope you agree."

"I do, Professor, I do. Personally, I hope Mr. Harvey gets the job done."

"Last question please?" A young man stands.

"Professor, Castro nationalized a good deal of U.S. business assets shortly after the revolution. In a reconciliation strategy, how do you deal with that?"

"Ronald, ARC suggests that we negotiate a mutually beneficial resolution that results in a win, win, win for Cuba, the United States, and those American businesses that were nationalized by Fidel in the beginning. ARC believes that we can achieve that goal." Ronald retains the microphone, still standing,

"I continue to read about Fidel's activities to suppress the press, and opinions, and certain organizations, sending dissenters to jail. How would you deal with that?"

"We, the U.S., would have to negotiate an agreement that included terms, conditions and timing for Cuba to move toward a more free society, and a free press over time, as part of a larger agreement that would move them toward democratic institutions, free markets, rule of law, and a new constitution. Separately, we need to negotiate a deal that frees unfairly jailed dissidents." An unsolicited question comes from the back of the room.

"Professor, in your judgment, why has this hostile relationship continued to exist so long after the Cold War ended and Russia left Cuba?"

"A quick answer. In the U.S., the reason was, and is, U.S. politicians who pander to U.S. special interest groups at election time. In Cuba, it was and is the stubbornness of Fidel Castro.... With that, students, that's it for today. Thank you for your attention."

# XXIV

## AFCA HEADQUARTERS

**Miami, Florida**

Today Martin Alonso is in his Miami business office on the 26th floor of the U.S. Bank building on Brickel Boulevard, overlooking the Port of Miami to the north, and Biscayne Bay to the east and south. He enjoys a two-story office with floor to ceiling views. His secretary is preparing two cups of strong Cuban coffee at the $6,000 brass cappuccino machine sitting on the back of the bar area, one of many features in Martin's opulent office suite. Why not? Alonso Construction had built the building and Martin owned it, as evidenced by a large impressive company logo done in relief on the wall behind Martin's uncluttered 4-foot by 8-foot mahogany desk with matching credenza. Martin was not a tall man so he had had his desk and executive chair built on a platform, which raised his side of the desk by six inches so that whether he was seated or standing behind his desk, he could look down slightly on every guest. The guests sat in very comfortable, deep, red leather chairs, which lowered their butts slightly below their knees.

Martin was meticulous in his appearance, dress and business planning. He was a ruthless, relentless, political, egomaniac in all of his activities. This combination of characteristics had made him one of the wealthiest and most powerful people in South Florida and certainly within the U.S. Cuban community. Martin was the *'go-to'* guy when it came to the Cuban vote in Florida, particularly, South Florida.

One of his protégés was visiting him today. His name was Gabriel Vasquez, and he was one of the two Cuban-American lobbyists representing Americans for a Free Cuba Association (AFCA) in Washington. Ms. Warez, Martin's administrative assistant, served them each a demitasse of strong Cuban coffee from the sterling silver serving tray. She sat the tray on the corner of Martin's desk between them, with a hot silver carafe of coffee and a small saucer of lemon peel. No sugar, crème or Sweet 'n Low needed.

"Will there be anything else, Mr. Alonso?" Ms. Warez says.

"No," Martin says. "Thank you. I'll call you when I need you." As Ms. Warez exited the room, the two men took a sip of their coffee and settled further into their chairs.

"Ah!" says Gabriel, "Janice never fails to satisfy."

"If she didn't, Gabriel, she wouldn't be in my employment. Gabriel, all is well in Washington?"

"Yes, Martin, everything is as you would have it." With further emphasis, "As you have planned it!"

"That's good, Gabriel. It's been a long fight, an expensive fight. I realize I have said this before, but, I believe we're nearing the end. This is not a time to relax our vigilance."

"We're not, Martin. We push the envelope every day."

"Well then, I must ask you, Gabriel, and I would ask Bill, too, if he had made this meeting." (*His voice rising.*) "Where in the Goddamn hell did this ARC outfit come from?" (*His voice rising higher still.*) "Who in the fuck is this Nickolas Harvey asshole?"

"All we know right now is that he is the owner of a relatively small defense contracting business in San Diego. He has several contracts with the Department of Defense. He's a retired Marine officer. Obviously, as a defense contractor, he's a card-carrying, big-time donator to the National Republican party. We don't know much more at this time, but we will soon, as we have the FBI, CIA, NSA and IRS checking him out."

"Shit," Martin says, "if you got those guys checking him out, you won't know anything for 18 months!"

"No, we put a big priority on this. We understand it's important."

"Oh! A priority! That means you'll know a little bit in 12 months! Jesus! It's no wonder government is paralyzed. You work there every day and you don't even see that everybody in the whole system is sitting on their ass waiting for a free lunch and/or dinner, a twice-a-month check and the next automatic raise in pay!"

"Not true! Mr. Alonso! People just don't understand how the U.S. Government works, how big it is—all that it does and tries to do. We live in the greatest economy and democracy in the world. We lead the free world! It takes a lot of time and effort!"

"Jesus Christ, Gabe, spare me the bullshit! The point I am trying to make is that you and Bill have to do something to discredit ARC. Slow them down, whoever the hell they are, discredit Harvey somehow, find him sleeping with a minor, boy or girl, whatever. But, do it now! We can't wait one or two years. This guy is focused on reducing the power of the Cuban vote in Florida for Christ's sake. Don't you and Bill understand that! Among bigger issues that means your job in the Senate is being threatened, for Christ's sake. Wake up! Get with it! We have a carefully planned, professionally executed threat to all that we've been working on for what seems like forever! Now, that we're close to the end, this Harvey guy may take it all away! We have to stop him. Have you got it now? Do you understand? Can you deliver a strong message to Bill? It's time that you two guys show the organization that elected you that you're loyal to them! You guys owe me! I want a return on my investment. I want it now!

You got it?"

"Yes, I do, Martin, I always did."

"Show me then. Get back to Washington! Meet with Bill! Develop a plan! Let me know what it is by Monday noon! And you tell Bill if he ever fails again to show up for a meeting I've called him to, that I'll personally cut his dick off and stuff it down his throat! Now get the fuck out of here and get something done!"

# XXX

## CADC BARBECUE

### (Cuban-Americans for a Democratic Cuba)

**Miami, Florida**

The president of the Cuban-Americans for a Democratic Cuba (CADC) has invited his Board of Directors to a poolside barbecue at his home on Labor Day. The party started at 6 p.m., with drinks and food that would be served at 8 p.m. Fireworks at a nearby park would be visible at 9 p.m.

The host and hostess were Joe and Lily. They lived in a diverse upper middle-class neighborhood in the western suburbs of Miami. Joe was an executive in the food service industry and Lily was an assistant principal at the local elementary school. They were second-generation Cubans. Both their parents had left Cuba legally pre-Castro. They had met, dated and married while in college at U of Miami. They met while working part-time at an upscale restaurant in Coconut Grove, on nights after school, except Sunday and Monday. They were both attractive, smart, personable, hardworking and did well in the restaurant business at the entry level. They struggled financially for several of their early years, but lived like students even after graduation and marriage. They ultimately got better jobs and saved enough money for a down payment on a home before they had their first child.

Lily had been a teacher's assistant when she got pregnant, but got her degree and teacher's certificate before giving birth nine months, two weeks and one day later to a healthy eight-and-a- half pound boy. They named him Christopher. Lily was able to easily take a pregnancy leave of absence as a teacher's assistant and she did. She took 12 weeks leave at eight and a half months, wanting to wait only four weeks on baby Christopher to decide to enter the crazy world of humanity. He finally decided and everyone was happy, including Christopher. Three years later baby Mary came along and Lily got her tubes tied. Baby Mary fulfilled Lily's plan for one boy (first) and one daughter (second). The dog would be acquired when Christopher was five, and he could reasonably take care of him. Lily had it all figured out. She was a thinker, planner, organizer and leader. Some men called her a bitch and a controller. But that wasn't it at all, she simply, unexplainably, felt very strongly about certain, sometimes unimportant, little issues. Some thought Lily suffered from OCD.

Lily was picking up empty plastic glasses, some half-full and abandoned, and small plastic appetizer plates, some half-full and abandoned, and other odds and ends of party trash around the yard and pool. Some guests tried to engage her in conversation as she made her rounds. But Lily was on a mission and wouldn't be distracted from the next piece of garbage.

Joe was in the kitchen off the patio deck and had been since 5:30 p.m. Earlier in the day he had been in the kitchen, cutting up whole chickens, chickens were cheaper that way, and slicing pork ribs into quarters, babyback of course, and making hamburgers for the kids out of a 10-pound package of raw hamburger meat. Making hamburgers takes time. Why the hell didn't Lily buy a box of ready-made burgers? Because the meat is cheapest by the 10-pound package! As a result, he wouldn't be spending much time with his guests. He was getting hot, and tired, and perspiration from his face was dripping into his special homemade barbecue that he was also making because, Lily said, he had the time. Why in the hell hadn't Lily reminded him to make the sauce last night! Shit! I have to cook all this yet and I need to start at 7 so it's ready to serve at 7:45, 8 at the latest.

Joe finished off the barbecue sauce with two bottles of hot sauce and several swirls of a large stainless steel spoon. It appeared to be the proper consistency. He stirred it a few more times and then leaned over the bowl to take a taste with the large spoon, thereby adding at least a half dozen more drops of sweat off his face into the sauce. Joe took a taste, stood up, smacked his lips and yelled, "Whoo-wee! Is that ever good! That'll get their attention! I need another beer." Joe went to he fridge, grabbed his fourth beer, popped the lid and downed half of it in one continuous swig. "Boy that hits the spot! I think I'm dehydrated! Okay! Mr. Bar-B-Q, here I come!"

Joe headed for the barbecue grill with the pile of ribs, which would take the longest to cook. He sprayed the grill with some anti-stick material and started setting the rib quarters over the grill's cooking surface. The resulting fat-spattered fire hissed and blew smoke into his face. Joe paused for an instant, wiped his face and threw down the balance of beer number four, an act that Lily happened to witness. Joe and the beer was perhaps being the only single event that could have defocused her from her cleanup—the garbage mission. She stridently walked over to Joe at the grill with a stern look on her face.

"Joe! The party is only one hour old! I've seen you drink two beers, not counting the one you drank while you were getting ready to drink. You can't cook or be a good host or a good husband or a good father if you're drunk! Slow down, for Christ's sake, we have three to four hours to go! You better eat something. Get something into your stomach. I'll bring you some chips and dip." Off she went, dip and chip hunting, not waiting for any reply from Joe.

Joe thought, Christ, this is my party, my friends, my Board of Directors and she is telling me how to act. I want to have a good time, this is Labor Day, the end of summer. Americans are supposed to celebrate, get drunk and have a good time. It is us Americans, particularly parents, who need to perpetuate these traditions so that their kids will know what to do when they grow up and holidays roll around. Christ! What's the sense of holiday barbecues, family gatherings, what my father taught me to do, if it's not to get a little silly and have a good time together! That's what my father did. That's what I need to do. I need another beer, all this heat is dehydrating me. Joe headed for the nearest cooler and got another beer, meeting Alex, one of his Board of Directors, at the cooler.

"Joe, how the hell you doin'! You're okay? You look a little ragged!" Alex says.

"I'm good, Alex, although this heat and humidity is drying me out. I'm dehydrating, faster than I can drink! I'm drinking Miller Lite though, keeps the carbs down. Do you think light beer is absorbed by the body faster than regular beer? I'm drinking one of these every 15 minutes and I'm still drying up! I can't get ahead!"

"Joe, I'm not sure about the hydration issue; however, I do believe light beer, particularly Miller's, goes to the kidney, bypassing the stomach. I've tested it standing at the toilet. You can drink it in and piss it out at the same speed. The brewmaster who invented that stuff has got to be a billionaire! Pure magic! It takes a case to get a buzz!"

"Alex, can we talk a little business?"

"Sure, Joe, always. What's on your mind?"

"You've read or heard about this new coalition, Americans for Reconciliation with Cuba, ARC for short, this Nickolas Harvey, guys? I mean guy."

"Yes, I have. It's my job, Joe, to stay abreast of all of these kinds of developments, large and small, as your Chairman of the Board."

"Well, to me, Alex, this ARC organization looks big, successful, and it looks like it will get bigger. This Nickolas Harvey guy sounds good. He knows what he wants and he knows how to get it. He gets his message out the old-fashioned way—he works!"

"I agree, Joe. It looks like whatever he gets done it will be good for us. He's singing our song a lot louder than we ever could, and I was just thinking. Since he and we are both singing the same song, so to speak, why don't we consider joining forces with him. Jump on his train, get some of the glory, maybe some of the money. What do you think? We're small potatoes compared to his organization, but we are not without influence. We have 20,000 subscribers who pay annual dues, and we have about 30,000 ex-subscribers who don't pay annual dues anymore. I believe a large percentage of the ex-subscribers could be resuscitated if we linked up with ARC. We may even be able to crank up the annual dues on the 20,000. What do you think, Joe?"

Joe took a slug of beer, thought a minute, and says, "Alex, I've had three beers, but I think I like the way you think. In fact, I like your idea so much that I believe it may have an even broader application than your currently suggesting. However, I would have to think about it a whole lot longer than I did in the last two minutes."

"What is the thought?"

"Alex, okay. I'll tell you, but you have to swear this idea remains between you and me. Your idea was the genesis, or I wouldn't even tell you. That's how good it is."

"Well, I swear. Hold on, let's get another beer first." Which they do.

"Okay, Joe, tell me."

"Our organization takes this idea to the Free Cuba, ADCA and CAA organizations and convinces them to merge with us as a precondition to merging with ARC, and we go to Mr. Harvey with the three or four of the largest liberal Cuban-American organizations in South Florida and offer him perhaps 500,000 new supporters!"

"Joe! That's brilliant! Absolutely brilliant! That's why you're Chairman and head barbecuer and I'm a lowly board member and guest! What an idea! You're the man! After the barbecue, let's have a little meeting with the other board members in your study. It's a simple idea, shouldn't take more than 20 minutes to lay it out and get them thinking."

"You got it, Alex, 9:30 in the study, after the fireworks display. You put it together, but don't spill the beans. This will take a little finessing to sell, but I believe they'll buy it. What have they got to lose?"

"Just their Director jobs probably."

"Maybe we can control that."

# XXXI

## HAVANA, CUBA

OCTOBER

Priscilla Hernandez, 36-year-old wife of Antonio Hernandez, jailed dissident, arose at 5 a.m. in her small third-floor apartment in the Barcelona section of Old Havana to the noise of a crying baby and a slamming door somewhere down the hall of her 100-year-old building.

It was early dawn on a new day, that time when dark turns to gray and gray to light. Priscilla watched it happen from her lonely and simple steel-and-spring double bed, thinking about the special day ahead, which occurred once each month. She would see her husband Antonio today in prison. This visit would be her 28th conjugal visit since Antonio had been convicted of crimes against the Revolution and sent back to prison for the third time in the past 20 years.

She was excited to see her husband, but still dreading the long, hot, difficult trip to get to the prison. But she knew once she got the trip started, she would be okay. She stretched while lying in bed and then flipped the sheet off her body, rose to the sitting position and turned the small table-side light on, which cast the small bedroom into light and shadow. She was wearing a man's white undershirt, which covered her breasts and upper body down to her thighs. She walked to the sitting room and kitchen combination and lit a match while turning on a gas burner to heat water for coffee. She then entered the small half-bath, turned on the bare overhead light and commenced her morning routine and preparation for the day's trip. She had taken a shower the night before down the hall in the communal laundry, toilet, bath and shower room. It was a shorter wait to do so in the late evening than in the morning.

As she stood before the small porcelain sink and the cracked and blotchy mirror, she silently assessed the work necessary to get her face and hair into shape for public viewing. At 36, she looked 50, gaunt and tired. Life with Antonio had taken its toll. Twenty years of marriage, but only nine years together. She both loved and hated Antonio for the same great strengths of character. She had only survived and persisted to raise and care for their son, Anthony, now a young man and already trying to find his own way in a difficult world.

With her limited but adequate cosmetic supply and a good deal of experience and artistry in such matters, she brought her appearance under control to her satisfaction and went back into the small kitchen and prepared a cup of coffee and toasted some bread and then sat at the little table, where she put sugar in her coffee and honey on the bread and thought about the challenging day ahead of her—the bus ride downtown, the long bus ride to the prison, the walk, the embarrassment of getting through prison security, the apprehension of seeing Antonio. Anthony, who had seen Antonio two weeks prior, had said his health was declining rapidly now and that his time was getting short. Tears came to her eyes as she thought this visit may be her last to see Antonio alive. She shook her head to shake the bad thoughts away, stood up and started her preparation for the trip. She needed to pack some food and water, get dressed in her best dress, shoes and hat, and get down to the corner bus stop by six o'clock.

# XXXII

## EN ROUTE TO CHRISTOPAL PRISON

Priscilla prepared to exit the old rickety bus taking her to the prison to visit Antonio, her ailing, dissident husband. The bus was full when she started out, but now is empty except for her. The bus stops at a lonely three-way intersection marked only by an old sign that identifies the direction to the prison. She steps down to the familiar dirt road. The bus does a U-turn and disappears in a cloud of dust back down the road from which it came.

As far as her eyes can see, she is surrounded by sugarcane fields and an occasional palm tree. She shoulders her large cotton bag and starts walking down the road toward the prison two miles away. She is halfway there when she is passed by two speeding cars, one behind the other, which do not slow down as they pass her on the dusty road, raising a vortex of dust, dirt and pebbles behind them, which forces Priscilla to cover her face with her hat and leave the roadway and try to escape across a muddy ditch. She does so, stumbling in the process, but catching herself on the steep further bank. She hesitates, then scrambles to the top, realizing she has lost a shoe in the mud. So she scoots back down the far side and recovers her lost shoe from the mud and scrambles once again up the bank, breathing heavily now and on the verge of tears.

She notices a nearby grove of four palm trees that provide a small, shaded, grassy oasis from the sun and heat further down the ditch on her side. She needs to recover her control before proceeding, so she walks, one shoe on and one off, to the small patch of shade and slumps to the ground with her back to a tree to relax and regain her composure. She rests a few minutes, then reaches into the large bag and retrieves a liter bottle, half full of water. She uncaps it and takes two large swigs of the fresh water. Her breathing and composure are returning as she reaches into her bag again and pulls out a folded cotton handkerchief, which she then moistens from the bottle, careful not to waste any water. Using one square of the handkerchief at a time, she slowly washes her eyes first, her mouth second and then the rest of her face, moving on to her neck, chest, arms, hands and finally her legs, swooning softly in her feeling of recovery. She finally moistens the handkerchief again to clean the top of her muddy shoe and then slips it back onto her foot.

She reaches into her bag again, remembering she hadn't eaten any lunch on the bus, having fallen asleep. She hadn't slept well the night before in anticipation of her visit to see her husband. And the constant drone of the bus engine, the wind in her face and the heat of the late morning had all combined to put her to sleep, as it sometimes did. She withdrew a little package wrapped in butcher paper, which she unfolded to reveal her small lunch: a piece of bread, a little piece of cheese, some dried fish and two pieces of mango. She spread her small lunch on her skirt on her crossed legs and ate slowly, chased by sips of the water from the bottle, which she planned to refill at the prison.

It was early afternoon and a gentle breeze had arisen, playing a soothing melody through the cane behind her and the palms overhead. At another time and another place, she would have succumbed to a short nap. She realized, although she had slept on the bus, that she was still bone-tired from the excitement, stress and fears of this once-a-month visit to see her husband and all that it meant: the resurgence of so many memories, good and bad, the associated emotions, the pain, the heartache, the sacrifices—all still too painful, in some cases, to dwell upon very long.

Sometimes she wondered how it had all come to happen, why did it happen, why to her, what had gone wrong, which decisions back there somewhere had put her and her family on this path to anguish? How long must they pay? My poor Antonio, she thought, how long must he pay? You, my husband, my love, you give us no relief either! What is more important to you, your politics and your machismo or your family? Your machismo or your life? Antonio, why can't you realize it is not your life to sacrifice, it is ours! Mine and Anthony's! Isn't our love, our family more important than your fight with Fidel! Please God, make him stop. Make him realize he sacrifices all of us, not just himself. Please, oh please God! God, please! Let Antonio live, give him the will to save himself and us. What greater gift is there in life but life itself and family?

Priscilla weeps into her dirty handkerchief in total despair, unknowingly streaking her face with mud. She cries for quite some time before once again regaining most of her composure. Realizing she has been wiping her tears with the dirty side of the handkerchief, she refolds the handkerchief to a clean panel and wipes her face clean once again, and her hands, and blows her nose, and refolds the handkerchief to a clean panel and puts it back into her bag, extracting a small brush, compact and lipstick. She brushes her hair, adds a little blush to her cheeks and lipstick to her mouth. She sees that her eyes are red and puffy and hopes that they will clear up during the walk to the prison. She feels better, following her release of pent-up emotion. She feels stronger once again and in control.

Taking a few deep breaths, she arises, stretches, pulls her dress down through the belt, wipes a few crumbs off her chest and tries to pat down and pull out creases in the front and back of her dress. She thinks, I'm ready. She shoulders her bag and walks down her side of the ditch, looking for a drier place to cross back to the road. In a few yards, she finds a good spot and carefully eases down the bank and steps over the muddy center and scrambles up the other side to the dirt road without mishap. She stamps her shoes clean of any lingering dirt as she looks both ways. There's nothing to the left except empty road and the intersection in the distance—to the right is the prison, about a mile away. She starts walking toward the prison, and the humiliation and despair that she knows awaits her there.

# XXXIII

## CHRISTOPAL PRISON, THE VISITORS' ROOM

Priscilla arrives at the visitors' entrance gate to the prison tired and depressed, having spent all morning getting there. There were perhaps 20 cars, trucks and scooters in the parking lot she had just crossed, but only two had passed her on the road. She was an hour late and that was why there had been little traffic during her walk. All the other visitors had preceded her. She would miss the time in the waiting room talking to the other women while they waited for their men to arrive in the visitors' room. It always feels good to share one's problems with others who truly understand and sympathize with you as they are experiencing the same misery—none, of course, to the depths of Priscilla. Her husband, Antonio, had been under a death watch by his guards for the past 30 days because Antonio was on his second hunger strike in six months, protesting his illegal arrest and conviction for crimes against the Cuban Government.

Priscilla enters the guard shack, approaches the counter and says, "How are you, Paul? How are the Mrs. And the kid?"

"Fine, Mrs. H., thanks for asking. You're late today. Is everything okay? You'll only have an hour in there, you know."

"I know, Paul. Mr. Hernandez won't have the energy for more than an hour anyway. Last month they brought him to me in a wheelchair. He could hardly keep his head up."

"I know, Mrs. H, and I hate to be the one to tell you, but he's worse now. You'll be visiting him in the infirmary. They usually don't permit visitors in there unless the prisoner is near death. One of the guards will meet you shortly in the visitors' room and take you to him. I'm sorry, Mrs. H. But he's doing what he wants to do. It's not us doing it."

Finally the door to the visiting room opens, and Priscilla can hear the noise of the other women visiting with their husbands and sons. It closes quickly and the guard impassively walks across the room to where Priscilla has been waiting for more than an hour. He says,

"Mrs. Hernandez, I am Corporal Gomez, senior guard of the prison infirmary. I'm here to take you to your husband, who is too weak to meet you in the visitors' room. However, you have been granted a special pass to visit him at his bedside in the prison infirmary. I've been told by his physician to advise you that his condition has deteriorated greatly since your last visit as a result of his refusal to eat or accept liquids other than water, either orally or intravenously. Prepare yourself accordingly. Further, the doctor encourages you to convince Antonio to accept intravenous feeding immediately or he will die soon. You will have to submit to a strip and body-cavity search to enter this area of the prison. I'll take you to a female attendant. Follow me."

# XXXIV

## CHRISTOPAL PRISON HOSPITAL

Priscilla followed the guard back through the door between the prison reception area and the visitors' waiting area and through another door into the main prison complex, recognizable by a new set of noises, both mechanical and human. Over this door was a sign reading Prison Hospital. She follows the corporal down a long hall flanked by various offices, large and small, and storage rooms. At the end of the hall was a large steel barred gate, the other side of which was a small hallway and windowed guard room, followed by another steel barred gate.

The guard escorted her through gate one, stopped, and said a few words to the guard at the guard station in the middle, who let them through the second door and into the hospital ward. Priscilla recognized a new set of familiar noises and smells immediately from her own visits to Cuban hospitals.

Before her was a long narrow room with perhaps 20 beds on each side, some with their surrounding curtains drawn, some without. In the middle of the room on each side was a sitting area, a television set and a bookcase. Several patients were sitting on each side in wheelchairs, reading or watching TV or playing dominoes. The high room was lit by both skylights and suspended tube lighting. The stone walls were bare. Between each bed was a table covered with patient and hospital incidentals.

Corporal Gomez talked to an orderly while consulting a clipboard on the wall. He returns to Priscilla and says,

"This way please." Priscilla follows Gomez down the center aisle to the eighth bed on the right. The curtains were drawn.

"One moment please," Gomez says. "Just give me a moment to check on your husband." Priscilla waited. Gomez came back through the curtain and says,

"Mrs. Hernandez, he is very weak, very weak, but he is awake and anxious to see you. Remember, he has deteriorated a lot in the past month. Try not to show too much surprise at his condition. Also remember, try to get him to agree to taking liquid nourishment. Do not get him excited. His heart is weak. The Cuban Government does not want him to die, Mrs. Hernandez. Talk him out of this needless demonstration, it will help no one. You can go in now."

As Priscilla approached the curtained bed, a wave of anxiety and fear gripped her total being. She stepped through a corner of the curtain and set her cloth bag and purse down on the bottom of Antonio's bed. Antonio was covered with a thin white sheet up to his neck, one skinny forearm over his forehead and eyes.

"Antonio, are you awake, it's Priscilla." There was no response or movement. Priscilla seated herself in the wooden chair near the head of the bed and said again, a little louder,

"Antonio, are you awake?" She slipped her hand beneath the sheet and gently replaced his arm above the sheet so she could hold his hand. There was no response, but his hand was warm. She bent over and gently kissed his hand and then turned it over and kissed his palm. She left her face in his palm and wept, her tears running profusely, her weeping turning to muffled sobbing, her convulsing upper body shaking the bed.

She felt Antonio's grip tighten lightly twice, in a signal to get her attention. She raised her head, wiping her tears from her face with her other hand and looked sadly at her husband, whose lifeless eyes looked at her from deep, blackened recesses in his skeletal head. He pathetically tried to put a smile on his face, which accomplished the opposite of his intent, for he had lost most of his front teeth, the sight causing Priscilla to start sobbing again as she moved to the edge of the bed to embrace her husband, who was too weak to hug back.

She kissed his forehead, noticing that he had lost much of his hair and what was left had turned white. She kissed his eyes and his toothless mouth. She told him she loved him with all her heart, and her tears flowed onto Antonio's face and down his neck in a continuous stream of despair and heartache. She continued to hold Antonio for almost an hour, with her head on his chest. Her breathing returned to normal two or three times, only to once again fall into despair. Antonio had managed to pat her arm several times, whispering, "I love you, too, and Anthony also. Tell him for me please."

The guard came into the enclosure at the 45-minute mark and says,

"Mrs. Hernandez, you have 15 minutes left. You can't stay longer, even if we would let you, because you would miss the last bus of the day." Priscilla sobbed. "I don't care about the bus, please let me stay the night with my husband, please! Please! This may be our last time together ever. Please!"

"I'm sorry, Mrs. Hernandez. That's just not possible. You have 15 minutes." The guard left. Priscilla simply sobbed, laying her head on Antonio's bony chest.

Antonio patted on Priscilla's arm wanting her attention. She lifted her head, looking into his eyes, now full of tears. In 20 years she had never seen him weep. He motioned her to come closer and she repositioned herself, putting her head next to his and her ear near to his lips. In a haltingly emotional whisper, Antonio says,

"Priscilla, there is a cigar box in the bottom of that old chest I keep my Revolutionary gear in. It is for you and Anthony. It's all that I have of value after a lifetime on this earth." Priscilla continues to weep. "Priscilla, listen. Just listen, this is very important. I want you and Anthony to go to America on Manuel's boat when he takes Maria and the baby. Get on that boat. Talk to Rose, she can help you influence Manuel. If necessary, remind Manuel he owes me his life. There is nothing of value for you and Anthony in Cuba after I am gone. I go to my death knowing the three of us should have left years ago. Priscilla, I will love you for all of eternity. This is our last time together." Priscilla starts sobbing again, saying, "No Antonio! No! No! No! Don't do this! Please! Please! Please!" Antonio covers his eyes again with his forearm, but the tears continue to flow! Suddenly an ungodly long wail emerges from Antonio.

The guard comes through the drapes, quickly pulling Priscilla by the arms away from Antonio, who continues to weep, his face contorted in pain and despair.

# XXXV

## GUANABO, CUBA

**NOVEMBER**
*End of Year One*

Rose had arisen early as usual to prepare breakfast for Manuel. This day Miguel got to sleep in a few extra hours because he was going to spend the day with his mother, which was a rare event.

After Rose got Manuel off to work, she went back to bed to sleep another hour or two, arising when she heard Miguel rattling dishes in the kitchen. She then rose again to prepare Miguel's breakfast and sat with him, drinking her coffee as he ate.

They chatted about the day's agenda, the people they would be meeting and what they would each wear to the luncheon meeting in Havana. It was obvious to Miguel that his mother was excited about their trip together to see Aunt Priscilla and cousin Anthony. He was pleased to see her so happy and understood that much of her excitement was caused by the opportunity to spend the day with him. His father had cautioned him to be on his best behavior this day with his mother and to not say or do anything to damper her enthusiasm.

They finished breakfast and Rose started cleaning up the dishes, while Miguel went to the outside shower stall at the back of the cottage to start getting ready for the trip. Rose laid Miguel's best white shirt, trousers and sandals out for him on his bed. When Miguel finished his shower, Rose took hers, and then returned to her bedroom where her best clothes also had been laid out on the bed.

She began to brush and comb her hair and then make up her face, which she seldom did, and then dress. She had taken some extra time with her hair, pulling it all back off her face and into a ponytail. At 40, she was still an attractive woman, and the ponytail and colors on her face made her look younger than her years. After she finished, she looked at herself in the cloudy mirror, straightening this, patting that and pushing the other. She wondered if she had gained weight since last seeing Priscilla. When was that exactly? She thought. She was surprised to realize it was about six months ago. They would have a lot to talk about, she thought. She also thought about Anthony, her nephew, whom she only remembered as a boy. He would be a young man by now. He was the same age as Rose's daughter, Maria.

Rose heard Miguel yell from the kitchen, "Mama, are you ready yet? We need to go or we'll miss the Havana bus!"

"Yes, Miguel," she says, as she enters the kitchen through the curtained door from her room with a smile.

"Mama! You are beautiful! I've never seen you looking so, so, so beautiful! That's the only word I can think of to describe you! I haven't seen that dress in a long time!"

"Thank you, Miguel, and you look very handsome yourself. Please take that bag on the chair and let's go."

# XXXVI

## HAVANA, CUBA

Rose and Miguel had taken the bus to downtown Havana, and now had about a 20-minute leisurely walk to their destination in Old Town.

Rose couldn't help but smile in the happiness and pride she felt walking down the street with her handsome son, noticing the furtive glances Miguel received from the women sitting on stoops, as they passed arm in arm. She thought, I'm not so old or out of shape that they can't wonder whether Miguel and I are mother and son or companions. She smiled to herself again. What a beautiful day. Soon the coffee shop came into view and Rose was pleased to notice that there were several empty tables outside along the sidewalk under an old worn canvas awning. They took a table in the corner with six chairs. A waiter quickly arrived and they ordered coffee. Rose told him two more guests would arrive soon. They rested, sipped coffee and watched people pass by.

"I haven't seen Priscilla since last fall and I haven't seen Anthony in several years. He must be 17 or 18 by now," Rose says.

"Yes, I think he's 18. He's getting out of school soon. I saw him a couple months ago," Miguel says.

"He's about Maria's age then?" Rose asks.

"Yes. He knows about Maria and the baby because he asked about her, but he has not been around her since they were both kids."

"What did he ask?" Rose says.

"He just wanted to know if she was okay and did she have a boy or a girl."

"What did you say?" Rose asks.

"I just told him the story, and said that she was fine with the birth and had a boy."

"What's he look like now?" Rose asks. "You'll see in a minute. Here they come."

Rose turns to look up the narrow sidewalk. She recognizes Priscilla and smiles, then smiles again at the handsome young man accompanying her. Priscilla and her son smile back as they increase their pace toward the sidewalk tables and Rose's open arms.

"Priscilla! So nice to see you again! How are you? It's been so long! But you look wonderful, maybe a little thinner. You're so lucky!" Rose says.

"Thank you, Rose, so do you. It has been too long! Rose, I want you to meet my grown-up son, Anthony. Anthony, this is your aunt Rose. You met her last when you were about 14. Do you remember Anthony?"

"Yes, I do, of course. Nice to see you again, Aunt Rose."

Rose replies, "How are you? Such a handsome young man, Priscilla, just like his father. Priscilla, Anthony, please sit. You must be tired from your long trip. Anthony, the last time I saw you, you were 14. It was when your soccer team came to Havana for the play-offs. Do you remember?"

"Yes, Aunt Rose, I do. We spent a great weekend at your home by the sea, and Miguel and Uncle Manuel took me fishing. I remember we got a boatload of bonita, and you made a big pot of fish chowder. I still long for a big bowl of that chowder and your homemade bread!"

Miguel interjects, "Everybody says that!"

Priscilla says, "Yes, he does and I've tried a dozen times to make that chowder for him, but he says it is never quite like yours. You must give me your recipe before we part."

Rose says, "Anthony, Maria sends her regards, and reminds you of the great fun you both had at the beach years ago and to remind you that you owe her a letter."

"Anthony, I didn't know that you were writing to Maria," Priscilla says.

"Only the last year or so, Ma."

"Yes, and it has meant a great deal to her, Anthony, thank you," Miguel says. "It has been a difficult year for Maria. After Peter disappeared, she had no one except family and the baby in her belly. She felt deserted, devastated and alone. She looked forward to your letters."

"We did all we could, but nothing we did or said seemed to help," Rose says. "I believe your letters helped a lot, Anthony, and we thank you."

"I knew she was having a difficult time and I felt she was alone. She was very depressed. I just tried to be a good friend and remind her not all was lost," Anthony says.

"You're a good boy, Anthony. I should say, you're a fine young man. Maria is lucky to have you as a friend," Rose says.

Coffee arrives for the new guests. Conversation ceases while the waiter pours fresh new cups and refreshes old cups. The waiter leaves. Priscilla carefully looks around the mostly vacant nearby tables, assessing their privacy. She leans into the table and speaks to Rose in a conspiratorial tone.

"Rose, have you talked to Manuel about our last conversation?"

"Yes, Priscilla, several times. Obviously he would like to help you and Antonio. But the boat is full and has been for months. There is only so much capacity before it gets unsafe. There have been others, too, Priscilla, who also have wanted to go before you and Antonio. Manuel has been adamant in his denial—maybe at some later date. If this trip is successful, he will probably try again with another group, which might include Anthony. I'm sorry, Priscilla, but it's not my decision to make. The decisions for this trip's passengers were made almost a year ago. We didn't know then that Antonio was thinking this way. If we had…"

Priscilla, still trying to make her case, interrupts.

"Anthony is still a boy. He is tall, but very lean. He only weighs 170 pounds, but he is strong, a good athlete; he can row, sail, swim. He would be an asset to Manuel, like his own son Miguel is on the *Resolute*. Rose, please, there must be some way. He could take care of Maria and the baby during the dangerous voyage. He also can be of help in Miami."

"Priscilla, I never said Maria and the baby were going. Where did you get that idea?"

"Manuel has never before done this kind of thing. He lost his brother when he tried it. He wouldn't be doing it now unless a son or daughter or you and he were going. I know you and Manuel aren't going. If Miguel was going, he would have already left. It is a new life for Maria and your grandbaby that you and Manuel seek."

"I know you've been aware of Manuel's intent but we've told no one of the names of passengers for their own protection. But I think it has just occurred to me how you found out that Maria and the baby were going." Rose looks at Priscilla's son with meaning.

Priscilla says, "Rose, don't jump to conclusions. It doesn't matter, your secrets are safe with us. What family more than the Hernandezes hates the Castro regime more? I just visited Antonio at the prison infirmary two weeks ago. He has been on a starvation diet in protest for more than 60 days. They've been trying to force-feed him liquids for a month now, but he slowly deteriorates. They started too late. He will die soon unless they move him into a civilian hospital. We don't think they will. He's been too much trouble and he isn't as well-known as some of the others outside of Cuba.

"Rose, he told me to tell you to tell Manuel that he can die in personal peace if he knows his son is going to America with him. He trusts Manuel and his skills at sea. He knows Manuel will get his daughter and grandbaby to America. Rose, Antonio believes he will die soon. He is so worried about me and Anthony. I've told him I'll be fine, but he knows if Anthony stays in Cuba after his death that Anthony will join the resistance and follow in his footsteps, looking for retribution he will likely not find. Rose, Antonio believes this opportunity is life or death for Anthony. If he fails through me in persuading you and Manuel, he will feel like he has failed his son, along with everything else he has failed at in his life, in his mind.

"Rose, please, please, persuade Manuel to do this for Antonio and for me. Antonio and Manuel once fought side my side for the freedom of Cuba. They were… were… comrades in arms. Ask Manuel to remember those times in the mountains when Antonio and Manuel feared their next battle would be their last and the dreams and commitments they shared over the campfire. Please, Rose. Please ask him to do it for Antonio. And Rose, we need the answer soon. Please. Antonio is barely holding on, I believe, holding on only to achieve this result. I don't believe he can hold out much longer."

Rose pauses and then says, "I'll approach Manuel once again on this subject. But, I assure you, Priscilla, I have represented you and Antonio well before. It's basically a timing problem. The boat filled up well before you talked to me the first time. But, I will try again. Perhaps Antonio's words will make a difference. But, I do not want to give you or Antonio false hope. It is not my decision. It's Manuel's, and he must make decisions that are good for all those on the boat, regardless of what he personally might wish to do."

"I understand, Rose, and I hope you'll forgive me for being so pushy, realizing the situation. But, I must represent my husband. Knowing that I might not have a husband in a few weeks, I do not want to lose my son, who is my only remaining family. Anthony is the only reason I have kept my sanity in the past few years. I cannot imagine how I will get along without him. But it is my husband's dying wish. Nothing after that is more important to him or me."

"I'll do all that I can, Priscilla."

Rose asks Anthony, "How do you feel about the situation in which you find yourself? You're not even quite out of school."

"I would rather stay in Cuba and take care of my mother and help find a way to help free Cuba. My father, when he was home, inspired these feelings in me. I wish to carry on in my father's name. He has been a Cuban patriot all of his life. He will die fighting that fight. How can I really consider doing anything else? What would be more honorable than staying and fighting for freedom? However, my father has a different plan than me. I respect his decision. He has a lifetime of experience in this long battle, I have none. I'll pursue his plan and the dream that he has for me. I'll continue the fight following a college education in Miami, for however long it takes. I will get there, whether it is soon with Manuel, or if I have to swim the 90 miles!"

"I understand, Anthony," Rose says, as she takes Priscilla's and Anthony's hands in hers.

"I can feel your commitment in your words. I believe you'll do as you say. I'm going to try to help you. If I can get it done, will you take special care of my daughter and grandson not only on the voyage, but in Miami as well?"

"It's an easy promise for me to make. You have raised a beautiful daughter inside and outside. I would be watching over her and baby Jon, whether you asked me to or not."

"Priscilla, I'll do all that I can as fast as I can, starting tonight. Pray for us all."

# XXXVII

## WASHINGTON, D.C.

Bill meets Gabriel in front of Tamie Bananas Tavern on the corner of Commercial and Market in the industrial district of Washington, D.C. It is 6 p.m., and there should be a crowd of blue-collar types having an after-work beer or two or six, but there are only three men sitting at the bar, being tended by an overweight, middle-aged, bleached blonde, who is bent over the under-bar sink washing glasses. She is carrying a lot of her excess weight in her push-up bra. All the men are sitting in front of the sink.

Bill and Gabriel pass the bar and take a high-top booth in the far corner.

"Why did you choose this place?" Bill asks. "We've never been here before."

"It's got a three-for-one drink special from 4 to 7 p.m., with half-price appetizers. How do you beat that?"

"You can't beat it."

"What'll you have?" says a black-haired, black-eyed, dark-skinned, rough looking Haitian waitress, who arrived at their table, overhearing the end of their conversation. She leans way over, putting her elbows on the end of their table and pushing her ample breasts together, revealing the bottom of her white bra. She has 12 or 14 rings on 10 fingers with long, dark red nails with jewels embedded in them somehow. On her wrists are a dozen dime-store bracelets and chains. Another four or five necklaces are around her neck. Her earrings are wide and long. Her sweet, heavy perfume permeates the booth, making Bill's eyes tear. Bill thinks, what is all that perfume trying to hide? Then he quickly thought to himself, I don't even want to think about that.

"I'll have a Captain's Rum and diet Coke," Gabriel says.

The waitress says, "If you want the three-for-one, you can't order brand rum, only well rum."

"Okay," says Gabriel, "make it your Well rum."

The waitress says to Bill, "And for you, honey?"

"I'll have a Seven and Seven with Well whiskey." The waitress departs.

"Bill, I've never heard of Well rum, have you?" Gabriel asks.

"No, and I've never heard of Well whisky, either, must be a new cheap brand."

Gabriel looks at Bill. Bill looks at Gabriel and says, "So what is the message from the Ivory Tower in Miami?"

"I'll give you the whole story as soon as we get a little whiskey in our stomachs. The story will sound better to you that way."

"Okay," says Bill, "you're the boss."

"I can tell you this," says Gabriel, "Mr. Alonso was pretty pissed you weren't there. What happened to you? I told him you were sick as a dog with the flu, running a 103-degree temperature."

"Well, the first thing is I knew it wouldn't take two of us to listen to his ranting. Besides, you're the boss. He pays you to listen to all that shit, but not me. The second thing is on Monday night I was at Labruscoe's down on Third and I ran into the most beautiful woman I've have ever met. She was really hot to trot, but it took a lot of beer and shots to get her off the barstool and out the door and into my car. In fact, it was four in the morning and I was supposed to meet you at 7 a.m. There was just no way I was going to get my rocks off and also make that Miami flight."

"Are you telling me you missed a meeting with the big boss because of a piece of ass?"

"No, no, but hell no. I missed the meeting because I was so drunk I couldn't find her ass with both hands! I never did get that job done. I woke up in the backseat of my car alone at 10 in the morning with my cock in my hand. I am not even sure she was ever back there with me!"

"Jesus, I can't believe you Bill! You just continuously choose to live on the edge! One of these days the old man is going to order someone to cut your balls off if you don't get with it! It may be me. And if he orders it, I'll have to do it, no offense intended."

"None taken, Gabriel."

"We have a job to do that the boss thinks we should have already done, although he did not really tell us to do anything except watch. I'm talkin' about Nickolas Harvey and his ARC organization. He wants us to teach him a lesson he won't forget."

"He'll forget everything if we kill him."

"Yes, but the boss didn't say to kill him. He wants the next best thing. He left it up to us, but he wants it soon, very soon."

"So what are we going to do?"

"I don't know yet. You got any ideas?"

"I'd have to think about it. Where's that good lookin' waitress?" Gabriel asks.

"Probably looking for that Well brand of whiskey we've never heard of. Here she comes. She's something else, isn't she?"

The waitress returns to the table and tosses down two cocktail napkins and places three drinks and the bill in front of each of them.

Bill says in protest, "I didn't know on the three-for-one that we got them all at once."

"It's company policy," says the waitress, "easier to keep track of how many you got."

"The ice will melt."

"We'll bring you more ice of you need it. Most guys can drink the first three pretty quick."

"Well, we're here for a business meeting, not to get smacked."

"Sorry, I can send Tamie over if you want to talk to the boss. But, it won't do you any good."

"Okay, sweet cheeks," Gabriel says, "we understand, we're businessmen ourselves."

The waitress continues to stand there, looking at them with a smile.

"What?" Bill asks.

"The invoice. That'll be $3.99 each or $7.98 total."

"Well, we may have another round, can't you start a tab?" Bill asks.

"Nope, company policy. You got to pay as you go—much easier to keep track of."

"How about I give you a credit card then?"

"Nope, company policy, no credit cards. Cash only."

"Jesus," says Gabriel, "you gals run a tight ship!"

"As businessmen, you know it's live and learn, we've made every mistake in the book two or three times. Eventually you wise up. Running an upscale bar-n-grill requires a lot of skill."

"I can see that, sweet cheeks. Here's a ten spot, keep the change," Gabriel says.

"Well thank you, honey, you're a real sweetie pie. My name is Sunset. When you're ready for the next one, just yell."

The waitress departs their area.

"Boy, she's a looker isn't she? Did you notice that when she stops walking her ass continues to jiggle for another five minutes," Gabriel says.

Bill raises his eyes to the ceiling and says, "Getting back to business, what do you think we should do to teach Mr. Harvey a lesson he won't soon forget?"

"Well, let's review the traditional options. Let's see… we could beat him up real good, we could run him and his car off the road, we could wound him in an assassination attempt, we could kidnap his wife… that might be fun. We could bomb his empty car or ARC Headquarters, we could shoot him in the knee. Do you like any of them?"

"The ideas I like best are the ones that are the least complicated and have the least risk for you and me of getting caught, or something going wrong, or ones that don't have a long prison sentence attached to them if we do get caught. We're only getting $5,000 to do this job, $2,500 up front and $2,500 out back if it all works right."

"Okay, so what do you want to do?"

"Gabriel, I'm kind of an old-fashioned guy at heart. I prefer the nontechnical solutions. Simple is… simple. Know what I mean?"

"Yes, so… ?"

"So… I say, let's you and I kick the living shit out of this guy. You know, put him in the hospital for two or three days. Give him time to really think about the meaning of life, pursuit of happiness, family and good health. You got my point?"

"Yes."

"You're okay with that? You agree?"

"Yes, when, where, how?"

"I'll put it together in the next day or two, give you a call and then we'll get it done. We've done this a hundred times, what could go wrong? Say, this Well brand whiskey is pretty good. I wonder if they sell it by the bottle."

# XXXVIII

## CHICAGO, ILLINOIS

Nickolas and Tim have been on the road, putting on meetings one after the other, sometimes three a day. This particular tour had started in Seattle and was moving east back toward Washington, D.C. This day they were in Chicago, staging their last meeting of a three-day stint of nine meetings large and small. Their schedule required them to depart downtown Chicago's Midway Airport at 10 p.m. that night for Indianapolis, Indiana, and the next night to Columbus, Ohio, for the next day's meetings and then back to Washington, D.C., for the weekend. However, all of that was about to change as Nickolas' satellite phone rang. They were in a limo heading to the last meeting in Chicago at the Hyatt Hotel downtown. He could see it was Phil calling.

"Good evening, Phil, how is it going?" Nickolas says.

"So-so, Nick, that's why I'm calling. Have you got a few minutes to talk?"

"Yes, we're in a limo heading downtown to the Hyatt Hotel. We just finished a very satisfactory meeting in Naperville. The meeting report will be in your e-mail by morning for your follow-up."

"Nick, I want to suggest a change in your personal schedule. We have a payables problem again this month that I believe only you can resolve. This is the third month in a row. We need to fix this problem quickly and it's going to take a serious cash infusion to do so. I suggest that you let Tim carry the ball in Indianapolis and Columbus and you catch a late flight out of O'Hare for D.C. We need you in the office tomorrow by 1:30 p.m. for an emergency staff meeting. If we get started tomorrow, and stick with it, perhaps we can find an answer before the weekend. What do you say?"

"Phil, you're the Chief of Staff. I know you wouldn't call me back if it wasn't critical. Do I need to know more now?"

"No, tomorrow after lunch will be fine. There is an e-mail ticket on your laptop for American flight 267 out of O'Hare at 10:50 p.m. Can you make that work? It's the last direct flight."

"Yes, I'll have to."

"Well, you can sleep late in the morning and have brunch with Liz and we'll see you at 1:30."

"Okay, Phil, see you then. Oh! Hold on. Call Liz and let her know that I'm coming home late tonight, will you?"

"Already have, Nick. She said something about getting out the scented candles. I don't know what that means, but maybe you do."

"We won't go there, Phil. Thanks. See you tomorrow."

# XXXIX

## ARC HEADQUARTERS

*DECEMBER*

Nickolas, Phil, Carmen and Judy are meeting in Nick's spacious corner office at ARC Headquarters. They are seated in the casual seating area of leather sofas surrounding the oversized coffee table in front of the fireplace.

Nickolas has just joined the group, sits down and nods to Phil to start the meeting.

"Nick, we appreciate your willingness to come home on such short notice. We have another financial problem this coming month's end. Our cash income, plus cash on hand, won't meet our projected fixed and variable expenses over the next fiscal quarter. Look at these forecasts on page two. I realize we had this same meeting 90 days ago, but unfortunately, we again need you to inject more capital.

"As you can see, actual donations are not equal to the commitments made at meetings. When our telemarketing people follow up, we frequently get the old *'the check is in the mail'* response. We're raising more money each month, but it is taking more effort, which means more telemarketers, and more expense to bring it in. At the same time, our other expenses have risen substantially and are increasing monthly now that we are up and running three teams pretty much flat out. Everything has cost more than our initial financial pro forma plan for this time period."

Nick analyzes the data quickly. It's pretty simple. Monthly income and cash on hand must exceed monthly expenses. Fixed expenses include salaries, employment taxes, employer benefits, building occupancy expense, payments on leasehold improvements, computers, vehicles, furniture, fixtures, utilities, etc. Variable expenses include personnel travel expenses, marketing expenses, meeting expenses, airline expense, car rental, security, etc. He could quickly see, although he already knew, that a few months ago ARC's average monthly expense was $200,000 a month or roughly $2.5 million a year. In recent months, that average monthly rate had increased to $350,000 a month and $4.2 million a year.

This month was their seventh month since organizing. Ninety days ago Nick had written a personal check for his second $600,000 investment, believing that once they got into high gear and into the fundraising, that between his second check and increased contributions, ARC could become self-funding. Unfortunately, that hadn't happened yet.

He had the money to contribute further, but as a businessman, he was intent on assuring that ARC could fund itself at the earliest possible date. He knew he could achieve that goal. He just needed to focus on it. He had been busy getting the coalition organized properly and off the launching pad. He knew that that part of his plan had now been achieved. Further, he knew that he was the only person who could assure the organization's ongoing financial viability. He mentally accepted the challenge to take the organization financially to the next level, and to eliminate the worry over operating capital, which, in any business organization, was a debilitating, frequently disastrous handicap if not managed correctly early on. He obviously had a backup financial plan strategy.

"Phil," says Nickolas, "I understand the need here. I've been thinking about it since our last meeting. I believe I have a good final solution to the capital issue, but I need to evaluate my idea a little further."

"Are our Dunn & Bradstreet numbers up-to-date and correct?"

"Yes, we use them all the time to establish new credit."

"Okay, give me a couple days. I'll get back to you."

# XL

## ARC HEADQUARTERS

Nickolas is working at his desk. It's been a day since his last meeting with Phil and Phil's financial people on the lack-of-capital situation. Phil is sitting in one guest chair and Phil's assistant, Carmen Benson, is in the other, patiently awaiting Nickolas' finishing whatever he is working on. He finishes, picking up a sheaf of papers, which he staples together and puts aside. He sits back in his chair, relaxes somewhat, steeples his fingers and says,

"Phil, I said yesterday we'd meet tomorrow, but, I made up my mind last night, after some preliminary investigation and a lot of serious thought, that I need more time to make a bigger decision. Here's my current thinking. We could spend a lot of time and energy trying to fine-tune our current fund-raising strategy, and obviously there are some ways we could improve the amount of donations and accelerate the receipt of them. But, at the end of the day they are likely not going to be enough in the short term, based on current projected rates of expense. That leaves the difference up to me.

"I believe I told you I was willing to invest half of my liquidity or about $4 million to $5 million. As of last month I've invested $1.6 million and loaned ARC $750,000, for about $2.3 million. Therefore, on that basis, I have $2.5 million to go. At the current rate, that could be only eight to ten months. In effect, the coalition, based on plan, would be near the point of success and run out of money. That would be worse than giving up right now and writing this whole effort off as a bad idea. Phil, you know we can't do that. You know I don't ever give up. Quitting is not an option, whatever the excuse. However, some philosophical compromises are now necessary. "We said in the beginning that we wanted to lead a nationwide grassroots campaign effort to get this job done, a dollar at a time, so to speak. We thought in a year or so, we could raise $5 million minimum to go with whatever I needed to put in, up to $5 million. It hasn't turned out that way, at least not yet. As it stands now, I could put in $5 million, and we could run out of capital nine months from now and potentially before we have the job done. Therefore, we need to raise more capital very soon. The only way I believe we can raise all that we'll ever need for this campaign, and assure our success in the longer term, is to switch some of our focus from ordinary citizens' small donations to large donations from U.S. corporations.

"I know what you're thinking. We are not giving up the grassroots campaign advantage. We know we need one million to two million people willing to vote primarily or secondarily for a president who supports our strategic change of foreign policy and economic direction on Cuba. But, the only way we can continue this campaign, and in the end, assure success, is with much more investment. *'Money talks and bullshit walks'* in the good old U.S.A. I didn't make the rules, but I do realize we can't make new ones for someone else's game.

"We must enlist the financial support of a few large U.S. corporations that have an old stake in Cuba or a potential new future stake. I believe they are already hopeful that our initiatives will provide opportunity for them. By now, they have heard and read about us. Some of them have probably been to our meetings. I suggest that we go to work on a new business plan to develop a targeted communications package for selected large corporate sponsors and complete a test meeting with one in the next 30 days. Then we'll launch a new series of meetings, in conjunction with those now scheduled, focused on large corporations. What do you think?"

"Nick, we have no choice! I was hoping you would say that!" Phil says.

"Okay, provide me a Dunn & Bradstreet report for each of the top-50 corporations in America."

"Why do you want that? It'll cost us $3,000."

"I want the names of CEO's, addresses, phone numbers, business types, that kind of contact information."

"Okay. I can get you that information for no cost, using a different source. When do you want it?"

"The sooner, the better, but no later than Monday noon. In the meantime, I'm *'loaning'* the coalition another $600,000 interest free. Here's the check. Hopefully, it will cover us along with donations, large and small, for another 90 days while we initiate a new strategic financial plan. Give me a week from today. We'll meet here again next Thursday at noon on this subject. Get me the intel I've requested by noon Monday."

"You'll have it by noon tomorrow."

"Okay, Phil, I have the message and I have the ball. Don't worry about this issue any further. One way or another, we'll put the capital problem behind us and get back to the work of changing the hearts and minds of the American people on Cuba."

# XLI

## NICKOLAS' OFFICE

Judy entered Nickolas' office, introducing Edward Jones and Miss Tara Evans of Octagon Real Estate Investments Company to Nickolas, who had walked toward them as they entered. He shook hands with the lady first and the gentleman second, suggesting that they sit in the casual furniture in front of the fireplace. Ed and Tara sat on one side and Nick on the other side of the large coffee table in the middle.

"Can I get anyone something to drink—coffee, tea, soft drink, a Colorado Mountain River water? Ma'am?" Judy asks.

Tara says sweetly, "That's Miss. Yes, please, may I have a, ah—I see a full bar back there. Is it too early, Mr. Harvey, to order a cocktail?"

"Not at all, Miss Evans. This bar is open 24/7 and we recognize no social imperatives here. What would you like?"

"Call me Tara and how about a, ah screwdriver?"

"We can handle that. Mr. Jones, how about you?"

"Well, since Miss Evans is opening the bar, I'll have a double Scotch on the rocks."

Nickolas was no stranger to drinking before noon; however, he rarely drank before noon while doing business. But what the hell, he thought.

"Judy, I can't let my guests drink alone. There is an open bottle of Wintergarden Chardonnay in the fridge. I'll have a glass of that."

Judy headed behind the bar. Everybody around the coffee table smiled at one another, looked away and then looked back. Nickolas thought, Tara is a real looker, I wonder how old she is? In the new millennium it was getting harder and harder to tell once they got between 30 and 60.

"Mr. Harvey," says Big Ed beginning. Nickolas interrupts,

"Call me Nick, Mr. Jones."

"Okay, good, Nick. Call me Big Ed, that's how my friends refer to me, or just Big for short."

"Okay, Big, I understand that you support the platform and mission of ARC and that you would like to help us out as a corporate sponsor?"

"Yes, Nick, that is why Tara and I are here representing Octagon. Our Board of Directors has authorized us to investigate ARC and make a recommendation to the board to provide assistance."

Tara adds, flirting a little, "Assistance, of, ah *any type* you might need, and/or financial assistance. We've heard on the news that you might need some financial help. We've followed your progress quite closely over the past six months and we believe there are some synergistic opportunities available to both of our companies should we choose to work together."

"I see," says Nicolas. "I'm afraid I must tell you that ARC is a class 501, not-for-profit corporation. Our goals in Cuba are strictly humanitarian."

Tara goes on. "We just want to help anyway that we can."

"What help comes to your mind first?"

Tara smiles and thinks to herself, I could give him an exciting answer to *that* one! But Ed answers, "Nick, there are three or four major elements of our business that you might need that we would provide free of charge. They are: financial services, security, and leisure time hotel and resort development in the U.S. and Caribbean."

Nickolas smiles and says, "Are we talking leisure time resorts and hotels with casinos?"

Tara says, "Yes, the best in the Caribbean. Totally legitimate. Somebody's going to do it. Why not us? With us, you can control the outcome, with somebody else, you can't. Think about it. We're the reformed bad guys."

# XLII

## WASHINGTON, D.C.

*APRIL*

It was a sunny morning in April. Tim had planned this meeting and its venue weeks ago. The location was the banks of the Delaware River just east of the Jackson Bridge. There was a wooded area there in blossom, with a river view through the trees. He had ordered a 16-foot by 8-foot raised platform, a podium and large speaker system, placed at the corners. The stage was set up to optimize the view and position the speakers. To the right and left were two banquet tables, each with tea, coffee and ice water. Forward of the stage, but angled off to the right and left, were 10 rows of 20 chairs on each side with a very wide V-shaped aisle down the middle. A tall, colorful floral display decorated each front corner of the stage, partially hiding the speakers.

In the middle, and between the spectator chairs, were gathered 10 to 20 standing members of the media, representing all the major national and local outlets.

In the chairs on the stage were Nick's key staff and all the department managers of ARC, dressed better than Nickolas had ever seen them before. Nickolas was waiting for his introduction from Tim, who was within the media group, assuring them that the program was ready to begin. Some late arrivals were parking on the distant parking lot and others were rushing to a chair with a free cup of coffee or a bottle of

Nickolas' new branded, Colorado Mountain River water, a personal joke of Nick's, having lived in Southern California.

Tim returned to the podium and took a drink of water, mouthing silently a big wow while looking at Nick. Nickolas took a drink of Chardonnay out of his water bottle, and toasted Tim. Tim nodded at Nickolas, and Nickolas nodded back—it was show time.

Phil says, "Ladies and gentlemen, my name is Phil Bowen. I am Chief of Staff for the Americans for Reconciliation with Cuba coalition." *(There was a smattering of applause.)*

Phil says, "Thank you. Ladies and gentlemen, it is my honor to present Mr. Nickolas Harvey, Founder and CEO of ARC." There was a somewhat larger smattering of applause as Nickolas rose from his seat and headed to the podium, shaking hands with Phil on the way.

Nickolas says, "Ladies and gentlemen, the Americans for Reconciliation with Cuba coalition is officially seven months of age this month. From concept, it is 30 months of age. I'm sure you would agree that we've come a long way since our organizational announcement last fall. Thanks to many of you, your constituents and audience across our great country, the average American's awareness of our cause has grown from virtually no awareness or understanding to the more than one-half million U.S. citizens who have joined our coalition and donated money to our cause.

"I'm here today to report ARC's progress 16 months before the next national election, which we believe will mark the turning point toward reconciliation between the United States and Cuba.

"My comments will require only 15 minutes of your valuable time, and ARC's marketing staff will pass out a complete press release package to each of you representing the media. At that same time, cookies, coffee, tea and water will be on ARC, following our remarks.

"Let me begin by reminding you of our ARC Mission and Vision Statement. It is ARC's mission to achieve a reconciled relationship between the United States and Cuba. Strategically, we see this relationship as similar to our existing relationship with Mexico and Canada."

During his speech Nickolas tried to make eye contact with various important members of the audience on both side of the media section.

As he did so, he recognized various uninvited guests by name and others whom he did know, but knew were uninvited. He also recognized several senators and congressman who were invited and others who were not, including Senators Gibson and Gonzales from Florida. There were also several Ivy League, stern, lean, young men in dark suits, Ivy League ties and sunglasses that he believed were FBI, CIA or NSA. Additionally, he recognized two undersecretaries from the State Department. It's a good crowd, he thought, as he continued his speech and managed to gesture, emphasize and smile in all the right places.

He concluded what he believed was a real positive status report on ARC's accomplishments to date. The media seemed to like it and were on him like bees on honey when he finished his speech, to a very respectable level of applause, and approached them as he descended the stage.

As he concluded the fifth two- or three-minute interview with well-known members of the six o'clock news, he knew that ARC and he would arrive in a very high majority of middle-American homes that evening. They were pushing the big time.

The *'tipping point'* had arrived.

# XLIII

## ARC HEADQUARTERS

Nickolas was sitting at his desk in his Georgetown office on a Saturday. It was mid-morning. The office was not open for business. Nickolas had let himself in, using his master electronic pass. Nickolas had not been in the office all week and no one outside of his immediate staff knew of his intention to work this Saturday and Sunday morning. He was, therefore, surprised when he heard a buzzer from the main front door. His first impulse was to get up, go down to the door and see who was there, perhaps one of his staff who had left their electronic pass card at home? His second thought was no, not likely, and he sat back down. The buzzer came again—not long and impatient, but just a little more insistently.

Nickolas made a decision. He rose, went out his door, down the hall steps and into the first-floor ARC reception area. He listened at the large double wooden doors. He knew not what he was listening for, but he listened, maybe to detect voices if there was more than one person, and there was. He heard a female voice say, "Let's just call him on our cell phone. We know he is in there." He heard two people walk away.

Nickolas returned to his office. He hadn't recognized the voices. He sat at his desk, waiting for the phone call to his reception switchboard, which came shortly. He hesitated, watching for the light on his phone desk pad. While he stared at his main phone, his private phone rang behind him on his credenza. He hesitated again, somewhat perplexed, as only his key staff, certain security people and family had his private phone's unpublished number—even he was not authorized by his security personnel to give this number to anyone without their advance approval. Security approval required calling phone number identification, cell or landline, in order to get connected through the security system to Nickolas' private office phone or to Nickolas' satellite phone when he was out of the office. The same telephone security system recorded all incoming callers' conversations and prioritized his incoming calls to the office, which were also electronically recorded. You could not have a private phone conversation with Nickolas. Only the security people, Elizabeth and Nickolas knew this fact.

Nickolas' private office phone rang for the fourth time, and the caller ID revealed a number, but no name. Nick's security instructions were to not answer calls without complete ID on his private lines. But, he knew it was the door-knockers, and he wanted to know who was so insistent on seeing him on a Saturday morning without an appointment to do so.

He picked up the phone and says, "It's your quarter, go for it."

"Mr. Harvey," a deep voice with a commanding tone says, "we are the folks who just buzzed your office. I'm calling to assure you we are nice people and that it's in your best interests to have a private talk with us. We basically just want to introduce ourselves. We'll not need more than 15 minutes of your valuable time, and that small investment on your part could mean millions of dollars to your organization, which we both know needs the money. What do you say? We're across the street on the corner. If you look out your office window, you can see that we're just a normal, everyday peace-loving couple, just like you and Liz. What do you say? Take a look."

Holding the phone, Nick took a cautious look from the lower corner of his window. The man at the corner waved in a friendly manner. The woman was well-dressed. Over the cell phone the man says, "You're a cautious guy for a businessman!"

Nick responds, "In my current business, I seem to be attracting some people who disagree with my business mission. What did you say your name was?"

"John. Just call me John. My companion is Laura."

"Who do you represent?"

"I can't talk about that on the phone, but that's why I want to see you. You'll like what I have to say to you. What have you got to lose besides 15 minutes? If we wanted to hurt you, you would already be hurt." That comment revealed a lot to Nickolas.

"Okay. You do look pretty normal. But, I'm not sure about the pants-jacket combination. It's hard to be recognized as "peace-loving" anymore. It was easier in the '60s. I see two of you now, and that's all I want to see when I open the door. Come on back. Buzz me and I'll buzz you into the lobby. Come up to the second floor."

Nickolas watched the two cross the street, and a moment later he buzzed them in. A minute or two later, there was a knock at the door to Nickolas' office suite. Nick was partially around the corner from his office reception area when he says,

"The door is open, John. Come in slowly and have a seat."

The door opened slowly and John and Laura walked in cautiously, saw Nickolas, smiled, raised their hands, palms out, signing peace, and started to sit down on opposite sides of the double door.

Nickolas said from the corner of the hallway, "No, Laura. Sit next to John." Laura did so, smiling and shaking her head.

Nickolas says, "Okay, now cross your legs at the knee and stay that way while we talk."

"Christ!" says John, "give me a break will you. We're just here to talk."

"Okay, John, start by telling me who you are. I'm not talking to you otherwise."

"Fine, I was going to tell you anyway. My name is John Mendoza. Have you heard the name before?"

"Yes," Nickolas says, "I think I recognized the name, but I'm getting old, my memory isn't what it used to be. I'm assuming you're one of the New Jersey Mendozas, am I correct?"

"Yes, you are."

"What are you and Laura doing in D.C. today?"

"Well, Nickolas, Laura and I are down here for a meeting with our two Republican senators from the great state of New Jersey. We've been invited to a special White House Republican fund-raising event by the President himself. Are you going to be there by any chance?"

"No, John, I'm not. I wasn't invited, although, I'm a registered Republican of long standing and as you might imagine, as a defense contractor, a heavy contributor to the party."

"Yes," says John, "I can see where that would be true. Laura and I have followed your campaign with great interest. Laura thought we should meet you since we were in town anyway."

Nick says, "Laura, I appreciate your thinking about ARC and me and stopping by to say hello."

Laura says, "Mr. Harvey, John and I are co-chairs of a family-held philanthropic organization. We contribute more than a million dollars per year to a few organizations that we believe are worthy and needy. We hear ARC is becoming needy, and we would like to help you. What do you think?"

"Laura, that sounds interesting so far. We're always looking for more donations; however, we are not needy as you say, any more than usual. Where did you get the idea that we were?"

"As I said, we're interested in ARC and we did a little investigating, as we always do, and that information was revealed in the investigator's report. I do not know her source. Does it matter?"

"No, Laura, not really. What would your philanthropic organization require in exchange, for say, a, ah—$250,000 contribution?"

John answered saying, "Nickolas, that's a lot of money, a high percentage of our annual budget."

Laura interjects, "Yes, it's a lot of money, but within our capacity if you're willing to accept one of our organization's personnel onto your board to assure that our contribution is expended wisely."

"I see," says Nickolas, "how about at the $100,000 level?"

"We would then only need computerized access to your financial accounting system and access to a monthly board meeting, if necessary, in our opinion. A simple contract would cover the arrangement."

"What are your organization's objectives?"

"Simply to help ARC achieve their mission," John says.

"Your objectives then are humanitarian, as it relates to the Cuban people?"

"Yes," Laura says, and John nods his head in the affirmative.

"Let me think about this possibility a day or two, will you?"

John answered saying, "Nickolas, what's there to think about? I'll give you a check right now, anywhere between a $100,000 and $250,000." He takes out a checkbook.

Laura says, reaching into her purse, "And, I have two simple contracts here you can sign. One is one page, the other is two pages. You want to read them?"

Nickolas says, "Geez, guys, I really don't want to disappoint you, but I can't make this kind of decision that fast. I need more information about your organization and its goals and objectives. ARC has to be careful how we raise money. We're under scrutiny from the IRS and the public that favors ARC and the public that wishes to discredit ARC. I can't take chances with big donations from unknown sources."

"Look, Nickolas, we were hopeful that we could tell our friends in the Senate, and even the President, that our association had made a deal with ARC to help them out. Politically, that could open a lot of very important doors to you."

"I understand, John, but I just can't do it. Legally, it's against our corporate bylaws. Laura, if you'll leave me your business card, I'll have my assistant call you on Monday to get the basic information we need to check your organization's credentials. If everything checks out, maybe we can do business. That's my bottom line today."

John and Laura look at one another in irritation and disappointment, not knowing what to say or do next. Nickolas is sitting at Judy's desk, with his elbows upon it and his fingers steepled, studying their reactions. Nickolas sees John uncross his legs, putting both feet on the floor and his hands on the arms of his chair. His face reflects anger, under control, but barely. Nickolas says quietly, but firmly,

"John, sit back, relax, cross your legs, or we're through talking, and I will have to ask you to leave the building."

John stops in motion, not moving forward nor back. Laura is moving her head between John and Nickolas, wondering what will happen next. It starts to happen.

John loses his cool, jumps up yelling, "You son-of-a-bitch, you can't play us for fools." As he rushes the desk and Nickolas, Nickolas rises quickly, crashing Judy's chair against the back wall. As he does so, he grabs the phone on the right-hand side of the desk, just as John lunges over the desk to grab Nickolas by the neck. Nickolas sweeps the phone over the left arm of John and into the left side of John's head, hitting John hard above the ear. John is down and out and lying on Judy's desk. Nickolas watches John to see if he needs to hit him again.

Laura is on her feet. Nickolas yells, "Sit down and cross your legs!" She does so. Nickolas determines it's not necessary to hit John again right now and grabs the telephone receiver cord, pulls it out of the phone base and receivers, and ties John's hands behind his back as he lies there unconscious, drooling on Judy's desk pad.

Laura says, "You son-of-a-bitch, you have no idea what you've just done! No idea!" She is on the verge of hysteria, barely able to contain herself, squirming in the chair, wanting to attack.

Nickolas calmly says, "Don't blame me, Laura. It's your buddy here who decided to get physical."

"You, you, you, intimidated him! You, you provoked him. Yes, provoked him. It's your fault, you asshole!"

"Sit still Laura and calm down. Don't do anything foolish. You can walk out of here with John in a minute or two, or you both can leave with the emergency services people."

# XLIV

## GUANABO BAY, CUBA

The late night is warm, with a light breeze off the ocean from the southwest, as Manuel leaves his home out the back door, pausing on the back stoop to light his pipe. He casually looks around. Satisfied that no neighbors are in sight, he steps down the stairs to the garden path, which leads to the dilapidated old garage at the rear of his property. Entering the garage through a side door, he finds his bicycle and wheels it to the alley, where he mounts and cycles down the moonlit alleyway, leaving a trail of sweet aromatic pipe smoke in his wake. His thoughts are angry as he revisits the strained dinner conversation with Rose. Why is it she has to bring up the most difficult problems at dinnertime, right after he has returned from a hard day at work and only wants to relax? Life could be simple and peaceful if she would just let him run things. He shook his head side to side as their argument reran in his troubled mind, and he tried to sort out the good points from the bad points in Rose's arguments.

While he was deep in thought, he subconsciously navigates his bicycle through a maze of back alleys and side streets in the half dark toward his secret destination on the waterfront, about 20 minutes away in an old run-down fish market warehouse district east of Old Town in Guanabo.

Manuel didn't like the idea of changing plans now, following a year of preparation. He also knew that the more new people you brought into the plan, the more likely you were to be discovered. More importantly, he was a seaman who understood the threat of the sea and was aware of the planning and the preparations that were necessary to reduce those threats when going to sea. He knew that all you could do as the captain was to plan properly for the voyage; you could never, ever eliminate all that could go wrong. Even the ship Titanic at 800 feet and 440,000 tons had sunk in just a few hours into her maiden voyage to America.

Manuel had been judicious in his planning, including the design and building of the little boat, to make the journey across the Florida Straits as safe as possible. He paid special attention to assure that it was capable of carrying the planned load under the severest of conditions. He had spent many hours at the library gathering and then computing the various critical variables involved. Realizing the variables and his many years experience offshore as a fisherman and the value of his cargo, he was led to the decision to plan and build the right boat, which he would pilot himself to and from the Florida Keys. He had discussed the design criteria with Rufus, who had built and helped build boats all of his life. Rufus had agreed with Manuel's design and specifications for the purpose. However, Rufus had reminded him that the design was neither less nor more than what was likely needed, including the probable margin of error.

Rose's suggestion that he should try to add Priscilla's son was crazy at this time. It was way too late to add an extra man and perhaps 200 pounds to the boat, with man and baggage! Rose just couldn't understand the various implications of adding a person to a small boat already full, the effect on displacement and freeboard in heavy weather, the effect on balance and speed with or without the small sail, and the crowding it would cause. There was only so much room on the four seats and on the floor boards for people, their possessions, boat and safety gear and supplies.

Before Manuel was aware, he was halfway to the pier and its dilapidated, old fish storage shed. He thought he had better get hold of his mind as he didn't remember anything about the bicycle ride so far, other than his frustration with Rose. He hadn't been watching for anyone following him.

He stopped his bike at the next corner and made a fuss about emptying the bowl of his pipe, refilling it slowly from a bag of tobacco he carried, tamping it down, then carefully lighting it, getting a good draw while looking around slowly for anything moving, particularly back along the long street he was now leaving. He could detect nothing unusual, although it would have been easy for anyone following to be in the dark and shadows of the many buildings, alleyways or trees along the sidewalk.

He got an idea. He mounted his bike and rode it around the corner for half a block, leaned it against a tree and quietly returned to the corner and stooped to sidewalk level to look around the corner. Nothing. No one. He returned to his bike, satisfied that none of his neighbors had seen him leave the area on his bike at night and had followed him. He wasn't paranoid, he thought, I'm just cautious. A lot was at stake for him and his family. Neighbors could not be trusted. That thought reminded him again of his irritable confrontation with Rose as a result of Priscilla's insistence that he make room aboard the boat for Priscilla's son, Anthony. It was way too late to consider such a thing!

Manuel was mostly upset by Priscilla telling Rose that he owed this favor to her husband as an old debt of honor! Rose had asked Manuel what the debt was, but he had said, "There is no such debt, honorable or otherwise, I do not know of what she speaks." Rose then said, "Priscilla says he saved your life during the Revolution." Manuel continued to tell Rose he knew of no debt and he had never saved his life. He continued to believe that to be true as he continued to wonder what Antonio could conceivably be referring to.

He thought about the war once again. They had fought with Fidel against Batista together, young men, really boys at the time, schoolmates who had run away to the Sierra Maestra mountains to join Fidel's Revolution to bring democracy and freedom to the people of Cuba. They fought and killed side by side, comrades in arms, one looking after the other. He thought about those times most dangerous. There had been only three or four incidents to consider, and as he did so, he could not think of any event in which Antonio might have thought he saved his life. He pondered it all again. From first hearing of this alleged debt, he had thought about this issue four or five times to no avail.

After the war of the revolution, they had parted, going their separate ways, Antonio had stayed in the Cuban military and Manuel had left to return to his family and join his father on the boat fishing. Later he met Rose and married, had two children. When his father later died, he took over the fishing boat. Later his mother died. One of his two brothers escaped to America and the other brother was lost at sea while fishing in a storm. Manuel brought his own son Miguel into the family business.

Manuel then thought about the more recent years. He and Antonio would always be spiritual brothers; however, their paths had diverged. Manuel had become increasingly disenchanted with Fidel's postwar revolution, although he shared his true feelings with no one outside his family and closest friends. He feared not for himself, but for them.

When his last living brother was discovered missing from Havana and reported to be in Miami, the whole family had been interrogated, then investigated and interrogated again. Fortunately, Manuel's brother had been smart enough not to let the rest of the family know anything about his intentions, method of escape, or those who assisted him. But, of course, the escape had been by boat and Manuel captained a boat and was a man of the sea, and thus became a major suspect in the escape of his brother. That had been five years ago, but he now wondered who had inspired Alonzo to escape and helped him do it, along with five others? Could it have been "uncle?" Was his brother's escape before or after Antonio had been let out of prison and joined the opposition again? He couldn't remember.

He had to think, maybe ask Rose. Maybe ask Priscilla. Then it hit him, so obvious he had overlooked it, focusing on shared fire fights in the war long ago.

Antonio had been in prison six years now, actually put there by his old comrade Fidel for anti-revolutionary, dissident activities. Antonio had certainly been tortured repeatedly and had much information he could have given up to improve his lot in prison. He hadn't done so; in fact, he was now engaged in starving himself to death to prove he was a stronger man with greater convictions than Fidel and his henchman. He hadn't given up Manuel's brother or his helpers when he likely knew of Alonzo's plans, and through Priscilla, Rose's sister, had acquired intimate family information. He could still give up that knowledge, maybe even get himself out of prison after six years if he bargained smartly.

That's what he was trying to tell me! He was desperate to get Anthony off the island before he died and could no longer use the leverage of his knowledge. That was it! That was saving my life! It was unwillingness to give up the names and illegal deeds of Manuel's family, past and present, that had been proven each time he had been tortured.

Manuel thought, figuring that out was a real challenge, but I did it—at least I think I did. The question is, what do I do now? Do I accept the debt and do what he wants? Or do I test him as a longtime friend and refuse? He said to himself, I'm going to have to think about that for a while. In any event, Antonio won't live much longer if he stays on his hunger strike—a bad thought, he said to himself.

It was only minutes now to the cyclone fence across the front of the rickety old building and storage shed. The pier and the ocean were just behind the building. He thought, shit, I've done it again, so engrossed in my thoughts that I've paid no attention to my security! He stopped again just past another corner, stepped off his bike, leaned it and himself against the wall, silently waiting, looking and listening for anyone following him. After five minutes, he was confident no one was following him. He remounted his bike and peddled the last four blocks to the old pier.

On the shore end of the pier is an old, dilapidated two-story wood building that years ago had been a wholesale fish distribution point with two truck docks on the left front side of the building, a street-level double doorway in the middle and offices to the right. The upper level had been the owner's home. All the windows and doors had been boarded over years ago. Behind the building was an old wooden pier, perhaps a 100-feet long, which was connected to the back of the building. It provided a covered area in which to sort, weigh and ice the fish and complete the business of buying the fish from the fisherman, which then were resold by the buyer to Havana restaurants, hotels and others for that day's luncheon and dinner consumption.

The same process still prevailed in Cuba, to a much lesser degree, on an off-market basis, mainly outside the greater Havana area. Otherwise, the Cuban Government controlled the catching of fish and the price of fish for commercial distribution. Those engaged in the independent business of catching fish now unloaded their fish at the main government fish docks in Havana and were paid a fixed-market price for fish that had changed little in the past 40 years. There was not even enough profit for the fisherman to properly maintain their boats, most of which were 50 to 60 years old and long ago unsafe for their purpose.

Manuel had exchanged the lock and chain on the front door of the building for one of his own, knowing the building and dock had been confiscated by the government and condemned as unsafe and unusable, having been abandoned long ago and ravaged by sea storms for years. Manuel looked up and down the street, then quickly unlocked the padlock on the chain to the double front office door and entered the building, taking his bicycle with him.

# XLV

## LATER THAT NIGHT

Manuel propped his bicycle against the wall in the old hallway and then, by pulling the two front doors toward him on the inside, he created enough of a gap to get his hand to the chain and lock, which he relocked from the inside. He then pulled the double doors back to their fully closed position and put a 2-foot by 4-foot piece of lumber across the inside of the doors so that they could not be pushed in or out.

Although it was quite dark, Manuel knew his way and passed through a rear door into the warehouse area and through its open rear to the moonlit dock. From here he had to be careful, as he transited the old dock out to a small building on the end. The dock deck had many missing planks, but Miguel knew the safe path and in moments was at the back door of the second building on the end of the pier, whose doors and windows had also been boarded over. This building also appeared abandoned. Manuel knocked quietly, saying, "Rufus, it's me." He thinks he hears a strange growl. The door opens.

"Welcome Manuel, come right in, we've been waiting for you. What have you got there?" Rufus asks.

"Rose sent a little package for you, as usual—some fresh vegetables from her garden and two loaves of fresh bread and some smoked fish. How are you doing, everything okay?" Manuel asks.

"We're doing fine, making good progress—no problems, no interruptions. A private boat came in close yesterday, took one look at the dock and then headed back east," Rufus says.

"Are your supplies adequate, got enough food for another week or so? Got enough water, beer? Need any materials?"

"We're in good shape, maybe next week you'll need to have Miguel make another midnight run. Have him bring more ice next time. Nothing beats a cold beer or two at the end of a long day."

"Will do, make me a list. I'll see you again by the end of the week. I'll know then when Miguel can make the run. Now, let's have a beer. Have you got a couple left in the cooler?"

"Yes, I do. I put them in there this morning to make sure that they would get cold."

"Good! I'm ready! Let's enjoy a beer or two, then inspect your work and then I'll be out of your way."

"No need for you to rush, Manuel. You know I don't get much company out here besides you and Fidel."

"What do you mean, Fidel?"

"Look over there by my bedroll."

Manuel takes a few steps to get a closer look in the nearly dark corner of Rufus' sleeping area. He sees a quiet, resting multi-breed dog, a combination of this and that, looking kind of skinny and spent, but he looks up at Manuel and starts wagging his tail. The dog rises to meet Manuel, licking his fingers as Manuel scratches behind the dog's ears.

"Aren't you afraid that Fidel's barking will give you away out here?"

"Did he bark when you arrived?"

"Well, no, I guess he didn't. I think he growled is all."

"Fidel and I made a deal when I found her a few nights ago. I told her I would look after her, but that she couldn't bark. Like all females, it took her a day or so to figure out I meant what I said. But she's got it now."

"What are you feeding her? Did you say Fidel is a *female?*"

"Yes."

"Why call a female Fidel?"

"It's my way of saying Fidel's a pussy. She eats whatever I get. I fish a little for both of us. She was starving to death when I found her. She'll eat anything. She won't bark now, but she'll growl and whine if she hears anything unusual, like the boat the other day. She provides companionship and security."

"Sounds like a fair exchange. I'll try to bring you a ham bone or something next time I come. Now, let's see the boat. How's it coming?" They walk over to the opposite side of the building where the framework of an incomplete, inverted small boat sits on five sawhorses.

"No problems with the construction although I'm still concerned about the age and condition of this old wood we scavenged."

"You're only using the best of it, right?"

"Yes. It still has life in it. But it is hard to tell the moisture content. It's not dry or brittle. When steamed, it bends very nicely, almost too nicely, maybe too easily if you get my meaning."

"Most of the wood on my boat is 60 years old. She still goes to sea almost every day."

"Yes, and in this case, you're only planning on going over and back, right?"

"Yes, that's the plan. But when you're sailing, the wind determines your arrival time. To get back, I have to unload in America the second night. If I am in American waters, the second day of daylight, it would take a miracle to land without detection."

"Well, in four days I can't see how you can get in any trouble as a result of my boat construction or the wood. The wood is taking the screws quite well. It shouldn't absorb much water in four days."

"Let me borrow your screwdriver a moment, will you?"

"Sure. Here, use this one." Rufus removes a screwdriver from his apron.

Manuel withdraws a screw halfway, testing the tightness and then re-screws it tight.

"Yes, I agree. It's tight and when the boat gets in the water and the wood expands, it should even be tighter, right?"

"Yes."

Manuel walks around the boat skeleton. "Rufus, it looks very good. You have not lost any of your skill. I'm very pleased. It looks like a piece of art. There's nothing more beautiful than the lines of a carefully laid out boat, except those of a woman—and they're just as dangerous in the hands of an unskilled master."

"Well," says Rufus, "we must remember that it takes both a good boat and a good master to make a long journey successfully. Also, a successful marriage."

"Well said," Manuel says.

"Rufus, I am being put under a lot of pressure to add another passenger to the boat, a young man. What do you think?"

"Where would he sit? The seats are full."

"He would have to sit on the aft seat with me."

"He'll be in the way of the tiller and the toilet seat."

"We can redesign the toilet seat to flip down and latch on the outer hull, and he'll have to get out of the way when I turn the tiller into him."

Rufus looks at the skeleton of the boat inverted on the sawhorses, walks to the aft and studies the narrow, slightly lifted stern area where the captain will sit and the tiller will be mounted. He wipes his forehead with a dirty rag from his rear pocket and says,

"I can't recommend it, Manuel. We've designed a little leeway into this boat but not enough under severe weather conditions to add another two or three hundred pounds. We already added four more inches of freeboard you remember. In the final analysis, it will depend on the weather. If you can predict the weather for me, I could give you a definite answer. You're the owner and the captain, it's your decision."

"I understand, Rufus. I guess I was just hoping you would say it'll probably be okay."

"I can say that, Manuel, but you know Mother Nature better than me, and we both know she is unpredictable."

"Yes, I know. But a debt of honor might be involved here that I am being called upon to repay. Maybe we can figure out how to weight reduce the boat and payload by a couple of hundred pounds?"

"Have everybody lose 20 pounds each before the trip."

"That's an idea, but most of these people are half-starved now. They'll eat better on the trip than they do at home if Rose has her way."

"Well, there are some things we can look at, like the mast, boom, sails, sea baggage, anchor, fresh water load, floor boards, safety gear, canvas covers and oars. Maybe I can get you a hundred pounds. We already lightened this boat once, remember?"

"Yes."

"Well, Manuel, you got to do what you have to do and after that, worry won't change a thing. Make your decision and we go with it. Just let me know very soon."

"Is now soon enough? We're adding a 170-pound young man with probably 30 pounds of personal baggage, so 200 pounds."

"I'll do everything I can. You do everything you can and then let's forget it. It will be what it is."

"How about another beer?"

# XLVI

## WASHINGTON, D.C. - EN ROUTE TO THE BLUE NOTE

Nickolas had returned to D.C. via the HDI corporate jet only an hour ago. It was now 6 p.m. and he was in the Friday afternoon post-work traffic headed to Georgetown and a dinner meeting with his executive staff. He was very happy and excited about the outcome of his initial four meetings with several Fortune 500 corporate CEOs in Dallas, Chicago and Detroit, and was impatient to share his good news with his close friends and associates.

Nickolas had called the office from Detroit after the last meeting on the way to the airport and invited Phil, Tim and Mike to dinner at the Blue Note at 7 p.m. He told Phil he had important news, but he didn't say more. He had requested that Abraham pick him up, instead of Tony, as he had not talked to Abraham in a while since security had taken care of most of his transportation needs. In his exuberant mood he was breaking his own security rules agreement just this once. It was good to see and talk with Abraham again and get up-to-date on the usual subjects they discussed: family, sports, current events and politics. Other than the slow traffic, which irritated Nickolas, it was pleasant conversation and it helped pass the time until Abraham says,

"Mr. Harvey, there's a black Suburban back there that has followed us through the last four turns. Do you want me to verify that it is following us?"

Nickolas unconsciously looked back. "No, in this traffic, there's little you can do. Wait until we get off the interstate and see if he continues to follow. Also, move into the right lane and slow down a little, see if he passes or keeps his distance."

Abraham did as instructed and a minute or two later says, "He moved into the slow lane, too, Mr. Harvey. He's keeping his distance. There's a white van two cars behind him that made the same move. Maybe it was incidental. It's hard to tell in this traffic, could be a team of two following us."

"Give it another two to three minutes and move one lane to the left. Stay in that lane until we reach our exit ramp. We'll see what happens."

Abraham waited a few minutes and did as instructed. "They haven't moved, Mr. Harvey. They may know our exit is coming up soon."

Nickolas says, "Maybe."

"Oops, number one just moved over. I can't see number two anymore."

"We'll see what happens when we exit. If we are going to avoid them, we'll do it in the village, but we don't want them to realize we've spotted them."

"How are we going to do that?"

"I'll tell you when I see the right spot."

"Okay. The exit is coming up. I'm moving over. Number one is moving over. Number two, I still can't see. Maybe I was wrong about the second car."

"Maybe, we'll see. Just proceed as if you were going to the Blue Note. But somewhere up here in the village, you're going to make a fast right turn and I am going to get out real quick, and you can proceed to try and take these guys for a long ride. I'll call you from the Blue Note. You call me if these guys stop following you after I get out. I'll walk the last three to four blocks to the Blue Note. See that three-story brick building two corners down with white trim? That's your corner. Is there now one or two back there?"

"Now two, about a block back."

"Good, make a normal turn. Stop quick, let me out and resume speed quickly."

"Are you sure, Mr. Harvey?"

"Yes, I am sure. If these guys were out to attack us, it would have happened on the interstate, not in the village."

"Okay. I hope you're right. Be careful. Thanks for the visit. Here we go."

The limo turned the corner in a normal fashion. Abraham jumped on the brakes. Nickolas jumped out the already open door, crossed the sidewalk quickly and stepped into a coffee shop. Abraham resumed his speed down the block. Nickolas saw three cars make the same turn, including the Suburban and the white van. The white van was an old Ford panel van lettered as City Locksmith Company. He couldn't identify anyone in the Suburban, due to the dark windows, and did not recognize either of two middle-aged, dark-haired white males in the panel van, who were wearing sport coats.

Nickolas didn't know what to think as he left the coffee shop for the three-block walk to the Blue Note. However, he thought it was unlikely that anybody would assign two cars to a routine surveillance. Nickolas had suspected that he was being followed previously, but this was the first confirmation. He went through the likely possibilities in his mind as he walked, watching the passing traffic coming up behind and coming at him from the front, as well as people on the sidewalk. He was not expecting trouble, just being alert and cautious. He quickly reviewed his personal defense options. He was ready, but needlessly. He was across the street from the Blue Note.

He ducked into another coffee shop, and ordered a cup of regular coffee. $1.98! He thought, a $1.98! Jesus, I remember when it was just a quarter! He didn't drink any coffee. He was already wired. Between the good news of the day and the adrenaline rush of avoiding the trackers, he could probably fly across the street if he wanted. He waited five minutes. He saw Phil, Tim and Mike arrive and enter the Blue Note. He thought, I hope they remember to order me a Chardonnay, I don't feel like waiting. He stayed a little longer, and in a few minutes, saw an old couple and a young couple enter the Blue Note. He got up, tossed the coffee and eased slowly onto the street. He paused, checked parked cars, checked for suspicious people loitering. There were none. He crossed the street and entered the Blue Note.

# XLVII

## THE BLUE NOTE

At the Blue Note, Nickolas was welcomed with familiarity by the hostess, Betty Lou.

"Your friends are already here. I'll take you to them," she says.

Phil, Tim and Mike were in their usual large corner booth, and there was a Chardonnay on a napkin at one end. Tony was at the bar. Nickolas slid into the booth with a sigh and a smile saying, "How we doing guys? Okay?"

They all nodded and replied in the affirmative. But Phil says, "You look frazzled. Bad flight?"

"No. Actually I'm a happy camper today. But Abraham and I did confirm a two-car surveillance team on us coming in from the airport. Abraham has probably still got them. He's going to take them for a little ride, see how smart they are. I'll call him in a little bit, see how he is doing. I don't believe there is any threat.

"But first, my friends, a toast! We've hit the big time in fund-raising! No more worries! We can focus on simply getting the job done. Cheers!"

The four of them touch glasses smiling, talking all at once in shared enthusiasm with Nickolas.

Phil was the first to say, "Sounds great! Tell us about it. What happened?"

"Okay, just a minute. I want to check on Abraham."

Nickolas calls Abraham on his cell phone to see how he's doing. Abraham tells a strange story. As soon as Abraham got to the state highway just outside Georgetown, the first car made its move on Abraham's limo, slamming the limo in the rear several times, trying to cause an accident. The heavier limo and Abraham handled the threat easily. At one point, Abraham, upon being struck in the rear, simply slowed down slowly to 20 mph, forcing his pursuer to also slow down. The offender backed off, slowed down and didn't know what to do. At that point, the passenger in the offender's car tried to shoot out the limo's tires with two shots from a handgun. Abraham sped up, putting some distance between his Chrysler 300 limo and the offender.

Watching in his rearview mirror, Abraham noticed a strange event. The second surveillance car, the old panel van, sped up from far back and overtook the offender's car easily, and then cut in front of the offender, effectively running both cars off the road and into a whole lot of dust, dirt and brush as they went far off the road into the tree line. Abraham simply turned around and headed for home. He did not seem to be at all upset about the event, according to Nickolas. Abraham considered it just another day at work, part of his job working for a secret agent!

"Abraham continues to surprise me," Phil says. "He has skills that were unknown to me before he came to D.C."

"There's a lot more depth to Abraham than anyone knew before we did a deep background check on him when we transferred him to D.C.," Mike says.

"Like what?" Tim asks

"I can't say, Tim, it would be an invasion of Abraham's privacy. He doesn't want people to know about certain aspects of his early life pre-HDI."

"Okay," Phil says. "Nick, you indicated you had some good news to share with us regarding your trip this week. What is it?"

"Just a second. Tony, come over here for a minute," Nick says. Nickolas sits back in the booth, smiles in a funny way, looks at each of them for a moment, getting eye contact and their total attention.

"Guys, you are not going to believe it. We've hit the mother lode, and it's called corporate business sponsorship! Nick reaches into his left sports coat pocket and pulls out an envelope, opens it and removes four checks. He says,

"Look at these." He hands one check to each of them.

"Holy Jesus!" Phil says.

"Yes, there is a God!" Mike says.

"You never cease to amaze me, Nick!" Tim says.

Tony says, "See you later boss," and pretends to be leaving with the check. Then says, "Nick, that's the most money I've ever seen at one time! Let me see the others." Everybody excitedly trades checks four times.

"Nick, if I added correctly, that looks like $200,000," Phil says.

"Yes, Phil, you're right. Now look at this one." Nickolas had held one check back. He handed Phil the check.

"I'll be a son-of-a-bitch! It's $100,000 from Roland Communications! How did you do that, or all of it, or any of it, for that matter? That's $300,000 from five corporate sponsors! Fantastic!" Phil says.

"And Phil, this is just the beginning. These checks are just seed money from these companies. If we show real tangible progress, there is more money. There are other corporations in America with a similar point of view," Nickolas says.

"What view?" Tim asks.

"All of these companies were doing business in Cuba when Fidel nationalized them, took over their companies and kicked their executives out of the country in 1961. Some of these guys wrote off millions, back when a million was 10 or 20 million! They've never forgotten what Fidel did to them. They want their money back and or they want the market opportunity back. Getting the money back is called 'reparations.' They want their reparations or their markets back."

"So Nick, what did you have to promise to these special interests people?" Phil asks.

"Phil, did you have to phrase that question *that* way? You wound me."

"Yes," Phil says.

"Fellas, life is full of compromises. Without compromise, human progress would stop. Think of your wife. We needed the money to get our mission accomplished. We gave up very little in the larger scheme of worldwide politics. I believe I made a very acceptable deal, but it is too full of details to get into right now. We've made a good deal, trust me; it's not the first time we've had to compromise some of our initial ideals."

"Okay Nick, we *trust* you, but as you say, '*we trust but we verify,*' but right now, it's WOW time! $300,000! That's a hell-of-a good week's work! Drink up guys. Here's to Nick!" They all emptied their glasses as Phil collected all the checks.

# XLVIII

## HYATT HOTEL - WASHINGTON, D.C.

Nickolas and Tony had arrived at the downtown Washington Hyatt at 10 a.m. at the invitation of one of the U.S. senators from Florida for a private meeting in Suite 1150, or so they thought, until their elevator stopped on the second floor and Bones and Butt got aboard with drawn guns.

"Punch the top floor button please. We're going to have a little talk upstairs," Bones says.

Nickolas and Tony are forced to the top floor, empty lounge bar/restaurant to be intimidated, thinks Tony, maybe beaten. Nickolas thinks, I have not taken the bad guys seriously enough. This is my fault. The four are walking toward a corner booth in the rear of the bar. Bones is pushing Nickolas with his gun and Butt is following Tony. Nickolas had noticed that both these guys had facial bruises and forehead cuts. The thickset guy had a broken left thumb in a small plaster-and-metal hand cast and was limping.

"Say," Nickolas says to the lead guy, "you guys look a little under the weather today. Have you been in a recent car accident or something?"

"No, just normal wear-and-tear in our profession. If you think we look bad, you should see the other guy. See him, that is, after he gets out of the hospital next month," Bones says.

They arrive at the corner, black leather booth, which will seat six easily. The boss takes a seat on one end and invites Nickolas to sit. Nickolas thinks, I wish this was the Blue Note.

"Slide in there Nickolas and let's talk. The place is closed until 5 p.m., but I can have Butt get you a drink if you want one."

"Well, since you're buying, have your '*boy*' bring me a bottle of Empire Three, a glass and a corkscrew. I'll handle it from there." Nickolas remained standing.

"I don't think so, Mr. Harvey. That sounds a little dangerous to me under the circumstances. Slide in there, Nick, let's talk."

"Well then, you must not be too confident in your ability to handle that 9 mm."

"Oh, I'm very confident with all the tools of my trade, Mr. Harvey, just as I am sure you are. Sit down, let's talk."

"No, I think I'll stand," Nickolas says. "If your '*boy*' wants to slip in there next to you, then we can all sit down. Otherwise, I'll stand. I'll listen. You have the gun. You have the floor, let's hear it."

"Listen, Nickie, I said sit your ass down, now, Goddamn it, or I'll have Butt put a bullet in your fucking knee! Then you'll sit your ass down!"

"I got a bullet in the knee once in Panama. The pain of a knee wound is overrated. It's one of those things like eating worms, sounds bad, looks bad, but it's not that bad. Let me show you the scar."

"Yeah," Tony says, "you should see that Goddamn thing." He moved a few feet to see it himself and to put himself between Butt's vision and Nick.

Before Bones could say no, Butt moved to see the old knee wound. Nick had moved Bones off the end of the table by planting his foot on the bottom cushion of the seat next to him. Nickolas raised his right pant leg, which everyone was focused upon, while extracting a long Italian stiletto, push-button switchblade, from his boot top while raising his pant leg. He snapped it open under the jaw of Bones, all in one very rapid, fluid motion. The blade was 10 inches long.

"Drop the gun, asshole! Drop the fucking gun!" screamed Nickolas, "or Bones will be wearing two neckties and one will be his tongue! Now! Now! Goddamit!"

Butt hesitated just a second, lowering the muzzle of his gun maybe two inches. That was all Tony was watching for, that involuntary signal of confusion, hesitation and uncertainty. He sprung toward Butt, pushing the gun barrel down and away with his right hand toward the floor and putting the web of skin between forefinger and thumb between the weapons hammer and firing pin.

"Son-of-a-bitch!" Tony yelled in pain. "You fuckhead, you pulled the trigger! Son-of-a-bitch!" He then brought his right hand and the gun back up fast and hard with his skin still caught in the hammer, into the jaw of Butt, who went over and down for the count with blood, spit and two or three of his teeth flying through the air. Before Butt was even halfway to the floor, already unconscious, Tony had hit him with a left hand karate chop to the neck and back-kicked him in the crotch.

"Goddamn that hurts!" says Tony, as he extracted his skin from the 9 mm in his hand and inspected his hand carefully and then stuck it in his mouth and sucked on it. "Shit!" he says. "I hate it when that happens!"

"Son-of-a-bitch!" Bones says, as he saw Butt go down the hard way.

Nickolas says, "Bones! Don't you realize you're messing with the best of the United States Marine Corps here!"

Tony, still looking at the web of his thumb, exclaims, "Hoorah! Hoorah! Nick, what do you want to do these guys? This one will require emergency room assistance."

Nickolas says to Bones, "What do you say, man? What do I want to do with you guys?" The stiletto, still under Bones' jaw, is now drawing a little red blood.

Bones says, "Actually I was in the Corps myself. If I'd of known you guys were jarheads, too, I wouldn't be here. Let us go. We'll forget the whole thing. You'll never see us again."

Nick says incredulously to Tony, "Can you believe this low-life bottom feeder was ever in the Corps!"

"Not no, but hell no!"

Nickolas says to Bones, "Okay, Bones, if you were in the Corps, show me your tattoo."

"I ... I don't have one," Bones says.

"No fucking tattoo, and you were in the Marine Corps! Bullshit! What is your first General Order!" Nickolas says.

"Ah, General Order?... I, ah... don't remember," Bones says.

"Don't remember! Then you were in the Navy—maybe. Okay, Bones, we're goin' to let you go because Tony and I are busy people and we don't want to have to fuck with your buddy here who needs medical attention. But, I don't think I should let you go without some lifelong memory of our meeting. Butt wouldn't think it was fair either. So which would you prefer, a broken arm or leg?" Nickolas asks.

"I can remember you guys from yesterday's car accident. Look at my face. I'll be looking at these scars every time I shave," Bones says.

"Yes, but you got those for a different bad choice, that you made yesterday. Today is today and I believe we all must be accountable for our bad decisions. Are you ready to be accountable for yours? It's the way we learn you know," Nickolas says.

Bones is looking into Nickolas' eyes. Nickolas' face is still only a foot away from Bones, and the stiletto is still under his jaw. Bones sees a refraction of the iris and screams, "No! No!"

By the second "no" Bones is missing the lower forward corner of his right ear lobe—a piece about the size of that bitten off of Evander Holyfield's ear by Mike Tyson—and which now was in the air, heading for the floor.

Bones, surprised and wide-eyed, screamed and grabbed his bloody ear as Nickolas and Tony left the bar for the elevator.

"Nickolas, you're something else!" says Tony, laughing.

# XLIX

## THE BLUE NOTE

MAY

Nickolas was at the Blue Note 45 minutes before his meeting with the president and a director of the Cuban National Freedom Association (CNFA), an old liberal organization of American Cubans, and he was 15 minutes ahead of Phil, who was meeting him there. CNFA had been around for more than 50 years, being one of several popular organizations that sprang up in the late '50s and early '60s. In the beginning they were one of the most well-known and had a Dade County membership of more than 25,000, which in the '70s grew to 50,000-plus. But in the '80s, as the membership grew old and less aggressive, the number fell to 20,000 or so. After a change in leadership in the 1980s and a focus on younger members with a more social agenda, lower dues and liberal philosophy, the membership grew again to 30,000-plus until the late 1990s when it fell again to 20,000 or so. The younger membership just didn't have the fire in the belly for the ideals of the first generation. However, the CNFA still claimed 20,000 dues-paying members and 20,000 subscribers. What subscribers meant, Nickolas did not know, but would soon find out.

Phil arrived 15 minutes later and headed for their designated corner table. Phil looked at Nick's Chardonnay glass.

"How long you been here, Nick?"

Nick put four fingers to his glass and says, *"That* long."

"I thought we were meeting here together a little early, to 'take the edge off the day,' as you say?" Phil says.

"That's right, you're here and I'm here, and that's what we're going to do. Do you want the usual?"

"Yes, they saw me come in. It will be here in a minute. Jesus! Nick, did you get here early to take the edge off of having to meet with me, so we could take the edge off meeting with others?"

"Phil, don't be silly. You're my best friend in the whole freakin' world. Why would I have to do that? I just got here early because the traffic was light."

"You're lying like a blanket! I read you like an open book!" Phil was smiling.

"It's a good thing you're smiling when you say that Phil, or I would have to kick your ass!" Nick says jokingly.

"You and the first Marine Division, you son-of-a-bitch. Drinking without me, your best friend, for Christ's sake! Everything we've been through! Goddamn!"

"Okay, okay! I'm sorry. I am sorry that the traffic was so thin, next time I'll wait on the street! Annie, get this shithead his Scotch! He's getting mean!" The Scotch arrives quickly.

"Thank you, Annie," Nick says. "Phil! Here's lookin' at you, you old fart!"

"And to you, Nick!" Phil says as he raises his Scotch on the rocks with three olives, and drinks about half the glass.

"Jesus, Phil! Don't get carried away here. The night is young. We have important business to do!"

"Don't pull that bullshit on me. I'm just trying to catch up with you, who had to get here early, to take the edge off meeting me."

"You're not going to let up, are you?"

"Yes, I am, because, as you say, we have business to do and it's important business. Do you realize the potential of tonight's discussion with these guys?" Phil smiles excitedly.

"Yes, I do. We could increase our membership and influence by 50,000 people in one shot, or a dozen shots. If we have to drink them, we will! There is no sacrifice too big!"

"I agree. If we can make a deal, that's exactly what we need to do. These guys must be seriously interested to fly up here from Miami for dinner."

"Yes, well, we have to make this deal, Nick. Where else are we going to find 25,000 to 50,000 dues-paying members tonight, here at the Blue Note?"

"I understand, Phil. I agree. We'll get it done, if it can be done on any reasonable basis. You ready for another one? Annie, two more!"

A few minutes later, two overweight Cuban men, typical suburban-looking executives, walked into the Blue Note, looking around for two other lean and mean executives, who they did not know by appearance. They huddled with Betty Lou, who pointed them to the far corner booth. They approached, swaggering and smiling, hands outstretched. Nickolas and Phil stood. Hands were shaken and introductions executed. The guests were invited to sit. They sat. Annie was called again to the table although she was almost there. Nick thought, as he sat down, these guys stopped somewhere on the way here to take the edge off.

"What'll you guys have?" Phil says, with Annie standing by.

"A dry vodka martini on the rocks, please," Joe says.

"A dry Miller Lite in a glass please," Alex says. Annie took their order and headed for the bar.

"Hey, Joe and Alex! How are you guys doing? Did you have a good flight?" Nickolas asks.

Both Joe and Alex answer at the same time, but differently.

"Great!" Joe says, at the same time Alex says, "Fantastic!"

Nickolas said to himself, they definitely had a meeting before they got here. "How is everything going at CNFA? Are you guys getting anything exciting done?" Nick asks.

"Oh yes," Joe says. "We're working hard to bring our dues-paying membership back up to 50,000, then 75,000, then 100,000. In fact, you're the reason we believe we can get it done. Your ARC organization has created so much visibility on the subject that everyone is talking about the U.S.-Cuba relationship. Our monthly meeting attendance is rising every month. One of the reasons we're here is to say thank you, we appreciate it."

"Well, Joe, you're certainly welcome. That is one of ARC's major objectives. But, I must ask you, if your dues-paying members double and your meeting membership requires that you meet at the American Airlines Arena, do you and Alex think you can get anything done? Just a business question, no offense intended?"

Joe thought a moment, looked at Alex and smiled. "No offense taken." Joe took a drink, turned to Nickolas, smiled, looked around the bar, took another drink, and said. "No, actually we don't think so. We've kinda run out of good ideas and enthusiasm. Thanks for asking. That's really why we're here, to see how we might do something mutually beneficial. We have some good numbers, some good names, some income, some history, but no excitement. You have the national media, some good numbers, some good names, no dues-payers, but you have excitement."

"Joe," Phil says, "we haven't really considered merging with any of the existing Cuban-American organizations for obvious reasons. But I'm interested in your proposition. Exactly what are you proposing?"

Joe says, "A merger, a partnership, a buyout, whatever. What do you mean, obvious reasons?"

"We're nearly the size of the South Florida Cuban-American voting bloc now and gaining every day. We've come from nowhere in a year to equal their voting power. Why would we merge with a group that is only going to complicate our business and potentially not contribute the benefits we're looking for?" Phil says.

"Well, we're not looking for very much. We've been dormant for a long time," Joe says.

"Dormant? Don't you think a loss of 50% of your membership is a decline? That sounds like failure to me," Phil says.

"Well, in recent years, we haven't worked very hard to retain membership," Joe says.

"Okay. You still got 50,000 names?" Phil asks.

"Yes, or more, but we don't have the money to chase them, especially when we haven't had anything new to say."

"Well, we can sure help you in the 'things to say' department," Phil says.

"Joe, Alex, we understand mutually beneficial relationships. I think you know ARC has achieved a lot of momentum and that if CNFA doesn't get some soon, you'll be out of business. So, what is the bottom line? Don't answer yet," Nickolas says.

"Annie, four more please," Nickolas yells.

"Have you guys had your dinner yet?" Nickolas asks.

"Let's save the food for the finale. We're here to make a deal tonight," Alex says.

Annie arrives with another round, sets them down and takes the empties. Nickolas picks his up and toasts Tony at the bar and gives him a wink.

"Okay, give us the bottom line and the steaks are on me," Nick says.

"As Alex said, we're tired and we want to make a deal. There are a lot of business issues to consider, but we know you guys are professionals and will handle all that. What Alex, all our Board of Directors and I want is to continue in our positions and retain our salaries and benefits, period. That's it," Joe says.

"And exactly what kind of money is that? And what is current monthly income?" Phil asks. And the meeting gained momentum from there.

After a big steak and rounds of drinks, a deal was agreed upon and memorialized on three numbered cocktail napkins. They all signed and dated them, and Annie witnessed them. Sam sent a bottle of champagne to the table with four chilled glasses and a plate of chocolate-covered strawberries.

# L

## ARC HEADQUARTERS

Nickolas picked up his desk phone. It was 1:30 p.m. and a common hour for Elizabeth to call if she was uncertain of his evening plans or wanted to meet for a cocktail. He was surprised when his administrative assistant said, "Mr. Harvey, the Cuban Foreign Office is on line three, a Ms. Cordoba."

"Thank you, Judy. I'll take the call." He pushed a flashing button and says,

"Nickolas Harvey here, how may I be of service?"

"Mr. Harvey, thank you for taking my call. My name is Juliana Cordoba and I'm an employee of the Cuban Government attached to the Cuban Diplomatic Corps here in Washington. I'm calling from the Cuban Foreign Office."

"Yes, Ms. Cordoba, and what is it you do over there, if I may ask?"

"I am the senior member of the Cuban Economic Development Committee here in Washington, D.C. I would like to meet you and discuss your organization's activity. I believe some of your goals are similar to mine. We might be able to help one another."

"I see, well perhaps, I'm not sure. You see, my organization's approach is to resolve each of our country's issues in a comprehensive all-encompassing fashion, requiring agreements ultimately forged at the very top by each country's leadership. Certainly there are huge economic development implications for both countries, but that is only one important issue of many requiring resolution. I do sincerely appreciate your call and offer of help, and if you'll give me your personal contact number, I'll have my Chief of Staff or his assistant call you with an appointment date for a visit with him. His name is Phil Bowen."

"Thank you for that thought, Mr. Harvey, but your suggestion will not fulfill my objective. I hesitate to be too candid on an open line. Let me see here, what to say, ah? Okay, yesterday I returned from Havana, following two days of foreign affairs meetings. In one of these meetings, it was suggested that I make this call and meet with you. I believe it is very much in your organization's interests to meet with me—the sooner the better. Please."

"How do we verify that you are who you say you are?"

"Have your security people start by punching onto the Cuban Embassy's website. You can call me anytime on the phone number listed by my name, plus code 007."

"Are you *kidding!* 007?"

"No. Call me soon."

"How soon is soon?"

"Hours, not days."

"Okay, we'll go to work on it. You'll hear from me one way or the other soon."

"Thank you, Mr. Harvey. Have a nice afternoon."

"You, too, Ms. Cordoba."

Nickolas hung up the phone and sat back in his chair and mentally replayed the phone conversation in his mind while reviewing his notes. He seemed to make a decision, picked up the phone and dialed Mike's extension.

"Mike, I just took a call from the Cuban Embassy downtown. Pull up the recording, listen to it and call me back."

"Will do, Nick. Give me 10 minutes. I'll come to you." Nick hung up, sat back and continued to think. He hesitated

to get excited too quickly, but this could be a major development. There was some chance that it was only an aggressive middle-level embassy person trying to leverage a meeting with him, but he didn't think so. His optimism was slowly rising, as he waited to get Mike's take on the call.

There was a soft knock on Nick's office door, followed by its opening by Mike, with a big smile on his face. Nick understood immediately that Mike was as excited as he was.

"Nick, I think this could be a major development. I did take a minute to click onto the embassy website. A Ms. Cordoba is definitely listed as the Economic Development Officer, including a picture. She is a real looker! I believe you will definitely enjoy the meeting. I wonder what they have in mind to do to help. There could be some big money here!"

"I don't know. There's no telling really until I talk to her. I'm not sure we could legally accept their money if they offered it, and even if we could, we probably shouldn't. We may be in a serious gray area of the law, meeting with a representative of an alleged Communist country. You need to talk to Larry and determine our legal boundaries in this situation. Just meeting this lady, realizing her job at the embassy, should be okay, but we don't know what she is going to suggest. We need to be prepared."

"Nick, you need to meet her somewhere where we can record the whole conversation, just in case something goes wrong."

Nickolas says thoughtfully, "Perhaps, if we can get away with it. Still this could be important, but it also could be dangerous. Like other recent events, this one is happening faster than we are able to plan ahead."

"Yes, but if you're just going to meet with this woman and basically listen, I don't see how that could get us in trouble. But I'll talk to Larry."

"Also Mike, call that guy you know over at the State Department and see if he knows anything about Ms. Cordoba."

"Good idea, I will. I'll be back to you before the end of the day."

Mike left Nick's office. Nick advised Judy to assure his privacy for the rest of the afternoon and went back to his deep thinking. He thought best with pen and paper in hand. He started reviewing various optional scenarios that could be developing and the potential consequences of various optional decisions relating thereto. Time passed. Ten pages of notes and two hours later, Nick arose from his desk, stretched his back, rubbed his neck and walked to his office mini-bar and extracted a cold Avian, and took a big swig. He then went into his private head and washed his hands and wet his face with cold water, dried himself and returned to his desk. Mike was sitting in the guest chair.

"Nick, I completed my snooping and got all the scoop that I think we need. Ms. Cordoba is the real McCoy. She has been on the Cuban Economic Development Committee in Cuba for several years, working for a couple of different men in Havana who reported to Raul Castro. She has been assigned in Washington only the past year. She is considered to be a very intelligent, experienced, loyal Cuban—a professional. She has a degree in international economics and a degree in business. Her father, mother and a brother are all doctors. She speaks four languages. She has been instrumental in recent years in helping to put together some big deals in Cuba with the Canadians, the French and the Spaniards. She obviously would have to be well-connected and respected by the Cuban leadership to be involved in these large international economic developments."

"I agree," Nick says. "What did Larry say?"

"No legal problem he can visualize. He suggests a meeting at a neutral public site. He reminds you that you will likely be recorded and photographed. He said not to accept or pass any paper—conversation only. Put a heavy emphasis on listening. No one has suggested that Ms. Cordoba is an undercover agent of the Cuban military police, but you never know."

"Okay," Nick says. "Let's give it a go. I'll agree to the meeting. You set the time and place and let me know. You can handle the rest."

"What day and time do you prefer?"

"As she said, the sooner the better. You know our wireless capabilities. Pick a place accordingly. Do you know where she lives?"

"Yes, on Vermont near 19th Street," Mike says.

"That's this side of town."

"Should I try for her after work?" Mike asks.

"I'd rather not have to think about this all night long!"

"Me too, let's do it. You call her back."

Nickolas called Ms. Cordoba's number on his satellite phone, and left a message. Within 10 minutes, he had a return call. Ms. Cordoba was driving her car today and was halfway home. Good, he thought. If he could get her to meet within the hour, she would have little time to arrange surveillance or electronics. She enthusiastically, immediately agreed to meet him at the Blue Note at 5 p.m. She would drive directly there from where she was now.

Mike was smiling, having heard enough of the one-sided conversation to know that a meeting at the Blue Note in the corner booth virtually meant he had no work to do. It was already done.

"Great! That was a break! Do you want me there?"

"No, I don't think so. Tony will be there. I can handle the equipment. I'll call you after the meeting. In the meantime, let's keep this little escapade between you and me. We'll tell Phil and Tim in the morning when we have the whole story."

"Always," Mike says. "I'm in security."

"Okay. I'm off to the races. Call you later."

# LI

## THE BLUE NOTE

Nick was sitting in the corner booth at the Blue Note, nursing his Chardonnay, which was especially full-bodied, with lots of character. Tony was usually at the bar during these situations, but for reasons unknown to Nick, Tony had removed his jacket and shoulder holster and donned a Blue Note shirt and apron and had become a waiter in Nick's section. Doing a good job, too. Maybe he had some experience in college. He also noticed Betty Lou was not sitting anyone in the adjacent booths or tables in Nick's section.

Tony, playing his role to the maximum, dropped off an ice water and said, "Sir, is your Chardonnay to your liking? We also have La Crema on special tonight, two for only $5, if you would prefer?" His eyes full of mirth.

Nickolas played along. "Yes, my good man, everything is good. I noticed that this wine was especially good. Your taste in wine is respected and your price almost unbelievable."

"We also have free appetizers tonight if you would like to nibble on something while you're waiting."

"Gee, this is a special night here at the Blue Note. How about the cheese and fruit board?"

"You got it, sir. Coming right up."

Tony headed for his computer-screen station at about the time a very attractive, black-haired, black-eyed, olive-skinned young woman arrived across the room at Betty Lou's podium— probably asking for the Harvey table. In a moment she was following Betty Lou toward Nickolas' corner table. Nickolas' second and third and fourth impressions were: she is very attractive, she is wearing at least $1,000 worth of clothes and shoes and carrying a $400 purse and a $500 briefcase. Lastly, she is walking on a million dollar pair of legs! Like Mike said, "This is the whole package!"

Upon arriving table side, Betty Lou says, "Mr. Harvey, your guest, Ms. Cordoba." Ms. Cordoba extended her hand beneath a large blindingly white smile and clear sparkling eyes, jeweled ears, wrists, fingers and ankle. There was not one hair, blemish, mole, ounce of fat or frown line to diminish the total package, and two bulges below the shoulders accented the entire presentation.

Nick accepted the hand and the firm, dry handshake, while making positive eye contact with a smile and saying, "So nice to meet you Ms. Cordoba. Please have a seat."

Before leaving, Betty Lou says, "Ms. Cordoba, can I have William bring you a drink?"

Nickolas says to Betty Lou, "Betty Lou, you mean Peter. Peter's working tonight."

"Oh yes, that's right, Peter. What would you like, Ms. Cordoba?"

"I'll have what Mr. Harvey's having." To Mr. Harvey, "I'm assuming that's a Chardonnay?"

"Yes, ma'am, and a very good one, too; however, La Crema is on special tonight, two for $5." Betty Lou looked at Nick like he was possessed.

"I'll have the La Crema then. Thank you." Betty Lou departed the table perplexed, looking for Peter to place the order. Ms. Cordoba turned to Nick with a smile.

"Mr. Harvey, thank you for meeting with me and meeting with me quickly. I, and the people I represent, appreciate your trust and cordiality. This won't take long. I'm going to be straightforward with you. I was told you're a man who appreciates candor. Is that true?"

"Yes, it is. I respect the art of diplomacy when it doesn't take too much time to get to the negotiation part."

"I understand. It is not uncommon among men for them to want what they want when they want it."

"Don't get me wrong. I understand that foreplay is important—an investment in the future. But when foreplay is the beginning, the middle and the end, I lose my attention, interest and patience. Did we just change the subject? You haven't got your first drink yet."

She says, "I understand. I live in a world of men. They all are powerful. They all have big aspirations. They are all successful, if nowhere except in their sphere of influence. I've dealt successfully with a hundred of them. If you'll give me a chance, I'll deal successfully with you and we'll both get what we want. The best deals are a win-win. That's always my approach in any deal or negotiation, how to achieve a win-win. I believe in the case of your cause, I can do that for you and of course, for me."

Ms. Cordoba's Chardonnay arrived, delivered by Peter, along with the cracker, cheese and fruit board, with about twice the food as normal, and two small plates.

"May I be of further service, Mr. Harvey?" Peter says with a wry smile.

"Looks good to me, Peter, thank you."

Peter winked at Nick and left the table.

"Ms. Cordoba, I hope you like cheese and fruit with your wine."

"Yes, I do. Actually I am famished. Thank you. I'll cut up some of this cheese if you don't mind." She started cutting and serving them both on the small plates.

Nickolas gave her time to take a drink of her wine, while he threw down a couple pieces of cheese with a grape. She did likewise and washed it down with another sip of wine and wiped her beautiful mouth.

"How's that La Crema?" Nick asks.

"Very good. Lots of oak accents, a touch of fruit, good body, character, very nice. Two for one too, that's a generous deal. Good choice. This is a nice place, very reasonable prices."

"Thank you. From my point of view, it could be a special evening."

"Assuming you're talking about business, it is."

"You're assumption is correct. What's on the mind of the Executive Director of the Cuban Economic Development Committee?"

Juliana took another generous sip of her La Crema and seemed to sit back and settle into the cushions of the booth and into business mode. She reached for her black leather business bag.

"I think we've already completed the foreplay. Let's forego further preamble, why are you here, bottom line? I only drink two Chardonnays when I'm doing business, and this one is almost empty," Nickolas says.

"I understand, Mr. Harvey, here we go. Bottom line, I'm here to invite you, take you, to Cuba, to meet with high echelon members of the government about your ARC coalition's progress, goals and objectives."

This answer was the answer Nick had been almost desperately hoping for all afternoon. An open doorway to direct communications with the Cuban Government was absolutely essential to the success of his plan. He almost breathed a sigh of relief while trying to assure that he physically revealed nothing.

Trying to be cool, Nickolas says, "I assume this would occur on the QT?"

"QT?"

"Quiet," Nick says. "No one knows except those involved?"

"Yes, absolutely. We don't know any more about you than you know about us. We need to fully understand your objectives, motivations and strategies. If they are, in fact, what we've been lead to believe they are, we may be able to help one another."

"That, *help one another* thing bothers me," Nick replies. "I don't think your help would be productive to me. Don't misunderstand me. I know it takes two to tango. Every negotiation requires that a minimum of two parties agree to try to compromise. If you're suggesting that following an understanding of each others current basic strategic objectives, we could enter into a long-term series of discussions, negotiations to resolve a long list of existing issues, I might be able to agree, after giving it some thought. On the other hand, trying to help ARC with advice and/or money might cause more trouble than benefits."

"I'm not empowered to set the parameters of any future negotiation or even to agree that there will be a future negotiation. I'm empowered to invite you to a meeting in Havana where you can discuss your plan and objectives with the people who will decide. I can tell you that you have impressed them greatly with your ability to change public opinion in America about Cuba. While you're improving understanding of the past and present U.S.-Cuba relationship and creating change here in America, the same kind of change is slowly occurring in Cuba. You have nothing to loose, everything to gain."

"Yes, I've heard that a lot lately."

"Would this be a private meeting?"

"Yes, at our end we can assure that."

"With whom would I meet?"

"Three members of the Cuban Senate who represent the forces of change in Cuba."

"Would you be there?"

"Yes, I'll interpret for both parties when necessary although all of these people understand and speak English. But, they are not fluent."

"When do you want to do it? And how long a meeting do you foresee?"

"The sooner, the better. I see this meeting requiring four to five hours on the ground in Havana. You'll fly with me. I'll arrange everything, including the proper diplomatic authorizations."

"How many of my people may I take?"

"You will have no need for anyone other than yourself. Your security is assured by the Cuban Government."

Nick thought, she's right. If I bring along two or three people, what are they going to do, other than listen. A security person or two would be of no help in those circumstances, probably just increase tension.

"What subject matter do I need to prepare to discuss?"

"None. You already know the answers to the questions they will ask. Think of this meeting simply as an opportunity to meet and get to know some influential new business or political contacts. The people you will meet just want to get to know you better personally and take your measure in an unofficial and casual manner."

"What's in this for me besides a box of good Cuban cigars?"

"The two senators are good friends of Raul Castro and as a result, the Cuban military. The opportunity is indirect influence and potential access—assuming they like you, believe you and trust you."

"Okay, is it a dress blues and tennis shoes event?"

"Excuse me?"

"What do I wear?" Nick explains.

"We'll fly casual. Take a suit bag with your best tropical blue suit, white shirt, tie. We'll change on the ground in Havana. If you can, I suggest we depart Thursday afternoon at 3. That puts us on the ground in Havana at 6:30 p.m. The meeting venue is cocktails and dinner at a Havana hotel at 8 p.m.—that's cocktail hour in Havana. We'll depart Havana at about midnight for the return, being back here in D.C. about 4 a.m. Friday. No one will miss you or know you left, except perhaps, your wife."

"Yes, she would miss me. She lets me play late outside at night, occasionally, but she doesn't understand 4 a.m. or 5 a.m., for some reason."

"Neither would I," Juliana says, "being the old-fashioned Catholic girl that I am."

"For me to be gone this Thursday p.m. and Friday a.m., I will need to move some meetings and appointments around a little. Also, I'll need to meet with my security staff. They will have to know what I am up to. I'm confident that I can make it all fit, but how about giving me 24 hours to firm it up? My security staff is completely trustworthy."

"It's your decision to make. Just keep in mind that if an article appears in the Washington Post this week on this subject, your credibility with the Cuban Government will be gone."

"I understand, don't worry. I'll call you by 2 p.m. tomorrow."

# LII

## ARC HEADQUARTERS

Nickolas had finished the staff meeting with security at 7 p.m. He had invited the attendees to dinner, but no one really wanted to go. He could tell on this occasion that they were tired and wanted to go home and relax. It had been a long, hard afternoon, trying to decide whether to go to Cuba or not, at this time and without security. Secondarily, if they accepted the invitation, what did the trip require in the way of preparations, legalities, security, etc.? There were lots of serious issues to discuss and agree upon. It had taken all afternoon and the early evening, but they had got through it all. He was going. They would see that he was prepared.

Nickolas finished reading his mail and cosigning some checks in the hour following the meeting. He cleaned up his desk and left the office at 7:45 p.m. He took the elevator to the P-1 level of the parking garage. He had driven to work today, which was not his normal pattern, but he knew he would likely work late, but he didn't know how late, so he called security to cancel the limo and give his driver an unexpected day off. Security didn't mind; in fact, they thought it was good for Nickolas to mix up his ways and means of transportation. Today he was actually driving Liz's Jaguar sedan as she was being picked up by a friend today and going into NYC shopping.

He got into Liz's black Jaguar and let himself out of the security parking garage below the office buildings and headed for his Georgetown townhouse only a few miles away. He was relaxed and pleased with the work completed this day. But, he recognized he was still a little stressed and hyped up and wished he had taken time at his office for a glass of wine. But he hadn't thought of it—too much excitement today. Think of it. He was going to Cuba and going well ahead of his original plan.

Four blocks later he decided to stop, turn around and go back to the Blue Note and de-stress for half an hour. Elizabeth wouldn't be back from the city until midnight anyway. She and Bette were having dinner at Bernard's at 8 p.m., about now, he thought. He remembered he hadn't eaten since lunch. Maybe some fresh oysters or green-lipped mussels would be good with a cold Chardonnay. Suddenly, he was hungry. He turned around the block and headed back to the Blue Note.

# LIII

## THE BLUE NOTE

Nickolas entered the Blue Note and headed for the bar, saying 'hi' to Betty Lou. The bar was going pretty good at eight o'clock, and the dining room was full. The three-piece jazz ensemble was playing "Moon Glow."

He had stopped here enough times on the way home to know that Sam was bartender tonight. Nickolas called him by name as they shook hands and Sam said, "The usual?"

"Sam, it's always the same—Chardonnay. You pick. I'm easy. But remember, show me the bottle."

"You got it. The house wine tonight is Estancia."

Sam served Nick his drink, showed the bottle and Nick took a sip as Sam looked on.

"Good choice, Sam. Thank you. You're still batting a thousand." He took another sip and then settled down to look around at the crowd and the jazz trio playing some cool stuff at the far end of the room across the bar. He started to enjoy the change of pace, and the music, and relaxed a little. This is good, he thought.

"Sam, I believe I'll have the Oysters Rockefeller with a second Chardonnay in a few minutes," Nickolas says.

A moment or two later, he notices a man sitting two stools down bar from him. He was a muscular, heavyset, balding older man with thick reading glasses and a black mustache, perhaps 50 to 60 years old, sucking, not smoking, a large, long dark cigar with relish. On his left ear was a wireless phone device. He was in an animated conversation as if someone was sitting across from him. He was making notes in a small, cheap coil-ringed binder—and doing all this while he drank a large beer and consumed a small Margarita pizza.

The man is wearing a pale green dress shirt, open at the collar, over a pair of faded jeans, providing a mismatched, retired middle-class Western look, at best. However, upon closer observation of his jewelry, he betrayed his middle-class look as he was wearing a large diamond ring on his right hand, an expensive appearing diamond-studded wedding band on his left and a gold Rolex wristwatch the size of a hockey puck on his left arm. He sucked the cigar in the manner of one thoroughly experienced at enjoying the activity. If it was me, Nick thought, I would have replaced the beer with a glass of good French Cognac to properly set the scene.

The man was studying the notebook but looked up and caught Nickolas looking. Nick says, "Good evening, what's on your mind?"

The man looked up over the top of his reading glasses at Nickolas, then looked at the hockey puck watch, removed the reading glasses and started chewing his gum. Where the hell had the gum been while he was eating his pizza, Nick thought. The man says, "Let's sit at the corner on the end of the bar. I have a message from Big Ed."

He got up, took a wad of bills from his left trouser pocket and threw down three tens. A good tipper, Nick thought, figuring his bill looked like about $15 unless he had more than one beer. As Nick followed him to the corner of the bar, he noticed the older man had two to three inches of height on him and maybe 15 to 20 pounds. But it was old pounds, starting to settle in the waist. Nick felt he could probably take him in a fist fight if he hit him first, and if not, outrun him in a foot race if he had to. Believing that living to fight another day was much more important than valor, running was number one in his defensive tactics repertoire.

He reconciled this strategy by always getting back to the guy who made him run, but getting back on his terms, turf and time. *The three T's.* Having done that a number of times over the years, he had only had to run the second time twice. As it relates to those two guys, time was the factor. Nick was waiting until they were about to die and then he was going to kick their ass! With these particular two guys, it would probably still be a hell-of-a-contest. Some older men get soft, but make up for it by fighting slower and smarter, avoiding speed, controlling their breathing and energy. Becoming better defensively by necessity, they avoid being hit. Explained another way, they get smarter and less emotional in their old age. As a result, some of them can be hell to reckon with and you never really know until you get in there with them. Sometimes, that was too late. They each sat down on their corner of the bar.

"So, what's on your mind? Or Big Ed's?"

"Let me first introduce myself, Mr. Harvey. My name is Helio. Helio Rojas. Big Ed said to give you this envelope after I introduced myself."

Nickolas took a sip of his wine and opened the envelope, which had his name and full address upon it. The content was a simple and straightforward. It only said,

"Nick, please meet my good friend and personal guard for many years, until our meeting last week when I assigned him to protect you. You will rarely if ever see him, but if you do, now you know his interests are yours and, of course, mine, but yours first. Please keep this knowledge between the three of us. Please be aware, this man will die for you if he must. Please avoid these situations. 'H' is one of my very best friends. Should you decide to go to Cuba, he can't help you there, so be very careful; we know there are those who vehemently oppose ARC's goals in Havana. Good luck, call upon me if you need me—'Big.'"

"Helio, your boss gives you a very strong recommendation," Nickolas says.

"Yes, and he also gives you one. You're fortunate to have such a friend."

"Well, I am not sure we are friends yet, perhaps, more like associates, with a common business purpose."

Helio touches his heart three times with his right fist, and says,

"No, Mr. Harvey. Let me assure you. We *are* friends, very good friends."

# LIV

## GUANABO, CUBA

*JUNE*

Maria had risen earlier than planned from her nap with baby Jon, having heard noises in the kitchen. It was late afternoon. She nursed her baby and put him back to bed. Then quietly she entered the kitchen and helped her mother prepare what was likely to be the family's last meal together for a long time. They were both conscious of that fact, and in their depression, had little to say to one another.

As the meal approached being done, Rose knew that it was time to wake Manuel and Miguel. She knew Manuel had slept fitfully, if at all, since he lay down at 4 p.m. Miguel was lying on his bed, fully dressed and wide awake, when she entered his room to wake him. The house was strangely quiet and devoid of conversation as all four went about their final preparations quietly, each carrying the weight of the undertaking of a dangerous journey that would commence in about an hour, and would dramatically affect the future lives of all of them.

What had seemed like such a good idea over the past 12 months did not seem to be such a good idea now to Rose. She was losing her daughter and her baby grandson. Maybe she would see them again in her lifetime and maybe not. The future, particularly in Cuba, was not something you could predict. Rose had been tearing up for days in anticipation of the loss, which was now at hand. Internally she felt lost, very depressed, anxious and helpless.

"Mama, your tears are falling into the eggs!" Maria says, as she pats her mother on the back in a half hug. "If you keep that up, they'll be too salty!" she says, trying to cheer her mother.

"I know! I know! I'll be okay after you and the baby leave. I'll have one last big, long, long cry and then I'll be okay," she says. "I love you so much, Maria, and little Jon. I don't know how I will get along without you."

"Miguel will be married soon and he will make you a houseful of grandbabies!"

"I hope so, but none will replace you and little Jon. I love you so much!" she cries.

"I know, Mama, and I love you, as does little Jon." Maria turns away, her own eyes filling with tears, as she pretends to straighten the simple table setting. She thought to herself, this is far harder to do than I thought. I have a loving family here! How could I have ever thought I needed to leave?

Miguel enters the kitchen, and sees the sad faces. "Mama, Maria, this is not supposed to be a sad day! It's supposed to be a happy day! It's a new beginning, in the new world, for Maria and baby Jon, who will carry on the family name in America!"

"I know, son, and I suppose someday I'll feel that way but not tonight. Forgive me for my sad face. It's just that… that…" Rose starts to lose control again.

"I know, Mama, but this may be our last family meal together in a long time. Let's try to get through it without tears."

Manuel enters the kitchen with a smile, saying, "Everybody having a good time?" He hugs Rose, gives her a kiss, and wipes the tears from her cheeks. He hugs her again and whispers in her ear, "Be strong, Rose. You can cry later, after we're gone. You'll upset everyone."

"Okay, Manuel, okay. I'll be strong."

Manuel takes his seat and says, "Let's everyone sit down and enjoy a nice family dinner together. It may be the last one in a long time."

"Jesus! Papa," says Miguel, "we all know that!"

Manuel says, "Let us hold hands while I ask for God's blessing on this family, the food we are about to share and the journey we are about to begin."

# LV

## EN ROUTE TO SECRET - EMBARKATION SITE

Miguel was driving and Manuel was in the passenger seat of an old 1940s International one-ton, stake bed truck with a canvas cover over the body and back gate. Maria and baby Jon were hidden in the back. It was 9 p.m. and there was not a lot of traffic, but still enough to make their vehicle inconspicuous among many, as they made their way west of Havana and toward the north, having picked up their other five passengers. The further they got out of the city, the less traffic there was on the roads, and the less likely anyone would care or notice.

Finally they left the paved road, turning onto a rock road that leads toward the beach. After a couple of miles, they turned north onto a sand and grass road and, at the proper spot, Miguel pulled off the road, and the truck followed a set of old tracks into a grove of trees, which closed behind them. He did a U-turn about a hundred yards into the grove and stopped, turning off the engine. Miguel turned to his father and says, "Papa, you sure you don't want me to do this?"

"We've been through that, son, don't start again now. You're engaged to a wonderful girl. When I get back, we're going to start planning on how to get you that cottage you two want. I got some ideas. Now, let's get everybody unloaded."

Manuel and Miguel exit the cab of the truck and move toward the rear. Manuel unties the rear tarp, and removes two rear slatted gates from the truck body, setting them against one side of the rear of the truck. He mounts the rear platform of the body and moves several stacks of lobster traps to one side, while saying,

"Okay everybody, you can talk now." They quietly stand up and stretch.

"You can hand me down your gear and then I'll help you off the truck."

Everybody slowly rose, stretching their backs, rubbing their butts and muttering to one another. They slowly get their belongings together, and start handing them down to Miguel, who sets the seabags and soft suitcases in a pile behind him. He then starts helping people jump down from the bed of the truck, which the two young people accomplish with ease, while the three older people have to sit down first, scoot off the edge with Miguel's help, and then jump the last couple of feet.

The last person off was Maria, who first handed little Jon to Miguel. Maria then sat down and easily reached the ground with the help of Manuel and Miguel. When she lands, however, Miguel did not let go and while holding his nephew, brought his sister into his arms along with the baby in his left, and in an unusual moment of deep emotion, held them both and wept silently on Maria's shoulder, saying, "Little sister, little Jon, I love you both so much! I am going to miss you terribly! I don't want you to go, but I know that you must." He kisses his sister, hugging her fiercely and says, "Don't forget me. Remember if you ever need me, just let me know. I'll swim to America if I have to."

"Miguel, I know, I know. We'll miss you, too. We'll never forget you, or Rebecca either."

Holding little Jon in front of him with two hands, Miguel says, "Little man, don't you forget your uncle either."

"He won't, Miguel. I promise. We'll all be together again one day. I know it. I just know it!"

Miguel hands little Jon to his sister, and notices that she is not wearing her baby sling, "Where is your baby sling?" he asks.

"In the rush, I forgot it. I'll fashion something when I get to the boat."

"Okay, but that's a long, hard walk from here."

"We'll be okay. Don't worry, I'm strong."

"I know you are. The sling just helps prevent an accidental drop of the baby if you fall."

The group is starting to get organized to move, following Manuel's instructions that it's time to move toward the beach.

"I know, I'll be careful," Maria says to Miguel. "Bye. Say bye for me to Rebecca. Be careful driving home, bye." Anthony, overhearing some of the conversation, walks over to Miguel and says, "Don't worry about Maria and little Jon. I'll help them to the boat and thereafter, as well." Miguel is too emotional to respond, and simply hugs Anthony tightly.

Maria, carrying little Jon, follows the group toward the beach. Miguel stands at the rear of the truck, looking after them. Manuel turns back to say goodbye to Miguel and help Miguel unload Rufus' three-wheel bike. That being done, Manuel says, "Miguel, you know I love you. I'm very proud of you. You're my best friend. Don't worry about us. I will get them to America and I'll be back home in two to three days. Take care of your mother."

Miguel hugs his father, unable to speak through his emotion. Finally, he struggles to say, "I love you, too, Father," as Manuel turns to follow the group and hoists his seabag back to his shoulder. They all disappear quickly into the tropical undergrowth and trees, their murmurs slowly fading into the evening breeze. Miguel pushes Rufus' bicycle into a grove of trees. Rufus will use it to get himself and Fidel back to town later that night.

Miguel finds himself suddenly all alone. He feels very emotional, lonely and apprehensive. He inspects the truck body. He repositions the lobster traps, and puts the two rear gates back in their slots on the body. He lowers the tarp down and ties it. He wipes his tear-streaked face with his hands and pushes his hair back. He re-enters the cab of the truck and drives the short distance back to the sand road. He pulls onto it, stops, gets out and, finding a proper-sized, freshly fallen palm frond, obliterates the truck tracks leading off the old road. He remounts the truck cab and heads for home, knowing his mother, especially tonight, wouldn't sleep until he got there. He knew she would require his constant presence until his father returned home safely in two or three days.

# LVI

## A DESERTED, OLD SUGARCANE PROCESSING MILL

Manuel leads the group through the sandy pine tree and palm forest toward the beach and the deserted, old sugarcane processing mill and its dilapidated pier. He knew the walk would take about 30 minutes, considering the likely pace of his passengers, carrying their baggage.

Manuel had planned for a full moon and a cloudless night; however, the old road had not been used in perhaps 25 years or more and was heavily overgrown. He kept getting too far ahead of the others, and every 50 yards or so, he would stop and let them pass, while encouraging those who needed it. About midway to the beach, Manuel was sweating and knew the older couple, Mr. and Mrs. Rafael, must need a rest. A rocky outcropping just ahead would provide some seating, and it was open to the moonlight, so he stopped there to rest the group.

In a minute or two, Maria and Anthony, carrying baby Jon, and Joseph Fernando joined Manuel, settling into and onto the rocks. Manuel asks Maria,

"Maria, you making it okay?"

"Yes, it's just a little warm in this forest without a breeze. There's a breeze in the treetops, but not down here."

"Anthony," says Manuel, "are you and baby Jon getting along okay?"

"Yes, he's a real good baby. I think he enjoys walking at night in the forest."

"Joseph," says Manuel, "how are you doing? Where's your mother?"

"She's right behind us, sir, leading Mr. and Mrs. Rafael. They don't see so good at night. Mrs. Rafael almost fell down, back there a ways, but I caught her in time. I carried her bag most of the way," he says proudly.

"You're a thoughtful young man for your age," Manuel says. I know your mother is very proud of you."

"Thank you, sir."

At that moment, Mrs. Fernando arrived with Mr. and Mrs. Rafael, who were moving a little slow, but otherwise in good shape. They apparently knew how to pace themselves for their age.

Manuel says, "Mrs. Rafael, are you okay? Joseph said you almost took a tumble."

"Yes, almost. I caught my toe on a tree root. Fortunately, Joseph was right beside me and caught me. He's strong for his age and size!"

"Thank you, Mrs. Rafael," says Joseph, "but also realize that your baggage doesn't weigh very much. You're pretty thin."

Mr. Rafael joins the conversation. "Yes, she is, and she keeps me that way, too. Of course, it's not hard to stay thin in Castro's Cuba. But still, I am told by my doctor that thin is good for long life, and Mrs. Rafael and I expect to live long in the land of milk and honey—the good old U.S.A!"

Manuel says, "I hope you do, but that milk and honey may put some pounds on the two of you, which probably won't hurt."

Mrs. Fernando says, "I need to talk to Mrs. Rafael to learn her dietary secrets. I could afford to lose some weight, although I have no idea what I weigh."

Joseph says, "Oh, Mother, you're always saying that. You look great the way you are."

"Thank you, son, but if I'm going to find you a new, rich American father, I'm going to have to improve my appearance."

"Oh, Mom! You're beautiful, don't worry about that. Men are chasing you all the time!"

"Yes, poor Cuban men with no future!"

Oh, Mom! We'll do just fine. In a few years, I'll be able to take care of both of us and send money home to grandma and grandpa. Just wait, you'll see."

"Well, like I've said, Joseph, if you're going to do that, you'll have to finish school and go to college, so plan accordingly."

Mr. Rafael says, "Joseph, your mother's right. In America you can achieve anything you wish. But, you have to work very hard and compete with a lot of smart people."

"I know, Mr. Rafael. I've got a plan for mom and me. I am going to work harder and longer than anyone else."

Mr. Rafael says, "Well, Joseph, long and hard goes a long way in America. Maybe I can help you when the time is right. We'll stay in touch with your mother."

Manuel looked at the group and smiled to himself and Maria, nodding his head in approval. The few people he had chosen to accompany Maria and himself were worthy of his extra efforts and risk. They had paid a fee, but each according to his own ability. The Rafaels, as retired jewelers, had paid the most. Only Manuel understood the potential outcome of Mr. Rafael telling Joseph that he might be able to help him at some point in time. He could only guess at how many diamonds the Rafaels were exporting to the United States via his boat on this trip.

Manuel stood, threw his duffel bag over his right shoulder, grabbed Mrs. Rafael's bag and threw it over his left, and said,

"Folks, it's perhaps 15 to 20 minutes to the beach so you'll hear the sound of the surf soon. Let's go to America!"

# LVII

## A DESERTED PIER ON THE COAST, WEST OF HAVANA

Manuel, nearing the beach and hearing the loud surf, rushed ahead of the others, running from the high dunes to the low dunes and onto the old wooden pier that was a feature of a long-abandoned sugar mill, warehouse and caretaker's home, which was nearby but not seen from their location. Manuel was concerned that a high surf may have disrupted their carefully laid plans at the last possible moment. But he found it was just his paranoia. He was so tense and stressed at this point that he thought his imagination had emphasized the sound of the surf, or had it? He stopped and looked again; his heart was beating like a drum in his chest. He leaned over, hands on knees, and took eight or ten deep breaths. In his mind, he was saying to himself, calm down, calm down, don't let Rufus see you out of control. He rose. Rufus was out there on the dilapidated dock beyond the surf line where Miguel and Manuel had left him late yesterday, using Manuel's boat, *Resolute*. Manuel's breathing returned to normal as those fastest among his followers caught up with him.

"Everything okay, captain?" Anthony says.

"Yes, son, everything is fine. You wait here until everyone gets here. When I see that everyone is here, I'll return and get you. Don't come onto the pier without me. It's too dangerous. Keep everyone right here in the tree line as a group. Let them rest, get their breath. I'll be back. Just wait here."

Manuel threaded his way slowly out the pier toward Rufus, using the bright light of the full moon and following a trail of small white seashells he had placed on the pier deck to avoid the danger areas. In a few minutes he was in the arms of Rufus.

"Rufus! Are you okay?"

"Yes, captain, it was a long night and day, but the sound of the sea is music to me, awake or asleep. The wind rose somewhat with the setting sun and increased as the air cooled. However, I believe in a few hours it will settle down. Our boat has been riding it out quite well. It's a little damp so let's be careful when we load. I've tied down the ladder and secured the boat to it. You can bring out the others."

"We'll have to be careful; it looks like we have three to four feet of running seas here right now. The old couple might be a problem."

"If we get Anthony on the boat first, he can help take care of them at the bottom. I'll handle the top."

"Good thing you repaired that old ladder."

"Yes, we'd be sitting here until this sea stopped running, otherwise."

"Okay, we'll start loading with the seabags. They'll use the bags to sleep on or lean on anyway. We just need to remember which bag goes with which seat."

"That will be the young fellas' job."

"Auh, yes, you're right. I think they're all at the beach, if these old eyes aren't deceiving me. I'll get them out here. We need to get under way. It's almost eleven o'clock."

Manuel returned to the beach. The group was sitting on their bags in the sand.

"Everyone here?"

"Yes."

"Everybody okay?" Manuel asks the group at large.

They all nodded their heads or murmured in the affirmative.

"Okay, on your feet and grab your bags. You two are to follow me step for step when we get on the pier. You others follow them step for step. We're going to hand your gear down to the boat when we get out there, and then you'll enter the boat in the order of your seating, and then we'll set sail for America and freedom. Let's go! Follow me. Be careful, this old pier is missing a lot of planks."

The group gathered their gear. Manuel is in front, and Maria's in the middle with little Jon. They left the sand and carefully followed their leader to the end of the pier where Rufus was waiting. They stopped, dropped their bags and with concern, looked off the edge of the pier at the 10-foot drop to the small sailboat below, which was bobbing on the swells of the rough and noisy sea, as it crashed against the aging piers underpinnings, shaking the entire surface. There were several gasps of surprise and fear. The old couple held one another close in excited, fearful conversation.

Manuel expected this reaction and did not want to give them too much time to think about it. "Quickly," he says to Anthony, "show them how easy it is to get into that boat. Rufus and I are going to hand these bags down to you. You put them beneath the proper seat. It's damp, so be careful, take your time."

Anthony says, "Aye, aye captain," and went down the ladder. Near the bottom he stopped, got the timing of the waves and on an upsurge, stepped easily onto the gunwale of the boat hull and then into the rear bottom of the boat. With Manuel in the middle of the ladder, Rufus up top, and Anthony down below, they handed down all the baggage. Rufus says,

"Now folks, Anthony made getting into the boat look a lot easier than it is. However, he's on the boat and he'll be telling you where and when to step in, and he'll help you. Just remember, only step in and let go of the ladder at the same time, when he tells you—not before, not later or you will likely get hurt. Trust Anthony, do what he says, when he says it, and you'll be okay. Remember, when you step into the boat, you must let go of the ladder."

Slowly, carefully, Rufus, Manuel and Anthony got everybody safely on the boat and seated. Manuel came up the ladder to the pier deck and Rufus.

"All aboard and accounted for, captain," Rufus says.

"Rufus, I can't thank you enough. Give me an embrace and your best wishes. Pray for us. Thank you! Thank you so much! Be careful going back to the city. God protect you. Good Lord willing, I'll see you and Miguel in 48 hours off point La Playa in *Resolute,* if not, in 72 hours. Goodbye Rufus, see you soon."

# LVIII

## SETTING SAIL

Manuel was down the ladder and in the rear of the boat moments later and at the rudder. He yelled to Anthony in the forward seat, "Release the forward spring line." At the same time, Manuel released the aft spring line and pulled all the line aboard. He ordered the bow dock line to be released and he released the aft dock line. The little boat, which was pointed seaward, fell a point or two to the port, and the onshore wind caught the partially reefed sail. The boat heeled and moved slowly off into the night.

As the boat left the pier, Manuel let out all the mainsail. The shore, and the noise of the surf quickly fell away, as the boat heeled further, gaining speed as the open sea quickly absorbed the little boat with the only sounds being those of the water hissing by the hull and the periodic tapping of the sail lines against the short wooden mast.

Manuel trimmed the mainsail, set the foresail and found a comfortable angle to the waves, whose intensity was relieved by the deeper water of the ocean. Suddenly, all the noise, stress and fear of the journey, from the truck ride to boarding the boat was gone. The clear night sky was bejeweled by a million diamonds as far as the eye could see. The sea air was so clean you could taste it. And the boat was driving through the waves like a hot knife through butter. Everyone felt the relief of being under way. Manuel could tell by just looking at the nearby faces and their body language. He thought that with the stress of tonight, and for that matter, the last several days, they would all fall asleep soon to the music of the sea. He smiled to himself, relieved to be at sea, in his element, in his comfort zone. He thought we're now in the arms of Mother Nature and in the hands of the good Lord. Please God, let me safely pilot these good people to America and to the better life there. And yes, a safe trip home for me to my Rose and Miguel. Please, help me do this.

# LIX

## AT 30,000 FEET ALTITUDE EN ROUTE TO HAVANA

Nickolas and Ms. Cordoba and two other U.S. Cuban Embassy personnel, returning to Cuba on annual leave, had boarded the Cuban executive jet aircraft at Reagan International about two hours ago. They were now somewhere off the coast of the Carolinas. All four guests had each taken a two-seat row for the five-hour flight and gotten as comfortable as one could get in this older commercial Falcon 50 ex-commuter carrier.

Nickolas had been reviewing his notes from the staff meeting of yesterday and creating an outline for the meeting tonight. He was in deep thought and, as a result, the time was passing quickly. Juliana was similarly engaged. She had unfortunately chosen a seat two rows behind him so he didn't have the pleasure of looking at her for five hours. When she passed him boarding the plane, she had said that they would visit later, before landing. He continued to think about Juliana. "Sharp cookie," he thought, and a real looker, as are many Cuban woman. It's in their genes—the black hair, black eyes, golden skin, white teeth, well-developed bodies, nice butts. What was the genetic purpose of those unique butts? Childbearing, he guessed, or maybe generations of stoop labor? He didn't know, but he found genetic development and physical variables in human beings interesting. He thought, I need to buy a good book on the subject, what would it be titled? Perhaps, the genetic development of boobs and butts by race? His mind returned to business and he continued his task until falling to sleep to the drone of the airplane somewhere off the coast of Georgia.

One hour later he awoke to the gentle shaking of his shoulder by Juliana, who was leaning over him from the aisle saying, "Nickolas, Nickolas, wake up."

Nickolas opened his eyes, but he was still in the fog of awakening. He looked into Juliana's ample cleavage, only a foot away. "Are we there?" he says, raising his eyes.

"No, we have maybe an hour to go. We had to change course and approach Havana from the west. There's bad weather coming in from the southeast. Nothing to worry about. Our change is just precautionary. Could be raining when we land. We're instructed to fasten our seat belts and continue staying in our seats for the remainder of the flight. If you need to use the restroom, now is a good time."

"I'm okay."

"Do we need to talk? Do you want me to sit with you?"

"Not necessary. I think we've covered everything. But you're certainly welcome to join me."

"We'll have time in the car once we land if there are any last-minute issues. I'll see you on the ground in beautiful Havana."

Juliana left Nickolas with a big smile and a pat on his shoulder and returned to her seat. Nickolas stretched, cleaned up his work, spread across the window seat and adjacent serving table. He flipped the table up and locked it. Filed his papers in his bag. Took a big shot of water from his bottle. Hooked his seat belt and settled in to his own thoughts again for the last hour.

The plane vibrated slightly as it hit the first rough spot on its way around the approaching weather. Out the right side of the plane, it was still sunny, the sun perhaps two, three hours from its resting place over the horizon. To the east out the left-hand window, Nickolas could see the darker clouds in the distance starting to pile up. He thought, too early in the season for a hurricane and if there had been a potential, he would have heard about it. It's probably a somewhat localized rainstorm, which occurred almost daily in the Caribbean in the summer. These thunderstorms could develop out of nowhere relatively quickly.

They were over the Gulf of Mexico now, west of the Bay of Florida. The Florida Keys could be seen off to the left in the distance. The pilot had reduced altitude in preparation for his landing in Havana.

The sun was falling in the far west in a spectacular display of red, yellow and orange as the pilot brought the plane heading into the northeast, in a slow descending bank, which lined him up to land at Havana's International Airport. Nickolas was intent upon seeing everything that he could from his elevated vantage point. He discovered quickly that Havana was not in the flight path, but was up ahead to the north. He could see the city in the distance and could tell that it stretched a considerable distance in all directions, much bigger than he had thought. He could detect little in the way of industrial smoke typical of heavy industry. The city was laid out by the Spaniards 300 years ago in a basic grid pattern, starting at the Bay of Havana and moving outward to the southwest and east.

# LX

## AT SEA
## TEN MILES OFF
## THE CUBAN COAST

Manuel rested at the rudder, realizing that when they got to the edge of the Gulf Stream and its fast river of water, moving at three to four knots, that they would definitely pick up speed and likely find some decent wind. Shouldn't be far now, he guessed.

The two younger men, Anthony and Joseph, had been rowing for nearly an hour. As they left shore, the breeze that had moved them off the dock had died a few hours later. The rhythmic sound of the oarlocks had lulled the other passengers to sleep. They were spread all over the bottom of the boat like sardines in a can, with their heads resting on their soft seabags and their bodies on the extra sails and canvas cover. The lines snapped the mast, as the short boom with mainsail switched back and forth, and the little boat glided over the slow moving ocean swells— soon to end their journey as they washed ashore in America.

# LXI

## VIP TERMINAL HAVANA AIRPORT

Juliana was suddenly sitting behind Nickolas on the edge of her seat and pointing out Nickolas' side window saying, "Welcome to Cuba. That's the Cuban coastline below us." As the plane continued on its approach from the northwest, the dark, stacked thunderheads in the distant southeast were readily apparent. But it was not raining yet.

Juliana continued to point out features of interest as they approached the airport. Suddenly, they were on the ground. A good, almost gentle landing. The roar of the engine brakes. The gravity effect, the brake release, and the turn onto a taxi runway. Nickolas thought, I'm in Havana! Life is an amazing thing!

The plane taxied to a smaller, private aircraft debarkation terminal, did a 180-degree power turn and shut down the engines. What a relief, he thought. They all gathered their personal items and awaited the opening of the door by the copilot. That done, they all threaded their way forward with their bags and down the planes narrow folding stairway to terra firma. Nickolas stepped to the side at the bottom of the ladder and let Juliana pass. As she did so, she says,

"Let's go, someone must be meeting us inside."

"Give me a minute, Juliana. I need to soak up this atmosphere a little."

Juliana stopped, set her two bags down and says,

"Okay, but just for a minute. We're a little late already due to avoiding the storm, and it will rain soon. That's probably why no one is here to greet us yet."

Nickolas did a slow 360-degree turn where he stood on the pavement, soaking up and mentally indexing all that he could see. Not what I expected, thought Nickolas, mildly surprised at the size and busy nature of the José Martí International Airport.

Nickolas' thoughts were suddenly interrupted by a tire squeal. He turned around quickly to see a large military type vehicle at speed, turning in his direction, having entered the plane debarking area from the right. He half turned to Juliana to ask her a question, but upon seeing the surprise on her face, he knew the answer. She was not expecting that kind of greeting.

His first thought, shit! I am going to die in Cuba! His second thought was, it's my own fault for coming down here without my own security or at least my weapon. Those thoughts flashed through his brain in a millisecond while, at the same time, his instinctive defensive body actions were being messaged by another part of his brain and his feet were moving before he even knew where they were taking him. They were taking him toward Juliana, who was near, but the one, two, three steps and leap seemed to take forever, and his skin crawled, anticipating the first gunshots hitting his back. He tackled Juliana at the hips, taking her down, as a burst of automatic weapons fire went over their heads as they fell. Another burst, then another burst. Then handgun fire.

Juliana, totally surprised, says, "Get off my back, I can't breathe!"

Nickolas now heard more tire screeching down by the airfield gate and more automatic weapons fire. The gunfire only lasted a few seconds and then stopped as the vehicle passed the rear of the plane. He says to Juliana, "Just stay still. We don't know what's going on. Where the hell are the people who were supposed to meet us?" Nickolas rises to his knees to look around.

Juliana, still on the pavement, says, "I don't know. The car should have met the plane when we arrived."

"Well, I hope to hell that wasn't it!"

"Obviously not. Don't even think that way."

"Let's move behind the boarding ladder." Nickolas rolled with Juliana in his arms about six times toward the plane's ladder. The car had passed behind the plane's tail, and Nickolas and Juliana were partially shielded by the plane. The pilot was at the top of the stairs, struck dumb by what he was hearing and seeing. He yelled at Juliana in Spanish to get up the stairs quickly and they both did, Nickolas pushing Juliana to the floor on her stomach between the seats, where he covered her with his body.

The pilot, still dumbfounded, stood at the head of the aisle in the flight deck threshold. Nickolas heard another screech of rubber, saw the pilot, and yelled, "Get down! Get down!" The pilot stepped forward instead to look out the passenger window for the car. There was another two long bursts of automatic fire from the car, which stitched a series of holes down the fuselage of the plane, both above and below window height. The pilot took one of these right in the eye and was dead before he fell into the seats across the aisle. Glass, aluminum and plastic rained down on Nickolas and Juliana, but they were not hit from this second attack. Juliana wiggled. Nickolas said, "Stay down! Stay still! Play dead!" They remained still for what seemed like 20 minutes, but was only five, before the Cuban military boarded the plane, having secured the area. The attackers were gone, disappearing as fast and unexpectedly as they had appeared.

In spite of the attack upon them and all the excitement immediately following that event, Juliana and Nickolas were gathered up by the Cuban Government security personnel and quickly whisked away from the government's private air terminal for the 18-mile ride to downtown Havana. Both Juliana and Nickolas were high on adrenaline. It would take the entire ride to downtown for them to get themselves back together and under emotional control. They were told that the meeting location was being switched from the Hotel Santa Isabel to the Hotel Inglaterra for security reasons.

# LXII

## HOTEL INGLATERRA - HAVANA, CUBA

Nickolas and Juliana were met at the back of the hotel's truck delivery dock by armed military and were escorted through a large storage room to a service elevator, where they were taken to the second-floor conference center and an area of meeting rooms.

"Stop," Juliana said in Spanish to the guards as they approached a restroom area. "We must clean up and change. We'll do that right here while you guard the doors. It will only take us a few minutes."

The lead guard looked at one of his crew, whispered to him and sent him on to the meeting room to advise the hosts of a short delay.

Nickolas and Juliana hurried into their respective restroom to clean up as best they could and to change clothes.

They both returned to the hallway in minutes and to their guards, looking totally refreshed and ready for a Saturday night date. They made a handsome couple. Moments later they were ushered into the meeting room, and Nickolas met his hosts.

Three men were standing in front of a portable bar in suits and ties, each with a highball glass in his hand and a smile on his face.

"Juliana, it is my honor to introduce everyone and to have you both here," Mr. Ramos says. "Mr. Harvey, although this visit is short, we look forward to having you back to Havana soon and to showing you our beautiful city in the full light of day so to speak."

"Yes," says Senator Perez, "and on your next visit, we guarantee no surprise welcoming parties. We heard about the trouble at the airport and do not yet know who the perpetrators were, but I expect to know soon. We can only apologize with deepest sincerity and thank God that neither you nor Juliana were injured. This kind of thing simply does not occur in our country. We're absolutely amazed that it did and we're very embarrassed. You're our invited guest, a secret guest. Very few people in our government know of your visit."

Senator Marini adds, "And, those who did know were close to us, other than the Cuban military security police, who are supposed to be above suspicion in such matters. However, in this case, I wonder, since it was the security police who failed to meet your plane at landing time. They say they were at the airport at your original landing time, but left for a break when your plane was delayed due to weather."

The senators were all members of the Cuban Government from various cities in Cuba, including one from Havana. They seemed to be friendly, animated and even jovial, probably trying to reduce any lingering tension from the airfield "incident," as they apologetically referred to it. There was no bartender and Nickolas was uncertain whether to help himself or wait for an invitation. He was certain he needed a glass of wine. Juliana read his mind, stepped to the bar and pulled an uncorked bottle of California Chardonnay out of its ice bucket, selected a large wine glass and poured him and herself a generous glass. She hands Nickolas his and then says,

"Gentlemen, a toast, *'Viva Cuba!'* It's good to be home, even if only for a few hours." Everyone joined in the toast.

Nick thought, I hope she doesn't get the kind of a reception we received at the airport every time she comes home. But, he says, "*Viva Cuba!*" raising his glass.

Senator Marini continues, "As I was saying, those personnel sent to pick you and Juliana up left for 30 minutes to get coffee down the street, leaving the gate closed, but unlocked. Your flight was actually 45 minutes late. Security heard the gunfire as they were sitting outside the café and returned just as the terrorists completed their second attack on your plane. Both terrorists are dead by the way, Mr. Harvey—one driver and one shooter. The only other fatality was one of the pilots, as you know."

"What happened to other pilot?" Nickolas asks. "I don't remember seeing him at the end."

Marini answers, saying, "The copilot's job is to disembark the plane first, assuring the ladder and rails are in place, and then to help passengers get off with their luggage. The first attack happened to occur when everyone was on the ground heading to the terminal, except you, Juliana and the pilot, who were last off. The others watched the attack from inside the terminal."

"Including the copilot?" Nickolas asks.

"Yes."

"Is that normal procedure?"

"No, but he said the women had both hands full of luggage, so he went to the building with them to open the door and protect them."

"Very fortuitous in retrospect," Nick says.

"Yes," Perez says, "but likely an innocent action. Mr. Lopez has been a pilot for our government for a number of years. Obviously, considering that he flies frequently between Washington and Havana, we trust him completely."

"Yes," Nick says, "you're right. I hadn't considered that implication."

Ramos, trying to conclude, says, "In any event, Mr. Harvey, once again, please accept our deepest apologies and be assured that we will get to the bottom of the matter. Obviously, there will be no publicity in Cuba about this near-tragic attempt on your life. I hope you will agree that there will be no publicity in America either."

"Yes, it's agreed. The publicity would not favor my efforts in America, nor yours here at home. I say that assuming that our goals are the same, the reconciliation of U.S.-Cuba relations?"

Ramos answers, "Yes, our general goals are the same." He nods at his two friends. "However, there are many others in government and elsewhere in Cuba who might not agree. Our purpose in inviting you here tonight is to privately get to know you better, Mr. Harvey, and to generally exchange views on the matter of what you call normalization or reconciliation. Does that sound agreeable, Mr. Harvey?"

"Yes, I would like to do that."

"Good. Juliana, will you refill our drinks and join us over by the fireplace?"

The men move to a grouping of two facing sofas with occasional chairs facing the empty fireplace. Mr. Ramos takes a chair, as does Nickolas. The other two men each take a couch. Between Nickolas and Mr. Ramos is a triangular side table matching the angle of the chairs, with a lamp and a nicely carved mahogany box toward the front. Mr. Ramos turns the top side of the box back and says, "Cigar, Mr. Harvey?"

"No, thank you. I used to do that but no longer."

"These are special, Mr. Harvey. You cannot get a better cigar anywhere in the world than this one."

"I believe it. I have some friends who would do almost anything for a good Cuban cigar."

"Tell you what, Mr. Harvey, when you leave, take this box and whatever cigars are left home with you as a little remembrance of this occasion."

Juliana had served everyone a fresh drink and was sitting down next to Mr. Perez. Mr. Ramos says, "Juliana, don't let Mr. Harvey forget. The box and cigars are his."

Juliana nodded in confirmation. Mr. Ramos completed his cigar preparation ceremony, using folding cutting tools and a gold cigar lighter from his right jacket pocket. The cigar ignited as he rolled it in his mouth, and he pulled on it three times to get lift off. Lift off achieved, he blew smoke into the higher air, settled back into his chair and took a sip of what had to be his third Manhattan. Nick was already starting to like the guy, who apparently was the alpha dog of this pack.

Mr. Ramos then says, "Mr. Harvey, would it be okay if I called you Nickolas?"

"Yes, it would. I would prefer it."

"Good, as I said earlier, we want to get to know you. You may call me Antoine, if you like."

"Thank you, Antoine, I will."

"And you may call Mr. Perez, Lewis, and Mr. Marini, Ramone. We are now all on a first-name basis. Let's all get comfortable, too. Let's get these jackets off. Havana has got far too much humidity for jackets. I much prefer the carbone. You know the carbone, Nickolas?" They were all removing jackets, folding them and laying them on the nearby sofa table.

"Yes, I do. I occasionally I wear one when I'm in South Florida or elsewhere in the Caribbean. It's a very practical style."

"Yes, Nickolas. In Cuba, even the well-to-do, do not have the level of air conditioning that the average American enjoys."

"I know, but remember, in America, the average American did not have air conditioning until perhaps the '70s, not that long ago actually. Many Americans do not have it today. My family did not have a television set until I was 10."

"In Cuba," adds Lewis, "almost every family has a television set."

"Yes," Nickolas says, "but black and white, not color."

"True," Lewis says, "but color is not essential to enjoying the news from around the world."

"True," agrees Nickolas, "my family did not have color TV until I was 15."

"Were you brought up poor, Nickolas?" Ramone asks.

"Not poor, maybe lower middle-class. We always had shelter, food, clothes on our back. I was the oldest of four, but I went to school. I didn't have to work, we got by. My father was a self-taught auto mechanic. He always had work. He had an eighth-grade education. He died shortly after he finally got that color TV set for the family."

"Antoine asks, "You lost your father at 15, Nickolas?"

"Yes, I did."

"And you were the oldest?"

"Yes, I was."

"I am surprised you got through high school and college. U of Illinois, correct?"

"Yes. You have done your homework, Antoine."

"You would be disappointed in me if I had not, correct?"

"Correct, Antoine." They raised their drinks in salute to one another and smiled. Antoine went on to say,

"We've all come from small beginnings in this room, Nickolas. Fidel and the Revolution are likely the only reasons we are here with you tonight. The Revolution, like your United States Marine Corps ROTC program, gave poor people the opportunity to become educated. We took advantage of it, all of us, and here we are. What do they say, 'Birds of a feather…'"

"Yes, Antoine, 'Birds of a feather flock together,' as they say. I do believe we are *all* birds of a feather, but we've not flown together in a long, long time. My dream is that all of us in North America, or should I say the Western Hemisphere, can ultimately fly together, starting with Cuba. We are very close neighbors. The U.S. only has four that close, Canada, Mexico, Cuba and the Bahamian Islands. It's unnatural that we can't get along after nearly 250 years of being neighbors and friends for most of all those years."

"True," says Lewis, "and that's why we're here."

"Yes," says Ramone, "we agree. Let's take a break. Juliana, you can refresh our drinks. It's getting late. Antoine, I think we need to get down to business or Juliana and Nickolas won't be back in Washington before daylight."

Rising, Antoine says, "Yes, you right, Ramone, the voice of reason, as usual."

They all took a break, the men heading for their latrine, Juliana heading for her commode. Juliana returned to the bar to refill drink glasses, while the men took a breath of fresh air and a stretch on the patio. Then everyone came back to their seats and their fresh drinks, two with their cigars.

"Nickolas," says Antoine, "Juliana is going to take some notes. You will see them first in Washington, and make any corrections you feel necessary. We'll memorialize it, whatever way you say it was. No one outside of very senior Cuban Government leadership will ever see these notes, besides you and Juliana. Is that okay?"

Nickolas hadn't expected that minutes would be taken or that they would ask for his agreement if they were. It was their party. He thought, they could have, or still could be, video recording the whole meeting from 10 hidden cameras in the room. How would he know?

He says, "I can think of no good reason to object."

"Thank you, Nickolas. We wouldn't ask, but we work for people who believe they want to see every word of the discussion we are going to have."

"Juliana must be a real good note taker," Nickolas says.

"She is," says Antoine, "and even if she didn't take notes, she could likely quote everything we said with 90% accuracy."

"Juliana," says Nickolas, "you didn't tell me you had a photographic memory."

"Not photographic. I'm just a very good listener with a good memory."

"Great," says Nickolas, "now I'm going to have to remember everything that I've said to you to see if I compromised my intentions somewhere."

"Not to be concerned. Nick, it's not in your nature to be devious."

"Well, thank you, Juliana. I do try to be an officer and a gentleman without being boring."

"And you are, Nick. Don't worry. You've been with a friend and you are with friends now. You may not know that for sure at this time, but you will eventually."

"I trust that to be true, Juliana, or I wouldn't even be here now."

"We know. We appreciate the fact that you trust us."

Antoine sits forward in his seat. He removes his already loose tie, folds it up, sets it upon his suit jacket, sets back and settles in.

"Nickolas, we know you're a successful U.S. businessman, who started a small business with a good idea, and with a lot of hard work built a large U.S. defense corporation. We know you're a multimillionaire. We know you served four years in the Marine Corps, spent some time in Grenada and Panama, came out a captain, and stayed in the Marine Reserves another six years. We know you're a card-carrying Republican of long standing. We know you have a good marriage and two grown children. Your son is running HDI while you pursue a new career in politics. Is this all true?"

"Antoine, you were batting a thousand until the end. I'm not pursuing a career in politics. Simply stated, I'm trying to right an injustice being perpetrated on the people of Cuba largely by the U.S. political fund-raising system and the way our political leaders come to power and stay there, including presidents. Having effectively retired from HDI, I remain Chairman. Last March, I committed two years of my time or more and several million dollars to organizing, funding and leading the ARC organization as a Signature Event in my life. I'm sure your people are familiar with ARC by this time?"

Antoine smiles and looks at his companions, sips his drink and then says,

"True, Nickolas, we've been waiting and listening with great interest since the beginning. Your organizational and leadership skills have taken ARC far in a short time. But, tell me about this Signature Event implication, what does that mean?"

"Perhaps, Antoine, you're not familiar with the term. It only means that it is my belief that accomplishing this goal will be the most important achievement in my life and the one most likely for which I will be remembered. It may be my last major undertaking, whether I succeed or not. Therefore, it is my Signature Event."

"I see. I think I understand. I want you to know that there are many in Cuba who hope you succeed and who want to help. However, on the other hand, and as you and Juliana discovered upon landing in Havana, there are some here who do not want you to succeed. They are very happy with the status quo or are otherwise optimistic about their future, post-Fidel, without America's help or influence."

"I understand, Antoine. The same lines have been drawn in the U.S. for sometime and that is why the U.S.-Cuba relationship has stalled in an uncomfortable place the past 20 or 30 years."

"Yes, Nickolas, thank you. Now if you don't mind, Lewis would like to ask a few questions." Antoine nods to Lewis, who scoots to the closer end of the sofa and smiles and says, "Nickolas, we are, of course, up-to-date, we believe, with your progress. Could you give us some idea of what your plans are for the immediate and more distant future?"

"Our current strategic business plan requires that we continue to hold our meetings around the nation in all the major cities, about 100 cities, and 250 meetings, at an average rate of four per week. We've held about 100, so far. We have two presentation teams on the road every week, plus me, or my chief of staff, who stage the meetings that we believe will be more difficult, like ones in South Florida, or with the media, government, or corporate America.

"Timing-wise, we are 12 months away from the next U.S. election. In another six months, we'll have finished our meetings at the same time the Democratic and Republican presidential candidates will have been selected, and supporters of ARC will have already become influential in the electoral process and become more influential in the run-up to the national presidential election.

"We intend to assure that this issue becomes a major discussion and debating point in the election process. Hopefully, both candidates will be pro-reconciliation by election day. We'll assure that there is a voting bloc of average U.S. citizens with a strong pro-reconciliation voting requirement to offset the anti-reconciliation vote in Florida and New Jersey, which, at maximum, I believe to be about one million votes today. At the same time, we are working especially hard in Florida to change the minds of those particular U.S. Cubans to lower our hurdle level. We do believe we are not far from reaching the tipping point on this issue. Once we hit that point, everything will come our way quickly."

Lewis again says, "Thank you, Nickolas, for sharing the basics of your strategy with us." Another question, What about money? We've heard rumors recently that you may be running out of money?"

Nickolas' mind clicked. He now knew why he was in Cuba much earlier than he had anticipated. They were worried his progress would falter for a lack of capital, a recently publicized situation. These guys have a pretty good pipeline of information, he thought. Nick paused, took a slow drink of his now warm wine to think about how he wanted to answer that one. He found the answer quickly. They would only believe the truth, no matter what he said, and he was here, among other reasons, for a veracity check. Nick answered,

"I wouldn't say we're running out of money, but we are expending my total initial commitment at an unexpectedly high rate, primarily due to a less or slower receipt of donations than committed—primarily slower I believe. We have the pledges, but not the cash, to be self-funding at current rates of expense. Higher future rates require that we accelerate income in order to complete the next 120 meetings or so. But, however, you look at it, I'll have a financial shortfall in six months or so, considering cash-on-hand and the current rate of donations. As a result, we've hired additional telemarketing personnel to increase the rate of collections. But it's slow and unpredictable." Nick had chosen not to talk about recent corporate donations.

Ramone interjects, "Perhaps we could help. There are many in Cuba who want you to succeed."

"I understand, Ramone, but it is likely many of these people in Cuba and in the U.S. are thinking great progress can be made without any political or economic concessions. It's my personal opinion that achieving the lifting of the U.S. embargo would be like the Berlin Wall coming down in 1988—an event heralded all over the world as the end of the Cold War, but, in reality, an event that did very little for East Berlin until West Berlin invested billions of Euros in rebuilding the East Berlin economy from the bottom up. In fact, even today, East Berlin is not fully financially recovered from their 30 years of enforced separation from the rest of the free world."

Ramone responds, "What are you saying?"

"I am suggesting that without a major new agreement between our governments, beyond lifting the embargo, there won't be adequate capital investment to move Cuba into the 20th century, to say nothing of the 21st. No good relationship can commence or be sustained without consistent investment from the participants. It's natural law."

"What are you talking about?" says Ramone, with an edge to his voice. "We Cubans have done well without American investment for years now. We suffered a two-year recession when the Russians left, but we recovered very well."

"I didn't mean to insult your country, Ramone, if that's what you believe. I meant, I apologize, forgive me please, that was not my meaning.

I was only trying to emphasize that those who believe that lifting the embargo will fix everything in Cuba have not thought through all of the issues."

Lewis interjects, "Have you, Nickolas? Have you thought through all of the issues?"

"I probably don't even know all of the issues, and I don't believe that anyone in either the Cuban or U.S. Government knows all the issues because they have not talked to one another on this subject for 50 years or so! Our two countries have been estranged for a long period of time. Many of those years we were enemies, on the opposite side of the Iron Curtain. Many conservatives in the United States believe we are still enemies, that Cuba is a Communist state that threatens the U.S. and peace in the Americas."

Ramone excitedly interrupts, "That is totally preposterous. The opposite is true. The U.S. constantly threatens the socialist lives of Cubans and others around the world with their big-brother brand of imperialism and insistence that all nations adopt their style."

"See what I mean, Ramone," says Nickolas, smiling at Ramone. "There are reconciliations that are necessary to achieve the best outcome for both parties. That is all I am suggesting. Phase I is getting the embargo lifted. Phase II is negotiating a long-range settlement of all important, outstanding issues and perhaps agreeing to a 10-year strategic business plan co-authored and agreed upon in principle by both parties."

Antoine says, "Nickolas, you're obviously a strategic thinker. You are ahead of us at this time. Or perhaps you recognize issues that we do not, hoped not to have to address. Let's take another break. Following that, Lewis, Ramone and I need a 'sidebar.' Juliana, after the break, why don't you show Nickolas the beautiful view from the patio."

"Is that wise after this evening, Antoine?" Juliana asks.

"Excuse me, Nickolas, you have me so entranced with your last comments that I forgot our new security concerns. Juliana, you and Nick stay here. We'll use the meeting room down the hall for our sidebar. Let's re-meet in 30 minutes. Also, Juliana, it's getting late. I've pre-ordered dinner; please advise the kitchen to deliver it at 11 o'clock. We'll return at that time and continue our discussion over dinner."

Antoine, Lewis and Ramone rise, leaving their drinks, and exit the room, leaving Juliana and Nickolas sitting at their seats and stretching, smiling at one another.

"Nickolas, another wine?" Juliana asks, as they both rise.

"No, I'll wait for dinner, but I'll take a cold bottle of that water, please."

"Certainly, glass?" Juliana asks, at the bar.

"Not necessary, thanks." Nickolas rises, takes a seat at the bar.

"Want to talk, Nickolas, or just rest and think?"

"No, we can talk, but thanks for asking. I think I'm doing okay, what do you think?"

"Nickolas, I think you're doing great. I believe they all like you and particularly Antoine, and he is the most important. He is very close to the leader of the Senate."

"Do you know if the leader of the Senate is aware of this meeting?"

"No, not for sure. I don't want to guess at such a question. I have not been told."

Juliana continues, "Nickolas, you surprised them with your Phase II thinking. I'm sure that is what they are discussing right now. Have you mentioned this Phase II thinking in any of your speeches or writings before?"

"Not publicly, no, I have not, because in my projected timing of events this meeting was not expected for another six months."

"What made you anticipate it at all?"

"It's simply the natural course of events for intelligent, thoughtful people on both sides."

"I see," says Juliana, then partly in jest adds, "maybe our leadership is *smarter* than I gave them credit for."

"The opportunity unfolding should be quite obvious to any informed Cuban politician or diplomat."

"Yes, should be. Probably is, but that doesn't mean that it fits Fidel's or Raul's grand plan or Fidel's high personal expectations."

"True. Fidel appears to be a unique and complex individual, one who does not fit into any prior mold."

"Yes, I won't say more."

At that moment, there was a soft knock at the door. Juliana says, "That's the food, I'll let them in, it's almost 11. Nickolas rose to his feet, stretched, rubbed his neck and walked around, watching the table being set. The guard in the open doorway was vigilant.

Nickolas had not paid much attention to the table previously, but he could now see it was set for six. He asks Juliana,

"Were we short a participant tonight or are we expecting a dinner guest?"

Juliana replies, "To be honest with you, I do not know. I just noticed the table setting for six myself."

The two waiters filled the six water glasses with bottled water, laid out two sets of bread baskets, butter, salt and pepper. Red and white wines arrived in silver buckets with hand towels around the bottle throats. The wines were uncorked at the side bar. One waiter started preparing a large bowl of Caesar salad from scratch on a roll-around table.

At 11:10, Antoine, Lewis and Ramone returned to the room. They appeared to be in a jovial mood, talking, smiling and laughing lightly. Antoine says,

"Nickolas, please forgive our absence."

"Nothing to forgive. Juliana and I enjoyed our visit. By the way, are we missing someone tonight? The table is set for six."

Antoine looked at the table like he was seeing if for the first time.

"Why no, Nickolas. I am sure I advised the hotel that we would be five for dinner, just a misunderstanding in the chain-of-command, I suppose."

Antoine then stepped over to the table to the side of the headwaiter and whispered in his ear. The headwaiter removed an end setting and moved the side settings a little further down the table, giving everyone a little more elbow room. Nickolas thought, I wonder who the sixth man was going to be and why he decided not to come to dinner. Was

Antoine's meeting down the hall with the sixth man to prepare him to join the group for dinner? If so, why did he change his mind?

Antoine says, "Nickolas, you're the guest of honor so please sit at the head. Juliana, you sit to Nick's left, I'll sit to his right. Let's all sit down and enjoy a nice meal together and continue our conversation."

They did as suggested and one waiter started serving the Caesar salad and one circled the table with bottles of white wine, filling glasses as requested, a choice of a German Riesling or a California Chardonnay. *"Bon Appétit!"* says Antoine, and everybody hit the Caesar salad, which was magnificent, thought Nickolas, maybe the best he had experienced in a long time or made just the way he liked it, with both anchovy paste in the dressing and strips of anchovy on the top. Nick thought, I haven't eaten in almost 12 hours, no wonder this tastes so good. He took a sip of the new bottle of California Chardonnay, a Firestone, and says,

"Antoine, this was an excellent choice of Chardonnay, did you select it?"

"No, Nickolas, I left that to the hotel wine steward. Personally, I wouldn't know a good American Chardonnay from a bad one. First, because my drink of choice is good Scotch and second, when I do drink wine, it's almost always a Chilean or Argentine red. We do understand that all markets are accessible one way or the other, and Cuba has had to learn the art of 'the other,' thus the California Chardonnay and thousands of other American necessities large and small are difficult for us to acquire, or acquire at a reasonable cost."

"I understand," Nickolas says.

"Nickolas, when we adjourned our meeting awhile ago, you had us on the edge of our seats with your Phase II thinking. We're all impatient to hear more. Please continue as best you can while you enjoy your meal. Forgive us as we continue to eat while you talk. I guarantee you, we'll all be listening intently. To help you get back on subject, what are all these issues that you believe must be, or should be, reconciled, as you say?"

Everyone stopped eating, lowered their tools and picked up napkins to wipe their mouths. Only Nickolas went for another big fork full of the Caesar salad with a whole anchovy. He was going for a minute of thought. He hadn't anticipated getting back on point before the main course, at the earliest. Proper diplomacy would require dessert, Cognac and cigar time. He says, looking for time, with a mouth half-full,

"Man, is this good Caesar salad! You can't find a table-side made Caesar salad anywhere in the U.S. anymore, and if you do, it's not made with the traditional ingredients. Too many people don't like anchovies, I guess. I love them," he says, smiling at Juliana, who he had noticed was enjoying hers, too. No comments followed his remarks. He looked around, chewed, swallowed, put down his fork, buttered a small piece of bread, swallowed and says,

"Okay, here we go. Phase II, okay, what are all those issues? There is a bunch," he says, while taking a mouth-clearing drink of his Chardonnay. Where to start? Where to start, he thought, trying to get back into it. He was hungry and it was a great Caesar salad.

"Okay, here we go. I'm just going to go through a mental list," he says. "Please realize I am not here tonight prepared to discuss all these issues." He was hoping that they wouldn't want to discuss them all, as it would take two days at a minimum.

"Juliana," he says, "you may just want to make a one-line item list of these issues for the record. At the top of your list, write the words. 'Not an inclusive list,' since I was not prepared to get into this subject on this visit. But, I understand the value to the senators of having knowledge of these issues to consider and to prepare for the next meeting. On that basis only, I'll give you the list, as I remember it. 'It is not conclusive!' It's my list, no one else's. I do not represent the U.S. Government."

He hesitates, "I can't prioritize them in my head so pay no attention to order. Here we go. This is my Phase II issue list, as I remember it."

"Most Americans think your form of government is communistic and/or a dictatorship. You need to move toward democracy. This movement could occur over time.

"Human rights, freedom for political prisoners, freedom of the press."

Lewis angrily interrupts, "You're the last people in the world who should criticize Cuba for human rights! At Guantanamo, right here on our island, you have proved that America owns no high ground in the area!"

Nickolas raises his hand, smiles and says, "Lewis, we'll be here all night if you want to debate this list. Let me finish please." Nickolas continues,

"Anti-American rhetoric and activity, constant confrontation, need to be replaced by diplomacy.

"Subversive activities, in U.S., Central and South America, need to be replaced by diplomacy.

"The past Cuba/Russian nuclear threat needs to be discussed and reconciled.

"Immigration policy. A new policy needs to be discussed and agreed upon.

"Free trade policy, markets open in both directions, and…

"Reparations for U.S. businesses and Cuban-Americans. Assets lost due to Cuban Government nationalization need to be discussed and reconciled."

Nickolas pauses, drinks, "Ah, that's all the major issues I can think of now on my U.S. list, although I am sure there are many more lesser issues." He senses a pause in the proceedings and says,

"Excuse me, I have to finish off this great Caesar salad."

Everyone went back to their food and, in a few silent minutes, finished off the salad. The waiters cleared the salad plates, refilled the wine glasses, and served the covered entrées from the portable ovens at the side of the room, placing the first one in front of Juliana. Lifting the heavy silver cover exposed a small filet of beef, over a slice of toasted bread, a large lobster tail thermidor and green beans almondine—all on a beautiful plate accented with a red pickled apple slice and a small violet-colored flower in the middle over mint leaves.

Nickolas says, "I'm impressed. This looks world-class," as he cut into his filet and deposited a generous piece into his mouth. While he was chewing, he looked up, making eye contact with Lewis, who says,

"Nickolas, the Cuban list, as you understand it. Share that list with us, please." The others were enjoying their entrée, but took time to look to Nickolas for his response.

"Sure, Lewis," he says, wiping his mouth, and realizing he was going to be challenged to simply eat this meal, disregarding the prospect of enjoying it. Nickolas sipped his wine. The attentive waiter immediately filled the glass. Were they trying to get him drunk? He thought, and smiled to himself in distain of the possibility.

"Here we go again," Nickolas says, "no particular order. Juliana, are you ready?"

"Yes."

"Remember, this is just my opinion, my judgment of what your major issues would be if I were you, issues I believe would require resolution from your side of the bargaining table."

"We understand." Lewis says.

Antoine says, "Proceed, please."

"Okay." Nick notes no one is eating, they are all listening.

"U.S. acceptance and respect for the Castro family and respect for the Cuban revolution.

"Past U.S. subversive activities to unseat Fidel.

"The Bay of Pigs invasion.

"The embargo and economic oppression.

"Lifting the embargo and a free trade agreement.

"Full diplomatic relations.

"Reduced tensions.

"Long-term peace treaty. Protection for Cuba.

"Support to bring Cuba into the world community.

"Support for Cuba to join the World Bank.

"Guantanamo base property returned to Cuba. U.S. military exits.

"Return of Cuba's U.S. cash deposits, plus interest.

"Again, I'm confident this list is incomplete of some issues. However, if you believe that resolution of all these issues would constitute a new beginning for both Cuba and the United States, the effort would achieve the objective of my Phase II concept. Do you agree?"

Antoine responds, "Nickolas, you've given us a lot more to think about than we had anticipated, much of it above this group's ability to influence. However, speaking personally, I believe your Phase II concept has to be initiated at some point in time soon or Cuba will be left so far behind in the past by the rest of the advancing civilized world that we'll never be able to catch up. We're already nearly a half-century behind in many, many areas. That, of course, is only my opinion. Please don't quote me. Many in Cuba would disagree with me. They are happy where they are." Antoine pauses, then continues,

"Nickolas, let us now put politics and government behind us. It has been a long day for you and Juliana already, a harrowing day as well. Let's finish our meal, enjoy our after-dinner liqueur and a cigar over lighter conversation. We will then get you and Juliana safely back to the airport and aboard a new plane for your journey back to Washington."

"Sounds good," Nickolas says. "This is a terrific meal and I'm really enjoying it!"

The ensuing conversation through dinner casually covered subjects from baseball to film, to oil and troubles around the world. It was obvious to Nickolas in most of these mini-discussions that the media Antoine, Lewis and Ramone read and listened to had a different slant to the news than the media Nickolas consumed. Being a world traveler he knew this was true wherever he went outside the U.S., but it was obviously more true in Cuba.

At the end they, all shook hands and thanked one another for the other's input. Nickolas thanked his hosts for their hospitality, humorously excluding the attack at the airport. They all said that they were hopeful that they all would meet again soon. Nickolas said the same, but doubted that, in fact, he would see any of these three again anytime soon.

Nickolas and Juliana were turned over to the six hallway guards, which now included their two table waiters in black suits, bulging with short and long weapons on both sides. Nick thought, very good multi-taskers. They were ushered down the stairs through the empty lobby and out of the front door to the center unit of three waiting black SUVs.

Each vehicle got two of their guards. Juliana and Nickolas' vehicle got the two waiters. As Juliana jumped into the rear seat though the door being held by the senior waiter impersonator, with Nickolas right behind her, he says to one of the waiter guards, "On the way to the airport, could you write down your recipe for the Caesar salad? Man that was good!"

They arrived at the new executive jet, which was well-guarded by Cuban military. As they approached it, Nickolas says,

"Juliana, we've been upgraded for the trip home."

"Yes, it's rare for me to fly in a large jet unless I'm flying with our ambassador to the U.S. We'll be at Reagan International in three hours. You can be home in bed with your wife by 5 a.m. If you sleep on our way back, and sleep a little late this morning, you should be okay later today. That's what I am going to do."

They boarded the plane, met the new captain and copilot, put their luggage away, found blankets and pillows waiting for them midwing, sat down, buckled up, and prepared for departure. Their guards boarded their vehicles, and led, and then followed the plane as it taxied to the end of the runway. The pilot powered up under brake, released the brake and they were off the runway and in the air within what seemed to be a hundred yards to Nick. He thought, these guys are getting out of Dodge in a hurry. Their angle of ascent was very steep, and the engines were screaming as the pilot took a sharp turn to the right and headed out to sea without incident.

Nickolas put his seat all the way back, spread the blanket over his body and tried to relax so he could sleep. The long day, the big meal, the wine, the stress all caught up with him at the same time. His last thought was, what a wild fucking day! He fell into a deep sleep.

# LXIII

## CROSSING THE STRAITS OF FLORIDA EN ROUTE TO AMERICA

The baby awoke at 5 a.m., and Maria was discreetly breast-feeding him under the baby's little blue blanket—a baby shower gift from his grandmother a year ago. The old couple were still sleeping in each other's arms, wrapped in a corner of the boat's canvas cover, as were the young couple. In the starboard aft, where a flip-over wooden seat could be tipped over the rail, Anthony was completing his morning toilet. Rufus had come up with this simple design, using an old wooden toilet seat, primarily for the convenience of the women.

Rose had packed them all a breakfast of boiled eggs, smoked fish, bread and tea, which would be warm at best after nine hours, although she had wrapped it carefully in her best bath towel and tied the towel with twine. In another package was a light lunch for everyone, prepared by Mrs. Rafael and her husband, the retired jewelers. Although Manuel did not plan to be on the water the evening of this day, young Mrs. Fernando and her son had prepared a light supper for everyone, to be consumed as they approached land, or on the ocean, if for some reason they had not arrived to go ashore that afternoon or evening.

The prior evening's clear sky had turned slowly to overcast clouds. Visibility was reduced to maybe a thousand yards. The seas had been calm, but with a gentle breeze since about 3 a.m., with the light wind only occasionally filling the lofting canvas sails and snapping the lines against the mast. The rhythmic music of the sail lines had first hypnotized the passengers and then lulled them to sleep last night. Only Manuel and Anthony remained awake to exchange an hour of vigil for an hour of rest throughout the night.

The gray turned to black as the false dawn of early morning was overwhelmed by the night's last struggle to prevail, signaling the imminent dawn's first faint light, soon to rise in the east.

Manuel was minding the rudder. He thought about the last 10 hours on the water and tried to estimate the rate of their drift east and their distance under sail to the north. Their last effort to measure their movement in the Gulf Stream had indicated an unaided drift northeast of about three knots at about 2 a.m. With sail, following the current in the gentle nighttime breeze, he estimated four to five knots. But they had not been moving completely in the direction of the Gulf Stream flow northeast. They were trying to move more to the north across the Gulf Stream. Therefore, their forward and northern progress was somewhat less. How much? He did not know. He would make more estimates in the morning and try to recalculate their progress. If his early planning numbers were right, they were 30 miles north and about 30 miles west of Havana. It was now almost dawn. One or two of his passengers were turning over restlessly, seeking more comfort in the early morning.

As the first light rays of a new day came over the horizon, Manuel said another prayer to St. Christopher for their safe voyage to America. So much was at stake, so much in his hands. He knew that the next 12 hours would result in Rose's and his dreams of the past two years coming true, or failure, and their return to Cuba. He had to outfox the U.S. Coast Guard in the air and on the sea, and other vessels that could report him. He also had to beat Mother Nature if she got mean, but his planning had considered those issues to the extent possible.

The sun continued to slowly rise behind the mostly overcast sky. Manuel looked forward to dawn, as did Anthony, who had just awakened. Manuel did a slow 360-degree visual inspection of the horizon, looking for any sign of trouble. Nothing was very apparent beyond a small scud of dark clouds on the southeast horizon, basically behind them, and a long way off. It was apparently a distant squall—nothing to worry about at this time. Squalls, when not associated with bigger storms, were usually small fast-moving cloud formations full of rain and wind. Some squalls were so small you could sail right through them in minutes. This time of year they were a daily occurrence in the Caribbean and virtually unpredictable, sometimes forming out of nowhere in a few hours, only to roll over the ocean and disappear again as they dissipated their condensation and wind. He smiled, shrugged and gestured with his free hand to Anthony to reassure him he was not concerned about the small cloud formation in an otherwise clear but overcast morning. The baby shuddered, stretched, whimpered again and stuck his little fist into his mouth for security.

Manuel smiled at the scene of his daughter and grandchild covered in the dark blue sail cloth. What fun lay ahead in the distant future, teaching little Jon about the sea, fishing and boat handling. If you were a good fisherman, you never needed to worry about where the next meal was coming from. A small garden of potatoes, corn, tomatoes, peppers, beans, onions, celery, lettuce and a few herbs, along with a couple of dozen chickens or so, and you were set. Add a few pesos for flower, sugar, salt and pork, and you could eat well forever. He thought, I must be getting hungry now, thinking about Rose's packed breakfast.

Baby Jon shuddered again, wiped his eyes with both fists, swung his little arms, kicked his feet and fully awakened to the new day with an appetite. He was not a loud crier, like many babies, but he was a constant whiner until he got what he wanted, which was usually pretty quickly, as his mother was never far away and was very attentive. Maria awoke with the first cry. She spoke softly to Jon, soothing him as she opened her blouse and her nursing bra and pushed her nipple into Jon's searching mouth. He was instantly quiet. However, the boat had awakened. It was 5:30 a.m.

Manuel noticed Anthony's interest in the feeding process now under way and particularly, Maria's exposed breast. As a man, he understood Anthony's interest in looking; however, as a father he thought it was inappropriate. He gave Anthony an impatient look and Anthony looked away—only to be caught looking again a minute or two later. Manuel managed to get Anthony's attention again and raised his eyebrows in exclamation, and Anthony once again looked away. Manuel leaned forward and covered the baby and the upper portion of Maria's chest from view with the little blue blanket. Maria smiled at her father, shaking her head back and forth to indicate she thought he was overreacting.

# LXIV

## FIRST FULL DAY AT SEA

The seas had slowly but increasingly become troubled since dawn and the rising wind. The colors of the water were changing from blue and green to purple, then changing to black and gray, then black and gray and white, as the first small white caps started to appear. An hour later the color changed to black and white, as the wind increased and blew a splatter of white foam off the top of the breaking waves, as the small boat rose from its trough to the wave peaks.

The wind started to whistle periodically though the sail lines, and at the same time, set up an alternate beat as the lines now rapped and snapped on the mast. The direction of the wind started to move, shifting from quarter to quarter, causing the sail to fill and then loft, snapping in the wind, suddenly pushing the boat ahead and then suddenly slowing it down, making it more difficult for Manuel to maintain his 45-degree angle to the approaching waves. The rudder was requiring more and more of his attention, skill and strength. Every seventh wave or so started to throw low spray over the boat and passengers, as they increasingly huddled closer together, trying to protect themselves and each other from the cold damp mist.

Manuel was focused on trying to keep the boat on a safe, dry tact, but there was no way to avoid spray from the largest of the growing seas. His passengers were slowly getting wet, even though they were now trying to stay covered with a large canvas he had brought along for this purpose.

He furtively looked from time to time, when he could, at his passengers as his boat continued to drive forward through the wind, waves and mist. Looking rearward from his higher vantage point, he could see a squall line, maybe five to six miles in the distance, filling the void between the clouds and the sea on the horizon with dark, gray sheets of thick falling rain. Subconsciously, he thought that he needed to avoid the squall, momentarily forgetting he was not in his powerboat, which made it far easier to avoid bad weather.

Manuel checked his passengers again to see if anyone had seen the dark squall line to their aft. Most of them who caught his eye smiled at him nervously, but were still displaying trust and courage in the face of increasing adversity. The captain weakly smiled back and nodded to some, trying not to show any concern and, at this point, he didn't really have any serious concern. He had experienced far worse conditions at sea many times, including a half dozen brushes with hurricanes, but, of course, not in a small sailing boat.

His eyes returned to his helm duties. He straightened his back, looked aft again, and raised his hand to look at the squall line approaching, trying to gauge its direction over the water. It was difficult to tell, but it seemed to be powered by a stronger directional wind than the shifting winds he was in now. He became apprehensive. He knew how angry the seas in the Gulf Stream could become, and he hoped this wouldn't be one of those days.

It was noon on the first and only planned full day at sea. The weather had continued to deteriorate. The wind had been increasing steadily since early morning, and was now directly out of the south. The clear skies of dawn had become partially cloudy and now were overcast. The seas had continued to rise and were now black and cresting. White spume was spreading over the surface as the wind blew the water off the tops of the crests. The temperature had dropped several degrees in the past three hours.

Manuel's efforts at the helm to keep the seas from breaking over the boat were becoming increasingly difficult. He had been forced to take down the mainsail at about 10 a.m. He was now running before the wind, using a small storm jib that still powered the boat at five to six knots. His passengers were using the dismasted mainsail to further cover the open boat in an attempt to keep the sea out of the boat and reduce the need to bail water every 30 minutes or so.

It had become apparent to Manuel a couple of hours earlier that the scud mark on the horizon was not a distant, early morning squall line, but the leading edge of an unexpected tropical storm front moving north toward Cuba and Florida. The imminent storm was moving faster then Manuel's boat and in the same direction. The storm front was wide and filled the horizon to the west, south and southeast; therefore, he could not sail either east or west to avoid it. He was sailing before the wind, which put the power of the waves directly behind him. He was forced to be vigilant over his right shoulder, watching waves approaching from behind and then to look forward over his bow to determine the forward wave conditions and helm maneuver necessary to steer the boat safely as the wave hit his stern and the boat picked up speed on the downside of the passing wave. Manuel knew this constant high level of focus, concentration and physical effort was slowly wearing him down, at the same time the sea conditions were worsening.

He thought, thank God, Rufus and he had designed their boat as a double-ender, which by design, diminished the threat of following seas in heavy weather. Within the same thought, Manuel wished that he had rigged a small sea anchor in case of severe weather, but, he had not, thinking at the time that he would not put to sea in conditions that could result in bad weather, and that the trip he had planned was only 150 miles and approximately 30 hours sailing time. Where this storm had come from, he couldn't fathom. He had watched and listened to the weather reports twice a day for a week.

Manuel's neck was stiff, his right arm and hand numb, his back was sore and his butt was tired, even though Rose had made him a soft cushion to sit upon, which was now wet. His passengers were out of sight below the two canvas sails, except Anthony, who sat to Miguel's right, facing aft, watching for the approach of the periodic heavier wave, which required special attention from Manuel.

"Captain, a big one is coming up—number three back," Anthony says.

Manuel could tell by Anthony's tone of voice that the wave was only an average big one. But he looked back to make his own judgment, and measure the two in the middle, and then looked forward at the depth of the troughs lying ahead into which the boat would accelerate when the big wave passed beneath the vessel. A quick look back and quick look forward and he knew this wave, like the thousand waves prior to it, wouldn't be a problem. He adjusted the angle of the rudder just before the wave hit the stern. The canoe-style stern split the wave, without permitting the wave to push the stern right or left, setting up a broach in which the boat slipped sideways into the trough, and would therefore take the next wave over its side, which would swamp the boat if not turn it over. As the wave passed beneath the boat, Manuel brought the bow to port at 45-degrees to take the next wave at a safe angle. He had successfully completed this maneuver a thousand times or more that morning.

However, as the wind intensified, the waves grew in height and the troughs narrowed as the waves accelerated.

Manuel knew that the main body of the storm had not yet arrived and tried to marshal his experience and skills. He already had everyone in a life jacket. What was left? He thought, then thought more, as best as he could, and still steer the boat.

He thought, water and food. Better to drink it and eat it than lose it in a capsize. He told Anthony to tell everyone to drink plenty of water and eat all that they had left. They would be ashore late today—one way or the other, he thought.

Manuel looked behind him. The darkness of the core of the storm was rapidly approaching. The gray vertical lines of falling rain were apparent in the distance. The worst of the storm was maybe 30 minutes behind them. He says to Anthony,

"When you can see the rain actually hitting the water behind us, let me know. Tell everyone to prepare for heavy wind and rain. Tell them we must bail water as fast as we can when it comes aboard. If we capsize, they are to stay with the boat. Even if the boat fills with water, they stay with the boat. The boat is made of wood. It may fill up, but it won't sink. Tell them to be brave, not to panic and to help one another. Do it and get back here!"

Anthony did as instructed, ducking his head and body under the canvas and moving forward to deliver the captain's instructions. He paused only a few extra moments to exchange a few words with Maria, saying,

"Maria, it's going to get a lot worse in maybe half an hour and then it should be a lot better. There is nothing special to worry about right now except more wind and water. The captain is just being cautious. However, if somehow we end up in the sea, I will find you and baby Jon quickly. Don't worry, I'll be watching. I'll be with you. Strap the baby high on your chest with this line twice around, top and bottom, so that you can use your arms and hands. Let me help you. My belt might help, here. Be calm. Don't panic. If you end up in the water, stay with the boat."

Anthony delivered his message to the other passengers forward, then turned around under the canvas and reappeared at the aft end of the boat where Manuel was fighting the tiller.

"Are they prepared?" asks Manuel, his voice elevated, as the wind had risen in velocity.

"Yes, they are as ready as they ever could be for whatever might happen."

Anthony looked around him in amazement. In a period of what seemed like two or three minutes, the whole world had turned dark gray and white. The seas were more turbulent, and the troubled seas were rising and moving in all directions at once. The wind had risen substantially as the cooler air of the rain clouds approached. White spume was in the air and everywhere on the water. The boat was being driven forward with only enough sail to steer by. The waves had steepened, the troughs narrowed, and each time the small boat slid down the back of a wave, its bow was plowing into the rising back side of the next one.

The boat was now taking on water and Anthony started bailing, as did the Rafaels further forward. But they had to come out from beneath the canvas to do so, which permitted more water to come in than they were bailing out. Manuel yelled at them to stay under the canvas and hold the canvas in a manner that would permit the water coming over the bow to drain over the side.

"Here comes the rain!" Anthony yells at Manuel.

Manuel turned his head to see a black wall of rain, maybe a hundred yards behind him, so thick and heavy that you could not see into it more than five to ten yards. At that instant, there was a tremendously loud crack of thunder, which sounded like it was right overhead, followed by a lightning bolt that quickly filled the air with a sharp smell, followed almost instantly by another of the loudest thunder claps Manuel had ever heard, which made both he and Anthony cower in fear for an instant.

Manuel thought, well it's finally here, may God be with us, as he and Anthony were enveloped in a rain so thick that they could hardly breathe without putting a hand over their nose and mouth.

The sea and rain become one.

The leading edge of the storm had hit them with a vengeance. First were the high winds, which turned the sea to white foam and froth, followed by a thick heavy rain, with thunder and lightning all around them. Everyone who had a bailing tool was bailing water now. The higher southeast winds on top of the natural easterly flow of the Gulf Stream in the Straits of Florida resulted in extremely troubled and high seas, pushing the boat at eight to nine knots and increasing.

As Manuel steered his boat down the back of each wave, his bow was now digging into the rising forward side of the next one. He could not take the waves at a greater angle to the direction of the wind without broaching his boat and turning it over as it got sideways to the sea. If he continued to take the waves over the bow, ultimately the boat bow might dig too far into one and not come up, causing the boat to fill with seawater as it tried to drive itself to the bottom. It was a wooden boat, and he knew in that situation, the boat would resurface, but he also knew it would resurface without passengers and any of the boat's supplies or gear.

"Captain, a big one is coming three back," Anthony says.

There was only one other scenario that Manuel was concerned about. It was the worse that could happen. The boat could "pitch-pole," a condition in which the stern of the boat actually flips over the bow, throwing everyone out and then smashes down on the water, bottom side up—a very quick and surprisingly violent event. But, Manuel didn't have time to think about it or anything else. A second later his boat was rising quickly on the crest of a particularly large, powerful wave.

As Manuel steered his craft over the crest and got his first look at the deep trough on the other side, he knew something bad was going to happen; he just didn't know what. At the top of the wave, he took a quick look around, nothing to see but water— big water everywhere. At that second, the big wave broke and pitched the boat end-over-end through the air. Manuel had a mini-second of awareness that his body was uncontrollably airborne; however, before his brain could process the message, he was underwater and fighting for the surface with his flailing arms. Buoyancy ultimately overtook his momentum, and Manuel reached the surface just in time to clear his eyes and mouth before he was buried again and pushed down by another huge breaking wave. He popped up again, as the wave passed overhead, and rode the next rising wave to the top to look for his daughter, his boat and his passengers. He saw nothing but big troubled seas. He spun around, now starting to panic, looked again, nothing. How was that possible?

He was now off the top of a wave heading for the bottom of the trough. He thought, Sweet Jesus! How could that be? How could the boat, everything and everybody be swept away that fast? Not possible, he thought. They just were in the troughs when he was on the crest, and he couldn't see them. He was rising again. This time he was yelling at the top of his voice, raising his arms. "Maria! Maria! Maria! Maria! Maria!" Nothing! Wind, thunder, lightning, rain, water, white spume everywhere! A whiteout!

# LXV

## ARC HEADQUARTERS

Nickolas awoke tired and sore from the long prior day's activities and the early morning flight back to Washington. He had slept fitfully on the plane, due to turbulence, and not much after arriving home. He had awakened Elizabeth, and she had to know every little detail of his trip. Nickolas down played the attack at the Havana Airport, but Elizabeth still got very upset hearing the severely modified version. They talked for two hours.

Nickolas called the office and then went to bed for three hours. Elizabeth got him up at 10:30 a.m., with a large, strong cup of coffee and helped him get ready to go to work. Nickolas had called the office earlier and alerted security to an 11:30 pickup and Phil to a 12:30 p.m. meeting with Tim and Mike in the conference room. They were all there when Nickolas walked into the room. Good mornings were shared, and Nick sat down at the conference table.

"Okay, tell us, how did it go?" Phil asks.

Nickolas smiles and says,

"You won't believe it when I tell you! It went better than anything we anticipated!"

"You're shittin' us?"

"No, I'm not. I just got back at 5 a.m. this morning! That's why I'm getting to work so late! We met until 1 a.m.!"

"You're shittin' us!" Phil says.

"No, I'm not." Nickolas reaches into a grocery store plastic bag and pulls out the fancy inlaid mahogany box from the Havana hotel meeting room and sets it on the conference table. Everyone looks at it.

"What's that?" Tim asks.

"It's a cigar box." Nickolas flips it open, lifts it up for them to see and says, "Take a whiff. These babies are the real McCoy—a gift from the government of Cuba!"

"You have to be kidding!" Phil, Mike and Tim are now smiling and half believing. "Let me see one of those mothers." Nickolas pushes the box into the center of the table. They each inspect the box and fondle carefully the hand-wrapped Cuban cigars, looking, smelling and admiring the handwork and apparent quality, although not one of them was a smoker.

"Nickolas, I'll be damned!" Tim says.

"You are serious, aren't you?" Phil asks.

"Okay, we bite, tell us the story," Mike says.

Nickolas says, "What you're about to hear is very confidential."

For the second time that day, Nickolas tells his story—this time not leaving out all the hairy details of the attack at the Cuban airport. Nickolas' friends listen in rapt attention, not interrupting at all, except with noises of disbelief or awe. As Nickolas wraps up his story, he is barraged with questions, including everything from the size of Juliana's breasts to the type and brand of weapons carried by the Cuban security police. Each man is somewhat focused on his business specialty or his favorite female anatomical features. Nickolas finally got through all those questions and tried to get his associates back on the proper track by saying,

"Gentlemen, we have made big progress in the past 24 hours!"

Mike says, "Nickolas, you're something else! You went to Cuba, almost got killed down there, and all you're thinking about is the progress of ARC! Nick, I am your security chief, I should have been with you!" Phil interrupts before Nickolas can reply, saying,

"Mike, you need to reread our organization's security agreement. You signed it. He can go solo if he wants."

"Phil, okay, okay, okay! I still don't like it. Shit! This whole program is getting much more complex and dangerous than I thought it would. And quicker!" Mike says.

Nickolas says, "Well, the quicker part of it is the good news. This development has accelerated our business plan by six months. Sometime very soon, we need to meet to readjust our business plan and schedule. In the meantime, Phil, we need to talk about a meeting with certain friendly representatives of Uncle Sam. We have made personal contact with the Cuban Government. We went to Cuba. We need to put that meeting on top of the table before they find out some other way."

"Okay," says Phil, "I would say in these circumstances we should meet with Senator Dobson or Senator Morris. Who do you prefer?"

"I'm not sure, you're the specialist. What do you say?" Phil thought a moment.

"I say, Dobson, we have more leverage with him and you never know, this unauthorized meeting of a U.S. businessman with an enemy of the U.S. Government could go down hard. If you had discussed the danger with me, Nick, I would have voted against your trip yesterday."

"I know. And you would have been right to do so. However, as the saying goes, there are *'Tides in the affairs of men when taken at their ebb, etc.'* However, it goes, that's what I did. If we can get through the next 72 hours of a heavy downfall of bullshit, we'll have gained six months. Which reminds me Phil, call Larry, tell him the whole story; I can't bear to go through it for the third time today. After you talk to our father confessor, I guess Dobson, coordinate a meeting day and time for everybody and let me know. Phil, try to make it happen in the next two days somehow. I can't make it with the burden of this uncertainty any longer than that."

"Okay, Nick. I'll get it done, don't worry about it. Give me the afternoon and evening. I'll call you no later than tonight."

"I know where Senator Dobson goes after work every day that he's in the Capital. If I can't reach him before, I'll catch him on the way home."

"Thank you, Phil, and get some people busy on advancing the business plan and don't forget to get Larry into the loop early."

"Will do, and, Nick, don't get me wrong. This is truly an amazing development. You always were one lucky son-of-a-bitch!"

"It's not by accident, Phil. I *plan* to be lucky."

The meeting adjourned with much enthusiasm, excitement, laughing, backslapping, and "macho-man banter." The group separated, happy with what they had learned, and were unable to share, but happy nonetheless. Big progress had occurred. They were now playing on the world stage, even if no one but them knew it.

# LXVI

## WASHINGTON, D.C.

Phil had found Senator Dobson at his favorite table at his favorite after-work hours bar, Jonathon's, not far from the Senate office building. The Senator was coaching a young male senate page, whom he needed to dismiss, after seeing Phil at the end of the bar. The Senator flashed five fingers three times, a code meaning, "I need 15 minutes." Knowing the Senator's bent for rhetoric, Phil knew he had to invest an hour minimum, if he was lucky.

Phil's story, the Senator's questions and resistance to Phil's needs took two hours, six Manhattans and a dozen oysters Rockefeller, for the Senator to get to the point of agreeing to Phil's plan, although both of them knew the Senator really had no choice from the beginning. But they both played their roles until the end. The Senator agreed to prepare the playing field for an ARC meeting with an assistant to the Assistant Chief of Staff at the White House and a young Undersecretary at the State Department, whom the Senator said would be sensitive to his needs. Phil thought, upon leaving, that he had achieved some control of what otherwise could be a risky legal or political situation.

The next morning Phil got a phone call from the Senator, saying that they had a luncheon date with both of the targeted officials. Over the phone, the opportunities and vulnerabilities were discussed, and an agreement of sorts was forged, which was perceived to be a win-win for everybody. The Senator had come through big-time! Nickolas would be set up for an immediate meeting with the President's Assistant Chief of Staff and a particular Undersecretary of the State Department, as planned. The meeting time would be determined by 4 p.m. that same day. The Senator or his assistant would call. Phil was happy.

The Senator called at 4 p.m., and the news was good. The meeting was at the White House at 4:30 p.m. tomorrow. Phil was very happy, and Phil called Nickolas, who was happy, too.

# LXVII

## THE WHITE HOUSE

*JUNE*

Nickolas, Phil and Larry were ushered into conference room three on the second floor of the White House annex. It was 4:30 p.m., late for an afternoon meeting at the White House. The room was dressed with white, traditional woodwork and the walls were painted a soft yellow. Three windows looked out upon an expansive lawn with Pennsylvania Avenue on the other side of the tree-dotted lawn and a distant iron fence. Coffee, tea, water and assorted soft drinks appeared to be left over from an earlier meeting on a portable wooden serving bar against the wall. The room was neat and clean; the chairs, orderly.

Nick thought, someone had given the room a quick organizational once-over, but apparently, had decided to leave the leftover beverages rather than replace them. What did that mean? Probably nothing, considering the late hour. They all took seats in the middle of one side of the table.

"Phil, sit on the other side across from me. We don't want to look like we expect a contest, one side against the other. Besides, I don't like the opposition staring at me dead-on from three feet away, too much direct eye contact, and I have a blemish on my nose today," Nick says.

"You got it boss." Phil moved around the table to the other side.

"Larry," says Nickolas, "please move over one seat, I need gesturing room. We're not going to fill up this table at this meeting." Phil and

Larry looked at one another out of the top of their eyes, smiling wryly, agreeing by body language that Nick was a little nervous and starting to micromanage, his mind going into overdrive. Nick apparently recognized that fact, too, and says,

"Excuse me, guys, it's been a long hard week. Too much coffee today."

Nickolas gets up and prepares a cup of coffee.

"Anybody else for coffee?" he asks from the coffee bar.

Larry responds, "I'll take a bottle of water, no glass."

Phil says, "I'm good. What I need at this hour of the day isn't up there."

"Don't remind me," Nick says. "We'll get you what you need after this meeting, providing I'm still a free man."

Larry says, "Not to worry. I have you covered."

Voices are heard outside the door. The door opens and two men and a woman enter. They reach over the table and start introducing themselves and exchanging business cards. One of the men, the Assistant to the White House Chief of Staff, takes the head seat. The Assistant to the Deputy U.S. Head of State sits to his right and the woman to his left. The men each carry the large briefcases with buckles, favored by attorneys, and they start unloading the tools of their trade. The woman tables a laptop computer, a steno pad and a pen. She is apparently ready to do it the old-fashioned way or do it the contemporary way. Nick, Phil and Larry watch, slightly amused, as this little preparatory drama unfolds. Each administrative tool coming out of the bags was kind of like watching strangers opening gifts at Christmas. Finally they are ready; the two men are barely visible behind the mountain of gear and files piled on their end of the table.

Nickolas says to Phil and Larry, but loud enough for all to hear, "I don't think we brought enough beans, bullets and bandages!" Nick looked at the crowded end of the table for confirmation of his humor. Only the lady smiled in appreciation of his wry wit. He liked her immediately. He gave her a smile and a wink.

"Mr. Harvey," says Reilly, "I believe you called this meeting. What can we do for you?" All eyes turned toward Nickolas. Nickolas thought Reilly was a little direct, but says,

"Gentlemen, yes, I am the instigator, and I appreciate your valuable time on such short notice. Thank you. I assume that you know who I am and what I do?"

Mr. Rafferty responds, "Yes, we do. It's almost impossible for those in government not to know in recent weeks, although many wonder why?"

"The why of it is a question I have to answer almost daily, usually from people who know my answer; they just don't believe the answer. My stock answer *is* the answer. My well-published reasons *are* the reasons. I am who and what I say I am. My record of honesty, having done business with our government for more than 20 years, speaks for itself—not to mention my contributions to the RNC."

"Okay, let's not get sidetracked. Why are we here?" Mr. Reilly asks.

Nickolas sits forward a little uncomfortably, folds his hands, uncertain where to begin. He makes an unconscious mental decision and says,

"A week ago I was contacted personally on a confidential basis by a diplomatic representative of the U.S. Cuban delegation here in Washington, who invited me to a confidential meeting with three Cuban Senators representing the Cuban Senate. I met with them at a hotel in Havana two nights ago for about five hours."

Mr. Reilly and Mr. Rafferty exchanged knowing glances. Ms. Fiora gave him a look of sincere concern. Mr. Rafferty says,

"Mr. Harvey, you have no authority to represent the U.S. Government with the Cubans or any other government just because…" Nickolas and Larry both interrupt. Nickolas says,

"Mr. Rafferty, obviously I know that. I was not there to represent the U.S. Government. I was there representing my organizational cause at their request. They, like you, simply wanted to verify my convictions."

"Do you realize, Mr. Harvey," continues Mr. Rafferty, "that it is against the law for U.S. citizens to travel to Cuba without the government's approval? You could be arrested, jailed, prosecuted, jailed again and fined."

Larry and Nickolas interrupt one another again this time, with Larry holding up his finger and superceding Nickolas.

"Mr. Rafferty, I know you're an attorney by education and previous experience. I think you know that I'm an attorney, as well. I assure you Mr. Harvey's short trip to Havana was carried out within the law," Larry says.

Mr. Rafferty replies, "We'll see. You can trust that the State Department will be checking with Treasury and the Office of Foreign Assets Control."

"While you're checking, Mr. Rafferty, with your OFAC people, please ask them to approve the application I made six months ago and which, in spite of biweekly follow-up, has not been approved or disapproved."

Mr. Rafferty says to Larry, "If Mr. Harvey illegally visited Cuba this week, that certainly will not bode well for a favorable approval of his application."

"We've already answered that allegation, Mr. Rafferty," Larry says.

"Mr. Harvey, the names of these various people, please," Reilly asks.

"I don't think that's important at this particular moment," Nickolas says.

Reilly asks, "Well, what is important at this particular moment, Mr. Harvey?"

"The fact that three senior members of the Cuban Senate were using me as a tool to confidentially explore the interest of the U.S. Government in some off-the-record discussions regarding a new accord between the U.S. and Cuba. Is this not a monumental diplomatic event, this signal that they want to enter into serious discussion?"

"We are constantly discussing certain issues with the Castro government, Mr. Harvey. Just because you don't hear about it, doesn't mean that it is not happening," Reilly says.

"True. However, if the meetings were addressing and achieving anything significant, I would hear about it."

"What makes you think this particular event of yours is serious?"

"Because I verified their interest."

"How?"

"By reviewing the major issues, as I understand them, on both sides."

"I believe that kind of discussion puts you dangerously close to illegally interfering with United States Foreign Policy with a rogue country," Rafferty says.

"I think you may be confusing the current administration's political strategy with foreign policy," Nickolas says.

"They can be one and the same."

"Not legitimately! Not ethically, not morally!"

"Trust me."

"Okay, I'm not going to argue with you. That's not why I'm here."

"Well, we're back to beginning. Why are you here?" Reilly asks.

"As I said, I came here to tell you I was there for a short meeting at their request to discuss the initiative I described previously."

"Why do you believe they invited you, as opposed to using existing diplomatic channels?"

"My guess is that they see the existing diplomatic channels as a waste of time, realizing the past and present political history, and that they see me and my association and its growing influence as one of the only friendly U.S. initiatives north of the Florida Straits in 20 years. I believe they have enough foresight to recognize a sea change on the horizon, one that perhaps the American government does not see or want to recognize."

Reilly and Rafferty look at one another briefly, the passing ciphered message undetectable to the others. They both hesitated, waiting for the other to say something intelligent.

Rafferty responds first. "Mr. Harvey, I would like to arrange a meeting with you tomorrow at the State Department to be debriefed, in detail, regarding your meeting in Cuba. Following that, we'll decide what we want to do about this potential initiative and for that matter, about your potential illegal trip to Cuba. Do you have time tomorrow a.m., say, at 10?"

Nickolas glances at Larry. Larry's look is saying, no, or let's talk first. Nickolas looks at Rafferty, then at Reilly, then Rafferty again, trying to determine what is in their head by looking through their eyes. Nothing, he thinks, with a small smile at his own little internal joke.

Nickolas says, "I'm sorry, but I am booked all day tomorrow and Friday. The weekend follows. My best suggestion is that I give you and Mr. Reilly a call on Monday, and we'll try to put a date together for later next week."

It is obvious Rafferty doesn't like that answer. He purses his lips, looks at Reilly. His body language is changing, and it's apparent that he is getting angry and ready to threaten Nickolas. He looks at Reilly, and Reilly imperceptivity shakes his head no. Rafferty wants to speak, but holds up for a beat or two, then says, "Mr. Harvey, I really would personally appreciate it if you could come down to State in the morning. We can't move on this information without knowing all there is to know about your meeting."

Nickolas says, "You know enough now, assuming you believe me, for this administration to decide how they wish to proceed politically and otherwise."

"Can I trust that there will be no leaks to the press of your meeting in Cuba and of this meeting?"

"Yes, pending the next meeting with Mr. Reilly and the White House Chief of Staff and advice of the administration's choice of option."

Reilly gets tense. "Mr. Harvey, that comment sounds like a threat to me!"

"You're overreacting, Mr. Reilly, I'm simply reminding you so you can remind your boss that this unprecedented situational opportunity isn't business as usual to me, my people and my organization. We, the United States of America, have the potential to tear down the last wall remaining from the Cold War! The one U.S. politicians built and maintain between the United States and Cuba! It is in our mutual best interest to work together to get this job done. It shouldn't take more than a few days for your boss and his boss to decide what they want to do. Have your boss let me know."

"He's not going to like this!"

"Sure he is. Once he thinks about it, he will realize it is the political opportunity of a lifetime—a major Signature Event for the outgoing president. If he doesn't do it, I guarantee you the next president will."

# LXVIII

## THE BLUE NOTE

Nickolas, Phil and Larry are at the Blue Note to bring Mike and Tim up-to-date on their meeting at the White House an hour ago. It is now 7 p.m., and the Blue Note is humming, nearing the end of the cocktail hour and the beginning of the dinner hour. They are sitting in the ARC corner booth. Betty Lou has brought Tim and Mike their first drinks and Nickolas, Phil and Larry, their second.

"Okay, you guys. I'm ready, lay it on me. What happened?" Tim says.

Phil responds for Nickolas and Larry, "It was a good match, but Nick and Larry out-danced them at the end. They threatened us, as you would expect. But Nick reminded them of the political reality of the situation and then there was no place for them to go. We achieved our objective, I think, because they are forced to look at their hole card and decide which way they want to go. The options for them are limited. You agree, Nick?"

"Yes, I do, the whole plan in my mind was to confess at a low level of government that we were in Cuba, visiting on the subject of reconciliation, before they found out otherwise, and to give them notice of the situation and time to think about what they wanted to do before we bounce these issues up the political ladder a level or two."

"Yes, and Nick gave them until next Friday to make up their mind!" Larry adds.

"Well, I wouldn't quite put it that way, but we let them know we see this developing situation, this opportunity, as a high priority for the United States Government and for this outgoing president and his party," Nickolas says.

"Nick, what do you think they will do?" Phil asks.

"I believe, that under the circumstances, they have no choice but to meet with us at the level we need."

"And that is?" Mike asks.

"President, Vice President, Head of State, White House Chief of Staff, somewhere right in there, or all of the above."

"That sounds great! Jesus we're really moving up on the ladder of political influence! Nick, you said that we could and would, but somehow now it's a surprise to me. I guess I was willing to help you try, but the reality of the potential achievement I never seriously considered. Amazing!" Tim says.

"Tim, you haven't seen anything yet. We're just now getting the respect nationally that we deserve and that we've been working hard to get. It's not accidental, we planned for this result. We got it now, I believe. We'll move onto the final phase from here, assuming that the White House, in the next four days, tells us what we want to hear, which is simply, come on over and visit."

"I don't think there is much doubt about that, you have them in a box. Fellas, it was a great day, just one of many, a toast to Nick, he continues to bat a thousand. I don't know how the hell he does it, but he does! To Nick!" Larry says.

They all toast Nickolas in an enthused, happy manner. They no more than sit their drinks down when Tony steps over to the table and says,

"Mr. Harvey, there's breaking news on CNN. You need to watch, we're turning it up for you."

Nick turns to the nearest big-screen TV and sees the news anchor with a big CNN 'Breaking News banner' over her head on the screen, saying,

CNN News: They all listen intently—"It is not apparent, according to the U.S. Coast Guard, why this small sailing vessel floundered; however, there have been a series of severe thunderstorms moving across the Florida Straits in the past 24 hours. Even small thunderstorm systems can unexpectedly develop in the Caribbean this time of year and they can create very high winds and heavy seas. The U.S. Coast Guard discovered the small sailboat about 40 miles directly west of Key West in the Gulf of Mexico. Only one person is known to have survived, who told the story of the severe storm and the overturning of the boat and the loss of the captain and six other passengers, which included an older married couple, two women, a young man and tragically, a one-year-old baby. The Coast Guard continues its search for survivors in the area. Stay turned to CNN for more breaking news as CNN continues to follow this tragic story. Reporting from Miami this is Adela Rodriguez."

Nickolas looks at his friends. The expression on his face reveals his deep feelings of remorse.

"Jesus, is there no end to these tragedies until we succeed! This is what we're fighting for—to end this kind of news. There's been no end to it in 50 years! Do we not learn anything? Are we totally oblivious to the value of human life in the world? Are our only solutions fences, guards and passing laws, useless laws? Jesus Christ! It's driving me nuts! It's like the U.S. war on drugs! We spend billions and the U.S. appetite just grows! How long does it take to figure out that what we're doing doesn't work? We're supposed to be the smartest people in the world, for Christ's sake!"

"You're right," Phil says. "This shit has been going on for years. No one has been effectively addressing it. The politicians don't want to lose the special interest voters."

"Don't get me going!" Nickolas replies.

"You're already going," Phil says.

"Okay, okay. I know, talking about it doesn't achieve anything. You have to take action. Go for the throat relentlessly, until you choke the life out of the problem. Life, being the money and influence, in most cases."

Phil, "Let's move on. We're here to celebrate. We don't want to get depressed trying to save the world tonight."

Nickolas' satellite phone rings. "It's your ten dollar bill, what do you want to say?"

"Mr. Harvey, it's Judy, our switchboard is going crazy. You've had probably 15 calls from media people wanting to talk to you about the Cuban boat tragedy."

"Just take messages, Judy. Tell them I'm at church praying that the Coast Guard finds survivors, which is, in fact, where I am going."

# LXIX

## THE WHITE HOUSE

The President of the United States is at his desk in the Oval Office when Vice President Russell Wentworth enters with Edward Thornton, White House Chief of Staff. Both men are carrying several file folders to two chairs in front of the President's desk. They both say, "Good morning, Mr. President," as they sit down.

"Russell, I think this is your meeting, proceed," the President says.

"Mr. President, I would like to bring you and Ed up-to-date on recent Nickolas Harvey, ARC developments."

"Sure, Russ, go right ahead," says the President.

"Well, as you both know, ARC came into being last January and they have been campaigning in a variety of ways ever since, for about nine months now, to normalize the U.S.-Cuban relationship or reconcile it. I'm not sure I understand the difference."

"What does '*normalize*' mean, Russ?" asks the President.

"They have described it to mean to commence a formal course of mutual action which, when complete, will treat Cuba in a manner very similar to the way we treat Canada and Mexico."

"But we don't treat Canada and Mexico the same way," says the President.

"I know."

"And Canada and Mexico are democracies and they are our friends and supporters, at least most of the time, and Cuba is not."

"True, of course, but they say that is a problem we created and now perpetuate for pure political reasons."

"Well, hell," says the President. "Does Harvey think we should be doing business with a Communist state, one who agreed to place nuclear missiles 90 miles south of Miami aimed at Washington, D.C.! One whose human rights record is one of the worse in the world?"

"Yes, Mr. President, he obviously does think that, and he is relatively quickly getting a lot of other people thinking the same way. We need to discuss the emerging developments on this subject of which you are unaware."

"Okay, Russ, go ahead. I have a feeling already that I'm not going to like what you're going to tell me."

Edward Thornton, White House Chief of Staff, says, "Mr. President, last Thursday some ARC executives met with Senator Dobson. They have some common background, and they asked Dobson to intercede on behalf of Harvey to arrange a White House meeting at the highest possible level in the very short term. Dobson called me and I arranged for my assistant, and an Undersecretary from State, who Andrew Wells recommended, to meet with Harvey last Thursday afternoon. They met. Harvey came with his attorney, Larry Downes, and his Chief of Staff, Phil Bowen. They met for about an hour.

"What was so important?" the President asks.

"The big news is that Nickolas Harvey had been contacted through the U.S. Cuban Foreign Office and invited to Havana for an off-the-record, unofficial meeting with three Cuban senators."

"You're kidding! I assume he did not accept?" The President says.

"You would assume wrong," the Vice President says. "He was in Havana for a meeting at the Hotel Inglaterra a week ago Tuesday night."

The President considers that news while scratching his chin, and says,

"You're kidding! Son-of-a-bitch! Everybody wants to be an ambassador! So what are we going to do about that? We can't have ordinary citizens negotiating with foreign governments and setting U.S. Foreign Policy, for Christ's sake! He has to have broken some laws! Didn't he?"

"He says he didn't. He's a smart guy with a smart lawyer, so it wouldn't surprise me if somehow he or the Cubans figured out how to do it legally. Anyway, we've launched a quiet review of the matter through Treasury. But, even if he did break some laws, I don't think we want to make an issue out of it."

"Why's that?"

"Well, there are several reasons, but let me finish my story."

"Sure, go ahead. What did these three senators have to say? Who were they? Do we know them?"

"At this time, we don't know who they are."

"What do you mean?"

"Well, Mr. Harvey is working under a confidentiality agreement with these three gentlemen. He says he will tell the three of us when we meet with him to discuss the meeting he had in Havana, and its ramifications on the U.S.-Cuban relationship."

"I don't want to meet with him. What's he want to discuss?"

"The three senators are suggesting that the Cuban Government may be ready to commence discussions on how to repair the U.S.-Cuban relationship."

"I can't believe that! Fidel blasted me and our government in a speech six months ago in Panama! He hates me, our party and everything else we stand for!"

"I'm telling you what Harvey is telling us. He, Harvey, wants to meet with us this week. He says he has to report back to the Cubans one way or the other by next Monday."

"By next Monday! Why now? Why now would Fidel want to become friends? This doesn't make sense!"

"Maybe Fidel doesn't even know. Or, maybe Fidel detects a change in the U.S. political attitude about Cuba brought about by ARC and Nickolas Harvey. His campaign has attracted a lot of media attention. Additionally, for the past three days, the search in the Gulf for the seven lost Cuban immigrants is on every news channel. The pro-con mix on this subject has changed considerably, according to several polls on the subject. This fact is true, even in South Florida. Each meeting ARC holds down there creates big media attention, and they all debate the hell out of it, and in the end, some Florida Cubans switch sides, and I don't mean they switch to pro-embargo. If my memory serves me correctly, ARC has held six meetings in South Florida in the past ninety days, not to mention that this current search at sea for immigrants has great PR benefits to ARC, way beyond what Harvey could stage or buy. Every other newscast has an interview with Harvey. Besides all that, we have an election coming up."

"I know, I know. I've never received more phone calls on this subject, both domestically and internationally. In fact, I got one this morning from Governor Smith of Florida, and one yesterday from Bud Jones from RNC. He shared the results of one of their quarterly polls. It wasn't good. Well, Russ, what do you think we need to do here?"

"The election is only 12 months away. I think we need to start getting on the right side of this issue while there is still time. The traditional value of the South Florida vote and money is slowly slipping away. Look at the progress Harvey has achieved in less than a year. In another year, the value of votes anti-embargo could be twice the value of pro-embargo—or even more. He has momentum in a lot of areas."

"Ed, what do you say?"

"I can't add anything to what's been said. I think you know, Mr. President, that I've always been pretty soft on this whole issue, but I've understood why we've had to do what we've done. I believe the *'tipping point'* is very near. When that happens, we're backing a losing proposition politically. Besides that, Harvey is taking control of the outcome of this situation away from us. I don't think that is going to improve our status around the world or at election time."

"How do we handle the U.S. Cuban senators? Those guys are not going to tip over very easily."

"Well, we need to invite Gonzales and Perio in for a little discussion and *'splain'* it to them," says the Vice President with a wry smile.

"They may not eat the dog food," says the President.

"What else are they going to do? We are the best friends they got—at least for another year," says the Vice President.

"That's what worries me," the President says. "Okay, let's put together a plan to shit-can our old friends and make some new ones! Is three days enough time to do that? We can meet with Harvey on Monday. Russ, tell Grace to reshuffle my schedule to make it happen. The goal here is to regain control, cut our losses in Florida and make us look like the good guys. If we do this right, we may come out of this situation smelling like roses, maybe even be the hero. Keep me advised."

"I have the ball, Mr. President."

# LXX

## WASHINGTON, D.C.

Nickolas had agreed to meet Juliana earlier in the morning at Jonathon's at noon. Nick had arrived at 11:40 to get the edge off and address other issues on his mind that morning.

Nickolas was halfway through his Chardonnay when Juliana arrived, and he stood to welcome her.

"Juliana, you've had me excited since your invitation to lunch this morning. What do my friends from Havana have to say?" They sat down.

"Nickolas, I've been equally excited. It's good news. Our friends have met with others in the Senate and they have decided that they want to meet with you again in Havana. Same time, same place, same kind of confidential, informal meeting," Juliana says.

"Do you know what's on their mind, what they want to talk about?"

"I'm not sure. I get the feeling that the people they talked to you about at your last meeting have some key questions they need to ask. So, I think, they just want to clarify a few basic issues before everyone moves forward to the next step."

"I see," Nickolas says. "Can we leave out the Cuban Mafia welcoming committee?" he says, smiling.

"I can assure you that our security will be much more effective. Will you come?"

"Well yes, I will, if I'm not in jail as a result of the last visit. I'm being investigated by the U.S. Treasury, OFAC office, over the legality of my last visit. I took your word that you would legally get me to Havana and back. I hope you knew what you were doing?"

"I was assured by someone I trust that you would be legal. I'll let him know right after lunch that the Treasury Department is investigating. I'm sure he had you covered."

"Here's my attorney's card. He is also a good friend. He is aware of the investigation. Have your guy call my guy. If I have to go to jail, I'm giving your cell phone number to my wife Elizabeth. I assure you that you would not want to hear from her on this subject."

"I understand."

Nickolas' cell phone vibrates on the table. "Juliana, I need to take this. It could be the President of the United States again." He smiles, he rises, walks toward a nearby patio door, and passes through to the outside. Juliana watches him through the window, smiling affectionately.

"Nickolas Harvey here."

"Nick, it's Phil. What did Juliana have to say?"

"The Cuban Senators called. They want to talk again. Is that why you called?"

"No, listen to this. I just got a call from the While House, one of the Vice President's administrative assistants. The Vice President, the White House Chief of Staff and the President want to meet with us next Monday afternoon at 1:30 p.m."

"Phil, that's fantastic, can you believe it? We're crashing through the concrete ceiling or whatever it is they call it! Amazing! How come no invitation to lunch? Listen to this, the Cubans also want another meeting! Great, tell them we'll be there with bells on! Anything else, Phil?"

"Isn't that enough? I called because I thought before you ended your meeting with Juliana, you should know that we reached the top of the 'food chain' here in America. Have an extra wine."

"You're right, Phil. It's important that I know that now. Thanks. See you in an hour or two."

Nickolas smiles and thinks, wow, a White House meeting with the President and little Nickie Harvey. Who'd of thought? He returns to his table and Juliana, while turning off his cell phone and any potential bad news. He wanted to savor only the good news for a while.

"Good news? You're smiling," Juliana asks.

"Yes. On Monday, I'll be meeting with the highest levels of the U.S. Government to talk about ARC. It may mean, like our friends in Cuba, that they see that the timing is right for a change in the U.S.-Cuba relationship."

"Nick, that's wonderful. I know how hard you have worked to get to this point. I'm happy for you and for our common cause. Our friends in Cuba will be excited to hear this news."

"Thank you, Juliana, you're a generous lady. This is a milestone event, but only one of many necessary on the road to success. Our major hurdles are still in front of us, the primary one being the agreement of a new accord between the U.S. and Cuba. That's the biggest challenge—convincing two old enemies to become friends."

"Juliana, I hope I don't say something next that disappoints you or puts you in an awkward position, but I need to say it. Take time to think before you answer."

"Okay, Nick, go ahead."

"The highest levels of the U.S. Government, as I indicated, know a little bit, not much, about our meeting in Havana early last week. They do not know of you or the senators specifically. But they know of my visit there and the purpose. They know it was a confidential, off-the-record, backdoor inquiry, which is not diplomatically that unusual. In four or five working days, this issue has reached the White House Oval Office. I'll be there Monday. As I've said, Juliana, this event on Monday accelerates my influence of these events in the U.S. considerably. I, therefore, need to accelerate my influence within the Cuban Government. Do you understand what I'm saying? I can't tell the U.S. President on Monday that I'll take his suggestions back to three Cuban senators for their consideration. We can't get the work done that way. You need to contact your boss and let him know that I am now dealing with the U.S. President here and that I need to be dealing with Fidel or Raul there. Do you understand? Do you agree?"

Juliana takes the time to think as suggested, and then says, "Yes, I do. I don't believe you have broken the level of confidentiality that was intended. However, you or your government is moving much faster than our people here thought possible. That could be a problem. I am uncertain how high up this initiative goes on my end at this time. The top may not be ready to more this fast. It is quite possible that Raul or Fidel do not even know about the meeting in Cuba last week. I understand your request. I agree that it is reasonable under the circumstances, but I don't know if we can get it done real fast."

"Well, you have until Monday noon to find out and/or, make it happen. I need to know before I meet with President Downing. I will not mislead him as to my level of influence with the Cuban Government at this time."

Juliana replies, "I understand. Give me until Monday. I'll let you know by noon. I'm buying today, we're celebrating. What do you want besides a Chardonnay? A dozen oysters Rockefeller?"

# LXXI

## THE WHITE HOUSE

Vice President Russell Wentworth is chairing a small meeting in his office at the White House. Those attending had only recently arrived and taken their seats at the small conference table. The Vice President exited his desk, took his chair at the head the table, and says,

"Mr. Harvey and Mr. Bowen, we thank you very much for coming in today to visit with us. You've met Andrew Wells, Head of State, and Chief of White House Staff, Edward Thornton. The President intended to be here, but an emergency requiring his attention arose, and he, therefore, extends his apologies. He did, however, request that I assure you that he is current on all recent events relating to you, ARC and your growing influence on the U.S.-Cuban relationship. Furthermore, he said to make sure that you understand that you and he are not at odds philosophically on the subject. Proof of that point of view is the fact that we are sitting here in the White House getting ready to determine how we can achieve a win, win, win for everyone involved."

"Thank you very much, Mr. Vice President. Phil and I are honored to be here and have the opportunity to discuss our cause with you and Mr. Wells. We are disappointed that the President wasn't able to attend, but we understand. We'll look forward to visiting with him at the next meeting."

"Very good then, let's move forward into the purpose of our meeting. As you've probably heard, Mr. Harvey, I'm a very frank businessman. I have only one approach—straightforward, totally candid. I believe it saves a lot of time and misunderstandings, so I will apologize now, right up front, if I insult your sensibilities in any way."

"Not to worry, Mr. Vice President, you won't be insulting a virgin. Tell it the way it is." Nick smiles, "I'll try to keep up."

"Mr. Harvey, I've looked into your background recently and find a very consistent level of personal achievement, college, NROTC, active duty with the Marine Corps, corporate career, started your own business, HDI—Harvey Defense Industries, and built that business into a major U.S. corporation. You do a lot of business with the U.S. Government, correct?"

"Yes, that's true. We've had a mutually beneficial relationship for a long time."

"And earlier this year, you retired, turning business operations over to your son, correct?"

"Yes, more or less. I'm still majority owner and Chairman of the Board and will remain so for some time to come. But, yes, it was my plan to semi-retire and refocus."

"And in post-retirement, you organized and founded ARC and entered politics."

"No, I wouldn't say that. What I would say is that which I've consistently said from the beginning, which in summary is: Life has been very good to me and I desire to give something back to this world in appreciation. I'm not a politician and I…" the Vice President interrupts.

"Why pick Cuba as an issue you wish to champion?"

"As I've said many times, it's an issue that currently results in a great injustice perpetrated upon 11 million innocent Cuban citizens primarily by self-centered U.S. politicians, for political purposes, which needs correction."

"You're a card-carrying Republican yourself of long standing, you donate consistently and generously. You periodically attend RNC fund-raising dinners here in Washington. You have many friends in the Defense Department. Why would you take this aggressive action counter to your chosen party's platforms?"

"Obviously, I don't agree with this specific piece of U.S. foreign policy. What I see is a continuing major injustice, whether Republicans or Democrats are in power, as they chase the same special interests money and related votes in South Florida. I could give you an hour on this subject, but I know that you already understand, probably much better than I do."

"Yes, I understand your position. I'm just trying to understand you and your motivations."

"I keep telling people this, but they don't seem to want to believe it. I am motivated for the reasons I have stated. I keep it all as simple and straightforward as I can, so that the guy and girl next door can understand it. I am who and what I say I am, for the reasons I say I am. What you see and hear is what your get."

"Well let me make you an offer, Mr. Harvey. I am authorized to offer you a position at the U.S. State Department as Chief Officer, Cuban Affairs, reporting directly to Mr. Bill Finley. Mr. Finley is here with us to tell you more about the position and its responsibilities. Bill, please proceed."

"Ah, Mr. Harvey," Mr. Finley says. Nickolas interrupts.

"Excuse me, Mr. Vice President. I appreciate your offer, I sincerely do; however, I just retired from a desk job about nine months ago. I still have the Chairman's job at HDI. Now I'm also Chairman, President and CEO of ARC. My plate is full and I'm happy as a clam."

"Well, realizing your goals, I thought the opportunity to legitimize your activities would appeal to you."

"I feel my activities are not only legal, but ethical, moral and spiritually on target. I'll go even further and say, politically correct, if you believe that politics in the U.S. Government should adhere to the principles of our U.S. Constitution, the Declaration of Independence and the Bill of Rights and the will of the people."

"Well said, Mr. Harvey. I see you can be pretty candid as well. But it isn't a perfect world we live in, is it?"

"No, it's not, but it sure as hell could easily be a lot more perfect than it is."

"Agreed, and that is why the President and I ran for public office—to change things for the better."

"If you really believe that, Mr. Vice President, you will support the objectives of ARC."

"Well, we're here today to try to determine if there is a good way to do that in a method upon which we can all agree. You just turned down a good job in an extremely persuasive position. Let me try another idea on you, see what you think. The Downing Administration will officially appoint you as its Senior Civilian Diplomat and Negotiator in a new round of discussions between the United States and Cuba in an effort to lift the U.S.-Cuba embargo. In that position, you would work directly for me but work hand-in-hand with Mr. Finley at State and with his Cuban desk people. In this capacity, the Federal Government would be funding the entire effort, and the full power and resources of the U.S. State Department would be available to you. What do you think?"

Nickolas takes a moment to think, realizing he wants to show respect for the Vice President's ideas. He pauses.

"No disrespect intended. I think, Mr. Vice President, considering where I am now and where I intend ARC to be, come election time, that your suggestion would simply slow us all down. Secondarily, I have an organization at ARC, and many there have sacrificed considerably to help me get to where we are. I couldn't abandon them. It is out of the question for that reason, if not others. But, again, I appreciate very much that you're even talking to me on this subject. I sincerely appreciate your offer to work directly for you, which would obviously be a great honor."

"Okay, can you agree to let the State Department assign to you some people to assist you in your discussions with the Cubans, your security, your media relations, whatever, legal issues?"

"Mr. Vice President, you said you were going to be candid and straightforward here. What is it you're really trying to accomplish?"

The Vice President hesitates, thinks, grimaces and shifts his weight.

"Mr. Harvey, I think it's obvious that you have the better hand in this poker game, but the U.S. Government has more chips than you and we can't afford to lose this pot—the *pot* being the negative political, domestic and international image and our reputation, if it is known or perceived that the current administration wasn't largely involved in this initiative, which now appears will be successful to some currently unknown degree."

"No disrespect intended, Mr. Vice President, but this administration seems to be coming to this realization kind of late in the game, don't you think, sir?"

"Well, you would probably say, it comes to us as it becomes politically expedient. But in reality, it comes to us in the normal course of politics and the realization of current economic and other reality in Cuba in a rapidly changing world. It doesn't matter if we come to this decision late, unless you want to punish this administration or take all the potential credit for yourself."

"I'm not engaged in this effort to punish anyone, achieve personal fame, nor fortune. I've expended $2 million of my family's retirement funds. If you've read or heard any of my speeches, you know I'm avoiding the blame game. I am, as you're saying, Mr. Vice President, a card-carrying Republication of long standing who has done, is doing, and wants to continue to do a lot of business with our government. What is your minimum need of me? Your last idea. I've heard your first three. Give me a bottom line that I can agree to."

The Vice President sits back, grimaces, looks at the Secretary of State, the White House Chief of Staff, takes a drink of water and smiles tightly at Nickolas.

"Mr. Harvey, would you mind terribly if I call you Nickolas?"

"Not at all, Mr. Vice President. Call me Nick, that's what all my friends call me, and I suspect that we are about to become friends."

"Thank you, Nick, and your suspicion is true, and you can drop the Mr. Vice President and just call me Sir, for short."

"Thank you, sir, I appreciate the informality."

"Nick, here's the bottom line. This administration has to have its fair share of the glory here. You're trying to achieve your Signature Event and we have to achieve ours. The President may or may not get re-elected. I want to assure that his legacy includes adequate credit for this foreign policy achievement. That's the bottom line, my friend. Now, how can we plan together to accommodate this need?"

# LXXII

## HAVANA, CUBA

Three days later Nickolas, Phil and Larry flew back to Havana aboard the HDI jet for another meeting requested by Senator Ramos and arranged by Juliana.

The meeting objective for Nickolas was to be introduced to some senior Cuban Government officials by Senator Ramos, while Phil and Larry met and discussed ARC initiatives with some Cuban Foreign Office attorneys, the people who actually drafted Cuban policy into law where necessary. Nickolas' job was to get agreement in principle with Cuba's leaders. Phil's and Larry's job was to memorialize the principle into written, detailed Cuban Foreign Policy and Law.

Nickolas, Phil and Larry and their two bodyguards arrived at the Cuban Government Center for each of their 10 a.m. meetings, and met Juliana in the lobby. Juliana introduced Phil and Larry to their meeting host, and they departed down a hallway.

Juliana then led Nickolas to the second floor and an executive office area meeting room.

"You seem to know your way around this building pretty well, Juliana. You spend a lot of time here when you are in Havana?" Nick asks.

"No, not really. When I'm in Havana, my office is in the building next door. The Foreign Office is in Building 12. The Minister, however, offices over here, and occasionally my boss brings me over here for meetings he has with the Minister."

"I see, are you the lead U.S. expert?"

"No, that would be the U.S. Foreign Secretary, my boss, Señor Cruz. I've told you about him before."

"Yes, I remember. But how come you're here and he isn't?"

"Because I'm the expert on a subject that he is not."

"And that is?"

"You, Mr. Harvey. I am the expert on you."

"I see. Did you get a raise in pay when you received that status?"

"No, but my clothing allowance was increased, and I was offered a better apartment."

"Hmmmm, I think I see. Did you take the better apartment?"

"Well, certainly, why wouldn't I?"

"Well, one reason would be your knowledge, once getting to know me, that you wouldn't have a need for a higher class apartment to impress me."

"Are you telling me there is no way I could get you to visit me in my apartment? What kind of friend are you?"

"Ouch! You outmaneuvered me on that one."

"I think your imagination was somewhere it shouldn't have been."

"My imagination, or the imagination of your boss who offered you the better apartment?"

"Ouch! You outmaneuvered me on that one. Let's let that subject rest."

In walk the three Cuban Senators, Ramos, Perez and Marini, with hugs for Juliana and backslaps all around—all old friends with fond memories of one another.

Ramos says, "Nickolas, it's so very good to see you again and so soon. You're a man of action! What's it been, 10 days?"

"You called. I came."

"That's why we're here, Nickolas—Perez, Marini and me, to manage your transition from visiting with us to visiting with Señors Vargas and Alvarez. Between us, with your assistance, my fellow senators and I have achieved the objectives we were challenged to complete. It was a pleasure spending a long evening with you, especially following such a bad beginning. You're an exceptional example of the American spirit,

Nickolas. I hope your people know that, or come to know it. Speaking for Señors Perez, Marini and myself, we must leave you in the capable hands of Juliana. It is necessary that we pass you and our common cause up the chain of command to those who can make the final, hard decisions and commitments."

"I understand," Nickolas says. "I have the ball, our ball. It was my pleasure and my honor to have met you and to have helped you get that ball rolling. I'll keep you informed as we move toward a successful conclusion. I sincerely thank you very much. It was your contact that started this process."

"No, Nickolas, it was your decision to organize ARC. We're not here to participate in this meeting and we must now go. We wanted to greet you and welcome you back to Cuba and Havana and encourage you to stay the course. We've done what we could to help you get to this point. Good luck!" The three senators exit the meeting room.

"Thank you all for stopping by to say hello, I appreciate it."

Nickolas happily sits back down. Juliana smiles at him, joining him in his pleasure at seeing the three senators again. At that moment, two men and a woman enter the room. Juliana and Nickolas rise to meet them, and Juliana makes the introductions.

"Nickolas, please meet Señor Juan Vargas, President of the Cuban Senate. President Vargas, please meet Nickolas Harvey, founder of the Americans for Reconciliation with Cuba Coalition, commonly referred to these days as ARC."

"My honor to meet you, President Vargas, I've heard about you for years and seen you on CNN many times," Nickolas says.

"It is my pleasure, Mr. Harvey. Thank you for responding so quickly to our request to come back to Cuba and visit with us. It is my understanding that this time you are going to stay another day or two and permit Juliana to show you around Havana. Is that true?"

"Yes, I didn't know Juliana was going to be my guide, but that will only make my visit more memorable."

"Good, I thought that would be the case. A car, driver and Juliana will make your tour much easier, more enjoyable and informative."

"Thank you. I'm sure you're right."

"Now, Mr. Harvey, permit me to introduce Cuba's Minister of Foreign Affairs, Señor Pedro Alvarez. You'll be meeting with the Minister today. I'll be joining you for dinner this evening, and the Minister and I will meet with you tomorrow. Please excuse me as I must return to the Senate. Have a good day." The President of the Senate left the meeting room.

"It's nice to meet you, Mr. Alvarez. I've heard nothing but praises for your good work over the years," Nickolas says.

"Thank you, sir, you are most generous. I add my welcome to the senators and must say that your good reputation precedes you, as well. It is my hope that our two nations can come to some reasonable new accord, beneficial to both countries."

"I hope so as well, Mr. Minister."

"I want to thank you for being so generous with Juliana. She is a big supporter of your agenda and of you personally. I wouldn't be here without her efforts."

"Yes, let us sit down and begin our important work, please."

The Minister pauses, and marshals his mental, emotional and physical resources for the combat of diplomatic negotiations. He opens his portfolio, reads briefly, and then says,

"Perhaps we should start by your telling me about yourself, your company, Harvey Defense Industries, and the creation of the Americans for Reconciliation with Cuba organization."

# LXXIII

## THE NEXT AFTERNOON

The President of the Cuban Senate, Juan Vargas, and Minister Alvarez commence the second meeting of discussions at the Hotel Inglaterra in Havana with Phil, Larry and Nickolas.

Juan Vargas says, "Mr. Harvey, we have followed with great interest your development of ARC and your organization's increasing U.S. national influence in recent months. You're a great organizer, planner and a persuasive orator. I am sure you must be very pleased with your progress at this point?"

"Yes, I am, Mr. President. Planning-wise, ARC is way ahead of where we thought we'd be in the national polls at this time. The path, however, has not been without its hills and valleys, but we've persevered."

"Yes, I recall reading about your organization's funding shortfall a month or so ago. Have you overcome that problem? Cuba is not a rich country, but I'm sure we could help you in some way. May we?"

"Thank you very much for the offer, Mr. President, but our appeal to certain U.S. businesses for financial assistance was well received, and we are now funded for the foreseeable future— actually, for the next 12 to 15 months, up to the next U.S. election, and that point is really as far as we believe we'll have to go. In other words, we will have succeeded or failed. Of course, we fully expect to win. The fact that we're sitting here now is evidence that the dynamics of the situation have changed a great deal in favor of ARC's success."

"I agree, Mr. Harvey. The world is in a phase of accelerated change. Even in Cuba, where there has been little change in many years, we recognize that we cannot move forward in the future using the methods of the past. We too, must change and we must change at a far more rapid rate, or the world will leave us so far behind that catching up will be impossible."

"In my judgment, Mr. President, Cuba is at the threshold of great new opportunities. The major question is, is she courageous enough to step through the door and into a bright, new future? To do so, she will have to let go of the past. Is she capable of doing that?"

"One might make the same corollary about the U.S. at this point in time as it relates to Cuba, Mr. Harvey."

"I wouldn't disagree at all, Mr. President, although ARC has done a great deal to change those old ideas. You need only to consult the polls on this subject to realize that the South Florida U.S. Cuban voting bloc has already been neutralized. As the ARC campaign continues into the final month before the election, ARC's broad-based citizen support will go positive two-to-one on the reconciliation issues. This lead is forecast, without the high-value consideration of large U.S. business interest support, which is just now developing."

"I thought you had large U.S. business support?"

"I have a modest amount of financial support from four large U.S. companies, which wish to remain anonymous at this point in time. These companies and others wouldn't become aggressive financially or politically without a full realization that they'd win and that there would be return on investment. That fact is just now becoming reality."

"I see," the President says.

"Even the U.S. Government, until recently, interpreted ARC's objective as only about lifting the embargo. As I believe you understand, lifting the embargo would unquestionably result in a significant economic boost for Cuba, depending upon the terms and conditions of the resulting agreement, which no one has yet addressed. However, disregarding a reasonable replacement agreement to the embargo, Cuba should have much higher aspirations and so should America. Those aspirations should go well beyond a simple replacement of the embargo and the continuance of a frictional relationship between our two countries. Do you agree, Mr. President?"

"Ah yes, I think I do. However, I believe it may be more difficult for Cuba to come to terms with such goals than America, even though Cuba would obviously benefit the most from a significantly improved relationship. It may be, probably would be, difficult for Cubans to move forward as boldly as Americans might suggest or desire."

"I understand. You must stand up to walk, you must walk before you jog, jog before you run. A good strategic, long-range plan would be necessary."

"Yes, a mutually agreed upon plan."

"That objective is manageable, Mr. President. Where do we go from here?"

"I have reviewed the list of major discussion points you shared with our three senators. I agree that they are as good a starting point as any for initial discussions at the highest levels of our two governments. If we can reach some sort of mutually acceptable informal accommodation over time, we can then proceed through the traditional governmental diplomatic and legal processes to reach the desired conclusion."

"Are you then saying, Mr. President, that Cuba is prepared at this time to enter quietly into these discussions?"

"No, I am not; however, Chairman Raul Castro is. I suggest we break until 10 p.m. this evening, when Señor Raul Castro will join us for dinner."

Nickolas was flabbergasted, but revealed nothing. He did not expect to meet Raul on this trip. He concluded his two-hour meeting with Juan Vargas and Minister Alvarez at 3 p.m. This was an early end of the business day by Cuba's standards.

He knew it was unlikely that Phil and Larry, at their level of government discussions, would finish that early. There was a plan to meet in the hotel bar at 9 p.m., which was also early by Havana's social standards. Nickolas decided to have a drink at the hotel's sidewalk café and then catch up on some reading and take a much-needed nap, followed by a long hot shower and a slow get-ready routine for the nine o'clock meeting.

# LXVIII

## HOTEL INGLATERRA SIDEWALK CAFÉ

Nickolas settled into a shady table on the sidewalk patio of the building next door to the hotel's restaurant-bar entrance. It was a beautiful, sunny late afternoon with a warm steady breeze out of the southeast. He ordered a Blanco wine, took out his iPhone and started reviewing various notes, schedules, business plans, goals and objectives. This task, done in private, in a nice atmosphere, at his own chosen pace, was one of his favorite and most relaxing activities. Nick liked thinking and planning and he was very good at it, always had been.

He was deep into his thinking, enjoying his wine, when he realized he had company at the next table in a seat almost next to him. He looked around. Half the tables were empty with everyone widely dispersed among the available seats. Yet, someone had decided to sit right next to him. He knew this was not by accident, but chose not to recognize the situation at that moment. But, he did decide to offset the intrusion by moving to his left one seat, which then had him looking directly at the profile of the intruder. He continued to work on his iPhone, while studying the man to his right front.

The man was dressed in a cheap, somewhat dingy, rumpled, white suit with large lapels and an open-necked white shirt with an oversized collar. Nickolas' quick assessment of the physical threat level was low.

The Cuban man was perhaps 40, thin, 160 pounds, stringy, but not muscular—soft stringy, and obviously had a bad case of acne as a kid. He had a mustache and long black hair under an aged, stained Panama hat, and wore large black sunglasses, a $20 watch on the wrist and a $10 signet ring on the little finger. Nick thought, if this is a hit man, he's not doing very well. The intruder felt Nickolas' eyes upon him, turned and said in accented English,

"How are you today, sir?"

"Very well, thank you. And you?" Nick answers.

"I'm well, also. Thank you for asking."

"It is a beautiful Havana day, is it not?"

"Yes, it is, one of many at this season. Are you visiting for long?"

"No, just a couple of days."

"A shame, you cannot see Havana in a day or two."

"I agree. However, I expect to be back several times in the next few months."

"You are indeed fortunate. Most Americans aren't able to visit Cuba at their leisure."

"I'm not just *any* American, as you know. Let's get to the bottom line here. You're here to deliver a message. What is it?"

"You are very perceptive, Mr. Harvey."

"Yes, I am."

"The message is simple and brief: *'Don't come back to Cuba.'* I understand you're a very intelligent fellow, a *'nice guy,'* as you Americans say. However, you're into something you don't understand and in it way over your head, as they say. I'm here only to give you some friendly advice, which my employers hope you take very seriously. You and your *'pussy posse'* do not want

to continue your misguided, misinformed crusade any further in Cuba."

"Or what?" Nickolas asks.

"I was told not to threaten you. I was told you were a smart guy, a family man, a family man with a beautiful wife and two beautiful children in San Diego."

"You know what? You just threatened me. Worse, you threatened my family. Now I have to threaten *you* so you'll know that if you or your boss even *thinks* about threatening me or my family, I'll kill the lot of you. I'll wait three weeks for you to die, taking one appendage of your body each day."

"Sounds serious, Mr. Harvey, but I must emphasize once again, you do not know who you are dealing with. They have forgotten more about torture and pain then you could ever know."

"I trust you. I realize I'll have to make an extra strong statement. Now get out of my sight before I lose control and make an example of your skinny ass right here and now!"

The intruder smiled, revealing a life of poor dental hygiene. He rose from the table to his feet and started to speak. Nickolas raised his finger to him and said, "Don't say it! Or so help me, I'll kick your ass right here and now!"

The intruder smiled again, with uncertainty and an unconscious feeling of fear. But he poked his left hand middle and forefinger at Nick twice, pulling the imaginary trigger, nodding his head as he departed the area. Nick only got really angry and agitated if it happened fast. This had happened fast. He was highly agitated. He looked around the other tables and down the sidewalk. No one seemed to have noticed the verbal altercation.

Nick made a quick decision, probably too quick. He stood, threw down a U.S. $10 bill on the table and stepped out to the sidewalk. He could see the antagonist about 50 yards ahead down the street and crossing to the other side. Nickolas immediately crossed the street and started following him. The white suit and old Panama hat made it easy. After about four blocks the man turned into a narrow alley between two old four-story buildings. Nick thought, *Is this a trap?* Was this guy just setting me up? He didn't think so. He cautiously entered the alley and could see the man down the center, maybe 30 yards ahead at this point. He took out his wallet and held it up, smiling and yelled,

"Hey man, you dropped your wallet under the table when you left. Here it is."

The man turned, surprised to see Nickolas holding a black wallet, which he apparently thought was his. He was momentarily confused. Nickolas continued smiling and walking toward him. The man didn't know what to do. Nickolas was holding up the wallet head high in his left hand, smiling, saying in a friendly manner,

"Jesus, I've been trying to catch up to you for four blocks buddy."

The man was still confused. He slapped his right rear pocket. His wallet was there. He checked his breast pocket, it wasn't there. This wasn't his wallet, but this crazy Yankee thought it was. It could be full of American dollars, having been lost near the Hotel Inglattera, he thought. He looked at Nickolas, now 10 yards away, smiling, holding the wallet high. The intruder, his mind still uncertain and confused, but greedy, hesitated five seconds too long and worse yet for him, he reached for the wallet with his right hand. As he touched Nick's wallet, he was hit square in the center of the face with a hard blow from the open palm of Nick's right hand. The blow splintered the intruder's nose bone and started a major blood flow, and knocked the man off his feet and onto his back.

The intruder slowly sat up, tried to quench the blood flow with both hands, but could not. The surprise of the blow, the power, the pain, the blood, the knockdown, all within a second or two, totally disabled the man. He was choking on his own blood; he could not see, think, scream or resist. Nickolas bent over him and removed his wallet and identified his name and address. He took the time while standing over his writhing, crying victim to punch it all into his iPhone, repeating it all verbally so the victim, Roberto Ortiz, 121 Garcia Drive, would know.

Roberto screamed, "You son-of-a-bitch, you'll pay for this if I have to track you back to San Diego!"

"You're not very smart, Roberto, you just threatened me again. Do you like pain? Is that it? Let's see."

Nickolas leaned down and lightly pushed on Roberto's badly broken nose.

Roberto screamed, followed by, "Oh God! Oh God!"

Nickolas looked up and down the alley. No visitors. So, he grabbed Roberto and pulled him between two large dumpsters to one side of the alley, out of sight of the sidewalks at both ends.

Roberto was still in too much pain to do anything except lean against the wall, his shirt and jacket covered with bright red blood.

"Now Roberto, what was that you were saying about seeing me or my family in San Diego?" Nickolas says

"Nothing, nothing!" Roberto says. "You misunderstood my meaning, you misunderstood."

"Okay," Nick says. "You're starting to learn to be a gentleman. Good. I don't want to hurt you, Roberto. I just want you and your boss to understand that my pussy posse and I are very serious about what we do. I have a few more questions, Roberto, who is your boss?"

"I'll die if I tell you that!"

"You may die anyway, and you're going to tell me. The only question is how many fingers and toes, legs and arms you will give up before you do. Would you prefer to be unable to walk or to wipe your ass? You decide. I don't care, tell me now."

"You don't know what you're asking. They'll kill me, my wife, my kids, and my mother!"

"Hey, you threatened mine. I told you, I believe you. I don't care! But I can see we need to get started here. Give me that finger you pointed at me back at the hotel."

"No! No! Please. I got the message! You're a bad motherfucker. I believe it, I'll tell them! Please don't touch me!"

"Roberto, I know you'll tell them, but a picture is worth a thousand words. You're the picture. Do you want to be a dead picture or a live picture? Give me that finger!"

"No! No! No!"

Nickolas reached out for Roberto's bloody left hand, grabbing it in his left hand. He had the index finger of Roberto's left hand in his left and he bent it back toward the upper wrist to the point of breaking. Roberto went to his knees before his finger cracked.

Roberto screamed, grabbed his left hand with his right and held it tight against his chest.

"Roberto, you're a real sissy, broken fingers don't hurt that much. Are you ready now? I'm going to do another one for you real quick. But first, who is your boss and where can I find him?" Nickolas asks.

"No! No! Please! No! I can't tell you."

"Yes, you can and you will in the next few minutes. I guarantee it!"

Nickolas grabbed Roberto's left hand again and quickly bent the middle finger back until it snapped. Roberto yelled. Nick put his right hand over Roberto's mouth and broken nose to muffle the noise. Roberto started choking on his own blood again. "Are you learning anything yet?" Nick asks.

"Yes, yes, I am! You're a mean motherfucker. I'm going to tell them!"

"Well, Roberto, let's go for the other index finger, which will really limit your ability to wipe your ass. But you'll still be able to walk to the toilet."

Nick grabs the other hand. Roberto starts to fight and kick. Nick pushes on Roberto's nose. Roberto screams and grabs his face. Nick grabs the right hand. "Who do you work for Roberto and where do I find him?"

"Okay! Okay! Jesus, look at my hands! Okay! No more! He is Captain Barrego Cherino of the Cuban Military Police. He'll kill me if you tell him I told you. Please don't tell him. I have a family. You can find him at Government Center at the Cuban Military Police Command Headquarters. He reports to Colonel Quertero Rojas, who reports to Raul. He has remained untouchable since the Revolution. He's a very powerful man. He wants to stay a very powerful man."

# LXXV

## THE NEXT DAY

Nickolas was having a small breakfast and a pot of strong Cuban coffee in the Hotel Inglaterra lobby restaurant. It was 9 a.m., and he was meeting Rose Rodriquez and Priscilla Hernandez at 10 a.m. at a coffee house on Mencione Boulevard overlooking the ocean. Juliana would meet the women first to assure them that their meeting with Nickolas was innocent and sanctioned by the government and that there was no problem whatsoever with their talking to him. Juliana would interpret. Further, they would know that Nickolas was basically meeting with them to introduce himself and to express his sympathy for their loss. Juliana would have already given each of them a letter signed by President Vargas, exonerating them from any legal complicity from the effort of Rose's husband, daughter and grandbaby and Priscilla's son from illegally trying to escape Cuba. It was a personal favor Nickolas had requested and received.

Nickolas knew that regardless of what Juliana said, the women may not be very communicative. But it didn't matter as far as he was concerned. He wanted to meet the two women, look into their eyes and tell them how very sorry he was that he had been too late in his efforts to bring change to the Cuban situation in time to possibly save their loved ones. He thought, if they had only waited another 90 days, the outcome could have been totally different in the lives of seven human beings who were now dead because they pursued freedom, democracy and the hope of the American dream. In America everyone takes those ideals for granted. They pay no price to have them beyond legality. Yet, for unnecessary political reasons, these seven people paid with their lives. What a waste. Why does daily life for many have to be so poor that people will risk their very lives to change it?

Nickolas pulled the file out of his leather portfolio that his security staff had prepared for him. It included all of the data available on those on the boat and the two women he would be meeting in less than an hour. Juliana had provided much of it from the Cuban Government files they maintained on every citizen, all 11 million of them. The file on Priscilla, due to her husband being a dissident, was quite extensive. Rose's was much less so. Her husband was a fisherman, but the file included four pages dated in the 1950s, covering Manuel's Revolutionary past as an officer in Fidel's small but effective Revolutionary Army.

Nickolas couldn't read Cuban, but he was familiar with military-type personnel records and could tell from the lack of written commentary in various remarks sections that it was unlikely to contain anything very noteworthy beyond Manuel's more-or-less standard military statistical data. There was one official looking letter, which appeared to be a commendation that Nickolas would ask Juliana to interpret for him, but that was all.

Nickolas, however, being a marketing guy, had enough basic sales skills to enable him to speak like he had known both of these women for years, if he had wanted to. He wasn't there to impress them, but he did want them to know that he was sincere enough to have done his homework.

He finished his second cup of coffee, wanted another, but thought he would wait to have the third one with the three women at 10 a.m. He put his reading material back into his thin portfolio, paid his bill in pesos and departed the lobby area, hailing a cab out front.

A 10-minute cab ride in a 1954 Oldsmobile, four-door sedan, at a cost of $2 American expressed in pesos, with a $1 tip in American, landed him in front of Tomaso's sidewalk coffee shop on the north side of the Mencione across from the ocean.

It was a beautiful sunny morning under a blue sky with the sound of the rhythmic wash and crashing surf carrying across the broad boulevard. He was in his element. He loved the sea.

As Nickolas had exited the cab and was enjoying the ambiance on the sidewalk, he heard his name being called and looked around to see Juliana standing at a table in the shade not far away, at which were seated two middle-aged, attractive Cuban women, who were smiling demurely at him. Nickolas thought, I hope Juliana told these women what a wonderful guy I am. It would ease his burden if he sensed they liked him and accepted him for who he was, as opposed to one or two of his less attractive media images. He proceeded to the table with his most friendly, disarming smile on his face. In his mind it seemed to work, as both their smiles and eyes brightened. As he approached, he bowed a little and said in Cuban,

"Good morning, ladies. It is my pleasure and honor to meet you." They both laughed at his introduction, touching each other's arm. He shook both their hands. Rose stood, insisting on a hug, which he gladly returned in appreciation of her early acceptance. Juliana and Priscilla looked left out so he gave them a hug, too.

Nick sat down a little nervously, giving Juliana a special smile and raised an eyebrow questioning if everything was on plan. She nodded, smiling perceptibly in assurance.

Juliana says in Spanish, "Ladies, this is the handsome man I've been telling you about, Nickolas Harvey, Founder, Chairman, President of the Americans for Reconciliation with Cuba Coalition, ARC for short. You may not have heard much about him here in Cuba, but in the United States, he is becoming a national leader, a champion, if you will, for a future of peace and goodwill between the U.S. and Cuba. Nickolas is working hard to achieve a new beginning in the U.S.-Cuba relationship, which will be mutually beneficial to both countries and their people.

"Mr. Harvey was distraught to hear of each of your losses of family members. He is here to share his feelings with you and invites you to share yours with him. He believes that the aspirations and goals of your lost loved ones are synonymous with his personally and his organization's. Further, that you and your lost loved ones have been, or are now, soldiers in a much larger, well-founded, well-led organization of committed citizens of the world who will, in due time, bring peace, democracy and freedom to Cuba."

Juliana then told Nick in English what she had just told Rose and Priscilla.

"Juliana," Nickolas says, "you have been paying closer attention to my speeches than I thought you were! That was very good! I have a good job for you if you want it."

Juliana interpreted for the ladies and they smiled and laughed, Priscilla touching him on the elbow.

Nick thought, what a beautiful pair of ladies. Why did they have to experience such tremendous tragedy in their lives? He looked at them, laughing at Juliana's story. His eyes filled up. He turned his head into the breeze before they flowed, coughed a fake cough, took out his handkerchief and blew his nose, wiping his nose and eyes in a quick swipe, then turning back to the table and the ladies, with a smile.

# LXXVI

## THE WHITE HOUSE

Nickolas had returned to Washington from Havana 20 hours earlier and spent a quiet evening with Elizabeth, followed by a good night of rest and breakfast this day. Per earlier arrangements, Tony had picked him up and delivered him to the White House for a mid-morning meeting with Vice President Wentworth. Nickolas was escorted into the Vice President's office.

"Nick, welcome home. How was your trip? You were there, what, two, three days?" Vice President Wentworth asks.

"Yes, one and half days getting there and back, one in a meeting and one and half days looking around. I flew back yesterday afternoon."

"I heard you had a little trouble over there again. The natives are apparently not as quiet as the government wants us to believe."

"Well, somehow the natives know some of what is going on, being considered, whatever, and they are trying to influence the outcome one way or the other."

"Which way?"

"Actually, I believe both. There are Cubans who want an American relationship, democracy and capitalism, and there are others who do not want social and economic change in Cuba. It's not surprising. It's human nature. It's business. It's fear of change. The same things are happening here in the good old U.S.A. If you don't believe it, go to South Florida."

"Well, bring us up-to-date," the Vice President says. "What's happening?"

"I had a good meeting with the President of the Senate, Señor Juan Vargas, and the Cuban Minister of Foreign Affairs, Señor Pedro Alvarez. We spent four hours discussing the issues on two occasions."

"I thought Raul had agreed to meet with you and Vargas?"

"Yes, he did, but he didn't show initially. They saved him until after Vargas and Alvarez thoroughly interviewed me."

"I see, but you did meet with him?"

"Yes, he joined us for dinner the last evening we were there. He was clear in stating that they were ready, on an unofficial, unpublicized basis, to commence discussions at the senior level. If the basics can be agreed upon at that level, we can turn our State Department loose on their Foreign Office and hammer out the details and a legal agreement. ARC's Chief of Staff and our attorney have had a preliminary meeting with Cuba's Foreign Office people."

"Hey Nick, that's great! That's what you've been working for right? That's what we all want now, to get rid of that embargo! You should be smiling ear to ear!" Nick wasn't smiling. "What's the problem?"

"They want far more than just the embargo being lifted. Raul says he wants a broad-based, comprehensive, long-range plan for a new U.S.-Cuban relationship, including a five-year economic aid and redevelopment plan. I assume their new demands are far more than you are initially willing to bite off?"

"I don't know, yes, probably, I would have to talk to the President. That's a big jump, you know, between an unknown replacement plan for the embargo and a broad-based bilateral five-year plan for the economic redevelopment of Cuba. That's a huge jump! It's a 180-degree jump! But on the other hand, all negotiations start with high expectations."

"We'll all have to talk, the White House staff, I mean. After thorough consideration, we'll visit again with you."

"Sure, Vice President Wentworth, I understand. But, remember, you don't need to agree to anything except to agree to talk about it. That's not much of a binding commitment."

"Well, that's true, but there is an implied intent of purpose."

"So what, you can stand strong on that point, but you listen."

"True, let us talk about it. Are they indicating any concern that you're representing the U.S. in these negotiations as only a citizen diplomat?"

"No, they believe that ARC and I have their best interests at heart. No one else in America has championed their country's needs. They trust me, I believe, to get done what I advise them is reasonable to get done."

"Don't become overconfident, Nick, there cannot be any real trust between the U.S. Government and Cuban Government at this point. They are just hopeful that you are who you say you are, and what you say you are."

"And, I am. I think they know that and trust in that. Where do we go from here?"

"We need to hold a few internal meetings, then meet with the President. We had him and others lined up to ease the economic embargo, but he is not lined up for what you have described they now want. This initiative is much bigger than we thought a couple of weeks ago!"

"Just remember, Vice President Wentworth, that the downside for the President's Administration remains the same. This foreign relations achievement can happen with your administration's leadership and on President Downing's watch and be a major positive accomplishment, which puts him into the history books, or not. He hasn't had many foreign policy successes. Or the next administration can do it, and get all of the credit. One way or the other, this major event will happen soon. In my judgment, for him, at this time, it's a no-brainer."

"Thanks for reminding me, Nick!"

# LXXVII

## EN ROUTE TO THE BLUE NOTE

Nickolas left the meeting with the Vice President satisfied that he had made a good argument for the current administration to undertake a major change and liberalize its current Cuban foreign policy before the next election, now about six months away. Of course, the proof was in the pudding, as they say.

Nickolas had called for his car near the end of this meeting, and it was now in the passenger pickup circle waiting for him. Tony was at the rear door and opened it for him as Nickolas got in.

"How did it go boss?" Tony asks.

"It went well, Tony. The next time we come back here it will be to visit with the President of the United States and the leader of the free world!"

"It doesn't surprise me a bit. I never doubted your ability to get us to the top. But it's still kind of amazing though when you think about where we were a year ago and where we are now, isn't it?"

"Yes, it is. It's amazing and exciting at the same time. But, we still have a lot to get done."

"Yes, I know, but you'll get us there."

Tony checked them out through the White House security gate and they turned right on Constitution Avenue. Tony had noticed that a black Suburban had followed them as they left the parking area, and also made the turn behind them on Constitution. It was too early to identify a follower, but he periodically kept his eye on the rearview mirrors.

"Boss, I'm going to make few turns off our track. We may have another follower, maybe two."

"Okay, check it out, but remember it is just as likely to be Uncle Sam as the bad guys."

"Yes, I know. That's the friggin' problem, you don't know if they're bad guys or good guys until they're shooting at you!"

"That's why we sent you to combat driving school, Tony. Escape and evade, as they say."

"Okay. We'll see here in a minute. Hold on."

At the next corner Tony turned left on a yellow light, and both the first and second car behind him sped up and made the turn.

Tony says, "Hmm, two cars made the turn with us. It was the second car I was worried about."

"Have they closed the gap?"

"No, same pacing after the turn."

"Let's do it again up there on Grand Boulevard. You'll have less traffic and more room to maneuver."

"Okay boss, but so will they."

"Tony, either it's going to happen or not, and it probably isn't. I am as ready now as I ever will be. Besides, they can't reach us with anything less than a .50-caliber. You know the drill. If necessary, you take the right front tire and I'll take the left rear tire. Get your weapon ready, but don't open your shooting port unless they've fired on us and are right alongside."

"Got you, boss. Here we go."

Tony took the next corner onto North Grand Boulevard and accelerated enough to test the pacing of the two cars following.

"Boss, everything I know says both of these cars are following us."

"Okay, stay in the right lane. With just the two of us, we are disadvantaged on the right. But if somehow they get us boxed, I'll take the car on the right or behind; you take the car on the left. Remember, the best place for them to initiate the box is at a stoplight. Keep making right turns if you have to."

"Got you, boss. Get ready. The Suburban just passed the Cadillac."

"Cadillac! That doesn't sound like Uncle Sam."

"Well, a Suburban does. Hold it. The Cadillac just sped up! They're both coming fast! Get ready! We're getting out of here."

Tony hit the accelerator hard, and the Hemi engine almost burned rubber at 50 mph. Tony put another hundred yards between him and the two following cars before they knew what was happening.

Nickolas looked back and witnessed something strange. The Cadillac overtook the Suburban and forced the Suburban to sideswipe about a half-dozen parked cars and then roll over about six times down the middle of the street, while the Cadillac sped on and turned right at high speed at the next corner.

"Jesus! Hey! Did you see that? What the hell?"

"We have an unknown benefactor! Wow! And one that plays for keeps! Who the hell do you suppose that was? Head for the Blue Note, Tony, we need a drink and to watch CNN! Also, call Mike and have him meet us there."

# LXXVIII

## THE BLUE NOTE

Thirty minutes later Nickolas, Tony and Mike were sitting in their corner booth at the Blue Note. It was 11:30 a.m., and the early luncheon crowd was starting to show up. Betty Lou was seating guests on the other side of the bar since Nickolas and Mike were in the corner booth. She would continue to do so until the other side was full or Nickolas and Mike left.

CNN was on the big screen in the far corner. Tony was saying to Mike,

"Mike, you should have seen it! We picked up two tails leaving the White House. We didn't know if they were good guys or bad guys. I made two right turns, staying in the right-hand lane so they couldn't box us and then we got on Pennsylvania and I gunned it! We had to be doing 90 when the rear tail car passes the front tail car and then the front tail, in an old Cadillac, guns it, catches up with the SUV that had just passed him and blocks him into about six parked cars! The SUV hooks his front end onto the last car and rolled himself about five or six times! What a mess. They'll be cleaning up Constitution Avenue for hours!"

"What about the Cadillac? Do you know who it was? For that matter, who was in the SUV?" Mike asks.

"No, we got out of the area as fast as we could and so did the Cadillac. We stopped here to watch the news with you, to see what they report," Nickolas answers.

"Well, no one I can think of in government is driving around in an old Cadillac trying to save your ass. So who is it?" Mike asks.

Nickolas' face was blank. He was thinking. Then he revealed a small smile and a barely perceptible nod of his head.

# LXXIX

## HYATT HOTEL WASHINGTON, D.C.

*JULY*

At the last Monday morning staff meeting at the ARC offices, Mike had called for a special meeting on the subject of security. He said that the reason for the special meeting was to identify ways and means to meet the rising threat level to the ARC organization, which Nickolas had experienced personally and that his intelligence sources had been identifying over the past 60 days. Mike further indicated that he had suppressed some of these threats. He didn't say how, but others said that he had been forced, by circumstances, to exceed his legal authority or current ARC Security Policy to get the job done.

Mike had chosen the Presidential Suite at the top of the Washington Hyatt for this secret meeting of the executive staff and all of the security people. Nickolas had questioned Mike on the dollars and cents of this choice of venue, and Mike had informed him that the Hyatt had donated the $5,000-a-night suite to ARC, including appetizers and booze for their 4 p.m. to 9 p.m. meeting.

It was four o'clock, and everyone was seated in the open living room, dining room, bar-kitchen area. Mike brought the meeting to order, standing in front of the large stone fireplace.

"Ladies and gentlemen, please take a seat. We are gathered here in the beautiful Washington Hyatt Penthouse to discuss ARC security issues, realizing our threat level has been rising quickly in the past month or two. This situation is both the good news and the bad news. It's the bad news because it is increasing rapidly. It's the good news because if the threat is increasing, it is because our organization is becoming more successful, more rapidly than anyone, besides Nick, of course, ever thought could happen.

"Human beings do not like change, particularly human beings who are in power, whatever their cause or source of power. ARC has created a lot of change and is at the threshold of creating much more. We have reached and exceeded the tipping point.

"The power and aspirations of some of these competitive stakeholders are huge. Yes, I said hhuuugge… ! In some cases, it's about money and the money is billions! It's hhuuugge! In other cases, it's power and prestige, and with those people it's hhuuugge! With others, it's emotion, and with them it's hhuuugge!" Everyone laughed at Mike.

"We, therefore, must become increasingly vigilant as our organization moves into the last phase of our business plan, which requires that our opposition move into the last phase of theirs. Our opposition's last phase is to stop us at all costs. All costs means no limitations on how they eliminate ARC as a threat. Some of our opposition, and we don't even know who all of our opposition is, is likely willing to attempt murder and mayhem to stop us! I cannot overstate the danger of the period of time we are moving into.

"We are here tonight to revisit all of our security plans, intelligence, strategies, tactics, personnel levels, equipment, weapons systems, communications, policies, procedures, strengths, weaknesses, operating environments, etc., etc. Some of you have been asking for this meeting for a couple of months. Here it is. Let's give it all we've got in the way of good input and good planning until 7 p.m. Then we'll break for some high class finger food and a drink. At 7:30, we'll hear the quarterly status report of all department managers. Following the status reports, we'll discuss and agree upon the next priorities and action planning steps. Thank you."

"Thank you, again. Nick, would you like to add anything?" Mike says, following the last of the applause.

Nickolas gets up, walks to the front of the fireplace, and says,

"Mike, I believe your calling of this meeting and its purpose is very timely and your stated objectives are right on the mark. I couldn't add much of anything without being redundant. However, since I'm standing here in a meeting, which is so important to our security, and the well-being of every one of us here, and to a bunch of our people who are not, I must tell you that I believe you've achieved a great result to date—better than most of you know. But, as Mike said, the hard work, the most dangerous work is ahead of us. We'll be challenged much more frequently in the next few months and by opposition much more serious than those we've faced in the past few months.

"You may believe that you didn't sign up for a job that could cost you your life. Or, that we're not paying you enough to risk your good health, and that might be true. I want you to know that no amount of investment on my part will come between your safety and well-being. However, I cannot guarantee your safety, long-term good health or life. There are lots of bad people in our country and even more of them off shore. So if you believe it is time for you to exit the ARC security department, do not hesitate to resign. There will be no hard feelings. There will be the opportunity to move elsewhere in ARC, or if you're leaving, there will be a great letter of recommendation and 90 days severance pay, and health and welfare for 18 months.

"Think about it. Today is Wednesday. If you need to do something else, let Mike know personally before Monday noon.

"I thank you all for your loyalty, dedication to our cause and hard work. Give Mike what he's asked for this evening. It's an investment in each and every one of us."

# LXXX

## ARC HEADQUARTERS

*Two Weeks Later*

Mike and his security team staff are seated at the table in the main conference room at ARC Headquarters when Nick enters the room.

"What's up guys? This is your meeting, Mike."

"Nick, our threat level has been rising for 90 days now. Our intelligence contacts have indicated a heightened level of activity. We've been personally threatened by three different groups, and our e-mail threats from unknown individuals have doubled. You're being followed almost everywhere you go by two groups, which we know about. There are likely others watching us who we don't know about. I am not including your adversaries in Cuba, as there is little organizationally we can do to help you down there, beyond your flight crew and personal bodyguard. Fortunately, you're in Cuba very little, and when you are, no one is supposed to know. But we know that somehow they do know.

"You have been physically assaulted twice when you were afoot. And you and Tony have been assaulted in your car twice— all here in the good old U.S. of A., land of the free, home of the brave!"

"Okay, Mike, I think I know this generally. I'm not keeping count, but I have a few cuts and bruises to remind me. What are you advocating?"

"Nick, I'm going to suggest that we go on the offensive in a preemptive effort to neutralize the bad guys. It's apparent to me that some of these people are not going to back off. Their violence is going to accelerate. They've been trying to scare you and when you don't get scared, the next thing they will do is try to teach you a lesson you won't forget! If that doesn't work, you know as well as I do what's next. We can't sit back and just give them a free shot at you, Phil or Tim, or let them pick and choose where, when and how they attack, because the odds are they'll succeed on that basis. You know I'm right. Right?"

"Yes, I believe you're right, but we're not without our defensive capabilities, and I'm not sure I can get my mind around an illegal preemptive attack. Do we even know who to attack, or are we just going to attack everybody and anyone we think is a threat?"

"I understand your feelings. I shared them in the beginning, but when you think this strategy through, pro and con, and value the advantages and disadvantages, the advantages of throwing the first good punch in an alley fight usually wins. You know that. We may not want to fight, but once we realize we must, then you go for a disabling first blow! We do know who to hit, at least some of them."

"Okay, what specifically are you suggesting we do against whom and when?"

Mike slid two red-colored file folders toward Nickolas marked Code Red on the face. Mike's people already had their folders, which everyone now opened. Nickolas realized that Mike had likely held a pre-meeting with his security team to prep them and to prepare himself for the boss.

Mike says, "These two guys and their two underbosses need to be taken out of the game in our judgment. You may see other options you wish to discuss. Read the files. The final decision is yours."

Nickolas opens the first file to reveal a large picture and a smaller picture on the inside of the front cover, with three or four typed pages affixed on the other side. He looked at the two pictures, recognizing them immediately as two hoodlums who had visited him in his Miami Hotel late one night about six months ago. He read the files created by Mike's staff, which included a good deal of personal information about the two men, including their criminal arrest records, charges and jail time, which was extensive. He closed and set aside the first file and pursued the second file, which was arranged in the same fashion as the first file. He recognized one individual, the other he had not seen before and he had no criminal record. However, there were several *Miami Tribune* newspaper articles on the man's activities as head of the Americans for a Free Cuba Association. Nickolas read all the newspaper accounts of this organization and a summary, opinion and recommendation from Mike, which revealed that Mike's organization had invested a lot of time in investigating both of these guys.

"Mike, do you have the backup photos you refer to with you, which go with this file?" Nickolas asks.

"Yes." Mike passed Nickolas another thick folder. Nickolas pursued the photos, several of which showed the underboss in file number two surveying locations where Nickolas had been spending time, including in the Blue Note and at the executive jet departure lounge at Ronald Reagan Airport and outside the White House visitor's parking lot.

"Mike, on the face of the existing evidence, it's going to be very difficult for me to agree to a permanent solution in these two cases, but I can agree to a decisive, disabling preemptive attack," Nickolas says.

"Nick, that's all we're asking for at this point. However, you realize that the kind of action I'm talking about could escalate?"

"Yes. That's always a possibility in these encounters no matter how well we plan. '*Murphy's Law*' and '*shit happens*' is always a factor. What are you planning?"

"You and I will talk about that later. Obviously, we'll try to insulate you from any involvement."

"No Mike, don't try to do that. We are a team, I am the leader. I don't ask anyone to do anything that I wouldn't do myself. If the best plan requires me as an element, you are to plan accordingly. Agree?"

"Yes, Nick, agreed."

"I mean it, Mike. Don't bullshit me. This is very serious business, particularly, if something goes wrong."

"I understand. I *always* take you at your word."

# LXXXI

## THE HARVEY TOWNHOUSE GEORGETOWN

A few hours after the Security Team meeting at ARC Headquarters, Nickolas was home and in his master bath area, sitting on a stool with Elizabeth attending to him.

Elizabeth was helping Nickolas for the second time this week with his disguise, which included darkening his face, neck, chest, arms and hands with artificial suntan coloring, and adding a black hairpiece, mustache, goatee and tinted glasses. Nickolas wore a black silk open-necked shirt over black jeans with a lightweight oversized black sport coat. To finish it all off, Nick added some cheap but authentic looking jewelry, including two gold rings, a large wristwatch, a neck chain with a gold dog tag, and a gold bracelet. Nickolas had worn this disguise with different clothes four days earlier to have pictures taken for his fake Florida driver's license and for a fake U.S. passport. In the end, he looked like a half-breed of unknown origin. It didn't matter what he looked like, as long as he didn't look like Nickolas Harvey, even upon close inspection, and he didn't.

"Nickolas, I would sure feel better if Mike or Tony were meeting you in Miami," Elizabeth says.

"I know dear, but this is not dangerous as long as no one knows that I'm going to Miami or knows I've been there after I return. That's why I'm flying commercial and incognito. I'll only be on the ground in Miami a few hours for a brief meeting."

"Yes, I know. But a brief meeting in the middle of the night in Miami doesn't sound like business as usual to me. Why couldn't Mike or Tony handle it?"

"Because I'm the boss and some business people who are bosses themselves won't do business with anyone but another boss."

"Okay, I give up. I don't mean to sound like a wife. I know you know what you're doing and that you plan everything in great detail. It's just that this whole ARC program seems to be getting more dangerous for you and your people."

"Well, it is, Elizabeth. But it is more dangerous because we are succeeding, and we're near the end. This whole mission could effectively be over in 90 days. Then we'll take a nice long trip together, relax and celebrate our victory. Just be patient a little longer, everything is going to work out just the way we want it to. Okay?"

"Okay. You be careful. I love you. I'll see you tomorrow about lunch time, right?"

"Yes. Bye. Don't worry."

Nickolas picked up his overnight bag, and left the townhouse by the back door to the alley, where Tony was waiting in his car to take Nickolas to the airport.

Tony says, "All clear boss." And Nickolas entered the limo carrying a small black overnight bag. Tony went around the vehicle and entered from the left side.

"Boss, is that *really* you? I would never have recognized you if I passed you on the street. Elizabeth really did a job on you! What airline do we want?"

# LXXXII

## MIAMI, FLORIDA

Nickolas' commercial air flight to Miami International was uneventful, which was the way he liked to fly. It was the last flight of the day on a Tuesday night so the aircraft was only half-full and he had three seats to himself.

Upon arrival, Nickolas walked to baggage claim, looking for someone looking for him, holding a placard with his new identity printed upon it. He found the man easily, right where he was supposed to be. Nickolas introduced himself and followed the man to a waiting limo where he was introduced to his driver, who asked him where he wanted to go as they left the curb. Nickolas checked his watch. It was 12:30 a.m.—right on schedule. He instructed the driver to head downtown and pick up Brickel south, and said that there was no hurry, he was ahead of schedule. Further, if the driver saw an open coffee shop on the way, he would buy. The driver nodded in affirmation.

"Will do, that sounds good. I have a package up here for your meeting. Do you want it now?"

"No, I'll take it when we get to my client's house."

"Okay, no problem."

Nickolas sat back in the big leather rear seat of the Cadillac limousine, relaxed and mentally reviewed his plan. About a half hour later they were on Brickel heading south, and the driver asked for the address.

"Stay on A1A heading south. In Coral Gables turn left on Coral Lane to number 301." About 15 minutes later they were on Coral Lane, and the driver stopped at the end of the street. The beach was in front of them and 301 was on the left. The neighborhood was wealthy with multimillion dollar two- and three-story estate-sized homes built in the 1950s.

Nickolas instructed the driver to turn the car around and wait for him. He said he would be in the meeting for about two hours. He asked for the package in the front seat, and the driver handed it back to him. Nickolas felt the package in his hands. It was flat on both sides, heavy and shaped like a large three-ring binder. But Nickolas knew that it wasn't. He exited the car, walked to the front of the house at 301, then took a sidewalk around to the rear of the house and into the backyard, where he exited through a back side rear gate behind the pool onto the narrow beach. He headed north, walking up the beach at a leisurely pace for about a mile to a large estate that he recognized by the unique architecture of the estate's boathouse. He checked his watch; it was 2 a.m. He was right on time.

The back of the house was dark. He stopped on the beach beside the boathouse and opened the package, which contained a set of night vision, head-mounted binoculars, a small frame 9 am automatic, and silencer. In a small black bag there was a vile of liquid and four hypodermic needles, three loaded, one empty. Nickolas checked the 9 mm. It was loaded, ready to go. He 'snooped and pooped' through the gate after visually checking it and the pool area for guards, lights, alarms, dogs or motion detectors. Upon entering, he took the first chaise lounge with an umbrella that he found and sat down to rest and visually inspect the layout. It was exactly the same as the plans and pictures Mike had reviewed with him three days ago, taken by a small drone with a digital camera.

But, Nickolas still took his time to rest and absorbed the layout of the house in his mind and its likely security, although Mike had said that there wasn't any. The person who lived at this location for 20 years had done so without any police-recorded incidents, and therefore, had no fear of intruders. The owner was a very rich and powerful man who likely believed he was invulnerable. Twenty years ago he probably was capable of protecting himself and his family. Now, at 83 years of age, that was unlikely, and he had no wife or family to worry about at this time anyway. He lived alone. He had a maid, chauffeur, gardener and administrative assistant, but they didn't live in the house. But, Nickolas knew that *'Murphy's Law'* and *'shit happens'* to people who ignore certain time-proven rules so he sat, watched, rested and planned every move in his head.

He became so rested after a while that he became concerned about nodding off. That was when he heard a gate creak open on the north side of the house and saw the rough, dark outline of a man walk onto the pool deck across the pool from Nickolas, but at the opposite end, perhaps 20 yards away. The man lit a cigarette, and in the glow of the lighter, Nickolas could see a large black man in a two-toned blue security company uniform with badge, patches and ball cap, with either a holstered handgun or mace. At his shoulder strap was a two-way radio.

Nickolas didn't move. His chair was in shadow from the boathouse and the angles of the umbrellas between him and the guard didn't give the guard a clear view. The guard stood next to a table upon which was an ashtray and smoked the cigarette, enjoying the beautiful night. Nickolas watched him through his night vision binoculars until the guard stubbed out his cigarette and headed for the gate, to return to wherever he had come from. Nick immediately rose, and moving silently, quickly crossed the head of the pool and turned down the other side, following the guard. He heard the gate close again. He reached the gate in time to hear the guard fumbling with keys to lock it from his side.

Nickolas heard the guard mutter, "Son-of-a-bitch, fuck'n keys." Then he could see light through the edge of the gate door as the guard resorted to his penlight to find the right key to the door. In the light Nickolas could see the guard leaning down forward with his keys and penlight, focused on the gate lock. At that time Nickolas stepped back four or five steps and then rushed forward, putting all of his weight and leverage into the gate door. The gate flew open, hitting the guard's head at high velocity, and the guard flew back on the concrete walkway with his heels in the air. His head snapped backward as his butt hit the concrete some distance from his gate. He was unconscious and out of further action. Nickolas relieved the guard of his communication equipment, keys, light and weapons. He used duct tape on the guard's ankles, knees, arms, wrists and mouth.

Nickolas was confident that the guard had some sort of check-in system to his superiors. It could be every 15 minutes, 30 minutes or 60 minutes. He, therefore, knew he only had 15 minutes left to get this job done He figured he needed no more and proceeded through the gate, locked it from the pool side and headed for the back door, which he opened quickly, matching the lock brand with the keys in his hand. He discovered that what he knew was true, that this door entered the kitchen and the casual dining area. He noticed the kitchen appliances and furnishings. He noticed the oversized, Sub-Zero refrigerator and thought he would take a look to see what the rich and famous kept there. He opened the refrigerator, only to discover nothing in there besides milk, orange juice, beer, three pickles and three apples. Nickolas closed the refrigerator door and opened the freezer side, discovering a dozen or so healthy frozen dinners and several pints of ice cream. Nickolas thought, this guy is definitely on a diet or eating out every night.

Nickolas went to the cupboards to find a wine glass. He found one and then went to the fridge to try the White Horse Chardonnay he had seen in there. He poured himself a glass, sat at the kitchen bar and sipped and thought, while listening to the noises of the house. He finished his wine and went up the stairs to the second floor and the master bedroom of Martin Alonso, chairman of Americans for a Free Cuba Association.

He slowly approached the master bedroom door and put his ear to the crack of the closed door. He listened intently, and after a minute or two, was able to separate his own body's harmonies from those coming from the bedroom. Nickolas had no doubt that his target was sleeping. He put his night vision binoculars back on, turned the knob on the door and quietly entered the oversized bedroom, furnished with oversized furniture. There was a night-light lit in the master suite bath, which Nickolas quickly extinguished, darkening the room, but he could clearly make out all of the furniture in the room and the sleeping body of Martin Alonso. Nickolas approached the bed, gently shook Martin awake, put his hand over his mouth, and says,

"Say boss, I want to make you an offer you can't refuse! On your back, Martin!"

Martin awoke with a start and tried to yell, in his instant sense of fear and bewilderment. But Nick's firm grip over his mouth muffled Martin's outburst. Without thinking about it, Martin turned, from resting on his side to his back. Nickolas swung a leg over Martin, still holding his mouth, and still wearing his night vision binoculars. He sat heavily on his chest, looking straight into Martin's terrorized eyes. With each of Nick's knees on Martin's inside elbows at his side, Nickolas now had total physical control of Martin, and says,

"Martin, before I take my hand off your mouth, I am going to let you experience what I will do if you try to yell."

Very quickly, Nickolas changed the angle of his hand on Martin's mouth and closed Martin's nostrils between two fingers, effectively shutting off Martin's air supply. Martin immediately began to struggle, trying to dismount Nickolas, thereby quickly using what little oxygen he had left in his lungs. Martin's eyes revealed total panic, shifting to total terror.

"Martin, do you understand that your life is in my hands now?" Nick says. "Nod, if you do."

Martin nodded very quickly and vigorously. Nickolas then removed his fingers from Martin's nose, but not his mouth. Martin sucked air as fast as he could through his nose. A minute or two later, Nickolas slowly removed his hand from Martin's mouth, saying,

"Martin, I'm going to make you a retirement plan that you can't refuse. Listen very carefully."

# LXXXIII

## THE WHITE HOUSE

Nickolas, Phil, Tim and Larry had spent the last several days at ARC Headquarters preparing for their most important meeting with the U.S. Government to date. They had reviewed all of the issues they could identify that existed between the U.S. and Cuba. Realizing that the troubles covered almost 60 years of the U.S.-Cuba relationship, it was a long list—more than 125 line items of potential issues. Some were large, like the Cuban missile crisis and alleged attempts to assassinate Fidel, and the Bay of Pigs invasion. Some were smaller, like Fidel's efforts to spread his revolution into Central and South America and the Caribbean and Fidel's relationship with Iran and Venezuela.

Many of these events seemed like ancient history as they were discussed by Nickolas and his people. But he believed they were subjects that would likely arise and have to be addressed and satisfactorily reconciled.

Interpersonal relationships, in Nick's experience, at certain points with certain people, or at all points with some people, including in business, in politics, even between government leaders, were sometimes deeply personal. Therefore, human emotions were a major factor to be considered and were not to be undervalued. Nations had gone to war over what their leaders had considered as personal affronts by another. Nick had thought at the time, if these sensitive leaders, and only the leaders, had to settle their petty grievances or philosophical differences on the field of honor with pistols at 20 paces or with swords, many wars could be avoided.

Nickolas and his team were as prepared as they could be, as citizen diplomats, when they entered one of the White House annex meeting rooms at 10 a.m.

Nickolas noticed quickly that the conference room table was a magnificent example of American woodworking artists, and that the table could seat 22. He could not see a seam anywhere in the mahogany table, which he thought must have cost a small fortune, and the 22 high-backed leather armchairs, another fortune. Bottled water, glasses and White House notepads and pens were on the table in front of each chair.

A dozen or so people were seated around the table, chatting with one another. Nickolas introduced himself and his people in an exchange of names, business cards and titles, and then they took seats at what Nickolas thought was likely the bottom end of the table. It was the end opposite the Presidential Seal on the wall at the other end. They sat quietly, admiring the pens and notepaper and filling their water glasses. It was almost 10:10 a.m. before the last government participants took their seats at the table. Others took seats along the wall, several brandishing laptops and iPads.

Suddenly, there was a pen rapping on a glass and Nickolas noticed someone standing at the left center of the table.

"Ladies and gentlemen, it's my privilege to introduce those gathering at this table today to discuss American-Cuban Foreign Policy, trade, business relations and laws relating thereto. Please be advised it is the U.S. Government that has arranged this meeting and the President of the United States who has asked that all subjects discussed here today, including the meeting itself, remain confidential among those invited, for national security reasons. I remind you that you all have signed a confidentiality agreement in advance of this meeting, a copy of which is in the front of your portfolio.

"Ladies and gentlemen, my name is Harold Jones. I am, as most of you know, the Director of the Office of Foreign Assets Control. I report directly to the Senior Assistant Secretary of the Treasury Department. It is my distinct honor to introduce all participants in our meeting today—first and foremost, the Vice President of the United States, Russell Wentworth." (*Everyone rises, applauds.*) The Vice President smiles, nods and waves a hand to sit. They sit. "Next to the Vice President of the United States are the President's Chief of Staff Edward Thornton, Assistant National Security Advisor Perry Norton and Assistant Secretary of State Bernard McNeil.

"Continuing left to right, I suggest that everyone else at the table introduce themselves with first and last name and title. Please…"

Everyone did as directed until it came to the ARC people. At that point, Nickolas stands, and says,

"On behalf of all the people at the headquarters of Americans for Reconciliation with Cuba, I thank you for this opportunity to visit with you. It is my honor to introduce the three ARC executives with me today." Nick did so.

Mr. Jones says, "Thank you one and all. We shall commence our discussion with an opening statement by Bernard McNeil, Assistant Secretary of State, which will reveal the current United States Government position on its Foreign Policy position with Cuba. Mr. McNeil?" Mr. McNeil stands.

Nickolas quickly stands. "Mr. Chairman, excuse me for interrupting, but you know that those of us who are visiting our government today have been advised that our time with you is limited to one hour. I, therefore, respectfully suggest that we who are visiting do not have time to hear speeches. Nor, do we need to be advised what the current Administration's Foreign Policy is with Cuba. It is a subject with which all of us are intimately familiar. We are here to communicate with you on that subject, not to listen. We've been listening for more than 50 years. No offense intended."

Mr. McNeil sits down, looking at Mr. Jones.

Mr. Jones rises. His feelings are hurt.

"Mr. Harvey, need I remind you that you are guests of the United States Government, which has agreed to host this meeting at your encouragement?"

"No, you need not remind me, that the U.S. Government, including you, work for me and every other U.S. citizen. We are here, as you should understand by now, to question whether the U.S. Government is following the will of the people of America in its Foreign Policy with Cuba and otherwise therein, perpetuating and demonstrating long-held basic U.S. ideals relating to freedom, justice and the American way. We are here, as citizen diplomats, to have a discussion in the interest of clarifying existing U.S. Foreign Policy as it relates to Cuba and to identify mutually beneficial, logical and acceptable ways to reconcile the relationship. No offense intended."

Nickolas pauses for effect and looks around the table, and then continues.

"The past and current political positions, of the past and current administration, are now a matter of public record. The position of ARC and its supporters is also a matter of public record. We wish to move forward, not digress into 50 years of U.S. Foreign Policy failure. Our time is limited. Let's get into the key hard issues that we must resolve to open a back-channel dialogue with Fidel and Raul."

"Mr. Harvey, that was what I was trying to do by establishing that the current policy is a result of its historical development over time," Mr. Jones says.

"Mr. Jones, I think you know that ARC supporters would never agree with the government's politically biased interpretation of the historical perspective. Therefore, let's just immediately move into the major issues we must reconcile without the preliminary political positioning please."

"Mr. Harvey, perhaps you feel you could lead this meeting better than the U.S. Government?"

"Yes, I do, Mr. Jones, and I thank you for passing the gavel to me. Your decision will save both of us a lot of valuable time. Ladies and gentlemen, we at ARC sincerely appreciate this opportunity to visit with you about U.S.-Cuba Foreign Policy. I think you know that ARC has opened up a channel of communications with leaders in the Cuban Government who wish to improve relations with the U.S. Government, if you will let them. As a U.S. citizen diplomat, I am championing this cause with the approval of the President of the United States.

"I know many of you here have been involved in a series of preliminary meetings in an effort to reduce issues relating to U.S.-Cuba reconciliation to the absolute minimum. I may be making some assumptions here on what my people have told me, and if so, we'll discuss those issues and determine whether we need to add them to the basic list, if I am wrong. As some of you know, the 'Issue List' in the beginning was 125 issues long. As a result of your good work, and others not present representing the government, the list now is down to 27 issues with eight considered primary and 19 considered secondary. Let's discuss the eight primary issues and determine how they might be reconciled through negotiation with Fidel and Raul. Agreed?"

Everyone representing the government looked at one another or at Mr. Jones.

"Let's proceed," Mr. Jones says.

"The number eight issue is…" Nickolas says.

Nickolas, Tim, and Larry are leaving the meeting room, walking down the hall.

"Nick, what the hell was that all about?" Larry says. "I thought you blew the whole meeting there for a moment. I thought we had agreed to a meeting strategy?"

"Well, we did, but when Mr. Jones started to review 50 years of history, I just lost it, I guess."

"Well, you did your usual great job of recovering from imminent disaster, but I am not sure whether the outcome favored the government or ARC?"

"It doesn't matter; we have them over a political barrel. The chiefs know it. But the Indians didn't. This meeting was just part of the process to get to the final meeting with the President. Jones needed to do it that way and so did I. It went well. The next meeting is the important one, and we have identified the key issues. I guarantee you they'll be up late for a week preparing the President for our next meeting in two weeks."

# LXXXIV

## THE WHITE HOUSE

It was two weeks following Nickolas, Phil and Larry's meeting with Vice President Wentworth and other members of the President's staff.

Following that one hour meeting, both Nickolas' people and the State Department staff had been challenged to reach final preliminary agreement on all of the issues. Not all issues were resolved; however, good progress had been made.

This day Nickolas and Phil were back in the White House, meeting with the President and his Chief of Staff Edward Thornton.

"Nickolas, I understand that you had a good meeting with my staff on Tuesday," the President says.

"Yes, sir, we did, and it was made possible by the prior two weeks of meetings to get us to that point. There's been a lot of constructive effort on both sides to get the job done."

"To get the job done? What job?" the President says, with some aggression.

"To reconcile the U.S.-Cuba relationship, Mr. President. I thought we had agreed to try to achieve that result?" Nickolas says.

"We agreed, in my memory, to discuss the possibility, the issues, see where they went. We didn't agree to try to get the whole job done in two weeks!"

"Perhaps I overstated the objective sir, I apologize."

"No apology necessary, I understand your mission and enthusiasm relating thereto. But, let's remember the U.S. Government hasn't agreed to anything yet—beyond a back-channel, secret discussion of the issues."

"Yes, Mr. President, You are right. I understand."

"Nickolas, I've been advised of your list of issues, both primary and secondary. I also know the government's point of view on each issue. We are prepared to discuss each of the 27 points with you in preparation for your next visit to Cuba. I believe I am prepared to be flexible. But, you must realize we must have an effective negotiation here. The United States of America is not going to bend over and grease up for Fidel or Raul. It would be sending the wrong message to a lot of people around the world. You understand what I am saying?"

"Yes, I do, Mr. President, and I wouldn't have it any other way. Mr. President, I don't believe it is necessary initially to discuss the 27 points of contention the U.S. has with Cuba before we discuss the strategic issues relating to and affecting the current relationship. If we can philosophically reach agreement on certain key historical facts, the balance of the issues may become less important."

"Nickolas, I've set this meeting late in the day so if it's necessary we can continue discussion into the evening hours."

"Thank you, Mr. President. I appreciate your commitment to the task before us."

# LXXXV

## HAVANA, CUBA

It was 4 p.m. on a beautiful sunny afternoon in Havana. It was 80 degrees with a nice breeze off the ocean. Raul spent the day at his desk in his office at Government Center. Fidel had arrived only moments ago from his home in the countryside. His only purpose this day was his meeting with his younger brother Raul. They met in their favorite meeting room, the Isabella Room, on the ground floor in the library building and just off the courtyard garden in Government Center. The sun shown through the library's high, leaded, paned windows into the long two-story high, heavily paneled library room. The main conference table could easily seat 40, but the room included a number of small tables along the window, overlooking the enclosed garden and fountain, which Fidel had always favored. They met at the library door, each arriving from different directions down a long open portico. Raul was dressed in his military greens and was the first to speak.

"Fidel, how are you today? All is well?"

"Yes brother, as well as it gets under the circumstances. How about you?"

"I am well."

"Good, let's go in, sit, and visit. I've arranged for a steward. We will enjoy some strong Cuban coffee with special rum I've ordered and decide what we need to do."

"Good! I am ready to do so, having thought about where we are and where we are going for some time. Things are changing rapidly."

"I have, as well. It's been a long, long trip—lots of water under the bridge, as they say."

"Yes, yes, I agree. It has been a long time since we left the mountains and entered Havana as the conquering heroes, more than 60 years, brother."

"Yes, we were just students at the time, what did we know? Nothing! Yet, we succeeded! How do you explain that?"

"Blind luck, is how I explain it! It could not happen anywhere else in the world at the time it happened to us, nor, the way it happened!"

"No Raul, it happened because we made it happen. You and I made it happen. Yes, we were lucky. But we planned to be lucky. Who would have thought this outcome at the time?"

"I agree. Fate has been good to us."

"No, not fate, you and me, brother."

"Okay, big brother, I agree, you've taken us to where we are and far further than I ever thought was possible."

"But not only far, much longer than I thought was possible. Where do we go from here? I believe that we have been at some sort of crossroads for a long time, don't you?"

"Perhaps, I'm not sure. We've been at many crossroads more easily definable than this one, if that is what you mean. This one is different. This may be the one we have been awaiting. But it is difficult to tell because we have a citizen diplomat involved with apparent large American citizen support, but he is not a member of the government. How do you negotiate with assurance with someone who does not have the authority to make a deal?"

"Raul, I don't know. I suppose it's a legal issue. But, this Nickolas Harvey guy…"

At that moment, three things happened at once. The steward walked up to their table holding a tray of coffee cups, a pot of coffee and a bottle of rum. As the steward, now between the table and glass windows, bent down to place the tray on the table, a bullet passed through the library window and then though the steward's back and exited his upper chest, spraying Fidel with all manner of blood, bone, coffee, rum and flesh. The steward had accidently saved Fidel from the sniper's bullet. In the same instant, Raul and Fidel dove for the floor as the steward's dead body collapsed upon the edge of the overturned table. Fidel and Raul both squirmed behind the tabletop, now on edge with the dead steward's body hanging over the table above them.

"Are you hit? Are you hit?" Raul yells, as he ran his hands over Fidel's chest.

"I don't know! I don't know!" Fidel replies, checking his own body, then his head. His face, beard, neck, shoulders and arms were covered with blood. In that instant, another two bullets went through the dead body and the thick mahogany tabletop, narrowly missing them both.

Raul grabs Fidel's shoulder and says, "We have to move. We're not safe here. I heard no gunfire, it's a sniper. We must move on our bellies toward the back wall and the special door to the basement. We'll turn over that row of tables to protect us as we go. Do not stop when we start. Do not stand up either."

"Where the hell is our security?" Fidel asks.

"The sniper is using a silencer, so they do not know what's going on in here. Let's go! Move now! Quick! Quick! Quick!"

Fidel and Raul squirmed across the aisle on their bellies to the next table. One on one end, one on the other, they tipped the library table toward the wall of windows to protect themselves from the direction of the rifle fire. They huddled together for an instant. Two shots pierced the table just to their left.

"We can't stop. He now knows exactly where to aim," Raul says.

They squirmed to the next row and the next row, doing the same to the tables. They were now at the wall behind the last table. No additional rifle fire had occurred. The firing angle had changed, possibly eliminating a clean shot by the sniper.

"Which way is the door?" Fidel asks.

"It's to my right, the one with the gold-covered encyclopedias. Follow me. Stay on your belly."

At that moment there was the noise of breaking glass, and soon thereafter, the sound of windows being unlocked and raised at both ends of the room as two men dressed in Cuban Army camouflage fatigues entered the room through the windows— one at each end of the room. Each carried a silenced Uzi. Except for the weapons and black hoods, they did not look any different from many of the military who worked in Government Center.

Raul quickly surveyed the scene from his end of the table.

"Shit," he whispers to Fidel. "There are two of them with Uzis! We have to get out of here now! Follow me. Be quiet. Stay low. I'll crack the door just enough for us to squirm through. Let's go."

Like snakes, they slithered down the last aisle next to the wall of bookcases. In a moment Raul stopped, turned his head to Fidel and put his finger to his lips, reminding Fidel to be quiet. Then Raul raised his head enough to see the two men moving toward one another, converging on the area where the dead steward lay. The original attack took place only two or three minutes ago, although to Raul and Fidel, it seemed like an hour. As the two assassins got closer to the steward, they slowed, carefully inspecting the floor for blood. As they did so, Raul could see they ceased their visual sweeping of the entire room and that's when Raul rose to his knees, reached into the back of the middle bookshelf, and turned a small old brass door handle, which, with a click, permitted a section of the bookcase to quietly swing out. As it did so, Raul held it until Fidel was ready to squirm into the passageway. He then opened it a little more and Fidel quickly went over the threshold, followed by Raul on hands and knees, who quietly closed the door behind him with another click of the door latch. As he did so, he noticed his brother had left a trail of blood on the library floor.

They both stood in the dark at the top of a set of stone stairs leading to the basement. They smiled and embraced one another briefly and moved quickly down the dark stairway. At the bottom they passed through another door, which Raul closed and secured. He switched on a light. They were in a cavernous basement below the library, filled with old library furniture in two or three past styles. Raul turned to Fidel, put his hands on shoulders smiled and says,

"You old fart! You have nine lives! They just can't kill you, no matter how well they plan it, can they?"

In the dim light Raul still could see pain and anxiety in his brother's eyes. He hesitated, then looked down. His brother was holding his belly; however, there was so much blood on Fidel that he couldn't tell who it belonged to.

"Fidel, what is it? I didn't think you got hit! I thought this blood belonged to the steward! Get on this table, let me see!" Raul says.

"No, I don't want to know," Fidel says.

"Bullshit! Okay! I won't tell you! But, I have to know. You aren't going to die on me now! Get on the table! Now!"

Raul yanked an old sheet off the old library table and helped Fidel up onto it.

"Lie down brother, I need to look at your belly."

Fidel did as he was told. Raul unbuttoned Fidel's blood-spattered shirt, exposing a white, sleeveless undershirt. The undershirt had a blood stain just above and to the left of Fidel's belt buckle. Raul unbuckled his brother's belt and unbuttoned the top of his trousers. The blood stain was larger now. Raul lifted the bottom of the undershirt and pulled Fidel's Skivvies down to get a good look. He took a clean handkerchief from his pocket and wiped the blood away as best he could. As he did so, he saw an oozing that looked more like a knife wound to him than a bullet wound. He cleaned it again and looked closer. The wound was not straight like a knife wound. It was jagged and upturned at each end almost like a third of a three-inch diameter circle. Raul thought, not a direct hit from a bullet or Fidel would be dead by now. Could it be a ricochet or a bullet fragment—or likely a flying fragment of some kind, maybe part of the table.

"Brother," Raul says, "you're going to lie down, you've probably got something in your belly, but it's not a bullet or you'd be dead. You're bleeding, but not a lot that I can see, although you're probably bleeding inside. If it's a wood splinter, and I think it is, it could do further damage just by your breathing before we get help. Therefore, I think I'd better get it out of your belly right now, if I can. You agree?"

"Yes, brother. You're the doctor."

Raul takes a folding switchblade off his belt, flicks it open, and using a Zippo cigar lighter, purifies the blade. He then removes his leather belt, and says,

"Fidel, this may sting a little bit so bite on my belt and count to 60 slowly. It shouldn't take any longer. Okay? Okay! Take a deep breath, here we go."

Raul probed the wound and fortunately made contact quickly, and slowly extracted about a two-inch piece of wood.

"Brother, I got it! Here, take a look! Hey, I didn't say to hold your breath through the whole ordeal. Breathe, brother, breathe! Okay, that's better. Look at this splinter. I'm going to have it framed for you.

"Now we need to get your wound wrapped up and get you to the hospital right now. Get up. Let's go. I will help you. We'll get to the street using the sidewalk freight elevator. Let's go."

"I thought you said you wouldn't tell me?"

# LXXXVI

## GEORGETOWN WASHINGTON, D.C.

One week later at Nickolas' office, Nickolas, Phil, Tim and Mike are sitting in the casual sitting area. Each has piles of files on the large center coffee table before them.

"Nick, I think that's my story for today. Unless you see something that we've overlooked, we have you ready to go," Phil says.

"Phil, it looks good to me. Good work! Express my appreciation to your staff. Now all we have to do is sell our plan to Fidel and Raul," Nickolas replies.

"Nick, the first thing we have to do is get you in front of Fidel in one piece so that you can sell him. Let's talk a little security," Mike says.

"Okay Mike," Nickolas says, "you're right, we have to get there and back safely. I am sure our enemies already know about our meeting at the White House. They've had a week to put together their own plans. So what do you think, Mike?"

"Well, first, let me ask you a couple questions. Have you decided who's making the trip, besides you and Juliana?"

"Yes, I've decided the four of us will go, as well as Tony, Larry and Juliana, of course."

"The four of us?" Mike says incredulously.

"Yes. You guys have fully supported me and the goals of ARC for well over a year. You have some of the glory from our progress, but not a lot. We are on the goal line with two minutes to play at the Super Bowl. We are first and goal. When we make the touchdown and win the game, I want you guys in play and on the field. You each personally deserve all the benefits of this historic win. This is the big payoff for all your hard work."

Mike, Phil and Tim all looked at one another with big smiles on their faces and uncertainty as what to say in response.

"Yeah Nick," Tim says, partly in jest, "but if the plane goes down with all of us on board, ARC is done! We would be leaderless."

"Tim, I think you're joking, but the comment warms my heart because it suggests you guys would keep ARC going if something happens to me. Thanks for the thought."

"Nick, some of us in the beginning may not have expressed enthusiasm for your plan, but hopefully, now you know we are thoroughly, completely committed," Phil says.

"Yes, I do. But it's always nice to hear a commitment verbalized."

Tim adds jokingly, "Besides that, Nick, our ARC bank account is now up to $16 million as we approach the likely probability of concluding this project. So we are all very committed to that!"

"Okay, enough frivolity. We're joking, Nick, but Tim is right. Is it wise for all of us to make this trip, realizing it could be the most dangerous?" Mike asks.

"Mike, you know the incidence of private jets going down is one in a million. Besides, most of this trip is over the heavily populated East Coast, with an airport every 100 miles or so. When you pass Key West at 400 mph, you're only 15 minutes from Havana International. At 20,000 feet, you could glide there from Key West."

"True, but you're forgetting we have to get to the airport. Secondly, the statistics of jets coming down when a bomb goes off is almost 100%," Mike answers.

"Mike, as head of security, I suggest you and your team make sure we get to the airport safely and that the plane we fly does not have any bombs aboard."

"Okay Nick, now I understand why you invited me on this trip."

"And Phil and Tim," Nickolas says.

"Mike, Tim and I want a meeting with you after this one is over!" Phil says.

"I understand. Nick, one last question, when do we go?" Mike asks.

Nick thinks a few seconds, hesitating to answer for security reasons. He trusted these men with his life, but his training suggested that he not set the day and time until the last possible minute.

"Mike, everybody should pack for two nights and two days in Havana, although I believe we will get it done in one. You pull the security plan together and let's visit about it in the morning. I have some security issues and ideas of my own that I need to evaluate. Hopefully by morning, I'll have my answers. I have also to meet with Juliana and make sure they are ready for us in Havana. Everyone should be prepared to go on a moment's notice anytime in the next 10 days—day or night."

# LXXXVII

# THE BLUE NOTE

Next morning Nickolas and Mike meet in the corner booth in the Blue Note. The bar and restaurant is empty, with chairs stacked on tables. The only light is through the windows. Nick is typing in his iPhone when Mike arrives through the kitchen door. A coffee carafe, cream, sweetener, cups and saucers are on the table.

"Thanks for making coffee. I've only had time for one cup this morning," Mike says. Mike sits down with two, one-inch, black three-ring binders in his hand and slides one to Nickolas.

"Thank you, Mike. Have you guys electronically swept this booth lately?" Nickolas asks.

"Since we found that one bug, we sweep it every day and before every use of this booth by the four of us. Tony was down here about an hour ago. We are clear."

"Good. Give me a few minutes to read your plan." Nickolas read carefully, making notes on those pages where he had questions. He completed the seven segments.

"Great job, Mike. I have only two or three suggestions for our discussion."

"Okay, what are they?"

"Number one, I believe we should use a different plane, one other than the two we've been using in the past."

"Okay, do you have something in mind?"

"Yes, I have an old friend in Boston, who hit it big in the dot-com boom, and he has a near new, fully equipped G650. I called him last night and he said he would be glad to donate it to ARC for two to three days. We pay for the insurance and fuel."

"Who are the pilots?"

"Our regular pilots, assuming they are qualified on the G650."

"You remember what happened to the jet you and Juliana used on your first trip to Havana?"

"Yeah, I remember. Fortunately, it belonged to the Cuban Government. I did hear it is back in the air again. They were lucky that it only needed about 160 plugs and a reupholstery job."

"Well, how would your friend feel about that happening to his new Gulfstream?"

"I told him it was a semi-risky trip. He said if I was willing to fly it down there with my friends, he was willing to take the risk."

"He's a good friend."

"He's also got more money than God."

"Okay, I'll check with our pilots to see if they're qualified on this plane. What else you got?"

"If I were you, I would make the usual plans for our regular plane when the time comes. But we won't use it."

"You're really concerned about this trip, aren't you?"

"Yes, aren't you?"

"You just read my security plan, isn't it obvious?"

"Yes, you're right."

"Nick, I am always concerned, but I haven't seen you this concerned before."

"I am probably just paranoid because we are so close to success that I am afraid something will go wrong to kill the deal."

"I understand. I feel the same way. What else you got?"

"I think when we leave for the airport, whichever airport we use, that we leave in two convoys and take different routes. This tactic will require any followers to split their forces or make a 50-50 bet on choosing the right convoy."

"Okay, that makes sense. What else?"

"Mike, that's it. I had some other ideas, but you covered them in your plan. Make these two or three adjustments and we are good to go. Make sure everybody is on standby and let me know about our pilots in the next hour or two."

"Mike, I will let you know where the plane is located and the departure time six hours before we fly. You will advise our pilots, passengers, drivers, security three hours before flight time, okay?"

"It sounds real tight, but possible, outside of high traffic hours. Hopefully our departure time will be at night. I know you know what you're doing and why. I understand why you're not telling anyone in advance. But, your level of concern makes me a little nervous. I may have to pack my secret weapon."

"What's that?"

# LXXXVIII

## ARC HEADQUARTERS

Seventy-two hours later Nickolas called Mike, and launched the plan to depart to Havana at 8 p.m. from the ARC office basement garage.

When Nickolas arrived at ARC headquarters at 7:30 p.m., Mike and some of his people were on hand, as he expected. Others of Mike's team were already deployed on the roof, in the garage, in the Blue Note and on the street.

As Nickolas passes Mike's area, he asks,

"Is everything okay? Are we on schedule?"

"Yes, boss. I'll come and get you personally in about 20 minutes."

"Okay, I'll be ready."

Nickolas went into his office, went to his desk, sat down and removed a snub-nosed .38-caliber revolver from his ankle holster, checked its readiness and replaced it. He then reached into a concealed right-side pocket in his overstuffed leather desk chair and removed his favorite personal weapon, a model 16 SIG Sauer automatic. He checked the 16-shot magazine, checked the action. Then he went into a lower desk drawer for a belt holster and a special belt-mounted magazine holder, which held four magazines for the SIG. He took off his jacket and got a bulletproof vest from his closet. He laid the vest and his jacket over the back of a guest chair and sat down in the other one. He looked at his black matte chronograph; it was 7:45 p.m.—15 minutes to think about what he might not already have thought about. He thought, am I little nervous, or did I drink too much coffee with Elizabeth before leaving the house? Or, am I pumping a little adrenaline in anticipation of battle? I shouldn't be nervous if I've done everything I could possibly do to prepare. Have I done everything?

He ticked off the six risky segments of this trip. (1) On the ground between the office and the airport. (2) In the air between D.C. and Havana. (3) On the ground between Havana International and Havana Government Center. (4) On the ground at Government Center and in the meeting areas. (5) On the ground between Government Center and their Havana hotel. (6) In the hotel, if they, in fact, stayed in Havana the first night, which he was going to try to avoid. If they did have to stay in the hotel, he was going to suggest the meeting be finished at the hotel the next day to eliminate one or two trips to Government Center. No one other than Mike knew of this plan. Of course, he did not know at this time whether he could complete negotiations between 10 a.m. tomorrow morning and tomorrow night, but he was going to try like hell to get it done. Everyone involved in the U.S. and Cuba anticipated a two-night, two-day trip to Havana and back. Nickolas believed that anything he could do to change the official meeting timing plan and locations would reduce risk to his people.

At 8 p.m., Mike tapped lightly on Nickolas' office door and opened it saying, "Nick, it's time to go."

Nick didn't rise and asks, "Mike, is everybody here?"

"Yes, Juliana just arrived. She's in the office lobby now. Everybody else is here ready to go."

"Good. Mike, keep everybody on station and advise them we will be one hour late departing the building."

"What's wrong, Nick? What happened?"

"Just following my gut instincts, Mike. We'll leave in an hour."

"Okay, Nick, you're the boss. I'll communicate the delay. See you at 9 p.m."

"Okay, Mike, thanks." But Nick had no intention of leaving at 9 p.m. either, and when Mike tapped on the door again at 9, telling him it was time to go, he says,

"Sorry Mike, but we have to delay another hour. Keep everybody on station until 10 p.m."

"Okay, Nick, but it's getting late. Some of my guys have been at their post for four hours already."

"I know."

"Okay, I'll spread the word."

"Thank you, Mike."

Nickolas returned to his thoughts and said to himself, "My guys can stay up later than their guys and still function at 100%."

Twenty minutes later, at 9:20 p.m., he stood up, put on his bulletproof vest and clipped his spare magazines and SIG Sauer on his belt. He downed half a bottle of water, put his jacket on and strode out of his office in a determined manner, yelling "Okay people, it's time to rock 'n roll! Let's go! Now! Use the stairway to the garage. Mount up! Let's go! Tony, you take the lead!"

# LXXXIX

## EN ROUTE TO REAGAN INTERNATIONAL AIRPORT

All six members of the negotiating team, including Tony, arrived at the bottom of the stairs in the garage at the same time. Their baggage had preceded them and was already loaded in the rear of each black SUV. The two drivers were at the steering wheels, and three other security people were at the side with doors open, only a step or two from the door to the stairwell. Tony opened the stairwell door, assured all was well, and waved everyone into the garage and into their assigned vehicle. Mike passed Tony at the door.

"Mike, I see Abraham is here with the limo. What's going on?" Tony asks.

"Just another last minute idea of Nick's to create additional diversion and confusion. Abraham will lead us out of the garage and take a long third route toward Reagan International."

"That could be dangerous. What if somebody picks the limo and goes after Abraham? He's a civilian!"

"Not to worry! They'll get the surprise of their life because he's got more firepower in that Dodge than we do, counting both cars! If he's followed, his pursuers will end up in an inescapable trap."

"Okay, you're the boss, boss."

Mike and Tony check the lineup. Abraham has moved to the front of the line. Tony gets into the first SUV and Mike in the second. Mike spreads onto his head a muted radio telephone headset. "Radio check, please."

"Loud and clear number 3," Abraham says.

"Loud and clear number 3," Tony says.

"Loud and clear number 3," says an unfamiliar voice on the street.

"Okay number 1, hit it!" Mike says.

"Here we go!" Abraham says.

Abraham punches his electronic garage door opener and the door slowly rises. Abraham, with his foot on the brake, pushes the accelerator to the floor, and after creating a terribly loud screech and a cloud of smoke from the spinning rear wheels, takes his foot off the accelerator and rockets up and out of the garage at an almost instant 60 mph, flying over the sidewalk at the top of the ramp and putting the rear of the limo into a perfect 90-degree slide as he turned left on the empty street.

"Jesus!" says Tony to his driver. "Did you see that? What was that about? Don't do that! We don't need to rush unless I tell you to. Jesus I didn't know he could drive like that, Nick."

"Well, if you stop and think about it, you would realize that he does know, since on occasion he chauffeurs Liz and me around when you're not available. We had to send Abraham to combat driving school. He's just showing us his skills under pressure again. He's not bad for an old guy, huh?"

The two SUVs entered the street turning right; however, at the next major intersection, the second SUV turned left.

Nickolas says into his two-way radio. "Good luck, Mike, talk to you in five, hopefully not earlier."

"Ten-four, boss," Mike says.

Nickolas sat back, a little relaxed of mind and body. The game had begun. He looked at his watch; it was 9:35 p.m. Depending on fate, he figured they had a minimum of 26 hours and a maximum of 50 hours to go to get home again with the prize— the prize being an agreement in principle with the Cubans, which the U.S. could agree to, that would end the last remaining icon of the Cold War. Of course, 26 to 50 hours was plenty of time for a lot to go wrong. On the other hand, in the past year, much had been accomplished by the ARC organization and success was close at hand. But Nickolas knew that *'Murphy's Law'* and the rule of *'shit happens'* were always at work, especially when success was close at hand. He realized his nervousness and feeling of stress was gone now that they were taking positive action.

They were soon halfway to the airport, maybe 20 minutes to go. He looked at his watch again, almost 10 p.m. They were doing a steady 70 mph, without much conversation, per the plan in order to stay on-line for communications. Everyone was alert, looking carefully at their side of the road for anything suspicious. Pete was in the rear of the SUV with the only automatic weapon on board, behind the luggage, watching the highway behind them. Nickolas dared to think to himself that they all might make it to their destinations without incident when his ear phone cracked.

"Number 2, this is number 3. I've just heard from Number 1. They've picked up a confirmed tail, which is currently maintaining distance. Number 1 is 10 minutes away from the quarry."

"Number 3, this is number 2, ten-four."

Well, thought Nickolas. That proves the value of the third vehicle tactic. Those people, whoever they were, could be on Mike or us, but instead they're on Abraham and company and a guaranteed one-way trip to jail or disaster, depending on how the plan plays out. They were now 10 minutes from the airport. Nickolas' earphone cracked again.

"Number 2, we are now 10 minutes from destination. Whoops! Hold on, we have flashing lights up ahead, maybe an accident. No, looks more like a police roadblock. Two police cars, lots of highway flares, some emergency signs narrowing the highway, police in uniform with flashlights flagging us in at low speed!" Nick yells.

"Number 3! Number 3! Right now! Right now a 360-degree! Now, a 360-degree turn, highest speed! Do not stop! I repeat, do not stop! If fired upon, return nonlethal fire upon vehicles. Deploy anti-vehicle tactics now! Go to alternate route B. I repeat, alternate route B. We will wait with engines hot. Do not bring pursuers to us! Escape and avoid! Confirm!"

Number 3 confirms, "We've completed a real scary 360. Going to alternate route B, lock and load, utilizing anti-vehicle devices, escape and avoid, will advise, ten-four, gunshots fired, vehicles in pursuit. Excuse me for a few minutes. We have work to do here!"

"Ten-four, number 3, good luck."

Nick's heart was beating much faster now. Two vehicles with six of his people were at risk, plus four contractors. But, he knew it was Mike's vehicle that had the largest challenge. He hoped that the *'souped-up'* SUVs could simply outrun the fake police cars for about 10 minutes as Mike's vehicle backtracked to the turnoff for the alternate route. He mentally calculated, knowing his SUVs could do 120 mph, maybe 110 with a full load. If they could do 10 minutes per hour faster than the cop cars at 100 or 110 mph, Mike would gain one mile every minute or 10 miles in 10 minutes. That should do it, he thought. The pursuers won't see them turn or know which way they turned getting to the intersection, 5 or 10 minutes later. He opened his radio.

"Number 3, this is number 2, how fast are you going?"

"Number 2 to number 3, we are doing 120 mph."

Number 3 to number 2, if you are maintaining or increasing distance, my calculations say they will have to guess when you get to the intersection for alternate route B."

"Number 2 to number 3, doesn't matter now, the anti-vehicle tactics worked like a charm. Both vehicles went off the road at high speed with flat tires! We'll continue at 120 mph just in case the other two cars are trying to catch up. But most likely, they are trying to pull their buddies out of the wreckage on the side of the road. We see intersection for alternate B coming up. We'll be 10 minutes late."

"Ten-four, number 3, good job. Thanks to Home Depot on that one."

"No, thanks to you and all those Sean Connery 007 movies you saw."

"If it works, number 3, it works, doesn't matter where the idea came from."

"You're right. It is what it is."

"Yes, a viable tactic."

"Yes, a viable tactic. I have the message, number 7."

"Okay number 3, number 7 out."

Nickolas sat back again, somewhat relieved. Just then his phone cracked again.

"Number 1 to number 2, come in please."

"Number 1, this is number 2, your message waiting feature must not be working. I've been trying to reach you for five minutes."

"Well, number 1, we had some serious threats on the number 3 vehicle to avoid."

"Did we succeed, number 2?"

"Well, of course, number 1! How about you?"

"We have succeeded, too. It went just as you planned. I don't know how you knew about that old rock quarry at that location, but it was the perfect situation to put the enemy in a box. Once they hit that curve at the top on the road to the bottom of the quarry, there was no turning back. They tried but not enough room. They had to go all the way to the bottom and try to turn around in the mud. One of our guys, an ex-Marine sniper, shot out their rear tires with two shots from what must have been 700 to 800 yards in the dark. After that they were smart enough not to try to get out of the car. The county police arrived about 30 minutes later. We'll probably spend the next few hours in the county jail but we know who to call. Don't worry about us. Reach the plane and get to Havana."

"Ten-four, Abraham. Call Larry right now. You don't need to worry about anything. He'll take care of you. See you in a couple days."

"Ten-four number 2, over and out."

Nickolas sat back again, even more relieved. Both other vehicles had trouble but not his.

"Hey Tony, it looks like we got a pass tonight. We're almost at the airport. They knew better than to mess with you and me," Nick says.

"You got that right, boss, but I am a little disappointed. I am going to have an adrenaline hangover if I don't get to work it off."

"Well, I think we got a pass, but it's still a thousand miles to Havana."

"Don't remind me. I wasn't trained in aerial combat. I like fighting on the ground, a lot less distance to Mother Earth either way you get there."

"I know what you mean. But on this trip there is virtually no risk in the air and high risk on the ground at both ends of this trip."

"Easy for you to say, boss. I'll believe you if you tell me I'm getting a parachute."

"I am your parachute, Tony. Not to worry."

"Okay boss, I am trying to believe you."

Nickolas sat back again and tried to relax, maybe another minute or two. That time passed and Nick says,

"Turn right on this road coming up. Stay on it for three and a half miles." A few minutes later, he says,

"See that old gas station up there on the next hill? That's the airport, pull in and drive behind the building."

Juliana says, "Nickolas, you have to be kidding! Where's the plane? Where's the runway?"

"You'll see in a few minutes," Nickolas replies.

"I'll be a son-of-a-bitch! I wondered where the hell an airport was out here!" Tony says.

"Well, actually we're on it," Nick says.

"You're kidding! Where's the jet?" Tony asks.

"You'll see it in a minute if it landed on time."

In a minute or two they pulled into the abandoned gas station and into the parking lot behind the building. Very surprisingly, behind the old-fashioned, dilapidated building sat a new gleaming $60 million G650 Gulfstream, a top-of-line executive jet. Its engines at idle were creating waves of heat above the aged asphalt parking lot, a contemporary apparition in the meadowland of rural Virginia. The stairway was down, with two pilots sitting on the steps drinking coffee. Nick checked his watch; it was 10:10 p.m., and they were hopefully only 10 minutes behind schedule. Nickolas instructed the driver to park tight up against the center rear of the building. He got out and walked toward his pilots to tell them the second vehicle would be 10 minutes late. As he approached the pilots, he noticed that he knew only one. Tony was next to him and Nickolas says under his breath,

"'*Shit happens*,' if not, it's '*Murphy's Law*.'"

Tony quietly responds "I see what you're saying. Who is this guy?"

"I don't know. But it is a major deviation to the plan. Stay alert."

"I am already in the red zone just anticipating the flight. Now I am flying with a stranger at the wheel! Does he look like a Muslim fundamentalist to you?"

"No, but we're going to find out. Stay alert."

"I am alert for Christ's sake!"

"Okay, okay, here we are, here we go. Hey Harold, how you doin'? Good to see you. Who's your new friend?"

"Nickolas Harvey, this is Bill Penn. He's replacing Jim, who came down with a real bad case of the flu yesterday. Bill was recommended by the D.C. Executive Pilots Association. I called the ARC office and told them about the change and they said they would check it out and call me back, but they never did prior to flight time, so here we are. Did you hear anything from your office?"

"No Harold, I didn't, and I am sure that means everything is fine." Pushing his hand forward, Nickolas says, "Bill, I am Nickolas Harvey, glad to have you aboard."

"Thank you, Mr. Harvey. Pleased to be of service, especially on a G650 Gulfstream. This baby is like driving a Bentley on the ground."

Nickolas thought, I could ask this guy a hundred questions and still not know whether to fly with him or not, and I need to get my team to Havana.

So he says, "Bill, it is our pleasure. Are you pilot or copilot?"

"I am copilot. Harold is the captain."

"Okay fine. Harold, let's you and I look at the flight plan and timing while we wait on the second vehicle, which should be here at any minute."

"Okay Nick. Bill, why don't you do the preflight while Mr. Harvey and I discuss the flight plan?"

Bill says, "Will do, captain." Bill stood up and headed up the stairway.

Nickolas asks Harold, "Are you sure this guy is okay? Did you talk to Jim? Is he obviously unable to fly?"

"Bill is very capable. I checked him out on the way down here. He's ex-Marine air, spent time in San Diego at the Top Gun school and later in the Mediterranean twice. He's the real McCoy. Jim always emphasized the security issues so I understand your concerns, particularly on this trip."

"Okay, Harold, I trust your judgment, but you know our ARC saying, '*Trust but verify*.' We need to verify. We are going to be at 25,000 feet with this guy for two and a half hours."

"Nick, I feel like I've already verified Bill, but I will give it another effort."

"Good Harold, we can't be too careful now that we are this close. When I say we, Harold, I include you. You are a member of the team. We can't be certain of Bill in a period of three to four hours. The person most vulnerable to some adverse reaction from Bill is you. You need to be careful up there and let Mike or I know the minute you become uncomfortable, okay?"

"Okay. I understand. I will."

"Good, Harold, here comes Mike and company, let's get ready to go to Havana."

Mike's vehicle arrived. Everyone disembarked and the driver parked tight against the first SUV.

"Okay, everyone, get your luggage and let's board the plane. We've made it through Phase I. Phase II coming up," Mike says.

Nickolas waited for Mike at the bottom of the ladder. They would be last to board.

"Mike, we got a surprise when I got here. Jim is not the copilot. We got a new guy named Bill Penn. Harold says Jim got a major case of the flu and had to be replaced. Supposedly, this guy checks out. Harold called ARC to verify, but we haven't heard anything from them, probably because it's after hours. Anyway, Harold says he's ex-Marine air and had all the right answers to an hour and a half of conversational questions. He is probably okay but you need to get in touch with your designated hitter back at the office and complete a personnel check. Have him call you on your satellite phone as soon as he can. I believe we need to take the calculated risk and go. What do you say?"

Mike looks around, hands on hips, looks up, down and sideways and says,

"I suppose the biggest risk is that Bill is willing to give his life to keep us from getting to Cuba. That is very unlikely. I can't imagine any conspiracy that could succeed against you, me and Tony. Let's go. We have a date with Fidel in a few hours to change the world!"

"Okay, let's mount up. Soon as you get settled in your seat, make that call."

# XC

## BOARDING PLANE FOR HAVANA

Nickolas and his team his had boarded their luggage and then ettled themselves onto the luxurious G650 Gulfstream executive jet as it idled behind the old gas station on Highway 414 outside Oxon Hill, Maryland. Nickolas, now seated, was not at all happy with the new, unknown copilot Bill. He continued to quietly worry about it, although he knew worry was mostly a waste of time, compared to decision-making analysis.

His worry continued as the jet engine's noise mildly increased in volume as the big executive jet reversed engines to back up from the building, decreased volume to shift to forward, and then moved past the building and over the old parking lot to exit onto the highway. The jet turned right, opposite the direction from which everyone had arrived, turned on its landing lights and took off quickly into the wind from the west by accelerating down the long hill, achieving air speed, rising with a slight bank to the left and gaining altitude quickly toward the south and Havana.

Nickolas thought, finally we are in the air heading for Cuba. The next high-risk period was landing in Havana. If anything happened in the air, thought Nick, it would be Tony's worst nightmare. He felt better now that they were airborne, although he remained worried about the unexpected change in copilots. He thought, it's pretty early for a Chardonnay, but I need to celebrate getting to Phase II.

He got up, went forward in the cabin to the refrigerator below the small bar, and opened one of the two doors, to find a great number of alcoholic options. Wow! This guy knows how to fly, thought Nickolas. But he picked a small airline-sized bottle of Estancia and poured it into a beautiful, classic, etched wine glass and returned to his seat to sip and meditate in a sophisticated manner. He relaxed somewhat. He couldn't see any trouble in the next three hours before they touched down in Havana unless it was Bill, and at this point it was Mike's job and Harold's job to keep a close eye on Bill. It was 10:30 p.m., and as concerned as Nickolas was about Bill, he finished his wine and took a nap, knowing that in the morning he needed to be at his best to face Raul and Fidel.

# XCI

## EN ROUTE TO HAVANA, CUBA

Mike comes up the aisle to where Nickolas is seated, and gently shakes his shoulder to wake him up.

"Nick, sorry to disturb you, but I just heard from Mr. Darby's assistant regarding the change of pilots. In my judgment, we don't have any reason to be confident; on the other hand, we have no reason to be concerned. But, you know what I mean!"

"Yes, we have big reasons to be concerned. How far away are we?"

"We are about three-quarters of the way there, based on time. Miami is to the east. With only a couple hundred miles to go, maybe we don't have a need to worry."

"Perhaps, the odds are we are okay."

At that moment, there was the crack of a gunshot in the pilot's cabin. Everyone in the passenger area jumped in alarm. Nickolas says to Mike,

"Well, that answers that question. Shit!"

Nickolas began to rise as the plane suddenly started a slow roll. Nickolas yells, "Everybody to your seats, buckle up!"

The plane continued to roll through 360 degrees six times. Coffee, soft drinks, paper, jackets, shoes and briefcases tumbled around inside the plane like clothes in a dryer as the rogue pilot tried to disable them all. He finally stopped.

At that moment, Nickolas signaled everyone to lie on the floor in disarray, which they did. Moments later the bulkhead door to the pilot's cabin opened, and Bill looked out, with a .38-caliber automatic in hand. What he saw made him believe his series of 360-degree rolls had killed or knocked everyone unconscious. Nickolas was lying the farthest forward on the deck, in the main cabin between the restroom and a small galley. The pilot stepped over him as he peered around the aft corners of the galley and restroom. The plane was on autopilot. Nobody moved. The cabin was littered with debris.

Bill was vigilant and cautious, standing astraddle of Nickolas, looking carefully at each passenger in turn. Nickolas saw his chance as Bill stepped over him, and in one motion, Nick turned over and kicked upward with his right foot as hard as he could, catching the pilot in the groin. Bill dropped the .38, grabbed his crotch, and fell to the floor in excruciating pain. Nickolas dove for the gun while most of the others jumped on the pilot, beating him senseless in a matter of seconds.

Nickolas says, "Maybe we shouldn't have done that last part unless one of you knows how to fly a jet airplane?" They all looked at Nickolas with empty faces.

"Okay," Nick says, "how many had the video game *'Fighter Pilot'* on their Game Boy?" They all looked at Nickolas with empty faces.

"Okay, it looks like I am the designated pilot. Mike, tie this guy into a corner seat and cover him with a blanket. I don't want to see his face again until we land." Nickolas headed into the pilot's cabin and took the pilot's seat.

Juliana, looking concerned and standing in the pilot's cabin threshold, says, "Nickolas, can you really fly this plane?"

"Yes, I believe I can fly it, but flying isn't the problem. Landing is the problem."

Mike returned to the flight deck, and Nickolas says, "Mike, get Harold out of the copilot's seat, and put him next to the pilot back in the aft corner. Tie him in, then come back up here and help me figure out how to get this plane on the ground in the good old U.S. of A."

Mike, enlisting Phil's help, got Harold unstrapped and out of his seat. There wasn't much blood, just a small entrance wound in Harold's left temple. They manhandled him out of the pilot's cabin, down the aisle and strapped his dead body into the seat next to the rogue pilot, and threw a blanket over his head, too. Mike returned to the pilot's cabin and took the copilot's seat while putting on the radio headset. Nickolas says, "Mike, can you hear me okay?"

"Yeah Nick, loud and clear. What now?"

"That's Key West to the southeast. We know that town and the airport like the back of our hand. That's where we're going to land or crash."

"Don't joke, this is a serious situation."

"Who's joking?"

"I thought you said you had flown planes on Game Boy?"

"Yes, a P-51 Mustang, World War II, single-engine gas burner.

Not a computerized, modern jet!"

"Well, the principles have to be the same. Only the propulsion is different, right?"

"Right, but would you rather crash at 400 mph or 60 mph?"

"You're the captain, show me your stuff."

"Okay, get on the radio. 121.5 is the emergency channel. The radio is on your lower left side. To talk, push that button there on the yoke. Talk to Key West International and give them a Mayday. Tell them our situation. Identify our plane, heading, air speed, etc. Tell them we need someone to talk us down. Meanwhile, I'll try to figure out the key controls."

"Roger, Captain." Mike went about the business of communicating with the Key West Airport tower. In a minute, he says to Nickolas,

"They said you are already in the proper flight path and at the proper altitude for a landing. They are asking if the automatic pilot is on or off." Nickolas looks.

"The automatic pilot is on."

Mike, talking to the Key West tower, says, "The captain says the automatic pilot is on."

Mike listened as the tower gave him instructions to pass onto Nickolas.

"Nick, the tower says you are very likely programmed to land at Key West. Do not touch the automatic pilot. If our plane steers itself through an upcoming way point, he will know you are programmed to land."

"Man, good, what a break! Don't tell them in the rear. I want to surprise them."

"Are you saying the automatic pilot can actually land this plane on the runway?"

"Hell, I don't know. I thought that was what you were saying."

"Well, I don't think so, no. But I'll check." Mike talked to the tower again and then says to Nickolas,

"Nick, he said the automatic pilot does have an instrument landing system. Punch it on now and he can tell if it's been programmed."

"Okay, here it is." Nick punched a button, which then lit a green light. "It's on."

Mike said to the tower, "It's on."

Mike says to Nick, "It's on! Jesus, are we lucky today! Hold on, he's telling me something else. Well, maybe not totally lucky, you still have to do some stuff."

"What? When? Christ, we'll be over old Key West in a minute! I can see the runway, and we're losing altitude like an elevator in free fall!"

"Relax Nick, we're almost there now. Even if we crash, we now stand a 50-50 chance of survival. We're only 1,000 feet up!"

"Okay! Okay! What do I have to do for Christ's sake?"

"The tower said, watch your speed. The automatic pilot will slow the plane down to land as our descent increases. When the air speed hits 130 knots, flip the switch to lower the flaps and then pull the lever to release the landing gear. The switch is on the dash on my side, and the lever is on the console. I see them. I'll actuate them as you read the speed on the way down."

"What if we are not lined up right? Or, we come in too high on too low?"

"The tower said the computer in the plane and on the ground takes care of all that."

"Ookkayy. I hope you are right. We are going to make the final way point in a minute, and then we're going to land one way or another."

"Oh! I am glad you said that, about landing. I forgot something. The tower said that after you land and you're sure all wheels are on the runway, you have to slowly but steadily apply the brakes."

"Where are the brakes?"

"On the tops of those big pedals down there. Make sure you only push the tops."

"Anything else? Are you sure that's it?"

A moment later the $60 million jet was on the tarmac and gliding slowly to a stop, with the engines at low power automatically. Nickolas looked at Mike, and Mike at Nick, and they both started laughing uproariously as the passengers all tried at once to get into the small pilot's cabin, screaming and yelling in amazement and relief.

Nickolas got them all quieted down by saying, "The bars open! You know what I want." The passengers retreated back into the main cabin in an uproarious manner.

Nickolas looked at Mike with a very serious look on his face, as half a dozen emergency vehicles pulled up to the plane.

"Mike, it just occurred to me, this plane was programmed to land in Key West. We were supposed to be heading for Havana with no stops. I believe it was our replacement pilot's job to make us land in Key West for some sort of emergency. Harold must have figured it out somehow, and the replacement pilot had to kill him. Otherwise, why are we here?"

"Shit! You're right. An unscheduled stop here with no security for you and Juliana. Even Larry, Tony and I were not originally scheduled for this flight! You're here to die, Nick! Jesus, lets get out of this place, and get our weapons. We have to find cover!"

"They won't kill us in front of all those emergency personnel. They thought this would be a private party. I saw ABC and CBS news teams on the tarmac as we passed the terminal. They didn't expect all this attention. We're okay until we're out of the spotlight."

"Well, what do we do now?"

"We'll have Juliana call Fidel and tell him we're going to be a couple hours late. We have business to do in Havana. We have to get there.

We need a new pilot and copilot. I'll have Larry call Darby Industries and determine what they want to do… unless you think we should get someone here to reprogram this computer, and you and I fly her to Havana. It's only 90 miles."

"No, Nick. I think we've stretched our luck far enough for this day."

"I don't know, Mike, we might be better off in the air in the next couple hours than here at the Key West Airport waiting for replacement pilots. This is where they wanted us in the first place. This is trouble with a capital T."

"Nick," says Mike, "the tower just advised us to sit tight for a moment and not try to drive the plane to the terminal. They will send out a tug to take us in."

"Good," says Nickolas. "That's a safer location to unload."

"Hold on," says Mike, putting one hand on his headset, and listening to further tower instructions.

"Nick, they also say to keep everybody in their sets when they arrive, as the local law authorities wish to board and investigate before anyone is allowed to deplane."

# XCII

## KEY WEST INTERNATIONAL AIRPORT

Within a few minutes Nickolas noticed the motorized tug approaching, accompanied by a black SUV with flashing red lights. Nick shut the plane's engines down. Moments later the G650's front wheel assembly was coupled to the tug and they were being moved to the Executive Jet staging area and placed well away from the other aircraft. Two fire trucks, several emergency vehicles, police cars and a SWAT van surrounded the plane. Their headlights and emergency lights lit the scene like daylight.

Mike says, "I'll get the door and extend the stairs."

Nick replies, "Before you open the door, remind everyone again to stay seated and stay calm. We're going to be in here for a while. The police have got to do their thing. After you drop the stairs, you better take a seat. They'll be coming in fast and hot!"

"I know, Nick, this is what I do for a living! I'll also be telling the police there are two legally armed men aboard with three loaded weapons."

Shortly, Nickolas heard the plane door being opened and the sound of the hydraulic motor lowering the stairway, followed immediately by the sound of feet moving fast up the stairs.

Nickolas watched as two SWAT officers quickly cleared the plane and took up positions fore and aft with their handguns in the ready position. The forward SWAT officer had a conversation with Mike and then, using his radio, advised his senior that the plane was clear. A moment later, an apparently plainclothes city, county, state or federal officer arrived in the plane's door well to converse with the lead SWAT officer. A moment later they both were conversing with Mike, and then included Nickolas and then Larry, for a 15-minute conversation.

Following the end of this discussion, the two SWAT officers manhandled Bill off the plane. Next, a police photographer came aboard and took pictures of everyone and everything. The photographer then left and was replaced by a male and female detective, who took all the passengers' identifications and initial statements. Tim, Mike, Larry and Tony were asked to go downtown while Nickolas, Phil and Juliana had further discussions on the plane with the senior suit in charge, Lt. Jeff Hodges, and officers from the Key West Police Department, NSA and FBI. Another officer watched and listened to these conversations, took notes, but never said a word or asked a question. He looked like a Marine to Nickolas.

Maybe two hours later the law enforcement officers were all done with their on-plane investigation and seemed satisfied with Nick's, Phil's and Juliana's statements. However, the three of them were asked to go downtown by Lt. Hodges, who indicated Nick's entire group would be reunited, their weapons returned, and if all was in order, they would be assisted in completing their travel to Havana. At that point, a potentially serious delay appeared to have been avoided, at the cost of four or five hours of sleep that night in Havana, before their morning meeting.

Nickolas, Juliana and Phil were invited to ride with Lt. Hodges downtown. They got their bags, briefcases, computers and handbags together and followed Lt. Hodges off the plane and to the Executive Jet baggage claim departure area.

# XCIII

## KEY WEST INTERNATIONAL AIRPORT

*A Few Hours Later*

As Nickolas, Phil, Juliana and Lt. Hodges entered the baggage claim area, they were suddenly confronted by a dozen or more TV reporters, their cameramen, local press and two police officers, all talking at once, asking questions, giving orders and pressing forward upon them. However, their pace never slowed, and Lt. Hodges yelled at them that there would be a press conference downtown at police headquarters in about an hour. That statement seemed to slow down the group momentum, and some hurriedly started dismantling their gear to head downtown and get a prime spot for the news conference.

Other members of the press started following Lt. Hodges and the ARC people to the parking lot, still firing questions and sticking recording devices in the direction of Nickolas, who remained silent. In the parking lot everyone headed for their cars, started engines, turning on headlights, and pulling out.

Lt. Hodges says, "Here we are." He opened his door and pushed a button that opened all the other doors. Phil was on the Lieutenant's side of the car, waiting to get into the rear seat. Nickolas and Juliana were on the passenger's side, waiting for their doors to click open, when Nickolas heard a motorcycle engine revving up its power to an unusually high tempo. Then almost instantly he heard the sound of rubber squealing on pavement. He looked in the direction of the sound and saw a single headlight turn on as the motorcycle rocketed toward them at high speed from only 30 to 40 yards away. Two men in black leather and helmets were aboard, with one carrying a machine pistol in his right gloved hand.

Nickolas barely had time to say, "What the HELL?"

At the same time, across the top of the car, Nickolas could see Lt. Hodges and Phil turning in the direction of the noise. Nickolas reached for his 9 mm, which wasn't there! In that instant, the shooter on the motorcycle passed the Lieutenant's car on the Lieutenant's side, and poured a whole clip, perhaps 30 rounds, into the car before the Lieutenant could even get off a shot. This all occurred in perhaps five seconds, but in those first two to three seconds, Nick saw Phil and the Lieutenant go down. The back of the Lieutenant's head was blown out, and as Nick moved to get between the shooter and Juliana, he also got hit in the head. Nickolas was stunned—bleeding, but not out. He quickly gathered his senses as he heard the motorcycle tires squeal again, perhaps while braking, turning and coming back for another strafing run. Nickolas says to Juliana,

"Sit behind the tire! Don't move! They may be coming back!"

Nick could hear the motorcycle accelerating, but he couldn't tell if it was leaving or coming back. He ran around the back of the car. Both Phil and the Lieutenant were down on the asphalt. The Lieutenant was inert, while Phil was struggling to get up, muttering something. Nickolas noticed there was blood on Phil's back legs, as he grabbed him under the arm pits and jerked him to the back of the car, closing the car's rear door with his elbow on the way past. Blood from Nickolas' head dripped on Phil's back as he leaned over him.

The motorcycle engine was now at high rpm and getting louder. The shooter was coming back, and Nickolas hadn't had time to look for Lt. Hodges' handgun. Perhaps it's under his body, he thought. He sat Phil next to Juliana, getting them as much behind the tire as possible, as the shooter roared by on the opposite side, unleashing another 30 rounds of ammo as they passed. Glass, metal, pebbles, asphalt and all matter of debris fell over the three of them as they hunkered down. The cycle passed. No one was hit.

"We can't stay here," Nickolas says. "On their next pass, they may stop to make sure we're all dead."

He looked around. Down the parking lot, beyond two damaged cars, sat a car that was partially backed out of its space with the driver's door open—probably abandoned by its driver after the first motorcycle attack. Nickolas says,

"See that white Lexus with the headlights on? I think it's abandoned. The engine is running, and the driver's door is open. That's where we are going right now! Get up! Quick! Juliana, helps me with Phil. Phil, where are you hit?"

"Left legs."

"Both left legs! Is that it?"

"As far as I know, right now."

"Have you checked your middle leg? That's the important one, Phil!"

"I'm afraid."

"Okay, I'll check your middle leg later. Either it's there or it's not. It'll be what it is. Can you stand?"

"I don't know. But let's go. Just help me get on my feet. I'll race you there!"

"Nickolas," says Juliana, "you get one side and I'll get the other. Let's go before they come back."

Nickolas says, "Okay, get him up. Phil, here we go!"

In a crouch, they ran, staggered, hopped and skipped to the Lexus. As they got closer, Nickolas could see that the car's windshield had two bullet holes in it. As they came up to the car on the passenger's side, to keep the car between them and the shooters, he looked in. The dome light was on. An older, gray-haired gentleman was lying over the console. Nickolas reached in, touched the man's carotid neck artery for a pulse. There was none. Nickolas wondered how many other collateral deaths had occurred in the last minute or two in the parking lot. Suddenly he was very angry. He yanked the old man out of the driver's seat and sat him up against the next car in line, while Juliana held Phil upright. The two of them then put Phil into the backseat of the Lexus.

Nickolas says, "Juliana, get back there with Phil and check his injuries. Apply whatever first-aid you can. I'll drive! I've had enough of this shit."

Nickolas put the Lexus in gear and pulled up behind the Lieutenant's car. He turned off the lights, got out and listened. No motorcycle was seen or heard. He walked quickly over to the Lieutenant's body, knelt down, and saw a big hole in the back of the head. Nick turned the Lieutenant over, and saw a small hole over the left eye. Obviously, the Lieutenant was killed instantly as he turned his head toward the noise. His gun was still in its shoulder holster. Nick removed the gun and checked the chamber—empty. Nick chambered a round, and grabbed two spare magazines from the Lieutenant's shoulder harness.

He stood up, looked, listened. Nothing. In that instant, he heard the engine rev up higher and higher three times and then the squeal of tires. The shooters had been hiding and waiting a minute or two to see if any survivors appeared. These guys are real pros, thought Nickolas, as he rushed back to the Lexus, jumped in, yelled, "Seat belts," put the car in gear and attempted to ram the shooters. However, the motorcycle was so fast it passed in front of the Lexus before Nick could get there.

"Son-of-a-bitch!" says Nick, as he missed them. However, Nick had probably scared the shit out of them, as it was a close call, and the cycle driver fishtailed several times as he avoided the collision, but almost lost control. The shooter had been too alarmed to aim and fire.

Nick says, "Okay motherfuckers, the race is on!" He hit the accelerator hard and fishtailed himself into a sharp right turn in pursuit of the motorcycle, now out of the parking lot, but it almost went down on the turn and headed toward the ocean and Ocean Drive.

As Nickolas took a right turn out of the parking lot at 60 mph, he could see the cycle make a right turn at the red light on Ocean Drive into fast-moving southbound traffic. Nickolas says,

"We're going to gain on them!" The Lexus was doing 80 approaching the signal, which was now green. Nickolas took the corner wide with no northbound traffic in those lanes and again stood on the accelerator. He had narrowed the gap on the motorcycle. He turned the headlights off as the speed came back up after the turn. Nickolas knew there was three or four miles of straightaway coming up, with beach and parking on the left, and not much on the right. The red taillight of the motorcycle was getting bigger, and the Lexus was humming at 110 mph, with power to spare, since the speedometer numbers read up to 140. He was gaining on the motorcycle, which now seemed to be running slower.

Looking ahead, he saw the bike was slowing to enter a small beachside strip of parking lot. The cyclist actually turned on his left directional signal, which gave Nickolas reason to believe that he hadn't realized he was being pursued, as strange as that seemed.

"Well," Nick thought, "he's going to know soon enough." Then Nickolas noticed that there was a black SUV parked at the far end of the parking lot, which was a likely dumping spot for the motorcycle and transfer for the shooters. Nick thought, "Well, this is, or isn't, very fortuitous! But, I am committed at this point." He was moving at 120 mph or about 200 feet per second!

The motorcycle, with its two riders, turned into the parking strip, and headed to the south end and the black SUV.

Nickolas downshifted the automatic transmission, jumped on the brakes at the last possible second, and read the geography of the turn in an instant, which was grass and sand berm. He knew he would roll if he didn't straighten out the turn, which he did. This move put the Lexus in the air as it hit the sand berm, and took out a sign between the parking lot and highway. The Lexus landed hard, well down the parking strip and right behind the slowing motorcycle as it approached the SUV. Two men were in process of exiting the SUV.

So sudden was the appearance of the Lexus on the parking lot scene that it was as if it had dropped in from heaven above— except that the Lexus had about 80 mph of forward motion at that time. The motorcycle, unfortunately for the two shooters, was now only 30 to 40 yards in front of the Lexus, as it took its second hard bounce, which put it maybe four feet in the air, and lifted the two shooters off their bike and spun them into the hereafter.

The Lexus touched the ground again on its way toward the black SUV, which the two passengers were now desperate to leave behind them. Nickolas wanted to avoid a collision, and as the Lexus hit the ground for the third time, he turned the wheel to the right, and missed the SUV, but lifted one of the SUV occupants over the Lexus. The car crossed the berm again, between the parking lot and the highway, went into the southbound lanes and headed for Old Town Key West. Nickolas says,

"How's that for defensive driving?"

# XCIV

## OLD TOWN, KEY WEST, FLORIDA IN THE LEXUS

Nickolas turned right on Duval Street. It was about 3 a.m., and the Wednesday night drinkers and diners were almost all gone. That's too bad, Nick thought, it would have been fun to see the sidewalks and street-side tables full of everyone having a good time, as he and Liz had done many times in the past. He loved Old Town in Key West, so he moved slowly west down the street, looking for unwelcome company at each intersection they passed.

"Nick, where are we going? I am not really in the mood right now for a night on the town! I am hurting like hell!" Phil says.

"Well, if that's the case, a couple of Rum Runners will make you feel better!"

"Okay, you're right. Stop at Sloppy Joes and I'll show you how fast I can drink two or three."

Juliana interjects, "Can you guys ever be serious? Nick, Phil is bleeding steadily! He's not pumping it out, but it's a steady flow! It has to be a vein. He needs help soon!"

"I know, Juliana. I am taking him and you to my boat where I have the proper tools and medicine to help him. We'll be there in 10 minutes. Can you hang in there, Phil, for 10 minutes?"

"Yes, I'm okay. I'm not going to die any time soon. But I am ready for those two, make it those three, Rum Runners.

"Not to worry, Phil. At the boat I have something for you that's even better than Rum Runners. Just hold on, we're almost there."

Nickolas reached the last right turn on Duval and turned north three blocks to the Galleon Marina. He parked quickly and illegally and exited his door, running around to the right-side passenger door to help Phil. Juliana exited to help. They each took a shoulder, and with Phil complaining, headed for the docks. A few minutes later they were aboard the *U.S.V. Escape*, formerly known as the *U.S.V. Glory*. Nickolas got everyone into the salon and seated. Phil sat on the floor by the nightlight. It was the only light on, and the shutters were closed.

"Everybody stay where you are and stay quiet. Don't turn on any lights. I have to go below to get the first-aid kit," Nickolas says.

Nick went below, but his first stop was at a hidden sliding panel in his stateroom, where there was a steel gun cabinet safe. He twirled the dial, opened the safe and exchanged the lieutenant's 9 mm handgun for another, which was fully loaded. He grabbed three extra clips, closed the safe, closed the panel and went into the head, where he kept the boat's severe emergency medical kit below the sink. He extracted the black leather medical bag, put the gun and extra clips in it and grabbed two hand towels and two bath towels. He wet the hand towels in the sink and ran back upstairs to Phil and Juliana. He opened the medical bag, extracted a pair of surgical scissors and handed them to Juliana.

"Juliana, cut his pant leg off below the crotch so we can see what we're up against here. I'll prepare a shot of morphine."

Juliana went about her job.

Phil says to Juliana, "Be careful what you cut down there."

Nickolas opened a packaged hypodermic needle, and found the proper small bottle among several. He removed the cap on the syringe and the bottle, and filled the hypodermic needle. Juliana had the pant leg off. Nickolas handed her a dampened hand towel and says,

"Try to clean up that mess."

Nickolas was back in his bag, looking for one of three larger plastic bottles. He found the right one, opened the container and a package with large swabs inside. He liberally wet the swab and used it to paint Phil's upper outside thigh, which had two relatively small entrance wounds and two larger exit holes on the back side.

"Phil, I have good news and bad news. Which do you want to hear first?" Nickolas asks.

"The bad news, I like happy endings."

"The bad news is you got shot twice. We got two entrance wounds about three inches apart." Nickolas starts injecting the morphine around the two wounds.

"And the good news?"

"You're alive and you will not die from these wounds. You're going to feel a lot better in a minute. No large veins were hit and you've lost some weight." Nickolas looked for another package in his kit, found it, and opened it.

"Juliana, please wipe down both wound areas again with this disinfectant."

Juliana did so, on the front of Phil's thigh, and Nickolas liberally spread a coagulant powder over the wounds. She then helped Phil turn over and they both did the same on the more heavily damaged back side of Phil's thigh. Soon Nickolas was back in his bag, pulling out two large absorbent cotton compresses, placing one on the front and one on the rear. He then found a four-inch wide role of cotton wraps and wrapped the two compresses firmly in place, followed by three layers of adhesive tape—top, middle and bottom. He then wrapped his work with a roll of four-inch spandex wrap, which would hold it all together with the expansion and retraction of the thigh muscle.

"Okay," says Nickolas, "that's it. How do you feel, Phil?"

"I feel much better, but I am not ready to dance. Are we not out of trouble or what?"

"We are out of trouble unless they know we changed the name of the boat and then moved it here. But, if they knew that, they would probably already be here. They are likely cruising the streets and parking garages looking for the car."

"What if they do find the car?" Juliana asks.

"Well, there are four marinas in about a quarter mile of the car, and they will be looking for the wrong boat name and slip number, I hope. We aren't going to stay here very long. Phil needs to get to a hospital and get those gunshot holes cleaned out and sewed up. I'll call the Coast Guard on the radio and have them pick up Phil and get him to the hospital. But you and I do not want to spend the rest of the night and tomorrow answering questions for the U.S. Coast Guard and the Key West police. We have important work to get done. So Phil, we are going to let you carry that load from the comfort of your hospital bed. Juliana and I will help you down to the other end of the marina for the pickup. Just tell the authorities the total truth, except about this boat and its name. Tell them you blacked out during our escape and woke up on the end of the pier. You don't know where Juliana and I went, or who gave you first aid, okay?"

"Okay. I got it. Let's go before this morphine wears off."

Juliana and Nickolas, half carrying Phil, exit the rear salon door quietly and cautiously. They are surprised from each side of the salon-side deck passageways as two, shadowy figures dressed in black battle gear and wearing night vision goggles approach Juliana and Nickolas with weapons pointed. Before either can say or do anything, one of the dark figures says to Nickolas quietly,

"Semper Fi, Captain Harvey, the U.S. Marine Corps is here. Relax, stay quiet, take a seat on the deck. We'll get you out of here safely in a minute or two, and on your way to Havana."

# XCV

## HAVANA, CUBA

Raul's convoy of four black SUVs pulled up to the side of the Marine helicopter just as its wheels touched the tarmac. A dozen armed military types exited the vehicles quickly and set up a perimeter around the helicopter. The Marine fire team leader aboard the helicopter lowered the stairway and exited, setting his four men up in a perimeter around the aircraft, as well. The helicopter pilot then walked down the stairs and saluted General Raul Castro, who was waiting there. They shook hands, exchanged some short commentary, and then the pilot returned back aboard, and says,

"Captain Harvey, everything is going as planned. However, Fidel has been injured and is in critical condition at the Havana Hospital and wants to see you as soon as you land. General Raul Castro will take you directly there. I told him you needed immediate medical attention yourself. He said you'll get the very best. He'll see to it personally. I am proud to have met you, Captain Harvey. You will be in the care of the Cuban military police when you exit this helicopter. They look very capable to me. I have been instructed to remain in this location until you and your people return to me for your flight back to America. Be safe, good luck and Semper Fi."

"Thank you, captain, we appreciate your time and attention. We'll stay in touch by satellite phone. If I have my way, we'll be back in the air by end of day."

"We'll be here, ready to go, whenever you get back."

Nickolas and Juliana met Raul Castro at the bottom of the stairs and were quickly ushered into the third black SUV in the line. Raul got in the front passenger seat and turned around to Nick and Juliana and says,

"Welcome to Havana. We are on our way to the hospital to see Fidel, after getting you some medical attention, Señor Harvey. That looks like a nasty gash. He missed your eye by only a centimeter, you're a lucky man."

"A lot luckier than he was, General."

"Do you know who it was that attacked you?"

"No, not yet, but the Marine Corps Criminal Investigation Division is now involved and they'll get to the bottom of it. They have both the rogue pilot who hijacked our plane and the guys who attacked us in Key West."

"Juliana, are you okay?"

"Yes, thank you, General Raul. Señor Harvey has taken good care of me. We've had quite an adventure the last eight hours or so!"

"Yes, I know, and so has Fidel, as I am sure you've heard."

"Yes, I hope he is going to be okay!"

"I believe he will be, but he was very seriously wounded in the belly by a large fragment of wood in an assassination attempt yesterday afternoon. It is only by chance that he is still alive. A steward who was serving us in our meeting in the Government Center library took the sniper bullet meant for Fidel. I removed the biggest part of wood from his belly myself in the library basement as he was in great pain and bleeding internally."

"He was lucky you were there," Nickolas says.

"Yes, he didn't think so at the time I was working on him with my pocketknife, but he was lucky."

"He must be a tough old man to take the bare blade without anesthetic?"

"You know that he is. His strength now is in his heart, not his body. But, that heart! It is the heart of a lion, as you know!"

"I can believe that."

Juliana says, "General, Nick had to treat two gunshot wounds on his friend Phil Dobson last night in Key West after the airport attack. You both must be good amateur doctors."

"In all probability, Juliana, we are both good soldiers trained to provide first aid on the battlefield. Do you agree, Señor Harvey?"

"Yes, General. You are right. All that I know on the subject I was taught by the United States Marine Corps."

"Nick is very proud of his Marine Corps heritage, General," Juliana says.

"Yes, as he should be Juliana. As you will remember the Marine Corps came to Cuba in 1898 to help us gain freedom from Spain. We owe them a debt of gratitude."

"You're right, General. I had forgotten that piece of our history."

The caravan pulled onto the hospital grounds.

"Here we are, Señor Harvey," says the General. "We are going to take the time to properly care for your wound. After we get you proper attention, I will go up and tell my brother you are here and that you will see him soon. Juliana will stay with you, okay?"

"Okay," says Nick, "I am starting to feel like I am running out of gas all of sudden."

The General says, "Yes, I can see it in your eyes. I should say your eye, as the one eye is almost swollen shut. You look like you just lost a 15-round boxing match, but the doctors will get you in shape to see Fidel. Don't worry, we have the best doctors in the world in Cuba."

# XCVI

# HAVANA CENTRAL HOSPITAL

As they arrived at the hospital, the caravan of cars stopped. The same dozen well-armed Cuban military police sprang out of their vehicles and set up a perimeter. Upon a signal, General Raul says to Nickolas and Juliana,

"Okay, we're clear, let's go."

He got out, opened the rear door, and assisted Juliana and then Nickolas out of the car. Taking Nickolas' arm, the General guided the two of them into the emergency room and into the hands of the half dozen or so nurses, assistants and doctors waiting with a gurney for Nickolas. They tabled Nickolas and like a group of white angels in flight, pushed him into the emergency room and stripped him of his clothes almost before he could cover his most private parts with his hands. But almost simultaneously, they had covered him with a sheet.

Nickolas hardly had time to look around and realize he was in a totally up-to-date emergency room, no different than he would find in La Jolla, California, at Scripps. The nurses were prepping his right arm for installation of a port device. Others were inspecting his body, high, low, front and rear, checking for wounds, broken bones or bruises. He was sure there were plenty of bruises.

The detailed survey of Nickolas' body only took a minute, with everybody talking at once in Cuban; however, he knew enough Spanish to recognize some non-medical commentary on his physicality. Very quickly his medical team had hooked him up to a drip with uncertain content, which almost immediately made him feel better and more relaxed. Within seconds, there was a sheet over his head, which left exposed only the raw, two-inch open gash to the left of his left eye and on the upper cheek bone. A local anesthetic was injected all around the wound, with what felt to Nickolas like a six-inch, dull needle, which was very uncomfortable, but Nickolas endured it stoically like the true Marine that he was.

Thirty minutes later it was over. He was stitched up, bandaged up and iced up. He felt like the left side of his head weighed 25 pounds, but, the pain was gone. He had no sight from his left eye and the whole left side of his upper face and temple was swollen under an ice pack bandaged to his face. Much of his strength had returned, he thought, but he did not remember being put into the bed he was in. A check of his watch showed it was only 90 minutes later, 5:30 a.m. Juliana was sitting next to his bed as he looked around trying to regain his senses.

"How are you feeling, Nickolas? You've been sleeping for over an hour and a half."

"Actually, I am kind of groggy, but otherwise I feel okay except for the anvil taped to the side of my head."

"The General has been down here a couple times asking about you. He is concerned about your health and ability to complete your mission here."

"He needn't be concerned in either case. I am going to complete this mission, no matter what it takes."

"Here he comes. Are you sure you're ready? Maybe you should rest a little more?"

"No, I'm ready, but maybe a large cup of strong Cuban coffee wouldn't hurt."

"Señor Harvey, you're back among the living! How are you?" Raul asks. "The look in your eyes, I mean the look in your eye is much better, although your injury looks much worse." He laughs. "Fidel is awake and has been waiting impatiently to visit with you."

"Is he okay?"

"Yes, he is still weak, still critical. Stomach wounds, they are very bad news, infections, you know."

"Yes, I know. I am ready, General. Give me a minute or two to get dressed and we can go upstairs. Juliana, while I am dressing, will you see if you can find me that coffee please."

Nick starts to stand up. Juliana stops him, insisting he get into a wheelchair—no need for clothes, because he is going back to bed in a few minutes.

# XCVII

## FIDEL'S HOSPITAL SUITE

A few minutes later the General and Nickolas arrived at the top floor of the hospital and exited the elevator. Nickolas noticed three military policemen at the end of the long hallway. They proceeded past many empty rooms, and Nick assumed that, for security reasons, Fidel's security had cleared the entire top floor. When they reached Fidel's hospital suite, the General knocked softy on the door and then turned the handle. They entered the spacious room. Fidel's bed was partially raised at the head. The only light in the room was from a reading lamp on a table to the left of Fidel's bed. Fidel looked very tired, underweight and weak. He looked up as they entered, putting a file he was reading on the table at his side and says,

"Captain Harvey, I understand that you, like I, have been severely challenged to get to this meeting?"

"Yes, it appears so, Mr. Chairman; however, perhaps you more than me."

"Belly wounds! You know they are very unpredictable. I wouldn't be here now if my brother was not only a good field medic, but one of the few who would not take my direct orders, for you can be assured that when he started cutting on me with his pocketknife, I ordered him to stop many times, but he kept cutting, pulling and tying."

The General interjects to Nickolas,

"Not only that, he came up with swear words that I had never heard, even in the worst days of the revolution." Nickolas says to Fidel,

"Field surgery is an uncertain venture, but obviously the General knows what he's doing."

"Yes," Fidel says, "in retrospect, I believe so. How about you? You don't look too pretty either."

"I'll be fine. Your doctor did a good job of sewing me up. It looks worse than it is. Most of this bandage holds an ice pack."

Fidel says, "Nickolas, I asked Raul to bring you here as soon as you landed because my future health is uncertain. We have had an emergency succession plan in place for years. I discussed implementing this plan with Raul prior to my surgery. It will be announced at 9 a.m. today that Raul is replacing me. As a result, he will complete the final negotiations with you and hopefully with President Downing."

"Nickolas, we want to reach an accommodation with the people of the United States. We have wanted a peaceful coexistence for many years now. We are willing to forget your country's mistakes of the past if you will forgive ours. We must have a mutual respect. We will not be treated like an errant child, who must accept punishment before being forgiven. Cuba has been a government dictated to by a chain of ever-changing U.S. presidents and other elected government officials, using Cuba as a political tool in the U.S. election process.

"It took America more than 100 years to get its democratic institutions and policies in place. You can't expect Cuba to do it any sooner, assuming the Cuban Government leadership believes the time is right. If reconciliation with the U.S. is going to require that we become a democracy immediately, it will not happen. We are not ready for Democracy yet. The institutions are not in place, and our economy is too poor. But, we are willing to move in that direction over time.

"I hope you understand and that you can sell this approach to President Downing. Raul has my authority on all the other issues. I wish you both, I wish us all, good luck in this cause. I am tired now, please excuse me. I must sleep. Realizing I may not see you again before you return to America, I thank you for your efforts on behalf of the Cuban people."

"I do understand, Chairman Castro. I will work with Raul to hammer out an agreement that you and President Downing both can agree upon. You rest. Raul, Juliana and I are going to go to work."

# XCVIII

## HALLWAY OUTSIDE FIDEL'S ROOM

As they leave Fidel's room, Raul stops Nickolas and says, "Señor Harvey, are you sure you want to get into business right now? You must be very weak and tired. You only slept one hour last night. It is only 6 a.m. Why don't we let everyone rest until 9 a.m., then meet for a good breakfast and start then?"

"Are your people on standby?"

"Yes, but they are on standby at home, awaiting our call. It would take them an hour or two to assemble at Government Center and be ready."

"Where are my people?"

"They landed a couple of hours ago and are now downstairs, resting and awaiting your directions."

"Okay, let me make a suggestion. I suggest you arrange for a couple of meeting rooms right here at the hospital for 9 a.m. Have your Foreign Office personnel come here for the meeting. My people and I will get some rest. We can have breakfast at 8:30 a.m. in the hospital commissary, meet at 9, and stay at until we are done. An important benefit of this plan is meeting here keeps everybody off the streets and out of harm's way and is a last-minute change that the bad guys will not be expecting, if you can keep this meeting and location secret. What do you think?"

"I think that your idea is good. I will also increase security here at the hospital, which is already good, as Fidel is going to be here for a while. We'll do it. Why don't you talk to your people, and then come back up to this floor and take the room right there next to Fidel. This is the most secure location in Cuba."

"Okay, General, I'll see you at 8:30 for breakfast. Be careful. Get some rest yourself."

# XCIX

## FIDEL'S HOSPITAL SUITE

*Early Morning*

Nickolas returned to the top floor about a half hour later, having visited with Juliana, Mike, Tim, Larry and Tony—all of whom were trying to sleep in the lobby reception area, their baggage and briefcases laid about. Nickolas checked the security, finding that the military police, who were guarding the parking lot entrances and the front door, were alert. The first light of dawn had just become apparent. They had all sleepily listened to Nickolas' plan that they rest and meet in the hospital commissary for breakfast at 8:30 a.m.

Nickolas thought that the long hallway looked the same as when he had left it. There were two guards at Fidel's door and a guard at each end of the hallway at the two public elevators. Another guard stood between the two centered private service elevators next to a nurses' station attended by one female nurse and a male aide.

Nickolas waved at the several military policemen on Fidel's door, indicating he was back and going into his own room. The guard nodded in recognition and assent, and Nickolas opened the door and entered his room, which was just like Fidel's, only half the size. Someone had prepped the room per Raul's instruction as the bedstand light was on. There was a vase with fresh flowers, an alarm clock, his bags and a split of Chardonnay on ice with a wine glass, cooling in the ice next to the split, and a lightweight robe at the bottom of the bed.

Nick smiled to himself, thinking these Cubans are more thoughtful and gracious than I thought—just what I need to relax a little and try to get to sleep, although at this point he had maybe two hours left. He checked the bathroom and shower. Everything he would need was there. He thought okay, decision time. I am hurting, I am beat, do I shower now or when I get up? He quickly weighed the merits. The wine first, the bed second, the shower in a couple of hours. He thought about the pain pills the doctor had given him and opted for three ibuprofens from his toiletry kit instead. He needed to be on the ball after his power nap. He checked the alarm clock. It was already set. He undressed down to his Skivvies, and poured a half glass of wine. He drank half, laid back and thought, what a fucking day! He was starting to fall asleep on top of the sheet when he heard a noise coming from Fidel's room, sort of a low moan. Nickolas was immediately wide awake, off the bed and at the adjoining room door. He quietly opened his side of the door, exposing another door and listened.

He didn't hear anything further. He tried the door. It was locked on Fidel's side. He continued to listen, but heard nothing. Then he was startled to hear a single loud gunshot from the other side of the door. He quickly slipped into the robe, pulled his belt out of his trousers, put it on and headed to his room door. He almost wrenched his arm out of the socket trying to open his now locked door. Why was he locked in? Safety? No, that doesn't make sense. He put his shoulder to the door, nothing except a bruised shoulder. Now his face was starting to pulse with pain due to increased blood pressure.

Nick screamed through the door, "Guards! Guards! Open up! Open up!" No response. He ran to his bed and pushed the emergency button on the patient console. Nothing. He was now certain something bad was going down in Fidel's room. He ran back to the connecting door to listen. Nothing.

He yelled, "Fidel, are you okay? Fidel! Fidel! Answer me. Fidel?" Nothing. He ran to his windows, which were 48 inches off the floor across the whole wall, but only had 24-inch vertical openings at each end. He thought, no patient dives from these rooms. He looked down and saw a very small horizontal, architectural feature, perhaps six inches wide, apparently circling the building's sixth floor.

He turned to the desk and chair in the room. He grabbed the chair and went to the end of the room wall adjoining Fidel's room and swung the heavy chair as hard as he could into the glass window and the vertical aluminum frame encasing it. The glass shattered in a hail of flashing, flying bits and pieces. With only one leg of the chair left in his hand, Nickolas quickly cleaned the remaining shards of glass from the window frames. He then jumped up on the air conditioner and swung out on the window frame with one arm still holding the chair's leg in his right hand and stepped down on the tiny ledge. Only half of his bare feet would fit on the glass-strewn ledge. He ignored the pain while trying to knock out the glass to Fidel's room with his right arm.

After five to six unsuccessful glancing blows, he realized he needed a more direct hit. Holding onto his window frame with only his left arm, and with only half of one foot on the ledge, he stretched out into space to deliver what he knew would be his only blow with strength. The glass shattered. He then pounded out the shards of glass, afraid that gunfire would blow him off the wall when he tried to enter. But he had no choice. He cleared the glass. He threw the table leg into the room, and at the same time, grabbed the window frame with his right hand and swung himself into the room, landing on the floor next to Fidel's bed. No gunfire. No enemy, no guard, no Fidel.

What the hell was going on, he thought, as he got off the floor with a lot of small glass shards in his legs, butt and arms. He was now bleeding from a hundred small glass cuts, with much of the glass still imbedded in his body. He went to the door. Locked, just like his. He pounded and yelled. Nothing. He looked around, he felt helpless. He went to the bed, felt under the sheets, still warm. He looked around, no evidence of violence. He threw the sheets off, turned over the pillows and checked the electronic patient monitor, flat-lined, no patient. Only one area left, the John. He removed his finger knife from his belt, went to the bathroom and listened, nothing. He thought if I am going in there, I need a diversion. He returned to the bedside, got a carafe of ice water, returned to the door and listened, still nothing. He turned the handle, but didn't open the door. Then suddenly, he opened it and screamed as loud as he could.

"Look out! Look out!" all the while throwing the glass carafe of ice water through the partially open door. It crashed and broke on the second "look out!" He went in, one second later, prepared to live or die! Nothing, except he stepped on more broken glass, his feet already a painful mess. He thought, well, at least my face is not as painful as it was. He looked around the bathroom, nothing. The shower curtain was almost, but not totally closed. Nick thought, I hate closed shower curtains ever since I saw that Hitchcock movie.

Nick stepped into the bathroom, stood face to face with the curtained tub, took a breath and with the speed of light brought his right hand back and around with the finger knife, which in an instant cut the whole plastic tub enclosure in half. Before it even hit the tile floor, Nickolas knew there was no enemy in there, but Fidel was. He was curled up at one end. Was he alive or dead? Nickolas felt his neck for the carotid artery. He was weak, but alive, blood seeping through his stomach bandage. Had Fidel saved his own life by somehow getting into the bathroom? Or was someone going to fake his murder by drowning him or what? Why was the bathroom door unlocked if Fidel was trying to hide? Or, was that part of his strategy, not lock the door, but close the shower curtain partway? Smart, thought Nick, real smart.

Nick leaned over Fidel. "Fidel, Fidel? Can you hear me? It's Nickolas! Nickolas Harvey!" Nick slapped him lightly a couple of times. His eyes flickered, but no response. Nickolas slapped him twice a little harder.

"Fidel, Fidel, can you hear me? Are you okay? It's Nickolas! Nickolas Harvey!"

Fidel moaned, his eyes fluttered and opened some, and he says,

"Nickolas, I know your last name for Christ's sake, we are trying to reach a peaceful coexistence between our two countries! Stop slapping me! My belly is killing me. I need to get back into bed and onto my drip!"

"Okay! Okay! I am so glad you're alive. What happened? No, never mind, you can tell me later. Let me get you on your feet. Can you help me a little? Can you stand?"

Between Nickolas and Fidel's futile help, Nickolas got Fidel on his feet, leaving a bloody lower body imprint in the tub where Fidel's belly wound wept blood. As Fidel got to his wobbly legs, he got his first good look at Nickolas, who appeared to be bleeding from every part of his body below his elbows.

"Jesus Christ!" he says, "You're covered with blood! We need to get you to a hospital!"

"We are in the hospital, Chairman Fidel, and we're both bleeding, both of us once again!"

"Nickolas, call me Fidel. Our blood is mixing as we hold one another. We, like your American Indians, are now blood brothers." Fidel collapsed back into the tub. Nickolas couldn't hold him, tried, and ended up in the tub with Fidel, as Raul and four military police burst into the room and then Raul ran into the bathroom.

"Jesus Christ," says Raul, "are you two okay?" Both waived a hand. Nick thought, all these 'Jesus Christs' coming from these guys! Maybe this nation is more Christian than everybody thinks.

# C

# FIDEL'S HOSPITAL SUITE

*Two Days Later*

Raul arrived in Fidel's hospital room at 11 p.m. It had been a long tedious two days of meetings. He was very tired. The last few days had been difficult. But he had promised his brother that when the negotiations with Nickolas Harvey were complete, he would report back to him before discussing the negotiations with anyone else or revealing the details of the agreement. Raul did not look forward to this meeting, as he and his brother had increasingly disagreed on foreign policy over the past several years. Raul felt Fidel might accuse him of taking advantage of his critical condition.

Raul arrived at Fidel's door, having a brief word with the chief nurse at her station and the senior guard at the door to Fidel's suite. He stood at the door for a moment, trying to gather his dwindling emotional strength for the encounter with his brother. Then he opened the door to Fidel's room, which revealed a room in a twilight atmosphere, lit only by one weak lamp. There was light in between two chairs where guests sat. He approached Fidel's bed and looked at his sleeping brother's rugged and drawn face. Fidel's heart monitor was beeping in the background, with a green light. He thought, how far we had come, he and I, from where we were in the beginning, to where we are now. In retrospect it seemed impossible, but yet here they were. He shook his head in disbelief.

"Fidel," he says, "Fidel, it is your loving brother Raul. Wake up, speak to me."

Fidel did not open his eyes, only his lips moved as he says, "Raul, I heard someone whispering in the hall. I heard someone quietly turn the handle on my door and enter. I heard someone breathing beside my bed. I thought it was likely you. But, if it wasn't you, I was ready."

At that point Fidel moved his left arm from beneath the sheet, revealing a large silver-plated, long barrel highly designed antique .44-caliber revolver in his hand. Raul says,

"Goddamn! I haven't seen that cannon in 50 years! Where's your white horse? In your condition, I'm surprised that you can even lift that thing!"

# CI

## ON THE NEWS

*Five Days Later*

**From a Talking Head
On CNN:**

A State Department source, who wishes to remain anonymous, told one of CNN's White House correspondents that 57 political prisoners indicted by the Castro regime in the spring of 2006 for inciting political arrest in Cuba will be released soon as part of the imminent new U.S.-Cuba accord to end the U.S. embargo against Cuba.

If true, this would be the first visible confirmation of progress on this potential event. Let's hope it's true.

**From a Talking Head
On Fox News:**

*In breaking news from Mexico City...*
We are told talks continue between U.S. Citizen Diplomat Nickolas Harvey, CEO of Americans for Reconciliation with Cuba and ex-President of Harvey Defense Industries of San Diego, with the Castro regime in Havana. We are told by sources, who will remain unnamed, that Harvey is once again in Havana this week trying to reach a

U.S.-Cuba accord that would, among other objectives, end the U.S.-Cuba embargo and restart normal diplomatic relations, ending the U.S.'s last Cold War adversarial relationship. Can he get it done? Two years ago nobody outside the Pentagon or defense industry had heard of Nickolas Harvey. Tonight he is in Havana having dinner with the Castros. What can I say? This guy plans his plan and then works his plan. Stay tuned...

## On the News

*Two Weeks Later*

## Late Night Interview
## with Phil Bowen,

## ARC Chief of Staff:

"So are you telling me the Cuban Congress is actually considering moves toward a democratic government?"

"Yes," says Phil, "but I wouldn't get excited about it quite yet. Considering where they have been and where they are now, these initiatives will face many hurdles and years of development before becoming effective."

"How many years?"

"It's impossible to tell as we have no track record of this activity in Cuba. However, my guess is that you could expect some experimentation within two to three years, and if successful, major activity in five to six years and perhaps full implementation in ten years."

"That seems like a long time."

"Well, in many nations, it hasn't even been tried."

"Well, that's true I guess."

"Yes, it is. However, I believe our cultures and our countries are close enough that the process could move quicker if we all work hard together to get it done. For example, land reform. That effort starts with the Cuban Government being willing to finance low-cost land sold to farmers, who will raise crops, live on the land long-term and prove their ability to make a living. Having done so, they slowly buy the land, create equity and have the right to resell, transfer it and will it to heirs.

"In a slow progressive process over time, everyone in Cuba can become an owner of their real estate, create equity, net worth, buy, sell, and borrow money. All of that activity creates banking, requires rule of law, etc. It's a process. It can take time. It took a long time in America."

"I see. Let's take advantage of this moment for a break. Stay tuned. We'll be right back with our guest after this brief commercial message."

# EPILOGUE

It was 10 a.m. on a beautiful early fall morning in October in Washington, D.C. The media, assorted government and meeting coordinators of government officials, military personnel and special guests were all taking a seat in the Rose Garden behind the White House. At center forward on the terrace, about two feet apart, were two podiums with microphones—one with the White House Presidential seal and one with the Cuban National seal.

There was a feeling of excitement among those in the audience as everyone knew memorable history was being recorded on this day. As a matter of fact, the American President and the Cuban Chairman were, at this moment, behind the French doors behind the podiums signing a comprehensive agreement that would start to normalize U.S.-Cuban relations for the first time in more than 50 years, and some would say, the first time ever.

Suddenly, there was the noise of many people clapping and yelling just inside the French doors, giving notice to the Rose Garden audience that the leaders of the United States of America and Cuba had signed an agreement that had been the source of a great deal of public discussion, excitement and expectation for the past several months in the media of both countries and around the world.

For the United States, the Cuba agreement was the foundation cornerstone and best example of a new era of diplomacy and economic development cooperation in the Western Hemisphere. For Cuba, it was a deal that assured their future social, economic and political development success as they pushed toward the 21st century from the mid-20th century, while maintaining their national dignity.

The row of French doors opened and President Downing and Chairman Raul Castro, smiling broadly, led the procession of enthusiastic dignitaries onto the terrace. President Downing and Chairman Castro walked to their respective podiums, while smiling and waving at those they wished to recognize in the audience, who had stood when the doors opened and were clapping enthusiastically.

President Downing, in due course, asked them to please take their seats, which they did. He then says,

"Ladies and gentlemen, it is my pleasure to introduce to you Raul Castro, Chairman of the nation of Cuba."

Everyone stood again and the clapping continued for some time until President Downing once again asked them to take their seats, which they did. He then says,

"Ladies and gentlemen, it is with great pride and sense of accomplishment that I stand here today with our distinguished guest Raul Castro and advise you that the United States and Cuba have entered into a strategic agreement, which ends the U.S. embargo of Cuba, restores full diplomatic recognition and provides economic development assistance to Cuba over the next 10 years. I will not go into the details of our agreement at this time as it is very comprehensive. However, the media will have all the basic information later today. In my judgment, this agreement is long overdue and is a win-win for both countries. This agreement concludes the uncertain and frictional relationship both countries have had with one another for almost 60 years."

"Chairman Castro, please share your feelings with us."

"Thank you, President Downing. I, too, share your pride and satisfaction with our new accord. I agree it is a win-win agreement for both of our countries and our people. I am very happy that finally we can end the animosity that seemed to pervade our diplomatic relationship for so long. I say diplomatic relationship because I have always believed that our two peoples have had a strong affection for one another for more than a century, which has transcended the ups and downs of our political and diplomatic challenges.

"Both our countries have taken way too long to settle our grievances. However, it is now done, and I pray that neither country will look back, but only look forward. We have much, much more in common then differences. Let us both focus on the opportunities of the future, not the problems of the past.

"Thank you, Mr. President, for your leadership in helping both of our peoples move forward with hope and in a new spirit of cooperation."

Raul turned to President Downing to shake hands at the conclusion of his speech. But to his surprise, he turned into President Downing's open arms and a big hug.

The audience clapped and yelled with excitement and enthusiasm, recognizing the major future significance of this announcement for Cubans and Americans alike.

While hugging, Raul whispered into President Downing's ear, "Mr. President, you didn't recognize the contributions of Nickolas Harvey and his ARC organization?"

President Downing whispers back, "He does understand my appreciation and knows why he is not being recognized at this particular event. But, let me assure you, we are very much aware of Nickolas' very special capabilities, and the U.S. Government will use them again very soon."

"Thank you, Mr. President," says Raul, "I understand, but you may have to compete with me for his services."

"Raul," says President Downing, "at this point, we both have to get in line with a major injustice he can get excited about."

Raul says, "I have one."

President Downing says, "I've got four or five!"

They cease the embrace, turn to the excited audience, which is still clapping, and bow in recognition of their appreciation for a job finally well done!

# AUTHOR'S ACKNOWLEDGEMENTS

This book would not have been possible without the significant contributions of the following family, friends and constituents:

My loving wife, Bobbie

My sons, Roderick and Cary

My daughters, Angela, Kelly and Shannon

My business partner, Toni Biong

My editor, Rose Marie Scott-Blair

My book designer and artistic adviser, Beth Edwards

My encouragement coach, author James Thomas Carter

Special thanks to Kathleen Meehan and Carol Garan

I hope you have enjoyed reading my book—and meeting Nickolas Harvey—for its entertainment value, and its ability to simplify what otherwise has been a complex political and foreign policy nightmare for the good people of Cuba, who are one of our closest neighbors.

# ABOUT THE AUTHOR

**Gerard Dion** is a self-employed marketing executive with an extensive background in the automotive industry.

Born and raised in Burlington, Vt., his family relocated to the St. Louis, Mo., area, where Gerard joined the U.S. Marine Corps and attended Washington University.

Later Gerard was employed by International Harvester Co., headquartered in Chicago. Their management program ultimately propelled him through a number of ever-increasing managerial challenges and relocations around the United States and internationally, including St. Louis, Kansas City, Omaha, Chicago, Fort Wayne, Boston, Los Angeles, San Diego and Melbourne, Australia. While in L.A., Gerard earned a certificate from the UCLA Graduate School of Management.

Most recently Gerard has lived in Southern California and Southern Florida.

"Cuba Unchained" is Gerard's debut novel. You can learn more about Gerard and his book at www.cubaunchained.com.

www.ingramcontent.com/pod-product-compliance
Lightning Source LLC
LaVergne TN
LVHW091613070526
838199LV00044B/784